CORPS

OF

DISCOVERY

D0757250

James E. Thomas

I hope you enjoy my taking you on this historical trip.

James E. Thomas

Black Forest Press
San Diego, California
June, 2002
First Edition

CORPS

OF

DISCOVERY

James E. Thomas

PUBLISHED IN THE UNITED STATES OF AMERICA
BY
BLACK FOREST PRESS
P.O. Box 6342
Chula Vista, CA 91909-6342

Acknowledgments

The works most frequently referenced are *Undaunted Courage* by Stephen E. Ambrose and *The Journals of Lewis and Clark* by Bernard DeVoto. Often in these works the authors are, in turn, quoting the actual journals.

Printed in the United States of America
Library of Congress
Cataloging-in-Publication

ISBN: 1-58275-101-3

Preface

Corps of Discovery is a fictionalized account of the Lewis and Clark expedition. The facts of the expedition were followed as closely as possible; the dialogue between characters and some situational scenes have been fictionalized. In order to make it as accurate as possible, journal entries were frequently paraphrased and used as comments as if the characters were making comments to one another instead of making journal entries. Usually these are paraphrased but some, more classic journal entries, are also copied as dialogue. Some scenes have been fictionalized and have no direct reference in the journals. The purpose of this story is to acquaint the average reader with a knowledge of and love for the story of the expedition, an important part of our national heritage.

For those who desire an exact account, read Thwaites' *Original Journals of the Lewis and Clark Expedition,* an account of the journals themselves. Another good source is *The Journals of Lewis and Clark* by Bernard DeVoto, a concise edition of the journals. For those wanting an easy-reading, accurate account of the expedition, with historical analysis included, the author found the best reference is *Undaunted Courage* by Stephen E. Ambrose, also used by the author as a reference.

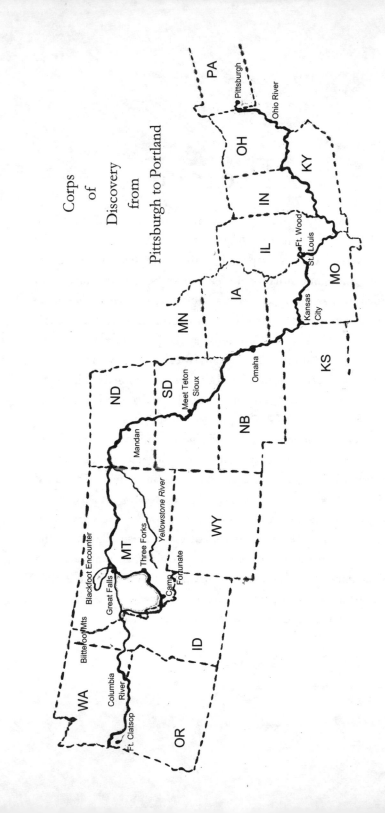

Corps
of
Discovery
from
Pittsburgh to Portland

1801 Washington, D.C.

Thomas Jefferson has been elected the third president of the United States. The North American continent is being populated by Europeans in ever increasing numbers. There are now 17 states of the young United States, and new territories are being added east of the Appalachian Mountains. Though the country is new, Jefferson, being a man of great vision, has challenging plans for the nation. Jefferson believes that finding a Northwest Passage to the Pacific will ensure wealth for the country by establishing trade routes to the Orient for furs and other goods. He believes he can acquire the Louisiana Territory from France, and then, by establishing a trade route to the Pacific, lay claim to the land from coast to coast. More than simply desiring geographical land acquisition, Jefferson wants to spread the new principle of democratic government into an empire. He believes this is the destiny of the United States. His vision will shape the future of the country and its people.

On February 23, 1801 Thomas Jefferson wrote a letter to Meriwether Lewis, at the time a captain in the Army. His letter indicated that he would be in need of a secretary, "not only to aid in the private concerns of the household, but also to contribute to the mass of information which is interesting for the administration to acquire. Your knowledge of the western country, of the Army and all of its interests and relations has rendered it desirable....that you should be engaged in that office. Further, service as my private secretary would make you know and be known to characters of influence in the affairs of our country, and give you the advantage of their wisdom. You will live in the President's House[*], as you would be one of my family."

Jefferson continued with the job description, "The office is more in the nature of that of an aide-de-camp, than a mere secretary. The writing is not considerable because I write my

---

[*] The current White House

own letters and copy them to press. The care of our company, execution of some commissions in the town occasionally, messages to Congress, occasional conferences and explanations with particular members, with the offices, and inhabitants of the place where it cannot so well be done in writing, constitute the chief business. You will be provided a servant and a mount. This position has been solicited by several, who will have no answer until I hear from you. Please answer with your decision as I need to fill the position early in my administration."

The mails were slow, but, upon receipt of Jefferson's letter, Lewis, in Pittsburgh, replied immediately. "I most cordially acquiesce, and with pleasure accept the office...I shall move expediently to get forward to the City of Washington with all possible dispatch; rest assured I shall not relax in my exertions. Receive I pray you, sir, the undisembled assurance, of the attachment and friendship of your most obedient, and very humble servant, Meriwether Lewis." Due to poor weather conditions it took three weeks for Lewis to travel to Washington.

Thomas Jefferson appointed young Meriwether Lewis as his personal secretary with a proviso that he retain his rank in the Army and his right to promotion. Lewis was to reside in the East Wing of the President's House. Jefferson's selection was based on the fact that he had known Lewis from the time he was a young man living only 10 miles from his home in Albemarle County, Virginia. Lewis was a bright young man and impressed Jefferson with his leadership qualities. Lewis had been serving in the frontier Army the previous six years. He had distinguished himself as a leader and had risen quickly to the rank of captain.

Meriwether Lewis and Thomas Jefferson were in daily contact. Many of Lewis' duties were menial, but he was also privileged to attend many presidential conferences and hear the various statesmen who regularly visited the president to discuss important issues. Lewis attended all White House gatherings, which were frequent with Jefferson, and became well-known in influential circles. Thomas Jefferson frequently sought Lewis' counsel on a variety of matters and asked for his opinion regarding governmental issues. He enjoyed hearing his more youthful opinion. Jefferson, being a man of means, had, on three different occasions before becoming president, tried to muster expeditions to the west. Each had failed. Now, as President of the United States, his ambition to launch the first expedition to reach the Pacific would begin to take shape.

January 17, 1803

President Thomas Jefferson and Lewis are having dinner. Jefferson spoke, "Meriwether, I have a plan I wish to discuss with you."

Lewis replied expectantly, "Yes, sir, what is it?"

The president continued, "Some say that I am an ambitious man, perhaps too ambitious, that the nation is not ready for my plans, and that I should only expect disappointment and grief from my dreams, but I believe, truly believe, that the time is rapidly approaching where we must grasp our dreams or see others snatch them from us."

"What plans are you speaking of, Mr. President?" Lewis inquired.

The president looked Lewis directly in the eye and spoke in a very calm and sincere tone. "Meriwether, it is my dream to have the United States become an empire on this continent, an empire that will stretch from sea to sea. We are living in a time where things are taking place rapidly. As you know, my dream is one of democracy. I want the democracy of the United States, the democracy of our noble experiment, to expand. Already we are hearing that the Spanish are moving into

positions of control up and along the western coast and even
into St. Louis. The French are the most powerful military force
in the world today, and they control the important port of
New Orleans. We cannot conduct river commerce unless we
pass through that port. I fear that we can lose this land, our
democratic dream, unless we act now. You recall in '93 when
you volunteered to join the westward expedition attempt and I
turned you down?"

"Yes, sir, I do," Lewis replied. "At the time, I thought I
lacked your trust, but I now realize it was not trust, you
wanted a more mature leader for the expedition. The
Frenchman who was chosen, Michaux, what happened to
him?"

Jefferson's eyes narrowed, "He played me for a fool, or at
least tried to. The bastard was a spy, but he never got farther
than Kentucky before I learned of his true mission as a spy.
He was trying to raise an army of American militia to attack
Spanish possessions beyond the Mississippi, all for his own
profit. The plot angered me quite deeply, for the element of
deceit and for the failure. I later insisted that the French recall
the man to their soil.... They complied, by God. They took the
bastard back."

Lewis responded, "I didn't know the details, but I am glad
he was discovered early on. I have heard rumors that in the
territories of Ohio, Indiana and Illinois there are people talking
of secession. They want to form a new nation that would trade
whiskey and other goods freely through New Orleans."

Jefferson replied quickly, "Precisely, Meriwether, precisely.
The Whiskey Rebellion and the physical fact of the mountains
separating our people of the east coast from those in those
western lands give rise to the question of their loyalty to the
United States. Distance separates, and those foolish taxes on
whiskey? Why, hell, doesn't Congress realize that taxation was
a major cause of our fight for independence from England?

Those citizens are fiercely independent people and they will revolt again if pushed to it. It's in their blood. But that's only one thing that I fear could happen if we are not decisive in our plans and actions."

Then, setting his cup down, he began to gesture with his hands. "Even if the territories remain loyal to the United States, and they should at least for the present, our nation would have its western border at the Mississippi River. All of the lands west of there will be developed one day. That is a certainty, and once they are developed, they will become powerful. If they are influenced by the French, Canadians, British or even the Spanish, our young nation will be at risk. I don't trust the Spanish or the French. If those far western lands are populated by people speaking a different language, with a different culture and politics, there will inevitably be troubles and war. The language will separate and the politics will exacerbate. If there is a war, our democratic form of government may perish before it has ever had a real opportunity to flourish."

"That is possible, Mr. President. It would be difficult for us to defend those remote regions from foreign powers," Lewis agreed.

"Meriwether," the president continued, "I have tried three times to muster an expedition to the Pacific. I want to locate and establish a mostly water route. I believe that there is a yet–to–be–discovered Northwest Passage to the Pacific Ocean. The commerce flowing through it will enrich and empower this continent. Three times I have tried; three times I have failed. But now, just now, conditions are changing to favor us, and I believe we will be successful. Listen to these plans; they are confidential."

Lewis stopped eating and moved to the edge of his seat, looking at the president. He knew that this would be an important moment; he was about to hear details of plans that few other men would know.

The president continued, "Napoleon is at war in Europe. That war has dragged on far too long and now he needs money to finance his efforts. The French hold the port of New Orleans and lay claim to all of the upper Mississippi and Missouri River basin. I have two choices. I can send an expedition into those uncharted lands, ignore the French claims, lay claim to them for the United States and face possible future conflict with France, or I can purchase the land from the French." The president paused for a moment and then continued, "Our minister to France, Robert Livingston, has already begun negotiations with Napoleon for the purchase of the Louisiana Territory. Things are going well; Napoleon is interested. He has had difficulties in the islands, losing troops that he can't afford to lose. He has found it's hard to rule a land from across an ocean. Half of our country's produce moves through the port of New Orleans. It will only become more valuable as the country grows and expands production. In short, we need New Orleans and Louisiana. Just think of it, Meriwether. The largest land acquisition in the history of the world could take place without firing a shot. Why, why, it's fantastic! With this single deal we would send notice to the rest of the world that the territory is now ours; it would be part of the United States. I find this extremely exciting. My pulse quickens at the thought, and I anxiously await each message from Europe regarding the subject."

Young Lewis, not taking his eyes off the president for a moment, was visibly excited. "All of the Louisiana Territory, sir? Why, if I'm correct that is more than double the size of the existing lands of the United States."

"Indeed it is," Jefferson said enthusiastically. "Nine years ago Captain Robert Gray in his ship *Columbia* fixed the longitude and latitude of the Columbia River. We know exactly how wide this great continent is, and one day it will all be part of the United States." Then continuing he added, "Our people look westward, and well they should. We are an expanding nation. We cannot let the Mississippi River become our western boundary. We cannot let the democratic concept have a fragile boundary at the river's edge. One day democracy will govern from sea to sea and the country will be ruled by a people held together by democratic principle more than mere geography. It will all be one country under our Constitution. The United States will be a great nation, but we must prepare now to make that possible."

Lewis replied to the enthusiastic president, "Sir, by negotiating for Louisiana you are taking a large step toward making your dream come true. When do you think it will be final?"

Jefferson answered, "I am not sure, but I am very encouraged by our preliminary negotiations. I still want to plan an expedition to the Pacific regardless, hear me well, regardless of the outcome. James Madison warns me that the French have the Spanish administering Louisiana for them and would most likely consider an expedition from the United States an invasion and an act of war. The Louisiana Territory extends to the Continental Divide. These lands are uncharted and unknown. We know the Columbia River empties into the Pacific and that its headwaters flow from the east. I personally believe that the headwaters of the Columbia River are separated by a mountain range that is near the headwaters of the Missouri River." Then, getting up from the table, the president moved to a cabinet and opened a drawer. He continued, "Look at these maps, Meriwether. Just look. They are confusing and contradictory. Except for the coastal map of Captain Gray, I can't believe any of them. They aren't worth the paper they are on. One shows the Columbia River going all the way to Hudson Bay. Another shows the Missouri River within a few hundred miles of the Pacific coast. I have strange reports that there are, now get this, large wooly mammoths, hills of pure salt, and large volcanoes in the lands west of

St. Louis. Other reports tell of blue-eyed Indians that speak
Welsh. You know, that rumor of the Welch prince and his de-
scendants that we keep hearing about." The president paused,
shook his head and gestured with his hands, then continued,
"I don't know what the hell to believe. You know me, I am a
scientist first, a scientist even more than a politician. I want to
know what is out there; I need to know what is out there."
Then gesturing toward the papers he continued, "I want accurate maps, accurate reports, from men I trust."

Lewis replied to the president, "These maps are incredibly
poor, sir. Many have large voids, and I agree, we should
explore these areas, record everything, map the area accurately
to permit future settlements." Then he shifted his focus from
the maps back to the president. "The expedition to these
lands, how large will it be? When will it depart?"

The president smiled broadly and put his hand on Lewis'
shoulder and said, "Yes, Meriwether Lewis, I do have a plan."
Then he gestured for him to take a seat as he sat down himself
and continued, "You will be the leader of the expedition. You
are young and intelligent; you are healthy and strong; you are a
leader; and, most of all, I trust you. Contrary to some of my
advisors, I want it to be a military expedition with military discipline. I want you to handpick the men that will accompany
you. Pick men with skills you will need along the way.
Woodsman with knowledge of the land, boatsmen to navigate
the riverway, carpenters to build forts, blacksmiths for tools
and rifle maintenance and men who know the Indian languages or at least how to make hand signs." Again moving to
his table, the president continued, "You will encounter many
native Indian tribes. Your orders will be to make peace with
them and to deal with them fairly. More importantly, you will
deliver a message to them from me. I want them all to know
that they are now part of the United States, that we value them
as members of a great nation. They should be told that they

will be given opportunities for trade goods only if they are peaceful. If they will build cities for trade, they will prosper. Also, Meriwether, they should be told not to make war on one another. Make that clear to them. If they are like the tribes we have known so far, they will have ongoing territorial disputes. They need to know that they are now part of a great nation and will no longer need to make war on one another." Then, putting both hands flat on the table and leaning toward Lewis, the president said, "Meriwether, this will be an enormous task requiring enormous effort, perseverance and skill. I have given it a great deal of thought and I know of no man that I would rather have lead this expedition than you. Will you accept, will you lead the expedition?"

Lewis looked at the president, paused, then smiled and said, "Mr. President, I do accept with pride, and I shall endeavor to be your personal representative throughout the mission, however difficult it is or how long it takes."

The president, smiling in return, extended his hand and said, "It is done then?"

Lewis, gripped the president's hand firmly, shook it and replied, "Done."

Jefferson said, "Good. Now let us have a glass of wine to celebrate this occasion. Tomorrow I shall ask Congress to appropriate funds to explore these lands." The president poured a glass of wine for each of them and lifted his glass to toast the agreement. Lewis responded in kind.

January 18, 1803

In the morning the president arrives at Congress to meet with Senator George Logan. Logan is the founder of the American Philosophical Society of which Jefferson is a charter member. It is a special trip because it is customary for the president to have the congressional members come to his office. Jefferson, however, eager to discuss his plans, decides that on this day he will go to Congress where he will meet his long-time friend.

After an exchange of greetings the president said, "Senator, I have proposed the leadership command of the northwest expedition to my personal secretary, Meriwether Lewis, I believe you know him?"

"Yes, I do," replied the senator. Then with a puzzled look he asked the president, "Was he your final choice? Did you consider other men?"

The president replied, "Does this require Senate approval?" Answering his own rhetorical question, he continued, "Of course not." Then continuing, "Yes, my friend, I have considered many other men, and none are perfect for the task, but young Lewis meets or exceeds my expectations in almost every area."

After a pause the senator continued, "Really, Mr. President, as I recall young Lewis has been subject to episodes of melancholy, rather serious episodes as I have been told. In fact, I have heard that his military career would have been at risk because his moods could infect his command. Is that true?"

Jefferson looked at the senator and said, "You are quite correct, Senator, Mr. Lewis has had moments where he is melancholy. And I must admit, when conferring with my cabinet regarding the northwest expedition and having Lewis in command, some spoke out in concern regarding his moods and his brash character. They were concerned that his brashness would endanger the expedition. But Senator, Meriwether Lewis, more than any man I can name, will be my eyes and ears on this trip. This expedition is very important to the nation at this time. It will provide a concept to unify the new states and territories into a union, a union that could slip away from us quickly if we are not decisive now. The people

will identify with our explorers, and when they return they will
have done much to bind the country together. As for Lewis'
occasional depressions of the mind, he is aware of this
problem. During those times he will usually confine himself
to quarters. It has been my experience that he recovers quickly
if left alone for a time and these episodes have not impaired
his ability to reason or think clearly. Even with this particular
personality trait, I'm quite sure he is the best man for the duty
at hand. I have known Captain Lewis most of his life. He now
serves in my office as private secretary. I know him as well as
any man. He is of courage undaunted, possessing a firmness
and perseverance of purpose which nothing but impossibilities
could divert from its direction. Careful as a father of those
committed to his charge, yet steady in the maintenance of
order and discipline. He is intimate with Indian character,
customs and principles, and habituated to the hunting life. He
will make exact observations of the vegetables and animals of
the country. And, very important to me, he possesses a fidelity
to truth so scrupulous, that whatever he should report to us
would be as certain as if seen by ourselves. To fill up the
measure desired, he has requested only to be educated in
technical languages and natural sciences. He is going to train
himself to make astronomical observations that are necessary
to establish the geography of his route. He has fine intellectual
and physical qualities that were refined while in the Army and
which are needed for such an expedition." Pausing a moment,
Jefferson pointed a finger in the air and continued, "I can go
on to point out that he is fiercely loyal to democratic principles, and that is extremely important to me, and he is
well–disciplined and flexible. Yes, he is prone to being moody
and speculative, but his other major qualities, his keen sense of
observation and knack of writing in detail will prove invaluable
for this strategic expedition. Senator, on this mission, we can
expect the unexpected, and Meriwether Lewis will document

it. I have, on occasion, noted with interest that during his times of melancholy, a firm hand from a colleague is his best medicine. Members of my cabinet have helped him greatly, and I have not noticed these moods in quite some time."

The two men began walking down the hallway. The senator continued, "Mr. President, I trust your judgment completely. I just wanted to point this trait out to you in the event you had an alternate choice for the command. Lewis could always go as the second in command, you would still gain the advantage of his positive character traits, and not put the expedition at risk."

"True," the president nodded in agreement, "I think there is merit in having another man in a command position for the expedition, but Lewis will remain my choice as its leading commander. However, the notion of a second, fully capable man has much merit. It will be a long and hazardous journey, and there is no guarantee that he will not meet with ill fate. I shall discuss this with Meriwether. He will most likely not have a problem with the idea of an alternate man to help command the expedition."

The senator then asked, "By the way, Mr. President, how much money do you plan to ask Congress to appropriate for this? You know we are already having closed discussions as to how much to offer Napoleon for the Louisiana deal."

Jefferson laughed, then put his hand on the senator's shoulder and replied, "At this moment in time, two-thirds of the population of this young nation resides within fifty miles of the East Coast. We need to secure our claims to the western lands now, right now, or forever lose them. We can make this happen without a war. That, my friend, is unheard of in history. As you know, I have tried to initiate an expedition to the west before, and it never came to fruition. This expedition will be made by our military, using military men, funded by our Congress. You ask me, how much do we need? The answer is, just as much as we can get, senator. Any amount to show a firm commitment and get it underway. I actually think we could make it as little as $2,500 but, knowing there is some opposition, maybe we should ask for more. What do you think?"

"You know the Congress well, Mr. President," the senator replied. "Just leave it up to me. I know how to handle the rival opinions. We'll get the funding; we will get it started. If there are cost overruns, we'll deal with those later. There is simply too much at risk if we fail on this one."

The senator paused and turned to the president and asked, "When I propose this to the entire Senate, what should we say our goal for the expedition will be? You know the purchase deal is still under wraps at this time."

The president stopped walking and turned to face the senator. He said, "Tell your colleagues that I will write a letter stating the purpose of our expedition. The official purpose will be to open the western trade routes to bring furs down the Missouri River and then eastward over the Ohio River to the 17 states. Our aim will also be to make friends and allies with the far western Indians while diverting valuable pelts from those rugged northern routes used by England. I am confident that our representatives in Congress do not want the English and French to continue profiting by diverting the riches of this continent to their benefit."

April 30, 1803

The terms of the Louisiana Purchase are complete. While not yet announced publicly, the entire Missouri River drainage basin is now the property of the United States. Lewis begins to prepare for the westward expedition following his conversation with the president. Evenings and other available time are spent with the president going over books and listening to Jefferson's explanations of the material. Jefferson, being of scientific mind, is knowledgeable in the current practices of navigation and celestial reading. Lewis pours over books on astronomy and cartography, learning all he can. He prepares a listing of materials he thinks he and his crew will need for the trip. Another list is made of special trade goods, anticipated as gifts and barter materials for the Indian tribes. He estimates the total bulk of this material and calculates the size of the craft that would be required to move the cargo. As he studies, he realizes that the library of materials he has at his disposal is not sufficient. After conferring with Jefferson, he decides to visit Philadelphia to study under the best teachers regarding the subject matter he feels he will need for the trip. He goes to meet the president to discuss his upcoming departure.

Lewis approached the Oval Office where the president was seated. He knocked on the door. Jefferson looked up and motioned for him to enter.

"Good afternoon, Mr. President. How are you today?" Lewis asked cordially.

"Fine, Meriwether, I am fine," the president responded. "You certainly have been occupied of late. What's on your mind this afternoon? Anything I can help you with? Have you set the date of departure?"

Lewis pulled up a chair and seated himself, then he began, "Sir, you recall our conversation when last we spoke of the expedition. You indicated that it might be a very good idea to have a second-in-command accompany me on the trip. To share the responsibilities of command, or in the event tragedy should befall me, fill in my stead."

Jefferson straightened in his chair, "Yes, I do. I believe that there will be times when this trip will be harrowing to say the least. You will need a good man with you, not only to share the responsibility or to replace you in the event of tragedy; Meriwether, you are simply going to need someone to confer with. I can visualize many times when you will need to ask for an opinion you can rely upon. I do not run the country by myself; I have a cabinet of advisors and I depend on their council. You will need a man you can trust, trust without question, a man who will assist you to make reliable decisions. That may be, and probably will be, a daily occurrence. On the other hand, ill fate, God willing, may not befall you at all, but you will most assuredly need a fellow officer for the daily rigors ahead."

Lewis listened to the president's words and nodded in agreement. Then he spoke, "Sir, the man you have just described, the one I could rely upon for counsel and to share the responsibility, that man is William Clark." Having made the statement of his preference for Clark, Lewis sat straight and waited anxiously for what seemed like several minutes for the president to reply.

The president looked up and fondled a pen in his hand as he spoke, "Clark, huh? William Clark. Yes, that is an excellent choice. As a matter of fact, Meriwether, I had his name on a list of candidates for this expedition before I talked to you. I had chosen his brother, George, for one of my earlier attempts." Then, laying the pen down, the president inquired, "Didn't you serve under Clark at one time in your career?" Lewis nodded as the president continued, "He is a captain, too..." Then looking up for a moment he changed his tone, "but I thought he resigned his commission awhile back and moved to Kentucky."

"Yes, sir, I served under Captain Clark," Lewis said smiling. "During the time I served under him I grew to respect his ability to handle men and to make sound decisions in times of stress. Also, during that time, we became good friends." Then Lewis paused and continued as the president listened intently, "Bill did resign his commission. He had family issues to attend to, but he is of military mind, and he is good...no, excellent, in command. I will need his ability to choose and recruit able-bodied men, and I believe he will accept re-instatement in the army to join me on this expedition. I want to ask him."

"Well then, I think that does it. Clark will be the man to accompany you on the expedition. Good choice, Meriwether,
good choice," Jefferson said encouragingly. "I like the decisions you have made already and you haven't even left
Washington. I shall write the orders today. I will…"

"Mr. President," Lewis interrupted. The president set his
pen on the desk and waited for the rest of the comment. "I do
have a request to make with regard to Clark. When I go west I
want a man to command with me, not under me. I know the
Army, and they will not readily agree to a split command; they
want a chain-of-command. However, I believe that this expedition is important enough to merit two captains. While it is
unusual to the military command structure, I ask that when
you write the orders for Clark to join us, that you would agree
that he should also be a captain." Then beginning to talk a
little more rapidly as if selling, Lewis continued, "Clark and I
will share the burden of command equally. Bill is good with
men and," looking down briefly, "good when I need an occasional escape from the routine of command. He is an
exemplary leader of men. His brother George was a distinguished commander of the Virginia troops and Bill learned a
great deal from his brother. While he served in the Kentucky
territory he learned, by example, how to construct forts, map
making and how to deal with the natives. He is able…"

"Now let me interrupt you, Meriwether." Jefferson said
smiling. "I could not agree with you more. You needn't sell me
or continue further. Clark will be your man. His brother
George, as I mentioned, was a man I had chosen for my earlier
attempt in searching for the Northwest Passage. Your man
comes from good stock. I like your choice, and yes, he could
have equal rank. That is a good idea." Then looking out the
window briefly he continued, "As you said, the army may
disagree. They like a singular leadership and linear chain of
command. Chain of command is important to the military

mind." Then looking Lewis in the eye he said firmly, "We cannot start the most important venture of this nation and not agree on such an important point. However, I do not choose to draft him for such a critical position. It must be of his own choosing. I want you to write him and ask him if he will join you on this expedition. You may inform him of our discussion, but I want him to join you voluntarily of his own free will. From top to bottom, every man that enlists in this expedition will be a volunteer. In fact, I would like to name it the "Corps of Volunteers for the Discovery of the Northwest Passage."

"Then that will be our name, sir," Lewis replied. "I understand and fully agree with you, from top to bottom, all the men, including Clark, will be enlisted by their own free will. By the way, Mr. President, there will be no problem of rank and dual captains. I *know* William Clark." Rising from his chair to leave the room, Lewis turned and said to the President, "Incidentally sir, you asked at the outset if I had a date set for my departure."

"Yes, I did," Jefferson replied.

"Today, Mr. President." Lewis said with a broad smile, "Today I will leave for Philadelphia. I plan to study information regarding rivers, known map distances and Indians. I will also enhance what you have taught me regarding zoology, botany, celestial navigation and medicine. Each of these disciplines will likely have daily use on the expedition. While not actually heading west, this is still an important first step."

"Quite right, Meriwether. Those disciplines will prove valuable to your success," Jefferson said. Then he added as he pointed a finger at Lewis, "I will expect a good accounting of the flora and fauna you discover. Prepare samples and return them to me on the first boat back from your winter encampment."

"Yes, sir, I'll take care to document everything I can…, as if you were watching me all the while." Lewis left closing the door softly.

June 19, 1803 Philadelphia

Leaving a study session on zoology and walking down the street, Lewis encounters a man selling dogs. The dogs are large Newfoundland dogs. Lewis, having never seen such a large dog, is immediately curious.

"Good afternoon, sir; what breed is this?" Lewis inquired.

"Do ya like him? He's a biggun, ain't he? Ain't nobody gunna give you trouble ifin you got him by yer side." The man had three dogs on separate rope leashes. Pulling a large black male near, he continued, "These here are Newfoundland dogs, they are. A good and hearty breed, loyal to their owners, good swimmers and sagacious. Why this here dog can hear a mouse in a haystack fifty feet away."

Lewis reached out and touched the dog which raised a paw in a handshake gesture, "Friendly, isn't he?"

"Yes, sir. This one has taken a likin' to ya right off. I kin tell you two would make a good pair," the breeder said with a big smile.

Lewis inquired, "How much are you asking for him?"

"Twenty-five dollars and I'll throw in the rope," replied the man.

"Really, the rope, too!" Lewis replied sarcastically, "Well, I have twenty on me right now. Will you take twenty and call it a deal?"

"Well, I dunno," the man replied. "If I go givin' five dollars away for each dog I sell, I'll be down fifteen dollars by morning."

"Twenty dollars," Lewis said and held the money in his hand.

"Well, then, young man, he's yours," he responded as he took the money. As Lewis walked away with the dog, the man shouted, "Just don't you tell how much it was you gave for him. I kin sell these other two fer twenty-five."

Lewis nodded and walked away with the dog. Kneeling beside the large animal, he said, "Well now, big fella, what am I going to name you?" He petted the dog on its head and shook the fur of his neck. "We are going west, a long way west. How about 'Traveler'? Do you like that name?" The dog kept walking. "Well, big fella, you're as big as a horse, how about I call you 'Hoss'?" Again the dog kept walking. "Jupiter?"

Lewis turned a corner and continued trying other names. Many names came to mind but not one that he really liked. He mumbled several names that came to mind as they walked, "Big Black, Napoleon, Missouri, Sergeant." Then finally, he said, "Hey big dog," the animal stopped and looked at him. It tilted its head to one side as Lewis kneeled beside him, "Most of this trip we are going to be traveling by water, on boats, and when we get to the end, do you know what will be there?" The dog looked at him as he grabbed its fur behind the neck and shook him gently. "Water!" Lewis said with a laugh, "more water. You are going to be a sailor with us on this expedition. How about I call you 'Seaman'?" The dog barked a loud "wharooooff." Lewis laughed and hugged the big dog, "Well, then, that's it. Your name is Seaman." Lewis picked up the rope leash and walked off, reaching down and petting Seaman as they went.

That evening in his hotel room Lewis penned a letter to his friend, William Clark, asking Clark to join him and share the command of the expedition. He added that he would need to actively recruit to populate the expedition with good and able-bodied men, knowledgeable in the ways of the wilderness. He closed saying, " I am pleased to add that President Thomas Jefferson has authorized me to offer you a permanent commission at the rank of captain should you decide to join me. Please respond to me in Pittsburgh as I will be there purchasing a boat and readying the expedition with provisions. I await your favorable response, your friend, Captain Meriwether Lewis."

July 4, 1803

The Louisiana Purchase is announced publicly. The purchase is lauded by General Horatio Gates who writes to Jefferson saying, "Let the land rejoice, for you have bought Louisiana for a song." The country celebrates its birthday with the announcement of the huge land acquisition. Newspaper editorials are full of compliments to the president with the opposing minority loudly questioning the judgment and expense of the deal. The result of the purchase is that the attention of the nation is turned forever westward. Other sovereigns, Mexico in particular, are reluctant to accept the expansion claims of the United States.

July 5, 1803

Meriwether Lewis was closing his quarters in the East Wing of the White House and preparing to leave Washington when the president approached him, "Well now, Meriwether, I see you have vacated your quarters. I must say I have mixed emotions; I am sorry to lose such a valuable aide and consultant. Contrastingly, I am pleased that my dream is taking shape under your stewardship. I know that you have prepared lists of requirements and have thoroughly gone over your estimates of provisions. You ordered a keelboat from Pittsburgh, didn't you? How is that going? When will she be ready?"

"Well, sir," Lewis responded, "I commissioned the construction of the keelboat with a firm in Pittsburgh. They should already be preparing for the construction with the final drawings and purchase of lumber. As soon as she is ready, I'll slip her into the Ohio and proceed to St. Louis. I'm going now to observe what should be the final stages of construction."

"How big is she?" the president inquired.

"She's 55 feet long and about eight feet wide. I have room for twelve oarlocks for rowing and a mast to engage the wind for sail. I think she'll hold better than twelve tons of cargo fully loaded," Lewis said as he unfolded a sheet of paper with a drawing of the craft. Showing the drawing to a very interested president, he added, "She's my own design, I named her *Discovery*. She'll have room for two blunderbusses mounted here on the stern which should prove useful. We will be able to demonstrate to the natives the power we have and encourage them to maintain peace with us as we pass by. Being well armed is the best means I know of to ensure tranquility."

Jefferson responded, "How right you are, Meriwether. Having demonstrable military might is a good idea. It will gain immediate respect from the natives who already know that a musket has more power than a bow. Hopefully, you will only have to demonstrate your power and never have to fire in defense." Then standing straight he looked at Lewis and added, "You named her *Discovery*? Excellent choice, for that will be her mission." Then continuing, Jefferson added, "I have gone over your list of provisions. It looks quite adequate. You're to be commended for your thoroughness and foresight in planning. The ample and varied amount of Indian trade goods is substantial. I do believe the natives you will encounter will find this merchandise interesting and valuable; it should impress them favorably. Let them know that if they are peaceful with your company, the United States government will establish even more trade with them in the future. It will profit them to be peaceful."

Lewis smiled knowing that he had Jefferson's approval for what he had done thus far. He added, "I've made a reservation on an additional smaller boat, too. It's a red pirogue* about 33 feet long. Once we get as far upriver as the keelboat will navigate, we'll need a lesser craft to proceed through the shallow waters. The pirogue will handle the bulk of the cargo, and we can fashion canoes and other boats for the men."

Jefferson smiled broadly and with hands on his hips said, "Meriwether, again I am impressed with your thoroughness. If ever a man had a doubt as to whether or not you were the one for this expedition, your attention to every detail should convince them otherwise. I am pleased, very pleased." Then leaning back against his table he said, "I do have one problem, however."

"What's that, sir?" Lewis queried.

"Well, Meriwether," the president smiled and said, "What am I going to do for a personal secretary now that you are leaving on this assignment? Your efficiency around here will be sorely missed. You know that, don't you?"

Meriwether looked around and then back at the president, "Thank you, sir, for being so generous with your comments. I'm sure that you will find another to fill in until I am able to return. I should be gone no more than eighteen months."

"Fill in!" Jefferson laughed and put his hand on Lewis' shoulder. "Lewis, Lewis, Lewis," he said with his voice trailing off. "When you do return from this epic voyage, you will be a national hero. I have no doubt of that. You will have stories to tell of your adventures and your findings. You and each of your men will be sought after. You will have grown larger than the humble office you now leave. To return to being my personal secretary will no longer be an option. You will be the country's own Christopher Columbus. Why, a career in politics would be yours for the taking." Then waving his hand

---

* A large canoe type boat commonly used for river travel.

in gesture he added, "An ambassadorship would be very possible. You could be a professor, or even president, of any esteemed university in the nation of your choosing. You are destined for greatness, my young friend, true greatness."

"I never thought of that, sir," Meriwether responded.

"Your humbleness of spirit will only endear you more with the people, Meriwether. Just you wait and see," the president said reassuringly.

"Well, sir," Lewis replied, "One thing is for sure. I have to be successful with the task at hand before any of those things can happen. As my mother always said, 'First thing's first.' For now, I know that I have to keep my mind and my focus on the problems of simply getting things moving. There seems to be something new each day to take my time. I cannot wait until Captain Clark joins me."

"Oh, yes, Captain Clark. When will Clark meet up with you? Has that been arranged?" Jefferson queried.

Lewis replied, "I have written him and explained the expedition. I told him of our conversation and asked him to join me after I leave Pittsburgh. I expect it will most likely be in the fall. I await his reply, I must say with some anxiety, but I am confident that he will answer in the affirmative."

The president said, "Meriwether, I will expect letters from you as often as you can send them regarding your progress and problems. This expedition has been a favorite hope of mine for a very long time, my darling project. Now, I believe, with the announcement of the purchase of Louisiana, it also has the eyes of our nation—quite possibly the world—all awaiting word of your fate. My prayers will go with you, and may heaven watch over you and your men as you make your way into those uncharted lands."

Then, walking over to his desk he turned and pulled some papers from the drawer. "Take a seat, I would like to go over a procedure with you that is important to me."

"Certainly, sir," Lewis replied as he seated himself near the president's desk.

Jefferson unfolded a paper with a matrix of alphabetic letters. "I want to leave nothing to chance here. I have developed a special code for you to use when writing sensitive papers to me. In the event they are intercepted or fall into the wrong hands, this code will protect your information. You needn't write everything in code as people will want to read your transcripts when you return. But the sensitive information regarding certain Indian tribes, fur traders, British and French outposts that have been established, those should be coded."

Lewis nodded his understanding, and the president continued, "You are to use this code and, in addition, begin each correspondence with the secret word, 'artichokes'. That way, should your code sheet fall into the wrong hands, even when deciphered, I will be assured the correspondence came from your hand."

"Very good, sir," Lewis said as he picked up the code matrix and studied it. "I had not planned for such an event. Perhaps I'm too trusting." Then holding the paper out he asked, "I assure you, all important communications will be written using this code. Is this copy mine?"

"Yes, yes it is," the president said. "I have another in my desk to decipher your letters." Then the president said, "We have another item to conclude before you leave."

"What's that?" Lewis inquired.

Jefferson pulled another paper from his drawer and put it on the desk in front of Lewis. "Your trip will be long and hazardous and God only knows what manner of difficulties you will encounter. When you reach the mouth of the Columbia at the edge of the Pacific Ocean, you may want to, or need to, consider returning home by sea. In the event you make contact with a ship, I have written for you this general letter of credit to ensure payment of your trip home. Any ship's captain should accept this letter. It has the full faith and credit of the United States government behind it, and it bears my signature and seal. Returning by sea may well be the best means of getting all of you back here safely and in a timely manner."

Lewis picked up the letter and read it. Then he commented, "This is good, Mr. President. You have told me how thorough you thought my planning for the trip has been. I must now compliment you. The code for private messages and now this letter of credit to friendly ships, indicate you have spent time planning on my behalf. Thank you." Smiling, Lewis folded the letter and the code matrix and put them in his pocket.

Lewis stood up from the president's desk, looked at the president and said, "I shall not disappoint you, sir; we will provide documentation of each new and different thing we encounter. I will keep my journal as accurately as possible. I'll write in code where needed, and each man that goes with us that can script will be encouraged to do so, to record observations from his point of view as well."

The two men looked at each other for a moment and then simultaneously gave a quick nod, shook hands and Lewis departed.

July 29, 1803 Pittsburgh

Lewis is now in Pittsburgh overseeing the final construction of the large keelboat that will be used on the expedition. He has also purchased a second, smaller boat, called a pirogue, to be used when the larger vessel can no longer navigate the river. He returns to his hotel room and asks the desk clerk for any messages. The clerk hands him a letter from William Clark.

Lewis smiled broadly, snapped his fingers, and said to the clerk, "Finally, my friend has responded. Today, sir, is a good day." Lewis proceeded to open the envelope with gusto. He walked over to a nearby chair and started to seat himself but was too excited to sit down. He stood to read the letter. As he read the letter he smiled broadly and then read aloud, "My friend, I assure you no man lives with whom I would prefer to undertake such a trip as yourself. Please accept this letter as my confirmation to join you. I will meet you in October at Clarksville on the Ohio side of the river across from Louisville. I shall immediately recruit and begin to train some men who will support our trip."

Lewis was ecstatic; he held the letter up high then ran over to the desk clerk, shaking the letter in front of him as he exclaimed, "William Clark, no, no, Captain Clark, is going to join me. We now have our destiny before us. We will explore Louisiana together for the United States. This grand and glorious expedition will soon begin."

The bewildered desk clerk smiled and looked down at the guest register book and commented, "Yes, Mr. Lewis, I am glad to see that you are pleased with the news that you have received today."

"Pleased? Pleased you say?" Lewis was exuberant. "My good man, a great burden has just been lifted from my shoulders. My best friend in all the world, Captain William Clark, will now join me in the task which was given to me by the president himself, President Thomas Jefferson. We are to explore and report our findings regarding the new lands just purchased west of the Mississippi River. The Corps of Volunteers for the Discovery of the Northwest Passage is now being formed and will begin. The lands of the Louisiana Purchase are now going to be explored and documented in the name of the United States for all posterity."

The desk clerk looked at him strangely and then calmly said, "President Jefferson? Indeed. Well, sir, I hope that your exploration will be successful. The Mississippi is quite some distance from here. Will Mr. Clark be joining you soon? Will he need a room?"

Lewis looked at the clerk and replied, "No, he will be meeting me later, and it is not Mr. Clark; it is Captain Clark." Then, re-reading the letter as he walked away, Lewis proceeded to his room.

August 31, 1803 Pittsburgh

Meriwether Lewis meets with the boat builder who, at long last, informs him that his keelboat, Discovery, is ready to launch. Lewis is very displeased with the contractor as he had planned on the craft being ready in mid-July.

"Mr. Lewis," the contractor said, "your craft is now complete," as the last nails were being driven into the deck planking. "She is ready for your inspection and payment."

"No need for me to inspect her now. I, unlike you, have been here nearly every day to witness the construction," Lewis said angrily. "If you had not had such a fondness for whiskey and rum, perhaps my craft would have been completed in July as I planned. You did promise early to mid-July when you took on the contract."

The contractor responded, "Sir, I lost two men to malaria, and one left without notice. It is not easy to replace competent carpenters. Those days when I was not at the construction site, I was recruiting new men to assist me in construction."

Not giving ground, Lewis replied, "Where were you recruiting them, in saloons? What quality of man would you find there? The same as yourself, no doubt." Then pacing back and forth in front of the contractor, Lewis continued, "Sir, you have delayed me greatly, delays that could cost me God knows what in the future. Now you ask for payment. I wish your contract were with me personally and not the Army; I wouldn't pay you in full for having missed the promised completion date. I would impose a debit charge for each week late."

"But Mr. Lewis, I have done…," the contractor started to say.

"Nothing but delay me," Lewis retorted pointing his finger at him. "Your quality of craftsmanship needed my constant vigilance or the boat would not float. I have tried shouting at you, cursing you, why, I even begged you to finish on schedule; all to no avail, and now you want payment. Sir, you have no conscience. During your delay, the river has gone down to the point where I am required to ship some of my goods overland to Wheeling in hopes that the waters there will support this craft. Fortunately, I have the pirogue to offload some of my cargo." Then pacing and stopping suddenly, Lewis again pointed his finger at the man and continued, "Your fondness of drink will put you out of business, and I trust, that will not be a bad thing. The boat building industry cannot withstand the likes of you. Pay you? Yes, I will pay you for I, at least, have honor, even to a commitment delivered late."

Lewis paid the man and handed him his voucher, "Now sir, if you will please leave my boat before I have you thrown off."

The man took the papers and walked off the boat mumbling about government contracts not being worthwhile.

While waiting for the boat construction to be completed, Lewis had recruited eleven men to join him. As planned, the men were recruited for their woodsman skills, river or boating skills, as well as their knowledge in certain trade skills. Recruiting men for the prestigious trip was not difficult.

Finally, *Discovery* was ready to launch, and by 10:00 A.M. she was loaded with nearly eight tons of cargo. The balance was placed into the pirogue with some heavy material being sent overland to Wheeling. These items represented all the material on the meticulous lists that Lewis had prepared. The material was categorized in groups:

Mathematical Instruments: contained telescopes, compasses, quadrants, sextants, thermometers and plotting instruments.

Camp Supplies: included many hand tools, whetstones for sharpening, fishhooks and line, mosquito netting, soap, portable soup mix, salt and writing paper with ink.

Gifts for Indians: included novel items such as mirrors, needles, scissors, combs, ribbons, tobacco, tomahawks that doubled as pipes, knives, brass kettles, face paint and beads.

Clothing Articles: included knapsacks, blankets, shirts, coats, frocks, pants and stockings.

Munitions: included rifles, gunpowder, lead, flints and one long-barreled air rifle.

Medical Supplies: included forceps, lancets, tourniquets, syringes, a powerful laxative called Dr. Rush's 'Thunderbolts' and assorted other medications.

Reference Literature: included books on botany, mineralogy and tables for longitude and latitude.

Lewis gave orders for the men to place these items in various locations as they stowed the cargo in the keelboat and the red pirogue. He knew where each item was located. Once the boats were loaded, Lewis gave the orders to shove off. Then *Discovery*, with Lewis in command, eleven new recruits and his dog, Seaman, moved westward down the shallow waters of the Ohio River. Lewis beamed with pride.

As they proceed downriver, Lewis became concerned about the weight of cargo in the keelboat. The water was low as it had not rained in quite some time. When the keelboat hit a sand bar, it would require considerable tugging to dislodge her and return to open water. Frequently Lewis had to engage the service of farmers to use their oxen to pull the boat through stretches of shallow water. Concerned about the river when he stopped in Wheeling, West Virginia, to pick up the balance of his cargo, he purchased a second, white pirogue. With two lesser vessels now at his disposal, Lewis ordered the men to move some of the cargo into the new white pirogue to disburse weight. When finished, they proceeded downriver toward their rendezvous with Clark. Fortunately, rains in tributaries were causing the river to rise, and he made better time.

October 25, 1803 Ohio River near Louisville, Kentucky Territory

As planned, Meriwether Lewis and eleven men meet William Clark at Clarksville, a small settlement near Louisville, Kentucky. Seeing one another from afar, the two men first fire a shot into the air and wave. The gap between them closes as Clark's group approaches the campsite. Smiling broadly, Lewis and his men wait as Clark and his group of ten draw near. Both groups of men watch on as Lewis greets Clark with enthusiasm. The two share a robust handshake as each man grips the forearm of the other with his free hand. Both smiling, they exchange a cordial welcome.

Lewis spoke, "God, it's good to see you again. I have never been so pleased as when I received your letter in Pittsburgh. I knew you would accept to join me; I just knew it. Still, I had to read it three times just to make sure. Bill, you look good. Are you prepared to spend the upcoming months on this expedition?"

Clark replied, "Good to see you, too, Merry. Of course, I would accept your offer, how could I do otherwise? This is the prize of all possible assignments. And to share it with a friend;

there really was nothing to consider. Needless to say, this expedition is ambitious in scope. I have spent many an hour thinking of how this command would face the rigors of the uncharted northwest. But I am as prepared as a man can be for such a challenge. And, as you can imagine, these men and I are eager to get underway." Then he walked over to the river's edge and looked at the keelboat. He turned and said, "Just look at this boat and all these provisions! Meriwether, you have outdone yourself. How much money did you say Congress gave you for the expedition?"

"Two thousand five hundred," Lewis replied with a smile. "With it I have furnished this keelboat. I named her *Discovery*; she's of my own design, and I filled her with provisions. Hey, I even have some money left over."

Clark replied, "You always were a prudent man with the money. I suppose that is why they made you paymaster." Then, still looking at the boats, he continued, "It looks like you have ample room here in the keelboat; why the two smaller boats?"

Lewis replied, "I have them to spread the weight out for times when the river's low. Fortunately, the recent rains and the river's natural depth increased as we moved on. That has kept me from needing towing. We had to tow her a couple times before I got to Wheeling. Another thing I have learned…" Lewis began as he gestured toward the bow of the boat.

"What's that?" Clark said inquisitively.

Lewis said, as he pointed to the cargo bags, "I'll need to repack and stow for proper weight distribution. I could use your experience there. Don't want the fore or aft sections loaded unevenly. It makes her too difficult to maneuver. I did use oilcloth to cover things, but the rains soaked it all pretty well anyway. Had to stop and dry things out to prevent rust and mildew." Then walking toward the pirogues Lewis continued, "You asked why the pirogues? Two reasons actually: first, to be able to shift the cargo around so the keelboat won't draft so low in the water. When we reach flat stretches of the river that have sandbars, I don't want to tow her. And second, more importantly, when we finally go as far up the Missouri as possible with the keelboat, we'll be able to proceed on through the more shallow waters with these two pirogues. They will actually become our mainstay when *Discovery* heads home." Lewis said proudly.

"Good thinking." Clark said, "I've always admired your attention to detail. I'm quite sure I can rest confidently knowing that we are well provided for on the trip." Then he said, "How forgetful of me. I should introduce the men that I have recruited for the expedition. We will, I am sure, get to know one another quite well."

"First," Clark said as he turned to the large Negro man standing closest to him, "This is my man, York. He has been with me since, well, since I was a lad, and he'll be with me on this trip. He's strong, follows instructions well and has never given me trouble. I've taken the liberty to teach him to shoot because on a mission like this, we may need every rifle we can get."

"York, I am pleased," Lewis said as he shook hands with the large black man. "Captain Clark has spoken of you often in the past, but I never knew you were such a big fella. Welcome."

York looked at Lewis and simply said, "Pleased to meet you Capt'n." Then, not moving too far from Clark's side, he stepped back and away.

Clark stepped next to another man and said, "This is John Shields, a blacksmith, a gunsmith and general mechanic. I'm sure we will often be able to use all of his talents. We will need him to keep all our weapons in good firing order."

Shaking his hand, Lewis said, "A pleasure, I'm sure we'll get to know you all. Meanwhile, feel free to proceed to introduce yourselves to the men that have come with me from Pittsburgh as soon as Captain Clark finishes with these introductions." The man nodded and stepped back as the next man stepped up.

Clark continued, "This here is Nathaniel Pryor, a sergeant, and his cousin, Charles Floyd. Both good men, both from Kentucky. Well, hell, for that matter, all these men are from Kentucky, so I guess I don't need to say that part any more." The men laughed, and Clark continued to move down the line of men with Lewis, shaking hands with each as he was introduced.

Clark then proceeded, "This is George Gibson and William Bratton, and this here is John Colter, and these two men here are brothers, Joseph and Reubin Field. And this last youngster on the end here, his name is George Shannon. He tells me he's just eighteen but old enough to go with us. His pappy agreed, so I consented to let him come. Young as he is, he may even grow some while we are on this expedition." He reached out and patted young Shannon on the shoulder.

Then Clark stepped back and with a gesture said to Lewis, "All these men were enlisted for their ability as men able to get by in the wilderness. Each should contribute to the success of our venture. They're aware of the hardships we might face, but each of them, to the man, has a frontier spirit, and each man wants to be a part of this great exploration. They know the native Indian ways and are able to make and understand hand signs."

"As I said earlier, men," Lewis said, with a pleased look on his face, as he addressed all the men. "I am proud to make your acquaintance. Now I will introduce you to those men who have come with me this far. We'll set up camp here for the night so that you can get to know one another. Tomorrow we will set out downriver." Lewis proceeded to introduce his group of men to Captain Clark and the men from Kentucky.

After the introductions, Clark stepped close to Lewis, waved
his hands out over the boats and turning to include the men,
he said, "So President Jefferson's dream is taking shape right
here in front of us. What'd he say we should call ourselves?"

Lewis smiled broadly, looked at all the men and replied,
"He said, since we are a group of volunteers, that we should be
known as the 'Corps of Volunteers for the Discovery of the
Northwest Passage.' They expect it will take us eighteen
months to reach the Pacific after we leave St. Louis in the
spring. How they figure that, I don't know except we know
from the longitudinal readings the distance from St. Louis to
the Pacific. That's over 2000 miles as the crow flies and not as
a river flows. Not to mention the mountains we will be
crossing."

Clark answered, "You plan on staying in St. Louis for the
winter? Probably best. After all, it's already late in the year, and
I would rather winter near a known settlement than
somewhere up the Missouri where provisions would be harder
to come by." Stroking his chin he continued, "Eighteen
months, huh? That's a long time to spend in uncharted
country. But on the way back, we'll have the river current to
help us along, so I suppose we can do it in eighteen months."
Then looking at the large black dog, Clark said, "What a fine
looking animal. Big too, why, I've never in all my days seen a
dog that big. What kind is he? Where did you get him?"

Lewis said proudly, "This here is Seaman. He's a
Newfoundland dog. He is big, ain't he? Got him in
Pittsburgh. Cost me twenty dollars, but I think he will prove
his worth when we're in rugged country. He's already been
catching squirrels swimming in the river for supper. Good at it
too; quite the hunter, this one."

Clark reached out and patted the large dog on the head,
"How you doing, Seaman? Are you ready to chase away bad
Indians and stand guard all night?" Then turning to Lewis,

Clark put his hand on his shoulder, and the two men began walking away from the others. Clark said, "My brother George has invited us to his home for dinner. I took the liberty of accepting for both of us. We've got a lot to discuss, Merry. I want you to tell me everything. George is eager to learn of our plans, and knowing him, he'll probably keep us up all night with questions about the trip, the president and our plans. Exactly what do we have as provisions in that huge keelboat? You spoke of studies in your letter. What disciplines have you learned to assist us? What did you do in Washington? Tell me of the president and your preparations. I am eager to catch up on everything since we last met."

"Yes, indeed. You've got more questions than a schoolboy, but I agree. I too have questions and we've a lot to talk about," Lewis said nodding to Clark. "I look forward to meeting your brother; he's a well-known patriot." Then turning to gesture toward the river Lewis continued, "*Discovery* is provided amply with many things. You can read the manifest whenever you please. Some of the other provisions that we will need, like whiskey and foodstuff, we can purchase in St. Louis before we depart up the Missouri in the spring. I have U. S. Army credit for supplies."

Clark nodded in approval, and the two men rejoined the others who were standing and exchanging information. The men made camp and talked late into the night, each man acquainting himself with the others and sharing stories of his home and people he knew.

Lewis and Clark departed early in the evening to visit the home of General George Rogers Clark for dinner. The next day, in the presence of General Clark, the men from Kentucky were sworn into the army in a solemn ceremony. After repacking some of cargo, they started down the Ohio River.

November 11, 1803 Ohio River, Illinois area

The expedition's crew is moving down the Ohio River toward St. Louis. The two captains exchange information, eager to share knowledge of a new subject. Lewis shares the recently acquired surveying information he has learned. Clark puts the knowledge to immediate use by practicing known distance measurements on the Ohio.

Lewis joked with Clark, "We already know these distances, my friend. They're all well-documented many times over. Wait until we reach the uncharted regions to ply your skills."

Clark replied, "I disagree. What better place to verify measurements? It's fascinating to know I can actually make accurate measurements without consulting the maps. Suffer me these lessons while I assure myself that I know how to use these instruments and apply the art correctly."

"You mean so you can play," Lewis chided Clark. "Yes, I agree. What better way to test your knowledge than on known stretches of the river. Are your calculations proving accurate?"

"With you as a teacher? Surely you jest," Clark responded. "I've made only two minor errors which I discovered all on my own, thank you. Actually, I'm very impressed with these instruments and this technology. One cannot resist the temptation to calculate when given these tools. In fact, I believe that once we set winter camp, I'll teach others of our party, at least those that can script, how to use these tools to survey."

"Good idea," Lewis replied. "There is no such thing as wasted knowledge, and training men to survey will be beneficial." Then he said jokingly, "I'm glad I thought of it."

Discovery came around a bend in the river where they could see Fort Massac ahead. "There it is, Fort Massac, just where it's supposed to be," Clark announced.

"Good," Lewis replied. "That's comforting to know. We'll spend the night there, and if all goes as planned we should meet a detachment of men from Captain Bissell. He was asked to send men, volunteers, of course, that would want to join the expedition."

Clark inquired, "How many do you think we will get? I believe that we should have at least forty men when we leave St. Louis. The first leg of the trip will be hard, and we need enough men to defend ourselves and handle the work of up-stream navigation."

Lewis responded, "I agree. We'll need men at the oars, men pulling tow ropes and some poling. If we have too many, it will be hard to feed them and coordinate everything. Forty to fifty should be enough, no more than fifty. Captain Bissell should have eight or more, but if he has too many, well, we will have the luxury to pick and choose which men we want."

The boats moved to a point on the river near the fort. Lewis ordered the men to drop anchor and to tie off the boats fore and aft. As soon as the boats were secure, the captains proceeded to Fort Massac. When they walked through the gates of the fort, they were approached by a uniformed officer.

The officer spoke, "Good day, gentlemen. I'm Captain Bissell, one of you must be Captain Lewis with the northwest expeditionary mission. I've been expecting you."

"Yes, we are," Clark replied extending his hand. "I'm Captain William Clark, and this is Captain Meriwether Lewis. We are the specially formed Corps of Volunteers for the Discovery of the Northwest Passage. We were informed that you may possibly have recruited good men to join us on our expedition."

The men nodded and shook hands as Captain Bissell invited them to sit in his quarters inside the fort. As they walked, Captain Bissell inquired as to the trip thus far and

explained that he had expected some volunteers from
Tennessee to join them. They proceeded to his office. Taking a
chair behind his desk and next to a U. S. flag, Captain Bissell
spoke, "Gentlemen, I have the names of eight men, possibly a
ninth, to join you on your expedition. They have not shown up
as yet and are now overdue. Eight will be regular army,
Tennessee regulars, and when they heard of the nature of the
trip, each man eagerly volunteered. Those eight will be turned
over to your command as soon as they arrive."

"Fine," Lewis said smiling. "We need and want disciplined
men, and we need them to be volunteers, too. That's
President Jefferson's wish. All the men on the expedition are
to be volunteers. I don't want to wait long. Are you sure they'll
be here soon? You said there could be a ninth, hasn't he
decided yet?"

Captain Bissell replied, "It's not a matter of his deciding.
He wants to go. It's just that the ninth man is not regular army.
He's a civilian. His name is George Drewyer, I told him he'd
be given an opportunity to talk to you. I can tell you this
much, Drewyer's a damn good man. He is half Canadian and
half Indian. He's good as an interpreter and with sign
language; God knows you'll need that. I also believe him to be
superior in judgment and cool as a cucumber. Further, I know
of no better hunter than George Drewyer, a crack shot and
able to be where the game is."

Clark looked at Lewis and then back at Captain Bissell.
"Well Captain, if this man is as good as your reference, we'll
need him. In fact, if you have a couple more like him, we
would want to meet them, too."

The officers laughed, and then Captain Bissell rose from
his seat and said, "I think it's time you met George Drewyer.
He's in our fort now waiting for you." Then the captain
shouted to a soldier outside his office door, "Corporal, go and
tell Mr. Drewyer to come to my quarters."

"Yes, sir," the corporal replied and left.

Upon his return, the captains walked outside. Lewis looked at Drewyer, a strong man with clear eyes in a weathered face. Drewyer stepped forward with his hand outstretched, and as Lewis shook his hand he said, "I'm George Drewyer, sir, and it's my pleasure to meet you. Word of this expedition has been spreading quickly. It'd be an honor if you would allow me to be a part of the trip. I love the idea of the frontier and I want to be with the men that see it first."

Lewis looked at the man and turned and said, "And see it you shall, Mr. Drewyer. God willing, you will be with us all the way to the Pacific Ocean and back. Captain Clark and I would like to offer you a position as interpreter and hunter. You are familiar with some native languages and how the natives make sign language aren't you?"

Drewyer replied, "Yes, sir, I speak English and French and can understand some of the Indian languages. I use sign language pretty good with them too when I have to. Sign language is universal with the Indians."

Lewis smiled and said, "Good, we can use you as an interpreter. There are lots of French fur traders where we are going, and being able to understand the natives will be most beneficial. If you join us, your pay will be twenty-five dollars a month."

"Thank you, Captain. That's good pay for being on such an adventure," Drewyer said enthusiastically.

Lewis said, "There's more. Captain Bissell has the names of eight men from Tennessee that were supposed to join us. I don't want to wait here for them to arrive. Your first duty will be to bring them to us. Will you get them and bring them to our winter quarters on the east bank of the Mississippi, opposite St. Louis? If you'll do this, I'll advance you thirty dollars now and meet you there later.

Drewyer replied, "Captain Bissell has already given me the names and locations of these men. I'll get 'em and bring 'em to the campsite, not a problem. I'll start tomorrow."

Clark said, "Good, Mr. Drewyer, good. We need a dependable man with your skills. Is it done then?"

"Done," Drewyer said as he grasped first Clark's hand and then Lewis's with a firm handshake.

Clark continued, "You'll earn every dollar of your pay, I believe, but if I judge men correctly, you will enjoy it even though it may be fraught with danger."

"Well then," Lewis said turning to Captain Bissell, "I will authorize a thirty dollar advance to Mr. Drewyer. Will you see that he gets the pay?"

"Certainly, Captain, not a problem; consider it done," Captain Bissell replied.

Fall / Winter 1803 Illinois Territory

The men of the expedition reach the confluence of the Ohio and Mississippi Rivers. Turning their boats into the Mississippi, they are immediately challenged by a very strong and powerful river, full of floating debris. They head north into the current using towropes, oars and sail. The power of the river is daunting, making navigation upstream with heavily laden boats extremely difficult. By the end of the first day, even though they have crossed the river several times to take advantage of lighter currents at the river bends, their progress is only ten and one-half miles. They now know firsthand what they will be facing as they journey up the Missouri.

Clark said to Lewis, "Ya know, we have talked several times of the number of men that we would need to accomplish this mission. Back east, they thought a small contingent would be best. Ain't no way, my friend. It's pretty clear now that the number we discussed, forty to fifty men, is more accurate.

We'll need numbers to make any progress against these kind of currents."

Lewis replied, "The river itself makes that point clear, not to mention that the men will need to relieve one another on a routine basis. This duty is strenuous to say the least. Sure could use those men Drewyer went to get. Anyway, we should be at Fort Kaskaskia soon. I'll use the draft authorization letter from Dearborn to get us more men. Until then, we'll have to do our best until we get there."

November 28, 1803 Fort Kaskaskia, Illinois Territory

The expedition arrives at Fort Kaskaskia, Illinois Territory. They order the boats anchored and securely tied and proceed to the fort where they are greeted by Captain Amos Stoddard. They introduce themselves and exchange cordialities.

"I'm Captain Amos Stoddard. You men gotta be the expedition the Army is sending into Louisiana. We didn't know whether or not to expect you. Everyone hoped that you would stop here. The whole fort is buzzing with anticipation of your visit. Let me extend whatever hospitalities our fort has to offer. A lot of men, quite understandably, want to join you."

"Captain Stoddard," Clark said with a smile, "we're very glad to have reached this milestone. Your fort is a welcomed resting point for weary travelers. In fact, we need to talk with you."

"Certainly," Captain Stoddard replied. "Come to my office. The entire Army is rumoring about your expedition to the west. We here at Kaskaskia are proud to welcome you and support you with any provisions you may need."

"Thanks, Captain," Lewis said as he reached into a pocket and produced a letter. "We will need some provisions, but more importantly, we will need your support by providing us with men. This letter from General Dearborn authorizes you to release men to me as we may require."

Captain Stoddard took the letter and read it then looked up at Lewis and said, "How many do you need? I know a lot of the men would like to volunteer for this mission. I can replace whatever number you require with new recruits or transfers from the east."

Lewis replied, "Thank you for understanding. We believe that we'll need fourteen more men. We can wait here a few days for you to make necessary adjustments. Besides, that will give time for the others who will be joining us soon."

Clark continued, "Yes, Captain Lewis is right. Fourteen men will enable us to make progress against this little stream out there. We'll trust your judgment and recommendations as to which men would best support our efforts."

Captain Stoddard looked at the two adventurers and said, "Fourteen. Well now, I had planned on possibly six or eight, but as I said, we'll make do. I would rather be shorthanded here for a while than have you struggle upriver. Your mission takes priority, national priority. We knew that, and Dearborn's letter makes it clear. We're proud to help. There should be no problem getting volunteers."

They talked a few more minutes about the expedition, their boats and possible hazards on the trip. Then they got up and moved outside. Captain Stoddard called one of his sergeants to muster all the men interested in volunteering for the expedition. Twenty-three men were assembled in a matter of minutes.

Clark walked around the men as Lewis mimicked his examination from the opposite side. They met off to the side and discussed the men. Fourteen were agreed upon and they reported their selection to Captain Stoddard. It was agreed that the men would be ready to leave the post by December 4 and join the expedition.

December 4, 1803

In the morning Clark takes the crew of men and moves out up the Mississippi toward St. Louis. Lewis travels up the Illinois side of the river on horseback. Five days later Clark and crew anchors near the mouth of the Wood River, across from St. Louis and opposite the mouth of the mighty Missouri River. There they begin to build winter quarters, which they name Fort Wood. The boats are pulled onto the riverbank as far as practical to avoid river action. One pirogue is left anchored to use as transport to cross to St. Louis as required. Lewis goes to St. Louis early to send and receive mail, to check out available supplies, to meet with the merchants and politicians and learn what he can about the area.

On his return trip from St. Louis, Lewis came into the camp at Fort Wood with a brisk walk. Seeing the Field brothers he asked, "Captain Clark? Where's Captain Clark?"

"Just over there," they pointed, "finishing up his lunch."

Lewis walked over to where Clark was eating. He set his rifle down and smiled; then he laughed and said, "You'll never guess what happened to me in St. Louis. I met the God damnedest pompous fool I've ever seen."

"What are you talking about?" Clark said. "Here, have a drink and tell me what happened." Lewis seated himself and poured a drink.

"Well, when I was in St. Louis, asking about starting the trip up the Missouri River, this Spanish fella came up; said his name was Colonel Carlos Dehault Delassus. He was all dressed in a fancy uniform, and he asked me..." Lewis got a broad grin on his face and continued, "You know what he asked me?" Then he leaned back and laughed, "He asked me, no, no, he told me. He had the audacity to tell me that he was the Spanish Commandant or something like that, and that if we were planning to go into Spanish territory, we would need to pay him for Spanish passports and that we could not explore the Missouri until after the official transfer of sovereignty had taken place in his presence in St. Louis."

"Spanish passports?" Clark said with an inquiring smile.

"Yes, yes, Spanish passports," Lewis said. "The arrogant bastard actually thought he could charge us for them, or better yet, that we needed them." Then in a more serious tone, he continued, "It just goes to show you that President Jefferson was right, absolutely correct. If the United States doesn't lay 'official' claim to those lands west of St. Louis, they will be open for grabs. Even with the Louisiana Purchase all wrapped up, there could still be disputes. We may have to defend the Louisiana Territory from the Spanish with military force."

Clark inquired, "Did he have any soldiers with him to back up his position?"

Lewis answered, "No, not that I could see. But there he was, all dressed up in fancy clothes and speaking broken English, telling me that we'd have to pay him for passports. I think all he wanted was the money."

Clark said, "Well, my friend, perhaps it's a good thing that we have established Fort Wood on this side of the Mississippi. I would not want to defend ourselves against Spaniards or give rise to any conflict before we leave. Remember, President Jefferson said we were to have a peaceful mission."

Lewis agreed, "Yes, his instructions are to be peaceful, but I am sure he meant with the native Indians. Even President Jefferson could not have imagined that the Spanish would be spouting sovereignty rights in our face over the newly acquired territory. But I agree with you, there's no need to have bloodshed with fools. Still, it points out quite clearly the need for our expedition to affirm the sovereignty of the United States over the Louisiana Territory."

"There's another thing," Clark said, "reflecting on his orders. I'm glad that the president told us not to explore any lands west of St. Louis this winter; I'd rather save everything for the mission up the Missouri in the spring, no need to take unnecessary risks. Do you think he knew we would meet this resistance? How did you leave it with your Spanish friend?"

Lewis waved a hand in the air and responded, "I told him that our mission was purely scientific, that we were to explore the upper Missouri and to set the longitude and latitude of all prominent points." Then shifting his position on his chair he continued, "As for the president's knowing we could run into this kind of trouble, I just don't know; he's uncanny. He's never ceased to amaze me with his knowledge and insight into problems. I think he knew it was potentially dangerous and he wanted us to stay focused on the Northwest Passage Expedition. He couldn't have known of this Colonel Delassus or the payment of tribute to the Spanish." Then looking around the camp he inquired, "Have we recruited any more men?"

Clark smiled and said, "Yes, I have talked to some, but they were incompetent. We wouldn't want their type on an extended journey, but I did get word that a man named Gass, Patrick Gass, I believe, wanted to join us. He claims to be a good carpenter and frontiersman. He's enthusiastic and we can certainly use a good carpenter. Building this fort is a real chore."

Lewis replied, "Any man with usable talent, willing to seek us out, will certainly be interviewed."

January 1804 Fort Wood, Illinois Territory

Patrick Gass is enlisted as a member of the expedition. The expedition is now forty-three members strong. They have named three men as sergeants: Charles Floyd, John Ordway and Nathaniel Pryor. Separate duties and details are delegated to each of the sergeants. The sergeants will be included on decision making when the captains feel they

need additional counsel. The captains decide that there will be a per-
manent party and a first-year party. They will consult the sergeants later
for advice in deciding which men will comprise the permanent party and
which men will return after their first winter stop at Mandan.

March 10, 1804

The winter has been long and the men at Fort Wood are bored. They
continually drill in military regimen, marching with precision handling of
their weapons. They play cards and use target practice to pass time.

The captains go to St. Louis to attend an official ceremony that will
transfer the Louisiana Territory to the United States. They leave the
sergeants in charge of the fort. In speeches at the ceremony they announce
that the Corps of Volunteers for the Discovery of the Northwest Passage
has a larger scope, larger than simply exploring and mapping the country.
Now, the trip has diplomatic importance as well. They put foremost on
the agenda that they will communicate to the Indian tribes that there is a
new Great White Father in Washington and that each tribe is now part
of a larger nation. They will inform all tribes they may happen to meet
that sovereignty has moved from previous French or English claims
completely to the United States. The tribes will be encouraged to cooperate
with the government and not make war on one another. Those that follow
the directive would enrich themselves with fruitful trade. This is the first
full disclosure of the true purpose of the mission. Those listening at the
ceremony applaud except for a small contingent of Spanish, who walk
away mumbling and pointing.

Upon return to Fort Wood the captains learn of a near mutiny.
Corporal Whitehouse, Privates William Werner, John Shields and John
Colter had ignored the orders of Sergeant Ordway to stay in camp and
left, without permission, to visit a grog shop where they got drunk. The
men are punished. Corporal Whitehouse is busted to private, Privates
Shields and Colter face a court-martial. They beg for forgiveness and
pledge not to be disobedient in the future. They are all permitted to stay

with the expedition but are given ten days of hard labor and confinement to quarters. Sergeant Ordway is admonished for not being more firm with the men. Captain Lewis calls the men together to tell them that whenever he or Captain Clark is not present, the orders of any of the sergeants carry the same weight as if they are orders from him or Captain Clark directly. Further, being military men, they should have already known that fact of military life and that future disobedience will be dealt with more harshly.

April 1, 1804

The captains meet with the sergeants and agree upon the names of the permanent detachment and the first-year detachment. While those names will be subject to review later, the permanent detachment will continue for the full duration of the trip. The first-year detachment will only go upriver until they reach the winter camp at the Mandan village. In the spring, when the permanent detachment proceeds on, the first-year detachment will be sent back down river with the keelboat to St. Louis. They will bring all accumulated information back as to how the expedition has fared with the Indians up to that time. They will carry topographical maps and letters to the president which will include all collections of plants and animals gathered along the way.

Today, from the St. Louis area, they prepare and send samples of plants and animals, scientifically documented, the first ever of this kind, back to the American Philosophical Society and Jefferson. This is the first pay-off of information from the expedition.

Clark orders the refurbishment of Discovery to install bulk storage bins near each oarlock with flip-up lids to double as shields in case of attack. Clark also installs a bronze cannon on her bow mounted to a swivel. It is a formidable weapon in event of hostilities. In addition to the cannon, additional blunderbusses are mounted to the aft of the pirogues to increase firepower. These items and many other supplies are purchased by virtue of Lewis' letter of credit from the president. The merchants of St.

Louis are among the first ever to learn how to profit from military contracts.

May 6, 1804　Fort Wood, Illinois

Winter at Fort Wood has been long. Clark frequently busies himself learning what he can from visiting boatmen and nearby settlers about conditions on the Missouri and its inhabitants. Lewis does the same in St. Louis. The men prepare foodstuff to be taken: they parch and pound corn into meal, pack honey and salt pork. For entertainment the daily shooting contest is made interesting by varying the type of targets and range; the winner gets a gill* of whiskey. Today a group of locals has come to the fort to challenge the soldiers to a shooting match.

Sergeant Pryor excitedly cames to Captain Clark, "Capt'n, there's a group of citizens out here that claims they want a shootin' match. How about it? Can we bring 'em in and show 'em what for?"

"Really, Sergeant," Clark said rising from his seat. "Where are they?"

"Just over there by the gate," Pryor said pointing.

Clark turned to Pryor and said, "Well now, Sergeant. It looks like today will be a good day. Get the targets and the stakes. Set 'em at thirty-five yards for the first round. Then go to fifty and seventy-five. And then we'll separate the men from the boys with a one-hundred-yard shoot. Any shooter can use an espontoon** for shots over fifty yards."

"Yes, sir!" Pryor said grinning broadly. "They said they wanted to wager. How about it, Capt'n? Can we make bets?"

Clark rubbed his chin and responded, "Sergeant, these men have been honing their skills against one another. It's high time

---

* Four ounces by weight

** A long pointed shaft, similar to a bayonet, which is placed in the ground and used as a brace to steady a rifle.

we had some fresh blood to make the competition interesting. A good wager will do just that. Just don't you, or any of the men, bet more money than you've got."

Pryor replied, "Alright, sir, I'll pass that word along. No advances of pay to make their wagers good. But Capt'n, this is a sure thing. I've seen these boys shoot, and they're good, damn good."

"I know that," Clark said patting Pryor on the back. "It's just that I never encourage reckless gambling among the men. I don't want any one of the men to meet a sharpshooter and lose more than he can pay. We still have a public image to maintain, you know."

Pryor looked at the captain and replied, "Sir, we're a pretty close-knit unit. Any man here loses money, all of us will make it good, and that's for sure."

"Really, Sergeant, that pleases me more than winning against these settlers. But I insist on my not-gambling-to-excess rule. Let's explain the rules to everyone."

The two men walked out to the shooting range where a group of men were quickly assembling. Pryor explained that the shooting would start at thirty-five yards, then fifty, then seventy-five and end with the best men in a shoot-off at one hundred yards. George Drewyer listened without expression. A slight smile crossed his face as he picked up his rifle, powder horn and musket balls and slowly walked over to the five lines of shooters forming for the first round of fire. The settlers, being guests, would fire first. At the thirty-five yard range and the fifty-yard range, all men but one qualified with three rounds on target. The losing settler paid up and then sat down to watch the rest of the match.

At seventy-five yards only six of the settlers could hold three rounds on target. The soldiers were consistently accurate. The losing five settlers paid their money and watched as the targets were moved back to the one hundred yard line.

At this range the targets appeared small. The settlers talked among themselves and then put money on the table to shoot. Only one of the six remaining settlers held three shots on target. All of the soldiers qualified at seventy five yards with Drewyer holding a close three shot pattern near the bulls-eye. In a final shoot off, Drewyer, using his espontoon, took careful aim and fired. His round found its mark, cutting the edge of the bulls-eye. A soldier positioned off to the side stepped up and called out where the shot had hit. Drewyer was expressionless as he prepared his rifle for a second shot. His next shot made a figure eight hole in the paper as the bullet struck almost exactly where the first shot had hit. The soldier called out the holes were overlapping. Drewyer carefully aimed for the final shot. The men were quiet as he squeezed the trigger on his rifle. The shot hit the target, forming an over-lapping triangle of holes with the last shot almost completely in the bulls-eye. The soldier ran to the target, removed it and ran back to the group of shooters. As he reached them he said, "Lookie what George did. It looks like a thirty-five yard target. Hell, I ain't never seen shootin' like that."

Looking at the target pattern, the last settler did not even step to the firing line. He mumbled something as he walked away. All the soldiers cheered.

Captain Clark had been observing this and spoke out loudly, "Men, welcome our guests and congratulate them. They did well, and I will authorize a gill of whiskey for each man here. We won, but that is what we have been practicing for. These guests are pretty game shooters in their own right."

One of the settlers came over to Captain Clark and said, "Thank you for the whiskey, although I think we really paid for it. That was some powerful good shootin' here today. Quite the exhibition. It was worth comin' here to see these boys shoot. That's for sure."

Clark smiled broadly and said, "It's our pleasure to host the competition. Please stay and share a drink with us." The settler departed for the table where Sergeant Ordway and Reubin Field were pouring whiskey. Clark walked over to George Drewyer and shook his hand as he said, "Good shooting, George, best I've seen. I'm damn glad to have you on our side."

Drewyer smiled confidently and replied, "The pleasure's mine, Capt'n."

The same day, Lewis and two men had made a regular trip to St. Louis to get provisions. They took the red pirogue and went to a general store where they purchased whiskey, beans, flour, tobacco and sundry other items to be delivered the next day to Fort Wood. Lewis signed vouchers for the Army at the store and then stopped at the post office to mail letters. While there, he picked up mail waiting for the men at the fort. Included was a letter addressed to William Clark from the Secretary of the Army, General Dearborn.

Upon return to Fort Wood they pulled the red pirogue in near the previously anchored *Discovery* and got out. Some of the men came from the fort to greet the returning party. Lewis instructed the men, "I have some provisions here to add to our cargo, including plenty of whiskey for those times when it is needed as a refreshment. The rest of the stuff will be delivered tomorrow." Then, taking the letters he had picked up at the post office, he proceeded to the fort.

Lewis walked into Clark's quarters, laid a satchel of material down and said, "I picked up the mail; here's a letter for you from General Dearborn. I'm sure that's your papers of commission, permanent rank of captain. Go ahead; open it up."

Taking the letter from Lewis, Clark said, "Thanks, I've been waiting on this. I'm glad it got here before our departure. Now it'll be official." Clark smiled as he began to open the envelope and remove its contents. As he read the letter, his smile vanished. His face turned to a puzzled look and then one of disappointment. Holding the letter, his hands dropped to his waist.

"What?" Lewis inquired with a puzzled look, sensing something was wrong. "What's the matter?"

Without speaking, Clark handed the letter to Lewis, shook his head, turned his back on his friend and walked over to the doorway. He leaned on the doorway and looked out across the courtyard of Fort Wood.

Lewis quickly grabbed the letter and began to read aloud, "The peculiar situation, circumstances and organization of the Corps of Engineers are such as would render the appointment of Mr. Clark, a captain in that Corps, improper. I, therefore, am authorizing a commission of Lieutenant in the Corps of Artillerists, which is enclosed." Then, holding the letter in his hand, Lewis lowered it slowly to his waist as Clark had done just moments before.

"This cannot be. It simply cannot be. Bill, I was told by the president himself. It was part of the deal. Jefferson agreed to it. He approved it, the whole package. Presidential approval before I left Washington. Damn, what do they mean announcing that you are **now** Lieutenant William Clark? This has got to a mistake. You were to be a co-commander, a captain, by agreement with the President of the United States, Thomas Jefferson himself. He made that agreement, that covenant, with me." He looked at Clark and continued, "He agreed, Bill; he agreed. That was weeks before I left Washington. This is a mistake, a horrible, terrible mistake. Secretary Dearborn just doesn't understand. This is a mistake of power I tell you, and by God I mean to correct it. I know the Army doesn't like to have dual command. They want a *'chain of command'*, one leader. I know the damn Army. I knew it was unusual when I asked for it. Why the hell do they think I asked the president himself to sanction dual captains? And, he did. He agreed. By God, he agreed to it. I'll write to President Jefferson right away. After all, the president is the Commander-in-Chief, isn't he? He should know about this. If the president cannot promote you to captain, then something is wrong."

Turning from the doorway, Clark said, "Meriwether, my friend, we will be leaving Fort Wood in a few days. Our final preparations are nearly complete. We're simply waiting for the weather to clear. The men are extremely anxious to leave. There's no time for a letter to reach the president and for a correction to reach the Army and return. Merry, I'll go as your subordinate, a lieutenant; they can correct the matter when we return."

Visibly upset, Lewis was pacing, "No, no, this is too damn important to me, and embarrassing to me, and," he paused with clenched fist, "and, it is patently wrong All the men call you captain. You have been introduced everywhere as Captain Clark, my equal, not my subordinate." Then, very animated, Lewis' voice was quaking and his hands were moving wildly as he continued, "This expedition needs two captains and it will have two captains! I'll write to President Jefferson and ask him to dispatch your corrected letter of commission with urgency. I'll ask for an apology from Dearborn. And," then stopping and looking directly at Clark he said, "further, I will tell him that his favorite project, the Corps of Volunteers for the Discovery of the Northwest Passage, will not leave Fort Wood until it has two captains in command as agreed. Not an inch."

Clark looked at Lewis and said somberly, "Your feelings are appreciated, my friend. But you must realize, this expedition is more important than the rank of one of its leaders. We should depart on time, as planned, with me as lieutenant and correct the matter when we return. I know the Army, and you're right, having two captains goes against the grain. They want

one leader, one commander. This concept of co-commanders
is simply too new to them to grasp. They can't handle it."

Lewis, eyes still flashing, said, "Just a moment. These
papers say that I am the only damned captain here. Then as
the God damned captain, I say we wait until you're also a
captain and can officially dispute my authority. I'll show them
they must honor commitments."

Clark looked at Lewis a moment and said, "I am honored
to have you as a friend. I believe that you're more upset than I.
But Merry, you must think of the expedition first. It's far more
important than the feelings of either of us. It must go on as
planned. If we wait here three more weeks for a letter, those
could be the same three weeks we'll need out there before
winter sets in. You must use sound reason here and not
emotion." Clark walked over to his desk and took the letter
and folded it, then put it back in the envelope.

Lewis, walking away, had started to exit the doorway. Then,
turning suddenly, he snapped his fingers and then clapped his
hands together loudly. His eyes lit up as he came back in the
room. "I've got it, by God I've got it. I know exactly how to
handle this situation. Listen. This is what we will do."

Recognizing the change in Lewis, Clark asked, "What are
you talking about? What are you up to?"

Lewis continued proudly, "As captain, and commander of
the expedition, I have the authority to make field commissions.
Appointments as, from time to time, I see fit. You know, a
commander's prerogative for the good of the mission. Well
then, I will just re-name the mission. It's not going to be the
Corps of Volunteers for the Discovery of the Northwest
Passage any longer. From now on we will call ourselves the, oh
hell, the 'Voluntary Expeditionary Force of the United States.'
No, no, how about the 'Corps of Volunteers to Explore the
Louisiana Territory'? Yeah, yeah, I like the idea. As such, you
will be a captain." Lewis continued, "I like it. You will be a

captain, and with respect to this mission your authority will be considered in all respects to be precisely as my own."

Nodding his head, Clark said, "It may work. You are clever, my friend, very clever. If it is that important to you, then we can do it. I must repeat, however, I would be perfectly willing to accompany you as a lieutenant."

Lewis responded, ignoring Clark's last comment, "Of course it will work, and it is the **only way** that I want you here. I'll announce to the men the new name of the expedition only. Your rank of captain shall never again be discussed, never. This is the last and only time we will discuss it." Then with a broad smile, "Please destroy that letter, captain."

Smiling broadly, Clark said, "My friend, this time it is you who breaks my mood. Your idea is clever and, more importantly, fully within your rights as the man in command. What did you say you would call the expedition?"

Lewis responded proudly, "Corps of Volunteers to Explore the Louisiana Territory." Then turning he said, "I'll announce this to the men immediately. We'll all have a gill of whiskey to celebrate."

Stepping out into the open area, Lewis looked around and then, spotting Sergeant Pryor, he motioned with his hands and said, "Sergeant, I want you to go to the red pirogue and get the barrel of whiskey just stored there. Bring it back to our dining area. Muster all the men. We're going to celebrate."

"Yes, sir," the sergeant said enthusiastically, and sensing the good mood of the captain he added, "Would ya want some tobacco, too?"

"Tobacco?" Lewis responded. Then he looked at Clark, who was nodding and smiling, and he continued, "Why yes, Sergeant, bring some tobacco, too. Assemble the men and come to our quarters when they are together. I have, we have," he said looking at Clark, "an announcement to make."

"Yes, **sir**, Capt'n, we all been a waitin' for this time."

The sergeant began walking toward the river. "You three men there, yes you, come with me. We're going to bring some whiskey and tobacco to the tables. The captains got an announcement to make."

The men stopped their conversation and quickly followed the sergeant as he led them to the red pirogue. They retrieved the whiskey barrel and the tobacco. Then, covering the cargo back up, they returned to the fort. The rest of the men were already gathering around the dining area tables.

Lewis and Clark were waiting for the return of the whiskey and tobacco. As it arrived, Lewis spoke, "Sergeant, put the whiskey at the head of the table here and the tobacco on the head of the next table over." Then raising his voice he said to all the men gathered, "Men, come up and get yourselves a gill of whiskey and some tobacco. When you return to your seats, I have an announcement to make, and I want to offer a toast."

Willingly the men obeyed the order as they fell into line and each man received a gill of whiskey doled out by Sergeant Pryor. Continuing on, they each took some tobacco and returned to their places around the tables. They were talking to one another and smiling. "This is the kind of meetin' I like. We should have more of these," Colter said with a laugh.

Waiting for the last man to reach his seat, Lewis looked at the assembly, smiled and then spoke in a loud voice. "Men, we have an announcement to make. I know that it has been a long winter."

"Boring, too," one of the men said.

"Yes, and boring, too," Lewis agreed. "We now want to tell you that we are making the last preparations for departure. The ice on the river is broken as far up as we can tell. I want to announce that next week, May 14, we will launch our expedition up the Missouri River." There was a loud cheer and banging of cups on the tables as the men whooped and applauded for a moment.

Lewis raised his hands to silence the group and then continued, "We've been in St. Louis often over the winter and many people there are talking of our expedition. Many of them don't know what it's called. Some know that we were named the Corps of Volunteers for the Discovery of the Northwest Passage while others think we're the Louisiana Territory Expedition and on and on. Some are really stupid and have names that don't make sense. Try 'The Army Sailors' Overland Cruise to the Pacific.' "

The men all laughed.

Lewis continued, "I want to put an 'official' name on our papers and documents that we'll be sending back to President Jefferson. Because of this, and to end the confusion regarding the correct name of the expedition, I want to create, here and now, our official name. We should properly recognize that we are made up of good men who volunteered and that we are on a mission of discovery. What do you think of," then pausing and looking at Clark, he continued, "men, what do you think of calling ourselves the 'Corps of Volunteers to Explore the Louisiana Territory'? Let's all drink to it."

The men cheered and each raised a cup and drank his gill of whiskey. Then they began talking among themselves. Finally Private Collins said, "So we are not the 'Corps of Volunteers for the Discovery of the Northwest Passage' any more? What did you call us again, sir? It was a big handle and I don't think I got it right."

"Corps of Volunteers to Explore the Louisiana Territory," Lewis answered proudly. "It's how we'll address our papers we send back to Washington."

Then Sergeant Ordway spoke up and said, "Captains, we're proud that you recognize us as a corps of volunteers. It's a good name and does recognize volunteers and all, but I think it's too big and long for all us men to remember straight. The most important part ain't that we are volunteers; it's the fact that we are going to discover new things, excitin' things. Why even our keelboat is named *Discovery*." Then he paused and looked at all the men who were looking at him as their spokesman, "Can we just call ourselves the 'Corps of Discovery' to keep it short and simple? Some of us wouldn't get it confused if it were simple. What do you think?"

All the men were nodding and buzzing in conversation. Lewis looked at Clark and back at the men then back at Clark. Both men smiled simultaneously. Clark raised a hand and spoke, "Men, 'Corps of Discovery' truly is shorter and easier to remember. But if the truth were known, after a long boring winter here at Camp Wood, I think you're just suggesting another name so you can have some more whiskey to keep on celebrating." He laughed and all the men joined in laughter and nodded their heads.

Lewis was pleased. He stepped over to Sergeant Pryor and said, "Today, men, you have found me in an exceptional mood. 'Corps of Discovery' is a name that you all agreed upon democratically; Jefferson would like that. Corps of Discovery it shall be, and yes, I do believe it's a two-toast day. Another gill of whiskey for all, Sergeant." Waving his hand over the group, all the men cheered and rose from their seats to line up for a second gill of whiskey.

Private John Shields reached out to grab York and the two began a tap dance on the table. Many other men joined in the dancing and they all talked enthusiastically. 'One more week' was heard often during the rest of the evening.

Lewis looked at Clark and said, "Corps of Discovery. I like it. Is it done?"

"Done," Clark replied smiling broadly. All the men shook hands and were jubilant.

May 14, 1804

The day before had brought continual rain. Today the weather is pleasant. Captain Lewis goes to St. Louis to settle matters, to get money from the Army post and then sign all open pay vouchers in final settlement for goods received. He also takes several letters to mail to the families of the men who can script. These will be the last letters mailed for a long time.

At 4:00 P.M. under the command of Captain William Clark, the Corps of Discovery bids adieu to a small group of well-wishing citizens and leaves Fort Wood. They cross the Mississippi and proceed to sail up the Missouri River under a gentle breeze. The great expedition of the Corps of Discovery has begun.

Clark is in the keelboat at the bow near the cannon, watching for river currents. Baptiste DesChamps leads nine men in the white pirogue. The red pirogue with nine more men follows. They use rowing, setting poles and pulling from the river bank with ropes to advance against the current. Against the mighty Missouri, fourteen miles will be a good day's travel.

Lewis remains in St. Louis and will join the party in a few days by horseback.

May 16, 1804 St. Charles, Missouri

Lewis remains in St. Louis working on arrangements for an Osage Indian chief's departure to Washington to meet Jefferson. He will catch up by horseback later. Meanwhile, the Corps of Discovery has reached the settlement of St. Charles in the Missouri Territory. Settlers from the village are at the river to invite them to a dinner and dance. St. Charles is a poor settlement of mostly French speaking people, a few Indians and some English speaking men.

Captain Clark ordered the men to anchor the boats near the shoreline. "Men, I will pay you all now as this is the last settlement that we will encounter that will take money for goods. Each of you line up and sign your name or make your mark on the pay voucher list, and Sergeant Pryor will pay you." Then pointing to the cargo of material in the keelboat, he continued, "I have noted that the cargo may be in need of shifting forward. With the weight redistributed, she should be easier to tow, and we'll get more benefit from the sail." Then he turned to Sergeant Floyd saying, "Sergeant, have the men move the cargo out and redistribute it as we discussed last evening. Make sure the front is packed tight and leave some room near the center keel. I'm going to see if we can add some supplies at this village. We'll wait here for Captain Lewis to join us."

Floyd responded, "Yes, sir. This should make towing from the riverbank a little better. That bank sure has been soft." Turning to the men he began to point and give orders, "Empty the entire front of the boat back to here, take those heavy items stowed there and the six cartons of lead and gunpowder and put them in the bow. Break this lighter pack into two parts and put them in the aft." He continued to instruct the men as to how to rearrange the keelboat.

Clark left the boats. Climbing the embankment, he proceeded to walk slowly and reconnoiter the row of houses and other buildings in the settlement. Seeing a general store, he entered to look for merchandise. As the storekeeper looked up, Clark said, "Good day, sir. Do you get much business from river trade?"

"Yep, sure do," the owner said proudly. "River men always need fishhooks, line, gunpowder and lead. I sell beans, dried pork and tobacco. Even have some fresh tobacco here, just came in two days ago. I've some very nice cooking kettles and a good supply of smith tools and supplies. What can I help you with?"

Clark replied, "Looks like you have a good variety, as good as any I've seen in St. Louis. Did you say fresh tobacco? Well then, I'll take all you have. I have a crew of men that'll enjoy fresh tobacco and I can trade it with Indians further up the river."

"Indians like our tobacco. Should be a good item for trade," the storekeeper replied.

Clark continued, "I am Captain Clark, United States Army, and my men are down by the river re-packing our keelboat. We're sent here by President Jefferson to explore the new purchase of Louisiana. I'll be waiting here until Captain Lewis can join me. He'll be along in a day or two."

With a surprised look of sudden realization the storekeeper said, "Captain Lewis? How dumb of me; why you **are** the official government explorers. How dumb of me; I shoulda guessed. You're the fellas that'll be exploring the Missouri. Hmmmm, Louisiana Purchase, what a deal that was. Yeah, I heard about that. I'll probably get a lot more trade now. Should be good for business, English speaking business. There's a lot of French here now. I expect I'll be going to St. Louis for supplies every month with business picking up." Then with a smile and pointing at Clark he continued, "I guess I'm in the United States again, and I didn't move an inch. Well I'll be; how many men you got with ya?"

"Forty-one men now. Lewis and I make forty-three," Clark said.

The storekeeper beamed, "Today is your lucky day, that's for sure. People here been talking about your expedition. Sorry I didn't recognize ya until you mentioned Captain Lewis. We've been expecting you almost every day. We're going to have a little celebration at the town hall here, soon as you're tied off and camped. How about 7:30, in your honor, to send you off in style; ya know, music, dancin' and some libation? There'll be pretty French ladies there to dance with."

Clark replied smiling, "It would be an honor, sir, an honor. I'll let the men know to be ready by 7:30, I'll have them dressed in their best uniforms for the occasion."

The storekeeper continued, "Now as for men to join up with yehs, I saw two Frenchmen, boatmen they were, that were askin' when you would be here. They were real anxious-like to join; been here two weeks or so. One of 'em got a patch over his eye, kind of a small and wiry lookin' feller. Said they were real good on the river and could talk some Injun, too."

Clark replied enthusiastically, "That's good news. I want to meet them. Shouldn't be able to miss them in a town this size, and with your description, I'm confident I will find them."

The storekeeper responded, "Not today, friend. They went out a couple days ago as guides a short way upriver. But they're due back in a couple days, probably by the time Captain Lewis gets here. Anyways you need not worry about finding them. They'll most likely find you first. They been real eager about your expedition." Then changing the subject, he looked out the doorway at the river and asked, "What do you call your expedition anyway? Is there a name?"

Clark grinned broadly and stepped closer to the counter where he turned and looked out the doorway and said, "Well yes, we are the Corps of Volunt…" He corrected quickly, "We call ourselves the Corps of Discovery, and our main vessel, the large keelboat there, she's called the *Discovery*."

The storekeeper said, "I like that, got a good ring to it, Corps of Discovery. It'll take real frontiersmen, true explorers, to get up this river and across the mountains all the way to the Pacific." Then with a reflective look he repeated, "All that territory from the French for a song. Jefferson sure did make a deal there." Pausing a moment he leaned over the counter, pointed with a finger and continued, "Next town upriver is called La Charette. Not much of a town; just a few settlers, but ol' Dan'l Boone lives there. Now there's a frontiersman for ya. Quite the frontiersman in his time, too, that's for sure."

Clark looked at the storekeeper and said, "Daniel Boone, huh? Well I'll be. I thought he was dead. Do you ever see him?"

The storekeeper responded, "Sure, he comes here. He's is one of my best customers. He's gettin' old. Must be seventy somethin' by now. He still gets out and hunts though; tough as nails that one. He likes tobacco and seems to know when I have fresh. Gets his whiskey from Kentucky, only the good stuff for him. One of my best customers, ol' Dan'l, for sure."

Clark gazed around the store, then said with a smile, "Daniel Boone. Well, if that ain't something. I think we will pay him a visit. It's certain I'll want to know anything he can tell me about the country out here."

Turning to leave the store Clark said, "Well now, it's been a pleasure, sir. I'm glad I stopped in. Could you put all the tobacco in bags and place it to one side for me? I'll take as much lead for bullets as you have here on the shelf and some dried beef and pork. Could you hold all these goods for me? I'll send a small detachment up to pick it up. Let me settle up with you now so all the men will have to do is carry it off." Clark paid for the material and the owner thanked him.

Leaving the store, Clark proceeded to the river's edge where the men were still working on redistributing the cargo. Sergeant Ordway had a group of men setting up camp and preparing food.

"We should be ready to eat in about an hour, Captain," Sergeant Ordway said. "The tents will be up at about the same time if I got things figured right. I'll have three fires, here, there and there. I got 'em all situated so the bugs won't bother us as much, specially if the breeze holds from the southwest."

"Good Sergeant, well done." Clark said as he looked over the camp activity. Then he walked over to the river's edge and said, "Sergeant Floyd, how's the work going?"

"Fine, sir," Floyd replied, "We should have it all ready by tomorrow."

"Good, Sergeant, good," Clark said.   Then turning to Sergeant Pryor he said. "It'll be evening in two to three hours. Do you think you could get a deer or two before it's too dark?"

"Yes, sir, we certainly can try. Game seems plentiful around here," Pryor responded.

Clark continued, "Good, then take four men and go see if you can get a deer or two to roast up. We could use the fresh meat, maybe even a good meal to spread out when Captain Lewis joins us. What we don't eat here, we'll dry for jerky or trade with the storekeeper for other goods. Don't be too late in returning because I want all you men to wash up tonight. The good people of St. Charles are going to have a celebration in our honor. It'll be the last celebration we'll have in civilized country. We've been invited to join them at 7:30 for music, dancing and some libations." Pausing a moment he looked the sergeant in the eye and continued, "None of you are to get drunk. There will be ladies present and I expect each of you to act in a dignified manner."

Pryor said, "Yes, sir." Then he turned and said, "Collins, Whitehouse, Colter, Gibson, get your rifles and be ready to head out on a hunt. Bring some fresh water."

Then turning to look at Sergeant Ordway preparing food Clark said, "Sergeant, you, Pryor and Floyd will be expected to keep the men orderly tonight. I don't want to leave the last friendly port of call with a bad reputation for conduct."

Ordway replied, "Yes, sir. These men are military and they know what to expect if they're disorderly. The other sergeants and me will inspect them before we go and watch 'em to make sure they act good in front of the ladies."

When Sergeant Ordway had finished the food preparation, the men sat down to eat. They were all in good spirits as they talked enthusiastically about this being their last settlement and a chance to listen to music and dance with ladies. When they finished eating, Clark turned to Sergeant Floyd and said, "Sergeant, take six men and go to the general store there in the village. I bought some goods earlier today and the storekeeper should have them ready to go by now. It's already paid for and he's expecting you."

"Yes, sir," Floyd replied.

"Do you have the place opened up in the keelboat for additional supplies?" Clark inquired.

"Yes, sir," Floyd responded.

That evening, at 7:20 when Clark had all of the men standing at attention dressed in military uniform, he addressed them, "Men, we're going to a gala event this evening in our honor. We here represent the United States Army and, more importantly, the Corps of Discovery. I expect that each man here will behave in a manner respecting his dignity." Turning toward the path leading to the village, he commanded, "Fall out." The men talked casually as they proceeded up the pathway toward the buildings of St Charles. Three men were left behind as sentries for the boats.

The early part of the evening went well. The men were gracious with the ladies and did not over indulge in liquor. Drewyer and DesChampes were popular as they could speak English and French and serve as interpreters for the mostly French speaking ladies.

During the evening, however, despite warnings to the contrary, Private Collins drank too much. He began to talk loudly saying, "I don't give a damn for this party. It's too stuffy and all fit 'n proper. Hell, I want to have a party where the women speak English and they don't parcel out the liquor in little bitty glasses with long stems. Come on, you guys, come with me. I'm going to see this damn town, or what there is of it to see. Who knows, maybe there's some good whiskey to be had."

George Shannon, hearing this nudged Sergeant Pryor and said, "Sergeant, did you hear Collins there? I think maybe he's going to be a problem."

"Yeah, I heard him. I just hope Captain Clark or our hosts didn't hear him spoutin' off like that," Pryor said. "The captain's over by the music and has been busy answering questions. I sure hope he didn't notice."

Shannon was shaking his head as he continued, "Captain Clark told us to be gentlemen and to represent the Army proper." Then pointing a finger at the doorway he said, "Look, there they go. They're leaving. Shouldn't do that. Do ya want me to go after them, Sergeant?"

"No, no, don't leave this room," Pryor instructed. "I'll go and say something to the captain and see what he wants us to do. Meanwhile, don't you leave this spot. I'll be back as soon as I let the captain know." Pryor walked across the crowded assemblage of people who were all talking and tapped Clark on the elbow.

"Capt'n, can I speak with you a moment?" Pryor said with a serious look in his eye.

Noticing the serious look, Clark responded, "Sure you can, what is it, Sergeant?"

Pryor said in a low tone. "Well, Captain, it's Private Collins. He's been getting rather out-of-line and not following your instructions none about actin' a gentleman. In fact, he was cursing loud enough for our hosts to hear. Just now he left by the back door over there, and he took Privates Hall and Werner with him. I think they're up to no good."

Clark's face lost its smile, his eyes narrowed as he listened to the sergeant while he looked across the room. He then sat his mug down rather hard on the table and said, "Sergeant, I want you to go find them. This town isn't that big. Take four men with you. I want you to be as quiet as possible so as not to let the people here know we're having a problem.

"Yes, sir, right away, sir," Sergeant Pryor said.

Clark grabbed Sergeant Pryor by the arm and continued, "When you catch them, put them under military arrest for desertion. Take them to the keelboat and tell the sentries there to hold them until morning. Instruct the sentries to shoot them if they try to escape. In fact, you better leave two of the men you take with you to increase the guard until morning."

"Shouldn't take us long to get 'em sir, not long at all," Pryor said.

"I'm glad you told me so quickly, Sergeant." Then he added in a low tone, "Tomorrow morning, we will have a court-martial for desertion for those three. When you have this matter under control, you and the other two men can return to the celebration here. When you return, behave as if nothing has happened. We don't want our hosts to think that we are an undisciplined lot of river rats. We will settle our matters with that lot in the morning. Go ahead now, get going. I don't want them loose in this town very long."

The sergeant moved across the room from where he had come and quickly recruited four men. They left by the back door without notice.

Privates Collins, Werner and Hall were apprehended within fifteen minutes of Clark's order. They were marched to the river where they were held, per instructions, until morning.

The next morning, Clark formed a military court martial for the three men, charging them with desertion and behaving in an inappropriate manner. Collins, because he was the ringleader, was sentenced to 50 lashes. The other men were granted leniency and were given 25 lashes each. Punishment was to be carried out at sunset.

Clark was stone-faced throughout the hearing. At the end he stood and spoke, "I am disappointed men, very disappointed. We are at the beginning of a long and difficult trip. The Corps of Discovery is a group of volunteers. To me that means you want to be part of this adventure. You want to be part of seeing new things, going where no white man has gone, making exciting and rewarding discoveries. If we're successful, and we should be, you'll be heroes. This trip will be difficult and will surely fail if we do not have discipline. We must start out on the right foot. Captain Lewis and I must know that each man among you can be depended upon completely and without question. For that matter, each of you owes that in full measure to the other. Your very survival may depend upon it. Dependability comes from discipline. It is my hope that after you receive the punishment that your peers and I have decided for you, that you will re-direct your efforts to be part of this expedition and not seek selfish pleasure." Then turning to Sergeant Pryor, Clark said, "Sergeant, get my journal, I want to record this event."

May 20, 1804

It had rained off and on the night before. The campsite by the river is wet and soggy. It is nearing midday and the men are preparing a midday meal. Smoke and the smell of food are wafting through the damp air. Clark is in his tent making journal entries when a shot rings out, followed by two more shots in rapid succession. It is Lewis. Clark runs out of his tent, rifle in hand and looks down the river with a broad smile. He fires his rifle in the air to respond and waves his hand.

Lewis and a small contingency were in view on the horizon against a stormy sky. "Hello, there. Would that be the Corps of Discovery preparing food?" Lewis shouted.

Clark approached him at a rapid pace as he rode into camp. "Glad to see you, Merry. Have any trouble?"

"None," Lewis replied as he dismounted, "but from the look of the river current along the way, I can tell you've been expending some effort. How's it been going?"

Clark responded, "You're quite right, there are strong currents and no shortage of large driftwood logs coming at us. This riverbank is unstable and there's a lot of debris to avoid. Hard to do with the long pirogues and near impossible with *Discovery*." Then turning to look at Sergeant Ordway preparing food he said, "Your luck holds well, my friend, you arrived just in time to test the good sergeant's mess. Have your friends join us, too."

"Certainly," Lewis said, as he motioned to the three men that had accompanied him. "You heard Captain Clark. Come into our campsite and join us for a meal before you head back downriver."

Sergeant Ordway walked up to Lewis, extended his hand and said, "Good to see you, sir, we been a waitin' for you. I just knew you'd be here today. The rest of the men said it wouldn't be until tomorrow cause of the storm and all, but I bet otherwise. I knew you could smell a good meal. Grab a plate, it's ready now."

As they were finishing the meal, two French Canadian fur traders, Francois Labiche and Pierre Cruzatte, approached the camp. Labiche, leading the way, approached Captain Clark and asked, "Are you men Captains Lewis and Clark? The ones going up the Missouri River?"

"I am Captain Clark, and this is Captain Lewis," Clark replied as he stepped back and took measure of the men.

Labiche nodded and said, "We been looking for you quite awhile. I was afraid we might miss you and then have to chase you upriver. We been a waitin' around these parts about two weeks now to meet up with ya. Word was you were to stop here. We want to join if you'll have us. This is good country and we would like to be part of exploring it. We would like to join up. Yes, sir, we would like to join ya." Then looking back and forth at Clark and Lewis, he continued with a broad smile,

"This here is Pierre Cruzatte and I'm Francois Labiche, can we join ya?"

Seating himself, Clark looked at the men, both of whom were small in stature, wiry, with weathered faces and had the look of frontiersmen. They were dressed in worn clothing and had intent looks of anticipation on their faces. Cruzatte had a patch over his left eye just as the storekeeper had described. Clark rose from his chair as he extended his hand, "Can you tell us more about yourselves? We can always use good men." They nodded and exchanged handshakes around. Then Clark continued, "Now hear me. Out here, we don't just want men to go into fur country to get wealthy. We are on a mission of exploration, of discovery. You must be able to contribute to the success of that mission. The work is hard; the territory is completely unknown beyond the Mandan village." Then pausing, he queried, "How did you hear of us, our expedition? Tell me something about yourselves."

Labiche was excited as he responded, "We know that. We heard you were exploring the whole West, over the mountains and all. That's real excitin'! Why, we could be part of history. We've never been beyond Mandan. We'd like to go with you." Pausing, Labiche poked Cruzatte in the ribs and said rhetorically, "Hell, who wouldn't want to go?"

Lewis had been silent to this point. Catching the eye of Labiche he spoke, "We will be going all the way to the Pacific Ocean. Our mission is to explore and document this territory. I know that the fur trading is expected to be good in these lands, but getting pelts is not our mission; establishing trade routes and contacting the native tribes is. We expect to meet many different Indian tribes. Our orders are to negotiate friendly passage with them and establish future trade."

Labiche nodding all the while answered, "We're interested, Captain. Both us are good riverboat men. Ain't nobody knows this river like Cruzatte and me. Ain't afeard of hard work neither. Trapping and just staying alive in this country is hard work." He paused and looked at the captains and then at his companion and continued, "Tradin' with the Indians, well, unless you want to lose your shirt, you'll be needing someone that kin deal with them, that can talk their language. Cruzatte and me have been trading with Indians a long time now. We could sure help you there."

Clark rubbed his chin, and looking at the men, inquired, "Has either of you ever been in the military, or even in a fort? Have you worked as scouts? I want you to know that this is a military expedition and if we take you on, you would become privates in the United States Army. You would have to obey orders and be subject to military discipline just like all the other men. I repeat, you would be subject to military discipline and duties, just like the rest. Would you want to join the Army?"

The two men looked at each other as Labiche explained in French to Cruzatte what Clark had just told them. They nodded, then Labiche turned and answered. "We've been in this land a good number of years, been to the Mandan villages, too. We been trading fur, and we don't got a lot to show for it. We'd like to be part of an adventure. Now it's true, we've never been in the military, but we know of it and its ways. We can serve as good as any man."

Lewis looked at the men and spoke, "Does the other man there, Cruzatte, speak English?"

Cruzatte turned toward Lewis and speaking for himself in broken English replied, "Some. I speak some, and I'm learning more all the time. I learn language fast. I just don't need English out here as much as knowing Indian. Labiche speaks English good when we need it."

Clark responded quickly to Labiche, "Do you men know the native languages?"

"Yes, sir, sure do," Labiche replied. "We know how to speak the important ones anyhow. Those on the lower Missouri are best, but we can sign real good to all the tribes the rest of the way to the Mandan. Gotta know some or they'll scalp ya."

Clark looked at Lewis and nodded, and then he continued, "We can use men that know the languages and practices of the Indians along the river. We're no strangers to hard work here. You and your friend will have plenty of work if you join us. Our corps is interested in volunteers, but you gotta know what you're volunteering to do. We cannot ask men to risk their lives and commit to months of hardship unless they volunteer."

Labiche replied, "Yes, sir, Captain Clark; we know the hard work you can expect out here. We'd be able to counsel you on that." Then he laughed and continued, "Pierre here don't look like much, one eye and all, but he's good on the river, knows every sandbar and knows how to read it good. River shifts all the time; he knows the shallows. Him and me, we work hard all the time. We're no strangers to toil. We both got good backs and calluses on our hands." Then he looked at Cruzatte and smiled, "Volunteering is why we traveled most of a week and waited two more here to meet you, sir. We want to join you and see this whole thing."

Cruzatte nudged Labiche and asked him in French, "Will they take us? What does this pay?"

Labiche asked, "My friend here is willing to accept the risk and the work. But, gentlemen, can you tell us what this hard work pays a man?"

Lewis responded, "Twenty-five United States dollars a month. But you will have to join the Army to get the assignment and the pay."

Labiche turned to Cruzatte and started to explain. Cruzatte raised a hand and stopped him, indicating that he understood what was said. Then he asked Labiche, "Does he care if I play my fiddle and tambourine?"

Laughing, Labiche turned to the captains and inquired, "My one-eyed friend wants to know if you mind if he plays the fiddle on occasion? He also plays the tambourine. He's good on some tunes and has a good variety of what he knows. Mighty entertaining on long nights for sure."

Clark smiled broadly and turned to Sergeant Ordway who had been listening all along and said, "Now that is a skill we had not planned to add to our crew, a musician, someone to lighten our spirits along the way and to provide a little entertainment around the campfires. Providence has given us these two delightful men to see if we are wise enough to accept them. What do you think, Sergeant?"

Ordway looked at Lewis and back at the men. "Well now, let me think, Captain. Two men that know the river, two men that know most of the native languages, men that have traveled and waited for two weeks just to join us as volunteers; they're not afraid of hard work and high risk. And now let me add, one of them can add music to our trip." He stroked his chin and said with a wry smile, "I'll just have to think on this one awhile, Captain." They both laughed while the newcomers looked on seriously. Then moving to get closer to Cruzatte, Ordway added, "With one eye, this man should also be in charge of our whiskey supply." They laughed again.

Labiche translated to Cruzatte, who was observing with a strange look, and then they all laughed.

Lewis then spoke, "Seriously gentlemen, we are pleased to invite you to join us as members of the Corps of Discovery. You'll be pleased to learn that a couple of our men, Drewyer and DesChampes, speak French. We'll observe your work for a few days, and if you perform as well as you talk, we'll enlist you in the Army."

Labiche said, "That's fair, Captain. Can we get to know the other men in your detachment?"

Clark replied, "Yes, you may. Feel free to introduce your-selves as boatsmen. They're all here except for a small detachment that went hunting."

Cruzatte and Labiche moved off to meet the other members of the Corps of Discovery. Clark moved closer to Lewis and nudged him in the ribs, "Some piece of luck here. I think these two will work out; I just have a good feeling. And you, for all your planning, didn't think about entertainment?"

Lewis replied, "Well, I knew you could whistle, and we did get plenty of whiskey."

Clark stepped back and looked at his friend, "Whistle, you mean your plan for entertainment on the lonely nights ahead in strange land was for me to whistle?"

Lewis replied, "I wasn't going to ask you until we were further upriver and away from civilization. The further out we are, chances are, the better you'll sound." They both laughed. Lewis said, "I agree, Bill. These two should work out fine. Do you agree we should enlist them after a few days' obser-vation?"

Clark said, "Done." The two men walked back toward the rest of the men; the Corps of Discovery was now forty-five men strong.

May 22, 1804 Lower Missouri

The river meanders in wide swaths as it stretches to over three miles wide at some points. Where it curves sharply, it cuts into the soft banks and makes them treacherous.

On one occasion the men are utilizing poling, cording and sail to progress laboriously upstream against a current that averages five miles per hour. Without notice, a large tree trunk appears in the water, and Discovery is heading directly toward it. Unable to swerve away, the large and heavily laden craft is struck just off the starboard side. As she swings uncontrollably in the water, she passes under a large tree near the bank which has a large, curved, low hanging branch extending out over the river. Though they try, the men can do little as the mast catches the branch and makes a groaning sound. The boat rotates in the water and exposes more of her side to the current. The force of the water causes the mast to crack with a powerful bursting sound. The large boat, adrift in a strong current and momentarily out of control, slams into the soft riverbank. The bank collapses dumping loose sand, mud and rock onto the deck, nearly swamping the craft. The pirogues are immediately ordered over and tied up. The men rush to the aid of their unfortunate companions and begin clearing the deck of debris.

Sergeant Pryor and Labiche immediately jump into action, directing the others as they clear the deck and correct her listing condition before she takes on water. Clark orders men to check the gunpowder stores and the paper and ink for moisture. He commands York to right several of the whiskey kegs that had been knocked over and are rolling about.

Lewis, walking on the shoreline with Drewyer, has been collecting plant specimens when he hears the mast snap and the excitement of men shouting. He instinctively runs toward the river. By the time he reaches the accident scene, the men are well underway toward righting the boat.

Observing the calamity Lewis shouted, "As soon as you can get the oarlocks clear, throw the ropes this way."

Clark added, "Sergeant Floyd, take ten men, and York, get those ropes secured and get her headed straight upriver. Soon as you can get clear of this high bank we will tie up and take measure."

Lewis shouted from above, "I'll go upriver and find a good spot to tie up. I think there's a good spot about five hundred yards ahead. Maybe we can use it." With that, he turned and ran upriver.

In a few minutes they reached the spot Lewis had selected. There they tied and anchored the boats. It had been a hard day thus far, and Clark said, "Men, even though we've made only about twelve miles, I think we'll stop awhile. Need to make a new mast and generally clean up. When you're finished cleaning the rubble and camp is made, a gill of whiskey is in order for this day's work."

The excitement of the moment waned as the men set about setting camp and preparing for the evening. Lewis noted several large bluffs along the river, some rising as high as three hundred feet. Many of these bluffs had caverns in them, exposing sandstone and rock surfaces.

Lewis said to Clark and Sergeant Ordway, "Think I'll go up and scratch my name on the rock face for posterity. Sergeant, want to come along?"

Clark replied, "Things seem under control here. I think York and I will join ya."

The four men moved out along the river's edge. Soon Lewis spotted a large open cavern and pointed to it. "That one looks good. It's high and conspicuous, as good a place as any to make your mark."

Ordway said, "Sure is steep. Can I go up first and see how tough it is?"

"Alright, Sergeant, go ahead." Lewis agreed.

Ordway started up the steep embankment toward the cavern opening. Going was difficult as some rock and sand dislodged, cascading downward. He finally reached the top and shouted down at the others. "Hey, Captain, I can see a long way from here. Think I'll put my name on the wall right here."

"I'll be up there in a moment, Sergeant." Then turning to Clark, Lewis said, "Come on. Today's been a rough day. Let's go put our mark on this bluff and show future generations we made it here today."

"I'm right behind you, Meriwether," Clark replied. "Stay here and wait," Clark said to York.

The two headed up the bluff face that Ordway had just ascended. Ordway was busy starting to carve his name in the face of the rock. As they approached the opening, Lewis was about forty feet in front of Clark. He placed his foot on a rock that was protruding outward. Reaching up to make his next step, the first rock dislodged and flew outward with sand and dirt as Lewis began an uncontrolled slide down the embankment. Rocks, dust and gravel struck Clark in the face as Lewis slid toward him. Fortunately, Lewis remained upright and did not tumble. He slid down the embankment for about twenty feet when he pulled his knife and plunged it into the face of the bluff. It slowed his fall and Clark grabbed him by the back of his shirt. His fall was arrested in a cloud of dust.

"What are you doing?" Clark asked. "I got dust and rock all over me."

"Just thought I'd drop in on you, Bill," Lewis quipped.

"Fine. Next time, could you let me know you're coming. It's rude to just barge in like this," Clark replied.

"I didn't really have time to announce myself," Lewis said. "Do you like my shirt? I think I'm done sliding for awhile. You can let me go now."

Clark looked at his friend and smiled, "Here you came, sliding in a cloud of dust, kicking rocks and sand in my face. I closed my eyes and reached out and grabbed for ya in self-defense just to stop the commotion. Lucky it was I got your shirt and not your crotch. How was it you got your knife out so quick? I never saw a man so quick with a knife. Is this your first try at that stunt?" Clark jibed.

"Why hell, Bill, I learned my dirt slinging and knife stabbing talents from watching those politicians in Washington. They used to do it all the time," Lewis retorted.

Ordway, hearing the sliding, immediately stopped carving his name and moved to the edge of the cavern, "Hey, Capt'n Lewis, you all right? What happened down there?"

Clark replied, "He's fine, Sergeant. He was just reminiscing about his political days in Washington. Spreading dirt around and kicking it on his friends."

The fall was enough of a scare to cause the men to abort the name writing excursion. Ordway stopped after only writing ORD[*] on the bluff. The three turned to go back to the campsite.

Lewis said, "I must apologize. This was a foolish idea. Really stupid. We're all alone out here and folly like this could get any one of us injured or even killed. We need each other far too much to put ourselves at risk for such folly. Let's get back to camp and see what it takes to get underway tomorrow morning."

Clark and Ordway looked at Lewis. York said nothing but followed behind Clark; the four continued on back to camp without saying anything further.

May 24, 1804   La Charette, Missouri

The Corps of Discovery has reached the small settlement of La Charette on the north side of the river, the last white settlement. It seems peaceful and inviting. Basking in the mid-morning sun, La Charette is a welcome respite. The village consists of a few rows of small houses and one large white house on a hillside overlooking the river. Clark orders the men to pull in ashore, drop anchor and tie up. While the men are securing the boats, there is a small group of people coming down to the river's edge to meet them. Anticipating that they are the much-reputed expedition from the United States, the group brings milk and eggs as a token of welcome. After greeting the welcoming party, the captains simultaneously gaze up at the large white house on the hillside.

---

[*] The letters ORD are still there today.

Turning to Lewis and punching him lightly on the arm, Clark said, "That's got to be Boone's house. Let's go and visit Mr. Boone, my friend. I'm sure it'll be interesting and informative."

Lewis stood looking at the house for a moment, "Well it's a sure thing he's not as dead as some people say. I'll wager he'll know a lot about this territory."

Clark replied, "My thoughts exactly. You know, I hear he still hunts on a regular basis. Imagine that, still plenty of frontier spirit in his bones."

"Can't argue with that logic," Lewis replied smiling.

The two men started to walk toward the village and the large white house on the ridge. Shortly they opened the front gate and were at the front step of the house. They paused a moment and then knocked firmly on the door. They waited for what seemed like a long time, shifting from one foot to another and looking around the town. Then the door opened. There, filling the doorway with his large frame, stood an elderly man in his seventies. It was Daniel Boone. His face was wrinkled with weather and age, but his eyes were clear. His hair was long and gray, but his posture was as erect as a man half his years. He wore buckskin pants and shirt and had an Indian beaded necklace around his neck.

Boone spoke, "Hello, may I help ya? Never seen you two before. You're new here, aren't ya? Well, come in. Come in, and welcome. Name's Boone. Daniel Boone. You kin just call me Dan'l, and who might you be?"

Lewis and Clark looked at the man and then at each other. Lewis smiled and spoke. "Well, sir, I'm Captain Meriwether Lewis and this is Captain William Clark. We are on a mission from President Jefferson to explore these parts, that is, the Missouri River to its headwaters, then on to the Pacific. We hope to find and map an all-water route to the West. We're a military unit, but our mission is one of exploration and discovery."

The elder Boone stood and looked at the two captains for a moment. Then a broad smile crossed his face as he spoke, "Well, well, I'll be damned. I heard we had purchased the territory of Louisiana from that French fella Napoleon. War-like bastard, that one. They never really owned this land anyway. I knew it wouldn't be long before civilization came pressin' in on me again. I moved away from Kentucky because it was getting too crowded. Didn't much care for the Whiskey Rebellion either. I don't want to be part of any anti-movement or cause. I like living where it's not crowded, where life is simple and clean. Moved as far west as I could just to get away from government and regulations. La Charette is nice because it's not crowded or nothin'. Fact is, it is the last white settlement that you'll see on the river here; rest is Injun all the way." Motioning for the men to follow him, Boone walked into another room. He continued, "I heard its all official-like now. Louisiana belongs to the United States. Now that it's all ours, people will be coming. Lots of people, just you watch and see. You men are just the first, that's all."

Motioning for the captains to sit, he continued, "Sit down, men, sit. So yer with the Army, huh? Going to explore the Missouri River? Would you like a drink of Kentucky whiskey? I got some good stuff here. How many men you got with you?"

The captains sat and Lewis said, "Why yes, Mr. Boone, I would like some whiskey. About forty-three now, we got forty-three men."

"Don't ya go callin' me Mr. Boone. Call me Dan'l. I like it better when folks calls me Dan'l," Boone said as he got a flask and poured three glasses with some whiskey. "Here ya go," he said, serving the whiskey. "Let me know if you don't like that. It's good Kentucky whiskey." He sat down slowly and looked intently as his guests sipped the whiskey.

Clark spoke saying, "We've got three boats, one large keelboat that Lewis here designed himself in Pittsburgh, and two pirogues. We've got 'em loaded with cargo and some trade goods, hopefully enough to last until we reach the Pacific and back."

Lewis added, "You're welcome to come down and visit our camp. We should have some fresh venison, the men put out a pretty good supper."

"I'd like that," Boone replied. "Don't get out much anymore and as much as I like to be away from civilization, I got to admit I like seein' you boys from the United States. It'll be a pleasure to see your outfit and say hello to your men." Then he looked at his guests and continued, "What do you call your outfit? Did they give you a name?"

"In fact," Lewis said nudging Clark slightly, "we're called the Corps of Discovery. That's what the men named themselves. We're an all volunteer group. Small enough to be mobile, big enough to be able to handle the elements and any possible hostiles."

Boone's eyes lit up; he looked toward the distance as if recalling times past and repeated, "Corps of Discovery, now that's a name; like it a lot, I do. I liked discovering things and going to new places. Fact is, I'd love to be going with you two. Why, if I was thirty years younger, I would pull up stakes right now and join you. That's the Lord's truth. Moving into the new territories and seeing things first, it gets in your blood. Dangerous sometimes and hard work most the time, but damn, that's when you know you're alive. You feel the blood moving in your veins. You feel the breeze in your face and walk on ground no white man has walked on. You see things for the first time. Yep, I'd love to go with you."

Clark listened to the elder Boone intently and responded, "Dan'l, if you were only **twenty years** younger, we'd take you quick as a shake. You're a legend, and you'd add to our company indeed."

Lewis, nodding his head, added, "You must have vast knowledge of this territory. And, coming from you, it would be experience that could help our cause. What can you tell us of the lands and Indians west of here?"

The captains moved to the edge of their seats as Boone nodded and began to speak, "I be honored to share what I know of this country with you men, honored. I guess I'd start with the Indians I know about. You'll meet the Oto and Missouri, of course. They're near these parts and mostly friendly. Curious, too. They like to see anything new and different. Good people and generous with their food and women. Then I think you'll see the Omaha, Assiniboine and Yankton. They're pretty good, too. But the ones you got to watch, I mean stay up nights on guard against, is the Teton Sioux." He looked at Lewis and then at Clark and continued, "The Teton can be just plain ugly. I ain't never met them, mind you; I only just heard things, but I heard it from reliable sources, and the story is always the same. They have the military strength to overpower the other Indians, and they do it, too, on a regular basis. They think they own the damn river. They have learned they can gain riches from the river traffic tolls and rob honest fur traders to grant safe passage. A lot of traders will go to great lengths to avoid the Tetons."

Clark asked, "Do you think they can be dealt with? What would you recommend?"

Boone sipped his whiskey and leaned back in his chair and responded, "Recommend?" Boone said, "Well I would recommend you sneak by them at night if you can. Make no campfires, stay on sandbars when possible, and double your guard. As far as can they be dealt with?" Boone paused and was silent a moment. Then he continued, "Yes, I do think you can get on with them with careful diplomacy. Trade fair with them, but most of all, don't show weakness. No fear. It's like facing a bear in the woods. If you turn and run, you'll be killed and et. If you stand your ground and hold your aim, that bear will most likely turn and walk back into the woods. Teton are like that bear."

Lewis asked, "Are they a large tribe? How well are they armed?"

Boone looked at him and continued, "I don't know. I think they are a large tribe, bigger than most. Can't be sure 'cause the pox has hit a lot of the tribes hard. I hear they're unusual. Some of their leaders can be made to understand trade. And trade they have. That's how they got their guns and ammunition supplies. They know the white fur traders have a value for their needs so they keep peace. They will always try to demand more than what's fair. What I hear is they'll use their strength to intimidate. They'll get their toll and then want more. If you can't sneak past them at night and you do have to meet them, expect them to show up in numbers. They may have guns by now, but they would depend on whites for powder and shot. Sorry to say, I have not heard how well armed they are in quite awhile. Not much good information comes here about them at all. One thing, they can't fix whatever guns they may have, no maintenance whatsoever, so they will trade with whites for repairs just like guns. In fact, they will want to learn gunsmithing real bad." Then he shifted his weight, sipped his whiskey again and continued, "Now, some of the young bucks, trying to make their mark, could get testy as hell. Real gutsy, and you have to watch that. It's my opinion to stay away from them 'cause they will get themselves in an awkward position that only killing can get 'em out of."

Lewis glanced at Clark as both men listened intently while the elder Boone spoke. It was obvious that Boone knew what he was talking about. Lewis felt fortunate that they had made this encounter. He then said, "Dan'l, your whiskey is good, best I've tasted. Would you come with us to our campsite, and we'll show you our vessels and have you meet our crew?

Supper will be ready this evening and we'll enjoy sharing your experiences with all the men. I know they'll all want to meet you."

"Yes, yes," Clark added enthusiastically, "Do join us. This will be an exceptional evening."

"Of course, I'll come. Fact is, it would take a team of horses to keep me away. Corps of Discovery. That spirit wakes these old bones. The honor would be mine to meet your crew. I'm sure they're exceptional to the man. One condition though," Boone said as he stopped and raised a finger in the air.

"What would that be?" Lewis inquired.

"Just this. I will purely enjoy having supper with yehs and visitin' with your men; talkin' about the West, lettin' them tell me about your expedition so far and all firsthand, but you got to promise me one thing for sure." Boone said, pointing his finger at the captains. "Tonight, after all our visitin' and enjoyment, you have to promise to sleep in my house tonight. This old man has to be host to the expedition leaders. If I can't join you, I sure can host you in my house this night."

"Of course, Dan'l, it'd be our honor," Lewis said nodding as he looked at Clark who was also nodding in agreement.

"It's done then?" Boone asked smiling.

"Done," both captains said simultaneously.

As they proceeded into the campground, Clark raised his hand and said loudly, "Men, gather round. I have an introduction to make." The men stopped what they were doing and moved to form a semi-circle around the captains and the elder Boone.

Clark said with a broad smile, "Men, it gives me great pleasure to introduce to you one of the great citizens of the United States. A true frontiersman, woodsman and hunter that we all have heard about. A legend, a man that left Boonesboro because it was getting too civilized and too crowded. He's settled as far west as he could. Men, let me introduce to you one of this country's best frontiersmen; this here is none other than Dan'l Boone." Then he stepped back and applauded. The men joined in.

Boone spoke, "You men have made an aging man very happy today. I'd give anything to be part of this expedition. You're part of the prize of all frontier travel. You'll make it all the way to the Pacific. You men will draw the first lines on the maps. Why hell, you will make the first maps. You'll be the first to do lots of things, meet Indian tribes, see mountain passes, see the fish, plants and animals of the West. I can't wait until you get back and tell me the tales of your adventures."

Boone began mingling with the men, and each man would shake his hand and introduce himself. The evening supper was roast venison and fresh vegetables.

Boone joined the captains at the dinner table and said, "I see you have a Negro with you? The men said his name's York and that he is your man, Captain."

Clark said, "Yes, that's my man. He's been with me since my youth. He's strong and he should be valuable along the way."

Boone said, "Never much liked the idea of slaves or slavery. It'll cause a problem some day. A man needs pay for his work." Pausing he continued in a reflective manner, "To my knowledge, the Indians have never seen a Negro. I've never heard talk of it anyway. Indians are curious and superstitious. They may be afraid of him, dunno. It could go either way, but one thing sure, he'll be a conversation item for them. Just pray it ain't raining hard with thunder and lightning when they see him because they **are** superstitious. Never know what they'll do. They could get in a religious fervor and take the notion they have to kill ya all."

Clark added, "It's my hope that by seeing the black skin and curly hair of a Negro, and then seeing my red hair and some of the men with blue eyes, well, I just hope they will realize that there is a great variety of people. More importantly, they will realize that times are changing. We'll be offering trade and peace. Perhaps they'll take us seriously and know that the future rests with people outside their own tribes."

Boone replied while nodding, "Jest play yer hand close. This'll be different and big medicine to the natives. Mebbie they'll accept the notion of being part of the Great White Father's land, especially if'n it benefits 'em. Mebbie they won't like it none." Then noticing Lewis' dog he said, "Where on earth did ya get that big black dog? I ain't never seen a dog that big." Then he laughed and asked, "Was his pappy a horse? You got a saddle for him?"

Lewis spoke up, "I got him because he was so big. When I saw the size of him, I just had to have him. His breed is called Newfoundland. I suppose because it was first bred there. I call him Seaman because we'll be spending so much time on the water, and, fact is, he helped me himself to pick out his name. Woofed at the mention of it, like he approved."

"Well, he sure is a bigun, twice the size of any dog I ever saw. Indians should be impressed with him too?" Boone said.

Clark replied, "They are. On the way down the Ohio, Meriwether was offered two beaver pelts for him by a couple of Indians in Illinois."

Lewis interrupted, "He's not for sale or trade. He'll make the whole trip with us. A good dog is better than a sentry. Although I must admit, I may be tempted to harness him to pull the pirogue if we need to."

The men asked several questions and stayed up asking about the river, the landmarks, Indians and animals. Cruzatte played the fiddle and the men began to dance around the fire. The captains were pleased and walked with Boone back to his house to spend the night.

June 1804 Across Missouri to Kansas City

As Lewis and Clark leave La Charette and point the bow of Discovery against the current of the Missouri River, they know that they are leaving the last white settlement they will encounter for a very long time. There will be no more letters or other communication with the outside world. From now on they will be a self-contained unit, all their needs will have to be met by each other as a team.

The last white settlement well behind, the river continued with unstable banks and a strong, steady current filled with debris. The combined efforts of the men rowing, using sails when possible, and towing with ropes yielded only an average of eighteen miles per day. The duties on board were split among the sergeants. One at the helm attended steering and the compass. One was stationed amidships to supervise the sails, watch over the rowing and keep lookout for notable points such as mouths of rivers or creeks and sandbars. The sergeant at the bow watched the river for serious floating debris that would be pushed aside by the bow man using a metal tipped pole. The sergeant also would watch for signs of Indians along the way, and then in the evening he was in charge of doling out the whiskey.

Mosquitoes became the bane of each day. Troublesome, thick enough to interfere with normal operation around the camp, the only sanctuary was the mosquito netting at night. They quickly learned to face the camp into the wind when possible and make fires to try to prevent the insects from invading the campsite at night. They saw frequent signs of Indian presence, abandoned campsites, but did not encounter any natives.

June 12, 1804

"Pirogues ahead, two of them, sir," Labiche shouted. The men in the two approaching boats waved as a signal of recognition and friendship. Lewis shouted to the approaching men and suggested going ashore to talk. The boats drew near. Lewis learned that one of the pirogues was loaded with furs and the other had supplies. Among those supplies was "voyager's grease," a mix of buffalo and bear tallow. This was especially useful on the river where mosquitoes ruled. Unpleasant as it was to apply and smell, it was much preferred to having a blanket of mosquitoes on arms, neck or any exposed skin, so thick they often interfered with normal breathing. During this meeting, the leader, Pierre Dorion, a middle-aged man introduced himself.

"I'm Pierre Dorion, and this is my wife, Two Birds, a Yankton Sioux. I've lived many a year just upriver. Who're you fellas? Why so many men and guns?" Dorion queried.

Clark responded, "We are a military group, the Corps of Discovery, sent here by President Jefferson to explore the upper Missouri waters in hopes that we will find a passage to the Pacific."

"The Pacific? You mean the ocean? Holy heaven, man! That may not be possible. All there is out here is prairie and this river. It's good land for fur trappers, plenty beaver, but I never talked to even one man that seen the ocean, not even when they's tellin' lies around the campfire."

Lewis had been listening to the man and perked up when he introduced his wife as a Sioux. "I'm Captain Meriwether Lewis, and this is Captain William Clark. Your wife is a Sioux, so do you speak that language?"

"Yep, sure do. French, too, when I get the chance. I was raised speaking French at home, played with English speaking kids. Got to know both. I sure do wish you luck in going to that ocean. I've never heard of any man even trying to get there from these parts." Then he stared at Clark for a moment and proceeded on. "Your name is Clark? I served under a George Clark back in '85 in the Illinois Territory. Good man he was. You any kin of his?"

Clark smiled broadly and replied, "Why yes, yes indeed, George Clark is my brother, now retired from the Army." Clark looked at the boats and back at Lewis, then continued, "Well now, good fellow, would you pull over to the river's edge here so we can make a deal? We can pay you for some of your voyager's grease there, as much as you'll sell us. We've been bothered by hordes of blood sucking mosquitoes. Sometimes we can't even work they're so thick."

"Sure, we can trade. I've got near three hundred pounds I estimate. It works if you can stand it. It's time we had a little break in travel. We can share a meal before we head on," Dorion said with a smile.

"Well, sir, we'd like that, like it a lot," Clark said. "So you served under my brother George in Illinois. Would you consider serving under me? This expedition could certainly use a man experienced in these parts, and knowing the Sioux language may just save us some fighting, even save lives."

Dorion looked at Clark a moment, then at his fellow travelers and replied, "It is a good thought. It's got merit to it, but my men here will want to proceed on to sell their furs. I gotta go with 'em to get my share."

The Corps of Discovery and the two southbound boats moved to the riverbank where they tied up the boats and the men got out. There they shook hands and continued the conversation as the sergeants directed the others to make camp and prepare food.

Clark and Dorion each sat down on a camp stool. Lewis, who had been directing the men, soon moved over to join them. Clark said, "Pierre, we are very serious about needing your help negotiating with the Sioux upriver. You knew my brother and he was good to you. I'll ask again, will you join our group and act as interpreter and guide?"

Dorion replied, "I really can't afford it, gentlemen. I have a lot of money due me when we sell these furs. I have to stay with them until this deal is done."

Lewis spoke in anticipation, "Pierre, if you would consider joining our expedition to assist as a guide, we will pay you for what the firs would have brought in St. Louis. I'll write you a note, which is acceptable at the bank in St. Louis or at the Army post. Knowing the language, you'd be a great assistance to our ability to accomplish a peaceful mission with the natives."

Dorion rubbed his chin and looked at his boat, then at *Discovery*. He gazed at his traveling companions and then the men of the expedition. "Good God, you are well-armed and well-provided. It seems as if I've stumbled across a once-in-a-lifetime opportunity. I believe I'll take your offer for pay now and maybe you could sweeten it for a dollar a day as guide going back upriver?"

Lewis looked at Clark and they smiled. They knew they could not let this man leave. Lewis responded, "Shrewd negotiator you are, Pierre, shrewd indeed. But the plain fact of the matter is we can use your services, and a dollar a day is fair." Looking at Clark he said, "What do you think, Captain? Is this man worth paying for his lost furs and a dollar a day?"

Clark stood, stepped over to Dorion who was also rising from his stool and extended his hand. They exchanged a firm handshake and Clark said, "Done."

Lewis added, "I'll have the sergeant there get one of the men to help you separate your personal effects from your boat and get it packed into *Discovery*. We'll leave tomorrow morning."

June 28, 1804

Hunting along the river is productive and hunting parties have no trouble obtaining fresh meat for the men. The hard work of moving three vessels against the river current gives each man a hearty appetite. The captains have decided that in order to save precious daylight time they will not make stops for breakfast or lunch. Breakfast and lunch are to be the leftovers from the previous evening's meal, eaten as the men take breaks as they move. They decide to have one large meal each evening and let the men relax at that time. Typically, the evening features a gill of whiskey per man while some dance around the fire to the music played by Cruzatte.

Mosquitoes continued to be a plague. Everyone uses the voyager's grease and mosquito netting for protection. During travel, the expedition camps on sandbars wherever possible. They consider themselves a military expedition in potentially hostile territory and, as such, vulnerable to attack. One day, as the expedition rounds a curve in the river and is making ready for evening camp on a sandbar, they notice a second island covered with vegetation.

York said to Captain Clark, "Capt'n, see that island? York thinks there might be green vegetables we can cook with the venison over there. Captain Lewis already showed York some of the good kind to eat. Do ya want York to go see?"

Clark replied, "Good idea, York; yes, go. It's not far, but the current's strong. Do ya think you can swim that far and make the return trip loaded with a sack of greens? Maybe we should just take the pirogue."

York smiled broadly and replied, "No need to take the pirogue; it'll need men to row it. That ain't no distance for York. York kin take these sacks, and if they's too many greens to swim with, York kin holler back. Then you can send the boat."

Clark looked at York and studied his face. He was expressing himself and using reason. He replied, "Sure, my man, go ahead. We could use some greens for our diet. Maybe even make some stew if you get onions."

York took two large cloth bags, tied them to his waist and plunged into the river. He swam powerfully, gracefully, and even against the current he reached the island quickly. Standing as he walked ashore, he turned and waved back at the crew. He shouted back, "It won't take long. This here island ain't very big at all."

York set to gathering vegetables; he pulled roots and cut greens. During his search he managed to find three duck nesting sites and each had six eggs. Then he loaded his two sacks, tied them to his waist and walked to the shoreline. He shouted, "Capt'n, York found some good ones; enough for supper. Even got a few eggs. No need to send the boat over. York kin swim good. This ain't no distance to go." With that he waded into the water, loaded with produce, and began to swim back to the campsite.

Clark, watching from shore, said to Sergeant Pryor, "I knew he could swim, but I had no idea he could **really swim**. Just look at him. It's like he didn't have anything in tow. Why I'd bet there ain't a man among us that could keep up with him out there, and him with all that dead weight."

Pryor responded, "Why, I ain't never. Sure enough, he can swim. No need to worry about him ever drowning. I wish every man in the Corps could swim like that, especially me."

They watched as York crossed the span of water and joined them on shore. "You done good," Clark said patting York on the back, "I never saw any man swim as powerfully as you just did. Why, if we get the keelboat bogged down, we can just hook a tow rope to York here and let him pull it free." York and the men laughed.

That evening they had vegetable greens and roots along with their regular diet of venison. Sergeant Pryor spoke to Sergeant Ordway saying, "York got these greens from the next island. Sure good, ain't they?"

Ordway responded, "Yeah, they are, and they make a welcome addition to the plate. I even heard Captain Clark saying he thought all these boils the men were getting was due to dirty water and not enough variety in our food."

Sergeant Pryor was chewing a mouthful of food and responded, "I dunno about the food curing the boils. Seems like we all got 'em. I think it's the water, but I have heard tell that men at sea need variety to keep from getting scurvy."

Ordway looked surprised and said, "Scurvy? Do you think these boils are the scurvy?"

Pryor responded, "Hell, John, I don't know. I ain't never seen the scurvy, but I do think that so many of us getting boils ain't natural. We eat a lot of meat. Meat's good, I always thought."

Ordway nodded and said, "There's lots of new stuff we're seeing out in these parts. Could be most anything causing these boils. I think it's the muddy water. Why hell, man, there could be anything in this water, from dead skunks to rotten tree branches."

"One thing sure," Pryor said as he chewed some of the roots from his plate, "eating like this can't do a body harm. I'd have seconds if there were more to have."

The meal was soon over and the men prepared to bed down for the evening. In the morning they would proceed on against what they knew would be strong current. Sergeant Pryor assigned Private Collins as first watch with Colter to relieve him during the night.

During the evening, Private Collins decided to take a small drink of whiskey. "No one will know," he muttered to himself as he pulled the cork. One drink became two, then three, then another. Noticing him with drink in hand, Private Hall came over.

"Hey, you sneaky varmint, is there some for me, too?" Hall asked in a low voice.

Collins, seeing someone to share his secret, willingly invited Hall to join. Drinking straight whiskey, it was not long before they became drunk and started talking loudly. Sergeants Pryor and Floyd overheard them cursing about the mosquitoes. They got up from the campfire to go down to the river's edge where the boats were moored to check on the two inebriated men.

Sergeant Floyd said, "Collins, is that you? Who's that down there with you?"

Collins replied, "Well Sergeant, it looks like Private Hall to me. Course I cain't tell fur sure, cuz his ugly face is all covered with moskeeters." He laughed.

"Get up here," Sergeant Pryor ordered sternly. "You men are drunk, and Collins, you were supposed to pull guard duty tonight. You can't be on guard in your condition. I'm putting the two of you under arrest. Drunk on duty, damn it man, you know better. You're also guilty of stealing whiskey without permission and of shirking your duty as a sentry. That whiskey is part of our supplies and not just there for the taking. All the men know exactly how much whiskey we got, and it belongs to all us men. It has to last the trip. There ain't no place around here to get more. Put the cork back in that whiskey barrel and get your drunken asses up here. Now! Move it, move!"

Sergeant Floyd moved closer to the keelboat and said, "Give me your hand, ya damn fools. You ought to know better than to steal whiskey." Taking their hands as they stepped from the keelboat, Sergeant Floyd pulled the drunken men up the bank.

Sergeant Pryor ordered, "Walk in a straight line back to the camp. The captains are going to see you in this condition and they'll decide what to do with yehs. Damn, you two ain't very smart, are yeh? Goddamn fools you are. You got yourselves in trouble back at St. Charles and now here yehs are again. The captains ain't goin' to like it none."

The two drunken men walked back toward the camp with the sergeants behind them. As they approached the campsite, the others quickly recognized that something was wrong and fell silent. Every eye was on the men as they moved toward the captain's tent. Lewis, hearing the men approach, came out of the tent.

Sergeant Pryor spoke, "Captain Lewis, Sergeant Floyd and me caught these two tappin' into our whiskey supply. Drunk as skunks, they was makin' all kinds a noise. I dunno how much whiskey they took, but it ain't right."

Lewis stiffened and approached the drunken men. "What have you got to say for yourselves?" He walked around them as they stood still. Then he continued, "You're lucky that the good sergeants here caught you. After your last court-martial, if I had caught you, well, you could have been shot for stealing government property. You two had to know this was wrong and now you will feel precisely how wrong it is. Tomorrow we will hold court-martial for the both of you."

Turning to the sergeant, he continued, "We cannot have the men helping themselves to supplies. We're a military expedition. The supplies are under Captain Clark's and my control. No man Jack among the crew has the right to help himself. Stealing supplies is stealing from the men, like stealing from family. I won't have it."

Sergeant Floyd spoke, "Sir, Collins here was supposed to stand guard tonight. I'll go get another man to take his watch. Do you want them bound with rope?"

Lewis' eyes flashed, "Stand guard!" He turned and looked Collins in the eyes, his face only inches away from Collins'; the private stood as erect as he could. "Any man that is scheduled to stand guard and then gets into whiskey. That man would simply be shot in any army. Why, I don't know what I'll do with you now, mister, but your punishment will be twice that of Private Hall here. Court-martial will be in the morning." Lewis walked a few paces and then continued in an angry tone, "Yes, Floyd, tie them with rope."

Lewis continued to pace for a moment and then said, "Sergeant Pryor."

"Yes, sir," Pryor responded.

Lewis ordered, "Get me five men for the court-martial; you, Gass, Colter, Newman and Thompson. Tell them that there will be a court-martial here by my tent in the morning. They're to sit in judgment of these, these, derelicts. Now get them out of my sight. I cannot stand the sight or smell of them any longer." Lewis turned to walk away and then turned back again and said, "And Sergeant," Pryor stopped and looked at Lewis. "If they try to leave their tent, tell the sentry to shoot 'em."

Sergeant Pryor took the men to a tent and set a sentry outside as guard. Meanwhile, Sergeant Floyd got another man to serve as guard on the encampment for the first shift. Pryor moved to advise the men Lewis had named that they were to serve on the court-martial in the morning.

Captain Clark had said nothing. Lewis had handled the situation firmly and firmness was required at the moment. Lewis, instead of returning to where they had been seated to rejoin in conversation, moved over to the river's edge and looked out over the water. After a few moments Lewis kicked the dirt and walked down toward the outer ring of the campfire and sat down. He put his head in his hands and sat motionless. Clark, recognizing the symptoms in his friend, picked up his rifle and went off to join Lewis at the edge of the camp.

"Merry, you acted as any man in command would have acted. What's the problem?" Clark queried.

Lewis replied somberly, "Bill, things are not going right. Here it is June and we aren't making good time on the river. We haven't met any Indians yet. I expected to be much farther along by now."

Clark knew that Lewis was in a dark mood. He replied, "The Missouri is a strong river, especially near its mouth. This current will not be as strong further up. Besides, think of it this way, on the return trip, that same water will be giving us a kick in the pants."

Lewis was still somber. "Look at this situation. The men aren't acting right. Stealing whiskey, why that's outrageous. I'm not sure what to do with them. Collins and Hall, why we just sentenced them to a good lashing. Dumb bastards, don't they have any sense? My command is slipping away from me. We have to set an example here. If we have this kind of disharmony this soon in the expedition, we'll never be successful. If discipline breaks down, we could fail in our mission or die."

Clark said, "You've acted as a good commander. Men will always be tempted, and some will succumb to temptation. Collins led Hall along. He also should have known that his duty as sentry later this evening was primary. He should never have dipped into the whiskey supply. Let us see what the men, their peers, on the court-martial will do. It will be interesting. You're not the only one disappointed here. The men don't like disobedience in their own ranks either. They know the risks. You'll be surprised. They will not be lenient in their judgment tomorrow. The men expect you to lead firmly and you did."

Lewis replied, "I need these men. I will need every last one of them to be successful. I cannot have the Corps breaking down this soon. I'm failing."

Clark reached over and lightly shook his friend's arm. "Damn it, Meriwether, you're not failing. This is to be expected in command. Tomorrow we'll have the court-martial and we'll observe the men. Note how they react to the charges and see what they exact as retribution. Now stop this cussed blame and pity." Then Clark slapped a mosquito on his neck. "If you want to get mad for a situation out of control, then get mad at these confounded blood-sucking mosquitoes. Come on, get up and come back over to our tent and under the protection of the netting. Staying here, why they'll suck you dry in an hour." With that, Clark stood and motioned his friend to follow him back to their tent.

Lewis looked at Clark for a moment. A smile crossed his lips as he got up and walked with Clark back toward their tent.

The next morning the flag was raised and the men stood at attention. The five men selected to judge were seated, and Lewis began the court-martial proceedings.

June 29, 1804

The court-martial is due to convene this morning. Lewis, in order not to show his emotions, sets about taking measurements of the moon and sun, accurately recording the time of day and position of each. These measurements can be used later to determine longitude and latitude.

The men of the Corps of Discovery are intense. They know there must be a trial and many are anxious to get it over with. On the river there is no means of incarceration; whatever punishment is decided upon will have to be dealt out immediately. To a group of men in the wilderness needing firm discipline, it is the only way. The trial begins at 11:00 A.M., neither of the captains presiding. This trial will be judgment from their peers. Opening the trial, Private Collins pleads not guilty. Then each of the witnesses testifies that he was obviously drunk. Further, many men add that he became drunk from stealing their whiskey. Others testify they are concerned he was drunk while on sentry and put them all at risk.

Collins is found guilty and sentenced to 100 lashes. Private Hall, witnessing the swift justice, immediately begins to attempt a plea bargain. He pleads guilty but tries to say he was coaxed into joining Collins, that he was baited with a sip of whiskey. The court listens to his plea but doubts his sincerity; they agree that he did not instigate the theft. After a brief discussion, Hall is found guilty of stealing whiskey and sentenced to 50 lashes. The men are all satisfied with their justice. The punishment is harsh, but the comments among the men are consistent, saying that they deserved it because "these men endangered our safety with their conduct." And, most importantly, "they stole our whiskey supply." All of the men seem eager to see the punishment carried out, all but York.

Shannon noticed York gazing in the distance with a look of gloom on his face. "What's the matter, York," Shannon inquired. "These guys got it coming, they stole the whiskey, we all know that for a fact."

York turned slowly back to Shannon and said, "Suppose so, Mr. George, but York done seen whippins afore, and I don' like 'em, even if the men getting the whippin' deserves it. It's an ugly thing and York just don't want to see it happenin' to us. York don' like seein' a lash on a man's back. If you don' mind, Mr. George, York will tend to other things while that's happenin'."

Shannon listened to York's words intently and started to speak in reply, but then said nothing. After a moment, he turned away from York, shook his head, slapped his thigh and walked over to join the other men.

Later that day, despite their sore backs, both Collins and Hall had to take their turns on the oars. In this group of men, no leniency was given or could be shown. The work of proceeding on was constant and had to be shared. The transgression had been paid for and now was to be forgiven.

July 4, 1804 Near Missouri / Iowa Border

It is Independence Day. The captains decide to have a day of relaxation and celebration. Drewyer, Sergeant Ordway and Lewis are engaged in conversation as Clark approaches.

"Men, just look at this land. Have you ever seen anything like it?" Clark spread his arms and rotated slightly from side to side, "Why it is a virtual Garden of Eden here. I ain't never seen so many deer tracks, they're as thick as cattle and hogs around a farm. Everything is so lush and green."

Ordway responded, "Yes, sir, it's truly beautiful here, lots of food too, just for the taking. There are raspberries all over. Plenty of fruit to eat, all kinds of it."

Lewis added, "It's relaxing, a fitting place for our Fourth of July celebration. Just look at the grasses on the plains with flowers everywhere. Pretty as any painting I've ever saw."

Drewyer added, "It is no test of my skills to get meat here. Do you want venison, buffalo, elk or bear? Any type of game is possible. Perhaps we could have a stew with some of each along with the vegetables?"

"Let's fire the cannon and give salute to the flag to celebrate the Fourth." Clark said enthusiastically. "Who knows? The noise may even attract some of these elusive Indians that we've yet to meet. Come on. Let's go to the campsite and celebrate. I believe that an extra gill of whiskey would be proper to celebrate the first Fourth of July ever held in these parts."

Lewis added, "Well, my friend, we could listen to you whistle a patriotic tune or we can encourage Cruzatte there to play his fiddle. Sergeant, would you ask Cruzatte to play for us. I really would enjoy listening to the fiddle awhile. Today, I don't want to think of anything but this beautiful place and our country's birthday."

Ordway said to Clark, "Given this festive occasion, Captain, do you think we could have more than one extra gill?"

The men turned and began walking back toward the rest of the camp. "I knew it, I just knew it," Clark responded. "Let us make a generous offer of whiskey and someone would consider it a weak moment and ask for even more whiskey." Patting Ordway on the back, Clark continued, "Sergeant, I have no problem with extra rations for the men, as long as it comes from **your** share." He looked at Sergeant Ordway and laughed, "Should I announce your generosity to the rest of the men?"

Ordway said, "On second thought, sir, I don't think so." They all laughed as they walked back into camp.

July 8, 1804

As usual, the day has been hard and long. Campsite is set an hour before sunset and the men have a large portion of meat to satisfy ravenous appetites. Typically, sentry duty is rotated among the men. It is extremely important to have sentries on guard each night. The Corps of Discovery has an enormous amount of trade goods and more guns and ammunition than any tribe of Indians has ever seen in one place. Any Indian tribe might be tempted to raid such a group if it is not constantly alert. The men have all retired to their tents behind the mosquito netting; the campfires are low and soon the conversations fade into silence as the weary travelers fall asleep.

Later in the evening Sergeant Ordway gets up to relieve himself and looks around in the direction of Private Willard, one of the sentries for the evening. Willard is not to be seen. Ordway panics. He quickly grabs his rifle and runs to the area being patrolled by Private Willard. There on the ground, Ordway finds Willard lying down, asleep.

The sergeant was furious; he muttered to himself, "I'll be damned." Then he slammed his rifle butt against Willard's feet. Ordway, with a stern look on his face said to Willard as he straightened up from the blow, "What the hell are you doing, man? You're **asleep** at your post. You stupid son-of-a-bitch. You're not new to the military. You know that can be a capital offense. And here I was worried I would find you with your throat cut." Then, turning his rifle around, Ordway pointed the muzzle toward Willard. "Get up. You're coming with me. I'll see what the captains will do with you."

Ordway woke George Field and told him to watch Willard while he informed the captains.

"Captain Lewis, Captain Clark," Ordway said in a muffled tone as he opened the flap of the captains' tent. "I've got a problem here you need to know about."

"What is it?" Lewis said, "Is there some kind of trouble?"

Clark added, "Have the boats broken loose? What's wrong?"

Ordway explained, "Well, sir, I woke up to go piss and noticed there was no sentry on duty. I went to investigate and found Willard lying down, apparently asleep."

Lewis clinched a fist and slammed it into his other hand, "Damn, damn, damn, where is he now?"

"I removed him from sentry post and put George in charge of watching him," Ordway replied.

Lewis fumed, "Good, Sergeant. Does he **know** the punishment for falling asleep on duty? I can't believe he doesn't know the punishment for falling asleep. The idiot! Tomorrow we'll hold a court-martial. I'm afraid he may force our hand."

Ordway inquired, "Shall I get men to serve, sir?"

Lewis shook his head and said, "No, Sergeant, the military is very clear about this. Where there is possibility of capital punishment, only the commanders preside. Captain Clark and

I will hold the court-martial. We alone shall hear this case and issue judgment."

"Very well, sir, I'll have the prisoner ready in the morning," Ordway said, then turned and walked away.

As the sergeant walked out of sight, Lewis continued to gaze in his direction, aghast with the news he had just heard. He spoke in a low tone, "What should I do, Bill? Just what the hell should I do? You know we are out here needing every last man and yet discipline seems to be a problem. Now I have to put a firing squad on a private for falling asleep on sentry duty." He sat down hard and said, "We must reconsider our list of men. Those that will continue on with us and those that will return to St. Louis."

Clark rose and stood looking out at the campsite, "Meriwether, my friend, this is not a fault of our command. This is a situation where a soldier, completely exhausted from a full and difficult day of fighting mosquitoes and pulling on a tow rope against upstream currents, was asked to serve as a sentry. He simply fell asleep from exhaustion, not dereliction of duty. You did the right thing in telling the sergeant that we would handle this ourselves. Whatever we decide, the decision will be removed from the conscience of the rest. Something like this, the men wouldn't want to sit in judgment. It's not like stealing a little whiskey."

Lewis replied, "A good thing it was that Ordway found him and not me. I may have acted irrationally had I discovered a soldier asleep at his post. Hell, Bill, I might have been tempted to shoot him right there."

Clark replied, "Perhaps it's a good thing that we have until tomorrow morning to sit in judgment here. There'll be cooler heads in the morning and I believe we'll reach a just decision tomorrow."

July 9, 1804

It is early morning and the camp is buzzing with conversation. The word of Willard's failure at sentry duty is on everyone's lips. The men are somber and anxious; they want to see what the captains will do in this situation. York has busied himself by adding small sticks to the campfire one at a time. He is not trying to build a fire or keep one going; he is simply keeping his mind off of the subject. He snaps the sticks and tosses them into the fire and then watches as they catch fire before he repeats.

The court-martial is held with the captains in military uniform. Full dress adds to the mood that this court is about to rule on a very serious matter. The evidence of Sergeant Ordway against Willard is presented first.

"Captain Lewis, Captain Clark, last evening I awoke to relieve myself when I discovered that Private Willard here was lying down, sleeping on sentry duty. I arrested him and charged him with dereliction of duty as a sentry."

Clark said, "Very well, Sergeant Ordway." Then looking directly at Willard, he continued, "Private Willard, you have heard the charges made against you this day by the sergeant. You are aware of the possible punishment. How do you plead?"

Willard was scared, his feet shifted, he looked at the ground and then at the assemblage of men all around. Turning slowly, he looked at the captains, "Guilty, sir, of lying down; not guilty of going to sleep."

Lewis asked in a somber tone, "Private, do you have any further evidence or anything further to say before we consider your case and make judgement?"

"No, sir," Willard said softly.

Clark asked the men, "Did anyone other than Sergeant Ordway witness the private sleeping on duty? If so, step up now and provide witness."

No one moved. Lewis spoke, "This court will take a few minutes' recess and announce our judgment." The two captains rose slowly and walked back away from the men and talked. The men could see them pointing upriver and sometimes shaking a head in disapproval and then nodding a head in agreement. Finally, the captains turned and walked back toward the men.

Clark seated himself; Lewis remained standing as he spoke, "Private Willard." There was a moment of silence as Lewis and Willard locked in a steady gaze, "We have found you guilty on both counts."

Willard began to shake visibly as the other men were looking at one another. Lewis continued, "As you all know, we are a military command. Even though each of you volunteered for this duty, we are still subject to military rules, military law. That law is very clear about a soldier sleeping while on guard duty in what is determined to be hostile territory." Lewis paused and then continued. "If this infraction had occurred at any fort in the United States, there would be no question but to carry out the military requirement for execution by firing squad." Then, pausing again as he looked at Willard, the other men and then at Clark, he proceeded, "We are but a few men, volunteers who work hard each day to make this expedition, the President's dream, a success. I believe that Private Willard was exhausted from a day of toil on the river. I do not believe he went to sleep from being derelict in duty. He was, however, still guilty of sleeping on duty. As a good soldier he correctly should have gone to his sergeant and told him he was not alert enough to continue to stand guard through the night. That is an error in judgment on Private Willard's part that could have cost all of us here our lives had hostile Indians discovered a sleeping sentry." Pausing a moment and looking directly at Willard, Lewis continued, "Therefore, Private Willard, it is the judgment of this court to exercise leniency in that you will not be put to death but instead be given 100 lashes, well laid on, on your bare back." Lifting his gaze to the entire assemblage, Lewis continued, "All of you should learn from this. Sleeping while on sentry duty is not excusable under any circumstance and being tired or exhausted from a day's work is not an acceptable excuse. Do not interpret our leniency as weakness. We will have, must have, a high level of discipline or we will fail. The Corps of Discovery depends on each man performing when he is called upon. We are in possibly hostile territory. All of our lives depend upon one another. Where one man is unable to perform, another must stand in for him." Lewis stood in silence for a brief moment and then said, "Sentence to be carried out at three o'clock today. This court-martial is adjourned."

Private Willard looked at Lewis and said, "Thank you, sir."

August 1, 1804 Council Bluffs, Iowa

It is Captain Clark's 34th birthday. To celebrate the occasion, there is a feast in his honor. That evening Sergeant Ordway presents Clark with a meal that includes beaver tail (a delicacy), venison and elk. In addition, there are freshly picked cherries, plums, raspberries and grapes, all of superior quality.

During the feast Clark commented, "This is a meal fit for a king; the bounty of this land is simply overwhelming. There should be no trouble getting people to settle and farm this country. If this kind and quality of produce is available growing wild, just imagine what farming would bring."

Lewis enjoyed the meal with his friend and they had an extra gill of whiskey to toast the birthday. Lewis commented, "My writing skill is being challenged by the sheer volume of new plants and animals that we are finding. Each night is becoming more and more a chore than the night before. Write, dip ink, write, I get writer's cramp after a few pages. I sure hope the quality of my penmanship proves to be readable. Documenting plants and animals in proper scientific notation is not as simple as writing a letter to a relative back home."

"Yes, I know you spend a lot of time each night writing in your journal," Clark commented. "And, I must add, when you are evaluating a plant or an animal, well, I have learned to just leave you alone and all to yourself. Don't want to break your concentration."

"The writing isn't the half of it," Lewis responded. "The real job is documenting new specimens, validating that they really are unique, and then analyzing them and writing down just how they are unique. With plants, I have to look at the roots, stems, leaves, flowers or fruit. I then must devise how to catalogue them according to latest botanical coding principles. And animals, well, first I have to shoot one, stuff it or skin it and then analyze its bones, claws, hooves, teeth, fur and horns. Then, if all this documentation isn't enough, I have to preserve and store them for the return trip. The real problem comes when I have to write about Indian observations or the potential for developing this land. Those types of entries I have to do in code in a separate journal."

"Code?" Clark questioned. "You mean after all this gathering and analyzing for the naturalists you have to write to the president in code? What the hell for? Isn't writing it down enough?"

Lewis looked at Clark and replied, "Because, my friend, the president asked me to make my journal entries in code in case the journals fell into the hands of the British or French. At the time, it seemed like a good idea, but out here on the river, day after day, well, I must admit it is a pain in the ass."

Clark looked puzzled and then asked his friend, "Why do you do it then? You already write most entries in plain English. Why continue with the code book? God knows it is taking up a lot of your time."

Lewis looked puzzled at Clark, then replied, "Because the President of the United States asked me to, and, as a military man I am obliged to follow that order as long as I am able. It's that simple." Lewis sat back and let out a sigh as he continued, "This expedition is not only important to the president, it is important to our country - to history, that we get it documented accurately. We have already found a great many new things and learned that some prior beliefs were total misconceptions. That's why I ask those among us that can script to do so, to make a practice of making their own journal entries. That way, we'll have different points of view on important observations along the way. That's why, next to our gunpowder and ball, paper and ink are the most important items on board."

Clark, listening to his friend, looked at him admiringly and said, "You truly are the president's man, the right man to lead this expedition. Writing in code for Jefferson has got to take time and patience. I don't think I could do it. Still, I note that you do write frequently."

Lewis replied, "Well, I'm getting a little faster at the encoding and I do keep the coded journal separate from other observations. I don't code that much anyway. Mostly it's ordinary writing."

The next day at sunset a small band of Indians arrives at camp. They are Oto and Missouri and are accompanied by a French trader. This is the first meeting with Indians. The camp is excited to meet the Indians; Sergeant Floyd notifies Captain Clark immediately.

"Capt'n, we have company," Sergeant Floyd announced. "Looks like a small bunch of Indians with a white fur trader. I think he's French."

Seeing the white man with them Clark told Floyd, "Good, Sergeant, we have been expecting some type of encounter for quite awhile now. Get Labiche to act as translator. If the white man is French, we won't have to use sign language to communicate here." Then a half moment later, he added, "Sergeant, while you are out, get Dorion, too. That way we won't have to trust that white man with 'em to translate accurately."

"Yes, sir," Floyd said and departed. In a moment Labiche was hurrying toward the captains along with Sergeant Floyd. Dorion was walking a few steps behind.

The captains met with seven Indians and the French trader. They ordered the sergeants to prepare food, and they sat around a campfire and exchanged cordialities. The sergeants delegated the duty for preparation of dinner and then joined the captains with the translators, Labiche and Dorion.

The Indians looked over the campsite and took immediate interest in York. They also carefully observed the men, noting that each man had a firearm and the campsite seemed orderly and disciplined. One of the Indians asked and was translated, "What kind of paint does the large man have? Is it from the ashes of the fire?"

Clark immediately called to York and asked him to come and join them. York, who was working near the river on the pirogue, stopped and quickly came and stood at Clark's side.

Clark spoke, "This man is York. He's a Negro, a race of people from far away, they have dark skin and curly hair. He is not wearing charcoal; all of his skin is dark. He is one of many Negroes that live among the white people."

The Indians looked at York intently for a few moments and then, seeming satisfied, began to talk about a larger meeting.

Another Indian spoke and was translated, "We have seen you on the river many days and now visit your campfire. We come in peace. Our chiefs want to meet with you and talk trade."

Lewis was excited as he hung on each word as it was translated. He looked around the group and spoke. "Tell them," he said to Dorion, motioning with his hands, "that we are pleased to have them with us now. Tell them we very much want to meet with their chiefs and," Lewis reached out and picked up some tobacco that was twisted into the shape of a carrot and handed it to the Indians as he continued. "Tell them we also come in peace, that this tobacco is a token of our pleasure in meeting with them. Tell them that we want a meeting with their chiefs as soon as possible, that if they will hurry back to their chiefs, we will meet again. Tell them that..."

"Merry, you're too anxious," Clark interrupted in a calm tone as he patted his friend on the arm. "This will happen. They will bring their chiefs back." Turning to Dorion he spoke in a calm tone, "Ask them how soon it will be before we can meet with their chiefs and where would be the best place to meet."

Dorion nodded and translated to the Indians who began smiling and pointing upriver. As they spoke Dorion translated. "They are eager to trade with us. As a token they offer you some watermelons in exchange for the tobacco and food you have given them. They want to be the first to tell their chiefs of the whites with so much to trade. They will come back here to this place tomorrow before midday."

Lewis, having calmed himself from the original excitement, said, "We will wait here at this campsite until you and your chiefs come to the council with us. We have a message from the Great White Father in Washington who wants us to trade with all friendly tribes." Then he sat smiling while Dorion translated to the Indians who listened intently to every word.

The meeting was a success. The guests finished their meal and left, saying that they would meet the Corps of Discovery at camp the next day before noon.

Lewis turned to Clark and the sergeants and proudly announced, "Gentlemen, our first meeting with Indians seems to be starting well. Let us make preparations to meet and hold council with them tomorrow. I think we shall name this place for our maps." He turned and looked around briefly, then continued, "Council Bluffs. What do you think?"

"Good a name as any," Sergeant Pryor answered smiling. "How do you want us to prepare, Capt'n?"

Lewis replied, "Good question, Sergeant. I want to say first of all that we must not allow the friendly meeting today to relax our guard. We must be vigilant and stand guard as always. The Indians know we are here; they have seen our boats filled with trade goods. I don't want to be a target. A target is a bad thing."

Clark added saying, "Tell each man to be on his guard and watchful of anything. Meanwhile, Sergeant Ordway, make sure we have a fine meal prepared to entertain our guests."

Lewis added, "Sergeant Floyd, get the bale from *Discovery* marked thirty and let's have a look. Tomorrow I want to present a uniformed, close-order drill. I want to impress these people with our discipline and military appearance."

"Yes, sir," Floyd replied. "It's a sure thing they ain't never seen people march before. How many men do you want out?"

Lewis replied, "All but six, leave six on the boats and at full alert."

"You can count on us, sir," Floyd replied.

Clark, observing the exchange commented, "Floyd, you all right? Why the long face? Everyone else here is happy."

"Don't know, sir," Floyd responded. "I been having some pain in my gut; I think I must have eaten something I'm just not used to."

Clark looked puzzled and said, "Can't imagine what could be wrong with the food; everything here seems so good. Anyway, look after yourself, and if this persists, let me know. Captain Lewis has medical supplies. Maybe some 'thunderbolts' will help ya."

"Thank you, sir, for the concern," Floyd said. "I'll check with Capt'n Lewis for medications after the meeting tomorrow. I'll be all right until then."

August 3, 1804

The night has been restless for many of the men and they are anxious to start the day. It will be their first major encounter with Indians. A fog is hanging over the river as the sun rises across the morning camp. Some men are preparing breakfast; others take the mast from Discovery and erect a sun shade for the coming meeting. Opening the bale with Indian gifts as directed by Lewis, they lay out some of the trade goods: blankets, medals, flags and red leggings, previously prepared for an Indian encounter. A staff is erected at the edge of the camp and the fifteen-star flag is hoisted. At 9:00 A.M., under the flag with all but six men in uniform, they begin to practice close-order drill. The captains, also in uniform, look on.

Lewis spoke, "Bill, I just can't wait. Why, this is like Christmas for me. This is what we were sent to do, meet the Indians and spread the word of trade with the United States." Then pausing he looked around briefly and said to his friend, "Do you think they'll be impressed? What do you think will happen when they get here?"

Clark replied, "It'll be alright, just fine, I'm sure. You've gone over your speech ten times or more. These Indians have more to gain by being friendly and setting good relations with the United States than to just let us pass through. This is good for them, too." Then he looked at Lewis and said in a calm tone, "Merry, they have to know that trading with us will work to their benefit. All the information that we have gathered in St. Louis, from Dan'l Boone, from every source, has indicated that all the Indians we will meet should be friendly, at least until we get to the Tetons."

Lewis paused a moment and then said, "Yeah, you're right. It's just that it's already August. August, my friend, and we left La Charette in May. We didn't see any Indians until yesterday. Oh sure, lots and lots of tell-tale signs that they were around but this will be our first meeting. I'm anxious as a schoolboy for all to go well. The ones we met with yesterday seemed friendly enough, no surprises there; today should go fine. God, I wish they would get here."

Clark smiled at his nervous friend and nodded, "They will be here soon. They wouldn't miss this for the world. Put yourself in their place; would you miss seeing a group of white men with three boatloads of trade goods, more rifles than you've ever seen in one place, and a cannon for God's sake. Bet they've never seen a cannon. They'll hear all about York and his dark skin and about your big dog, Seaman. Why hell, Merry, they'll be curious to see all that, not to mention the funny looking captains in charge of the whole outfit. They'll be here, just relax a little."

Within the hour the Indian delegation arrived. The captains sent the sergeants and Drewyer to greet the Indian delegation and bring them to the campsite. They exchanged cordial greetings and stood for a moment looking at one another. The best interpreters for the Corps of Discovery were there, Dorion, Labiche, Drewyer, seated near the captains. There were six chiefs from the group and twelve other men accompanying them, evidently without rank.

Captain Lewis asked for translation as he spoke, "On behalf of the Great White Father in the United States, we welcome the opportunity to meet with you chiefs of the Oto and Missouri tribes." He waited while the translation took place before continuing. "We have many trade goods with us to show you the kind of material goods that are available to you if you will trade with us."

The Indians, listening to the translation carefully, smiled and whispered brief comments.

Lewis continued, "While we're sure you are accustomed to trading with whites, trading is not our purpose. We are a military unit, as you can see by the uniforms that the men here are wearing. We will soon show you with our performance, as a unit, some of what we are capable of doing. We're able to defend ourselves very well. The most we can demonstrate is the least we can do." He waited for translation and continued, "Our mission is not to trade but to explore this great river until we find its source, to meet with all tribes along the way and to make peace. The United States is now sovereign over this country; the French and British will be replaced. The peace we establish with you and other tribes will benefit the future trade with all Indians."

Dorion, acting as interpreter stopped and turned to Lewis and said, "Sir, there ain't no Indian word for sovereign." Labiche nodded in agreement.

"Well, Mr. Dorion, tell them it is like a gracious God that takes care of them and rules the land," Lewis added. Dorion continued with the translation.

One of the Indian chiefs spoke asking, "We are confused. You have boats full of trade goods and we came to trade. If not trade, what do you want of our meeting?"

Lewis waited for the translation and replied, "We are from a great and mighty nation with cities that number as the stars. We have come to show you what trade goods we have and to explain the advantage of friendly relations with us and your neighboring tribes. We want to help you build trading centers that will prosper and provide centers for future whites that will come to live with you on this land."

When the translation was completed, Lewis looked pleased. Then, turning to Sergeant Floyd, he continued, "Sergeant, I see the targets are on the trees and the cannon is ready." Stepping back and looking over the men who were waiting at parade rest, Lewis commanded, "Sergeant, take the men through close order drill. At the conclusion have them fire at the targets at the south end of the camp."

Then turning to shout at the men on *Discovery*, he added, "Sergeant Ordway, when the demonstration here is concluded, fire the cannon." Ordway nodded his understanding of the command.

Standing at attention, Floyd snapped a salute to Lewis and replied, "Yes, sir." Then turning to march the few steps to where the men were standing in four rows at parade rest, he commanded, "Atten-shun!" The men snapped to attention in one quick movement. This command was followed by a series of commands: "Forward, march," "column right, march," "left flank, march" and so on through the series of precision drilling commands they had practiced over and over last winter. They were good, very good. They handled their weapons with precision and there was one synchronous sound with each command. The Indians were riveted to the show. They had never seen men in uniform marching with precision as if they were one. Frequently they would look back and forth and nudge one another.

Then, as they marched across the camp, the order was given for them to prepare to fire. The men formed a front row and dropped to one knee and aimed; the second row formed, stood behind the first with rifles over their heads. At the command "fire" all the rifles exploded with one sound. As the smoke cleared, the Indians were wide-eyed and poking at each other, pointing and talking in a buzz. At that moment Lewis waved to Sergeant Ordway and the cannon on *Discovery* blasted with a tremendous noise. A tree near the riverbank crumpled and fell into the river. The demonstration of military might had been impressive. No native tribe west of the Mississippi had ever seen precision marching, precision handling of weapons or firing on a target in unison. It was a first for all the Indians to see and witness the might of a cannon.

Lewis stood and waited for the smoke to clear. All could see the targets had been hit squarely and nearly completely destroyed. "Parade–rest, Sergeant," Lewis commanded.

Pryor barked out the command, "Parade–rest," and the men resumed the posture they had had at the beginning of the exercise.

Lewis next began a speech that would become his standard with every tribe encountered by the Corps of Discovery. "Children, we have been sent by the Chief of the seventeen great nations of America…" the speech droned on with how they expected to establish peace between Indian nations and that this peace was necessary to ensure they would qualify for trade goods from the whites. He told them that they had been sent to learn of the wants and needs of the Indians so that when they returned, they would be able to tell the president who would then see that their needs were met. He promised a fort to be built at the mouth of the Platte River to serve as the center for trading. Later in the speech, Lewis changed the tone from being the fatherly provider to add a cautionary note and warning to the Indians that, "if they displeased the Great Father, he would consume them as the fire consumed the grass on the plains. They must do as they are told or else there would never be other white men to come to trade with them; their tribe would be alone. Only those tribes that do as the Great Father wants will benefit from his trade."

At this point Clark ordered Sergeant Floyd to get the gifts from the boat. Floyd left with three men and returned bearing sacks of materials. They began to disburse the gifts to the Indians.

"We do have some gifts for you as a token of our appreciation and to show you the quality of goods available if you follow our instructions," Lewis explained through translation. "There are not large amounts of gifts for the Oto and Missouri because we have a long way to go and many tribes yet to meet. There must be gifts enough for all the others that we will meet."

One of the chiefs replied, "Our chief, Little Thief, is not with us today. We shall tell him of your offer of goods and of peace. How will we know that you will keep your words? What will you do for us?"

Lewis replied, "Tell your chief that if his people acknowledge the United States as the only people to govern the land, that we will build the fort at the mouth of the Platte River that I spoke of. The new fort will be filled with many trade goods. The Oto and Missouri will be able to trade furs for many kinds of goods and their people will become strong."

George Field nudged his brother Reubin and whispered, "Did ya hear that? Their chief's name is Little Thief. What do you suppose he's like?"

Reubin replied, "I reckon we should be glad his name is not 'Big Thief' because then we'd have to double our guard." They nodded and chuckled.

"Take these gifts we offer you today," Lewis said. "Tell your people about the promise of wealth from trading with the United States." Then he continued as he looked the Indian guests in the eyes, "We want Chief Little Thief and any other chiefs that will go with him to go east and visit with the Great White Father in Washington. There, you will see the benefits that peace and trading will bring."

Another Indian asked, "What of our old white trading partners of the past, the French and British? Will they not also provide trade goods as you promise?"

Lewis listened to the translation and paused a moment before answering. The Indians waited for his reply. "Your old friends and past trading partners will be welcome in the forts of the United States as long as they agree that the United States has jurisdiction. They are now part of the United States."

Dorion looked troubled as he said, "Captain, there ain't no word for jurisdiction that I know of. Can I just say 'will be present here' or 'will occupy'?"

Lewis replied hastily, "Alright, then tell them as long as the French and British will work under our flag and not their own, it will be all right. Tell them that. These Indians may not understand the full meaning, but the French and British they talk to sure as hell will."

Dorion proceeded with the translation and then the Indian chief said, "We understand you save your trade goods for other tribes. Some of them are our enemies. We expected more from our visit than these few trinkets. Can you give us gunpowder and shot? You have lots of gunpowder and shot. And whiskey, can you give us whiskey? The French always give us whiskey." The Indian then stood waiting for the translation and looked at Lewis' face for a favorable reaction.

Lewis looked at Clark and said, "They want more, just testing us or they may be greedy. What do you think about them asking for powder and whiskey? There is no way we can permit that until a fort is built."

Clark replied, "You are asking them to have their chief go to Washington. I think a little powder and some whiskey are a good investment. I would only make it one canister and one bottle of whiskey. That way they don't have enough of either to cause real trouble, and, we would have met the request."

"Done," Lewis said enthusiastically, "Sergeant Pryor, get a canister of gunpowder, fifty balls and one bottle of whiskey." Then almost as an afterthought he said, "And Sergeant, get my air rifle, too. I want to demonstrate a gun that does not require powder."

The sergeant went to the boat and started to explain to Sergeant Ordway what the captain had ordered. "I heard him," Ordway said, anticipating Pryor as he was retrieving the materials from the boat. "Here ya go." He handed the materials to Pryor.

Sergeant Pryor took the materials as George Shannon joined him to bring the air rifle up. He handed it to Lewis. As he quickly loaded and prepared the air rifle, Lewis turned to Dorion and told him to translate, "Tell them to watch this. We have a rifle that does not use powder, it uses the air and can never run out of powder."

As Dorion explained to the Indians, who were now getting accustomed to works of wonder, they looked at one another but did not comment. They waited patiently for this new display of white man's technology.

Lewis proudly raised his air rifle and shot it, hitting a target some sixty feet away. The Indians began buzzing conversation again, pointing and nudging one another. The natives then departed, and Clark gave each chief a Jefferson Peace Medal. After the Indians were gone, Captain Clark congratulated the sergeants on the behavior of the men and the precision of the marching. Later that night he asked Lewis, "Well, what do ya think? That was our first meeting. I thought it went pretty well. How about you?"

Lewis nodded as he replied, "I was very pleased. I thought the men performed very well, excellent. I've never seen drill in any fort that was better. They were good. I was disappointed that Chief Little Thief didn't make it. It's hard to judge his personality when he's not here. I'd say from the reactions of the others that they were impressed."

Clark said, "It was good. You were a little windy here and there and used some terms I have no way of knowing whether or not they understood. They had the eyes of a startled calf part of the time."

Lewis replied, "I think the real test of the meeting will be if they keep the peace and if they send a delegation to Washington to meet Jefferson. God, I hope they send a delegation. It will be proof to the president that we are effective out here."

The first meeting with the Indians has been successful. The Corps of Discovery moves out to continue its trek onward up the Missouri. Mosquitoes continue to be a plague and the men seek seclusion each evening in their tents with mosquito netting. Those that have to be away from the safety of the netting use voyager's grease as their only defense. They all complain, even Seaman howls from the misery of constant insect attack.

Later in the evening, Private Moses Reed approached Sergeant Floyd with a request. "Sergeant, I done left my knife back at the council. I was cuttin' some tobacco back there at the council camp after the Indians left and I think I left her sticking in a log there by the fireside. Can I go back and get it in the morning? I'll catch back up right away."

Floyd, who was not feeling well, looked at the private, sighed and said, "Get in here or get out. You're letting those damned skeeters in here."

Reed replied, "Sorry about that; they are dreadful thick, ain't they? It's just that I paid good money for that knife and I would like to go get it back in the morning."

Floyd was in a light sweat and breathed heavily as he replied, "I don't know. If your knife was so damn important to you, why did you go off and leave it? Dumb ass. You're a dumb ass; ya know that, don't ya?" Floyd was irritated and pointed toward the captains' tent. "Go over and ask one a the captains. They may let you go. Tell 'em you asked me an' I said it was alright provided you get back right away."

Reed nodded and replied, "I appreciate it, Sergeant, I appreciate it. A man's gotta have a knife out here."

Reed moved quickly across the campsite and stopped outside the captains' tent. "Capt'n Clark, Capt'n Lewis, it's Private Reed. I left my knife back there at the council site. I already talked some to Sergeant Floyd and he said it would be all right fer me to go back and get it if'n you would agree to it."

Clark moved to the edge of the netting and told him, "Go ahead, Reed. Get your knife in the morning. Move quick to get it. You'll be by yourself out there and that's dangerous. You can go; just you be careful and get back here inside a day. You got that?"

Reed replied, "Yes, sir, thank you, sir," and he faded into the night.

The next evening Private Reed reached the council site. After searching through the rubble of the campsite, he found his knife and put it in its sheath. Then he turned and started back in the direction he had come. Suddenly he stopped. He paused a moment and looked upstream and then downstream. Finally he mumbled, "The hell with it" and moved out downriver. He had yielded to his desire to desert.

August 6, 1804

Three days passed and Private Reed had still not come back to join the Corps of Discovery. Clark approached Sergeant Ordway and commented, "Sergeant, Reed's been gone three days now. I was expecting him last night at the latest, and now I'm getting worried. I think he's either been killed or deserted."

Ordway looked at Clark and studied his captain's face. He could see he was serious as he replied, "Capt'n, Reed was acting strange, not talking much with the other men the last couple of days. I think the hard work, skeeters and boils finally got to him. Not to mention the prospect of meeting the Teton. My bet is he's deserted. Just plain wants to get back to Kentucky. He's probably up and gone. I figger he thinks you won't go after him, only one man and all, not a big loss. He figgers that you will just go on upriver and he will take his chances getting back to Kentucky by winter."

Clark listened to his sergeant carefully then replied, "Damn, I think you're right, Sergeant. I want to discuss this with Captain Lewis. I'll get back to you right away."

"Yes, sir," Ordway said as he turned and walked back to the boats.

Clark immediately went to Lewis and explained Ordway's opinion of Reed's absence. "I've been worried too. Fact is, I believe Ordway is right. I just didn't want to admit it to myself. What you think, Merry? Should we go get him?"

Lewis looked over the campsite and then upriver and said, "We can't have deserters here, especially here. We need to get a detail formed to go after him. Use Drewyer. He's the best hunter and tracker we've got. Have him take Labiche along. He's familiar with local languages in case they need translation with any Indians they might meet. I think we should have Ordway choose a couple other men to go with him. If he's been hurt and needs help, that's one thing, but if he's deserted, that's another. We can't leave men on the trail that might be injured, nor can we have men that would desert us here; we need everyone." Looking at the ground and then at the sky, Lewis continued in a low, serious tone, "Tell them when they find Reed, that if he doesn't give up readily and peaceful, shoot him."

Clark, slowly nodding all the while said, "I agree, my friend, a hundred percent. No army unit can tolerate desertion, least of all this group." Then he said, "I like your idea of using Drewyer to find him. He's got to be the best hunter I ever saw. I think we should instruct them to keep an eye out for the Oto Indians too. That chief that we didn't get to meet with…"

"Little Thief," Lewis volunteered.

"Yeah, Little Thief," Clark nodded. "We need to meet with him to tie the knot on that meeting. If Drewyer can find Little Thief and bring him here, then the detachment's search for Reed won't be a total waste."

"Done, my friend," Lewis said firmly. "I think giving the detachment a dual purpose is good, very good. Do you want to talk to Ordway or should I?"

Clark turned to walk away saying, "I'll do it, we've already started on the subject." Clark walked across the camp to where the boats were anchored. Seeing Ordway he called to him, "Sergeant."

Ordway stopped what he was doing and came to the captain. Clark explained the orders to him, "Take three men and Drewyer to find Reed." He also explained the need to try to find the Oto and Missouri Indians during the trip.

Ordway listened to the orders for the detail then inquired, "Shoot him, Captain?"

"Yes, Sergeant, tell Drewyer to kill him if he offers resistance. If he comes back peaceful, we'll hold a court-martial. Tell them to move quickly and take food with them so they don't have to stop to cook or fire their rifles or anything that would give away their position." Clark began to walk away and then turned and said, "Sergeant, we have to have discipline out here. If men think they can desert, we'll all be at risk. Besides, he may not have deserted; he may be injured and need our help."

"I understand, sir. The detail will be on the trail right away," Ordway said as he picked up his rifle and moved across camp.

August 17, 1804

Near dusk Private Labiche came into camp as the lead member of the detachment sent out earlier. He was excited as he turned to his friend Cruzatte and asked, "Where's Captain Lewis, Captain Clark?"

Cruzatte pointed in the direction of *Discovery* and said, "The captains are eating their dinner on board *Discovery*, in their quarters."

All the men had noticed Labiche entering the camp. Many of them heard his questions and, being curious, followed as he went to *Discovery* to talk to the captains. Hearing the commotion, Lewis came out of the officer's quarters.

"Captain," Labiche said eagerly, "We got him; we got Reed. He was about three days' travel south of the camp. Drewyer spotted him and we all ran to catch him. He gave up peaceful like, 'specially when he looked down the muzzle of Drewyer's rifle." Then looking around he added, "He's cool as a cucumber, that one. Drewyer always knows what he's doin'."

Lewis responded, "Well done. How far are they behind you?"

Labiche said, "Not far. They'll be here in the morning." Then beaming, he put his thumbs on his hips and turned and said proudly, "Know somethin' else? We found that Oto chief, Little Thief. He and his group will be with them. They should all be here in the morning."

By this time Clark was also on the deck, wiping food from his mouth as he looked at Labiche. Lewis said, "That's good news, Private." Turning toward Clark he said, "What do you think, a gill of whiskey to celebrate this news?"

Clark nodded in agreement. The men quickly formed a line behind Sergeant Pryor who was opening the whiskey barrel. Then he said in a low tone to Lewis, "It's good to meet the Oto chief, Little Thief, but catching a deserter, well, I have mixed feelings about that." The two men walked toward the others around the fire, Clark inquired, "By the way, Floyd's been ill. What are you doing for him?"

Lewis said, "I'm worried about him. At first I thought it was just diarrhea, maybe from eating something not cooked right. But it's persisted too long. He said he has been getting a gut ache for quite awhile now."

Clark replied, "I noticed he was pale and sweaty. He asked to be off work details early and then didn't eat anything. The meal was good, too."

Lewis said, "I didn't learn anything about his symptoms in Philadelphia, so it's pretty much try the best we can and let him have plenty of rest until he feels better. I already gave him some of Rush's 'thunderbolts.' That usually cleans out anything bad that a body may have eaten."

"You got that right," Clark said, "I can safely say I have seen five men at a time squatting due to thunderbolts. But they always got better."

Lewis added, "I bled him, too. I'd bleed him again but it didn't do much good the first time. I think it may be colic; I tried a poultice but he doesn't seem to respond. I hope whatever he's got will run its course soon. We could use him back on *Discovery*."

"Yeah, me too," Clark replied. Then changing the subject he asked, "What do you think we should do about Reed? Desertion is another one of those capital crimes."

Lewis stopped walking and looked at Clark, "I've been thinking. This differs enormously from the incident where we had Willard sleeping on guard. Do you agree?"

"Yes, I do," Clark replied, "Desertion is a willful act that takes planning. Falling asleep was a matter of exhaustion. This incident should have a court-martial involving the men, too. We'll all hear the evidence and then pass judgment as a court. That way, even if we decide to the extreme, it will be a joint decision."

Lewis nodded and commented, "I think so, but we will have Indian guests here at the same time. Do you think we should we hold off till they're gone or proceed?"

"No, I think we should proceed," Clark replied. "The Indians should know that our discipline means our men must obey the law at all times. Obeying law brings order, disobedience brings punishment. It's that simple. After all, when the government later sets up posts or deals with Indian trading posts, there will be laws. The Indians will have to recognize and obey those laws. Hell, with a name like 'Little Thief' it is obvious that they need to see how our law applies to our own people. Having a trial by the men against one of their own will demonstrate to the Indians that the laws are for all."

"True," Lewis replied. "Indian customs differ wildly from white culture. But now that they are part of the United States and subject to our laws, it may be good for them to witness that the laws apply to everyone."

George Drewyer and a small band of Oto Indians arrived at 10:00 A.M. The Indians were told that the man Drewyer had brought in had committed a crime of desertion. They were further told that any man accused of a crime would have a trial to determine his guilt and then to determine punishment. They seemed to understand and they were brought food. They ate and watched while the court-martial began.

Reed confessed to desertion and pled guilty to charges of stealing a government rifle and provisions when he left. He knew he was in trouble and asked the court to offer him mercy to be 'as lenient as your oaths will allow.'

The men of the Corps of Discovery knew they were an isolated unit and could possibly face many difficult situations on their expedition. They decided against a death penalty verdict and chose instead the punishment of running a gauntlet four times. That way each man would partake in meting out the punishment. Everyone on the gauntlet would strike him with a whip as he passed through. He would have no shirt and would run the gauntlet at a speed set by the men.

The punishment was explained to Chief Little Thief. Dorion translated Little Thief's words, "Can this man who has become a cowardly warrior and stolen your rifle now be given a pardon? We also have men who require discipline from time to time. The Oto never beat a man; this takes from his dignity."

Clark and Lewis both had explanations translated to the chief, who remained silent, either satisfied with the explanation or he did not want to spoil his opportunity to gain trade goods with these powerful white men. Little Thief agreed that the punishment could be carried out while his party was there and that he would watch. They watched in silence as Reed was lashed by his companions.

When it was over, York, who had been listening to all of the translations, moved quietly to the edge of camp and began tending the boats. Reubin Field spoke to him, "York, he knew when he decided to desert that he would be punished, maybe killed if he got caught."

York replied quietly, "York don' like to see beatings. A man runs from the authority and take his chances, maybe that's brave, too. Mister Moses just didn't want to be here no more. He should be more careful when he chose to come along in the first place. Now he pay the price of tryin' to get away. That's all York knows about it."

Reubin nodded and said, "He made a commitment and we all depend on that commitment. Breaking his pledge has to be punished. He's lucky he didn't get the firing squad."

York didn't look up but said softly, "Maybe so."

The Indians left the camp, and Ordway and Pryor were issuing orders to prepare supper for all. Captain Clark came over and said to Pryor, "Sergeant, we have had a busy day today. I think these men need to get their minds on lighter thoughts."

Pryor looked at Clark and replied, "What do you have in mind, Capt'n?"

"Well, Sergeant, I think that we can have our best spread of dinner followed by extra whiskey. After all, today is Captain Lewis' thirtieth birthday. I think that we need to begin his next year on the right foot. How about you?"

Pryor smiled broadly, "Well, sir, that should do it. Extra whiskey is always a popular way to celebrate here. Think I'll get Cruzatte to play the fiddle some after dinner. That'll perk the men up. We'll build a hell of a big fire and dance a little. Can we fire the cannon?"

"I don't know why not. Good idea. Well then, Sergeant, I'm sure I can trust you to make the arrangements," Clark said as he turned to walk away. "Oh, by the way, tomorrow morning the Indians will be back again as we prepare to move out. This could be our last meeting with them. We'll probably see all their chiefs."

Pryor questioned, "Should I keep extra sentries tonight, sir?"

Clark replied, "Yes, we should, even though things are peaceful. We must remember our weapons and trade goods are valuable and tempting. Continue with extra guards on the boats and two on the campsite."

August 19, 1804

"Look at that crazy bastard!" Joseph Field said to his brother Reubin as he nudged him in the side.

Looking up, Reubin replied, "Why, I'll be damned, I ain't never."

George Shannon looked and added, "I just got to tell the captains about this, they ain't going to believe it. I can see it and I still don't believe it."

As Shannon ran over to *Discovery* to get the captains, the Indian delegation was arriving into camp. In the lead was a man riding completely naked.

Shannon shouted, "Capt'n Lewis, Capt'n Clark, there's Indians coming into camp and the one out front is buck naked! Don't know what he's up to, but there he is, sure as hell naked."

Clark stepped off *Discovery* and moved into the camp to greet the new arrivals. "Dorion, where's Dorion? I think we'll need an explanation of what's going on here."

Through the rustle of men in the camp, Sergeant Pryor had already found Dorion, and they were headed toward Clark. They and Lewis arrived at the same time.

Clark spoke, "Dorion, ask them why this man comes here naked; the others are wearing clothes."

Dorion translated the captains' obvious question and then translated back the reply, "His name is Big Horse, and he said he came here naked to demonstrate that his people have nothing. That the words of the white man are as flowers. He has heard that the Great White Father wants to know of his needs. He wants to show that by being naked that he and his people need everything." Dorion paused while Big Horse spoke to some of his fellow companions, then he turned back to continue the translation. "They once were a mighty people with many chiefs and warriors. Then the white man brought the spotted illness. Now they are no more. They are weak to all of their enemies. They are few in numbers and need much help."

Lewis whispered to Clark, "Smallpox."

Clark nodded. Dorion continued the translation. "He has come naked and fears that you will send him home naked. He dreams of the peace you talk of but wants the white leader to make peace with the Omaha. The Omaha have been their enemy and you talk of making peace. Making peace with the Omaha will let his people live."

Lewis looked at the Indians and instructed Dorion, "Tell him that we would negotiate peace with the Omaha but we've passed their camps when they were gone hunting in the fields. We cannot go back now but we will negotiate for peace when we return. We believe the Omaha to be friendly people who will listen to the words of peace. Only peace will bring them prosperity and trade goods."

Dorion translated for Big Horse, "They want trade goods for their warriors: guns, powder, balls and whiskey would be welcome."

Lewis smiled and replied, "Those items won't cover his nudity. Get him a shirt and a blanket. We've given them some items already. We'll give you some tobacco, beads and paint to show our good faith. We can provide more if your chief will agree to go to Washington to meet with the Great Father of the seventeen nations. There, your chief can explain the needs of your people. Upon their return, trading posts will be built to allow you to get materials for furs."

Next, Lewis instructed the sergeant to give them some tobacco, paint and beads. The Indian delegation was obviously disappointed. Next the captains handed out printed certificates which declared that the bearer was a 'friend and ally' of the United States. An obvious cultural gap occurred. The captains did not understand the Indians' failure to be impressed with papers they could not read or see any immediate value or worth. Lewis and Clark recognized the mounting disappointment and ordered a dram of whiskey for the chiefs, brought out the air rifle, and demonstrated starting a fire in dry grass by using a magnifying glass in the sun.

The Indians were impressed but not completely pleased. Chief Little Thief agreed to go to Washington to meet the Great White Father in the spring.

Lewis was ecstatic as he turned to Clark, "Did you see him? Did you hear what Dorion said? Chief Little Thief will go to

Washington in the spring. Bill, this is a success, just like the president said it would be. Why, I think we'll have a regular parade of Indian chiefs going to the president's house."

Clark nodded and said, "Yes, it's good, but keep in mind these Indians are friendly. We've got a long way to go and some of them just may be reluctant to travel so far."

Lewis replied, "The president said they would come and by God here they are. I can't wait to write this in the journals."

August 20, 1804 Near Iowa / South Dakota

It is early morning. Sergeants Ordway and Pryor walk slowly through the camp toward Discovery. They go on board and stand outside the captains' quarters.

"Captain Lewis, Captain Clark," Sergeant Pryor called out in a calm, low tone.

Clark opened the door and looked at the two sergeants standing in the morning sun. Their mood was solemn, their faces drawn. Ordway looked at the deck as he held his thumbs in front of himself.

Clark looked at them a moment and then said, "What is it men? What's wrong?"

Pryor replied with a broken tone, "It's Sergeant Floyd, sir. He didn't make it through the night."

"Damn," Clark said as he turned to speak to Lewis, just exiting the cabin. "We lost Floyd last night."

Lewis dropped his head and said, "I was afraid of that. I tried everything I knew. I hoped that since he was young and strong that he'd whip this thing. He just kept getting weaker. Providence must have needed him more than us." Then rising from his seat, Lewis walked out to where the two sergeants stood. He placed his hand on Sergeant Pryor's shoulder and said, "He was your cousin, a good soldier and a good man. This expedition will miss him. He was a damn good man."

After a moment Clark said in somber tone, "Form a detail and go to the hilltop above the river there. Pick a good spot overlooking the river valley below and dig a grave. When the grave's been dug, come back here and get into uniform. We'll all move the body up for interment with full military honors."

Lewis nodded but remained silent.

As instructed, the grave was dug, and the men carried Floyd's body up to the hilltop where he was laid to rest. After reading from the Bible, Lewis closed the book. He asked the men to join in silent prayer. After a moment of prayer, Lewis said to Clark, "Captain, would you note on our maps that this hilltop is now Sergeant Floyd's Bluff and the river in the valley below is to be called Floyd's River."

"Done," Clark replied softly. All the men nodded in agreement. Each man placed a stone on the grave mound as they moved out and walked back toward the boats.

August 22, 1804

"What do you think, Bill?" Lewis inquired. "We need a replacement for Floyd. Should we appoint one now, or is it too soon?"

"We proceed on," Clark said in reply. "That's what we've always done when things got tough; we simply proceed on. You're right. We do need a replacement for Floyd and waiting won't change that. The men expect us to name a leader. Do you have one selected yet?"

Lewis replied, "I've been thinking. Let me know what you think of this idea. They're volunteers, Jefferson's men. Jefferson is the father of democracy, right? Well, how about we just ask the men to elect their next sergeant?"

Clark rubbed his chin, waited and then replied, " Elect him, hmmm. It's not military to hold an election for such matters, but I do like the idea. They should be responsible enough to elect one of the stronger men. It's a good test of their judgment. As a matter of fact, I think it's a damn good idea. Brilliant. Ya know, the men will follow and support a man they choose themselves. That should eliminate any discipline problems that could arise from lack of respect. Yes, I like it."

Lewis said confidently, "Well then, let's announce to the men this evening at supper. Let them offer three names and then hold a vote on them. The chosen man will be Floyd's replacement."

As agreed, the captains announced their decision to permit the men to hold an election to determine the next sergeant. Three men were nominated: William Bratton, George Gibson and Patrick Gass. The vote was held and Gass was the winner.

Two days later, Lewis issued the formal written orders that Private Patrick Gass was now promoted to the rank of sergeant in the Corps of Volunteers for Northwestern Discovery. The full name was used on the orders to document the date from which the promotion was to start and the pay grade change.

That afternoon, Private George Shannon, the youngest member of the group, failed to return from a routine hunting trip. The captains were worried; they were about to enter Sioux country. A day passed, then another, with still no sign of Shannon. Private John Colter, a good trail man, was sent in search of Shannon; he found nothing. Next, George Drewyer was sent; he was gone two days and came back empty.

August 27, 1804

Dorion advises the captains that they are now entering the territory of the Yankton Sioux. These are friendly Sioux. This is where Dorion had spent the last few years and learned the language.

Lewis said to Sergeant Gass, "I want to send a signal so the Yankton will know that we're here. I want to meet with them as soon as possible. Do you think firing the cannon four or five times would get their attention?"

Sergeant Gass replied, "Sir, I think the cannon may well cause enough noise for any nearby Yankton to hear, but mebbie they would interpret it wrong; they might think it is being warlike, firing a cannon and all."

"Good observation, Sergeant." Lewis replied, "Maybe we could start a grass fire and hope they see the smoke. I think that's the custom of prairie Indians to call a meeting."

"Yeah, I think a grass fire could be seen for quite a ways, even further than a man could hear a cannon shot," Gass replied.

Lewis continued, "Start a fire, Sergeant, and let's see if they show up."

Gass moved off and took three other men with him. They proceeded to set a fire in the tall grass that extended for several hundred acres. The fire spread quickly and created large billowing clouds of black and gray smoke that rose high into the sky.

Discovery proceeded on and soon crossed the mouth of the James River where a teenage Yankton youth waved and shouted from the shoreline to get attention. When the men waved back, he plunged into the river and swam out to the red pirogue. Clark ordered the boats put ashore, and as the boats were being moored, two more youths appeared.

Dorion translated, "They say they are part of a large group camped nearby."

Clark ordered Sergeant Pryor to take Dorion and a couple others and go to the Yankton camp to invite them back to meet. Then he ordered Gass and Ordway to prepare camp. They would wait for the Yankton party.

Drewyer approached Captain Lewis, "I see tracks along the river's edge here and also further up. These are not Indian tracks; they must be Private Shannon."

Lewis' eyes brightened, "Shannon? Tracks? Where?"

Drewyer pointed to footprints in the soil along the riverbank.

Lewis was excited, "This is good. It means he's not dead, just lost. He's headed upstream. He must think we're ahead of him and he's trying to catch up. What do you think?"

Drewyer nodded, "Yes, he's moving upstream. Must be confused, believing he's behind us. He's young and not a good hunter. Do you want me to follow his track? We may find him soon."

Lewis said, "No, I will have Ordway select a man to go after him. I think our luck is turning. We should find him now."

Then seeing Ordway and motioning for him to come, Lewis waited until the sergeant was closer to speak, "Sergeant, we're in luck. We've found what have to be Shannon's tracks here. I want you to send a man with extra rations to follow that trail. We'll get him back before he gets hurt."

Smiling a broad smile, Ordway replied, "I was worried he'd be dead, sir. It's good to see a trail. I'll send a man right away, you bet." Ordway turned and half ran as he moved across the camp where the men were setting up tents and fires.

At four o'clock Dorion appeared on the opposite bank of the river. He had thirty Yankton Sioux warriors with him. Captain Clark ordered Private Colter to get a boat to go get them.

As the first boatload came close, Pryor was excited and began talking several feet offshore. "Captain, they are friendly as can be. Havin' Dorion speak their lingo sure does help a bunch. They sure are interesting, different than any Indians back East. They thought I was some kind of chief or tribal leader. They wanted to carry me on a painted buffalo robe all the way to their camp."

The canoe landed and several men gathered around as Lewis and Clark waited. "Are there a lot of them?" Clark inquired. "What are they like?"

Excited from the Indian encounter, Pryor continued, "Oh yeah, there's a lot of them. We brought thirty back with us, but they've got a regular village back there. Women, children, dogs, and except that they don't have a general store and streets, it's just a regular village. Dorion here really helped a lot. He knows some of the men; they recognized each other and it was peaceful right off." Then looking around at the crowd of men gathered to listen to his words, he continued, "Their tents are handsome and painted different colors. They's got sticks supporting them forming a cone shape. They have some larger ones for council meetings, but most will hold about a dozen people comfortably. As for the people, well, they are all dressed in elk skin and buffalo. A very interesting place to see." Then looking around a little he added, "And the land we covered, it's just covered with game."

Reubin Field shouted, "Do they have women? Ain't seen a woman in a long time." All the men laughed.

Clark said, "Hold on now. We'll meet these people and this should be a profitable meeting."

Lewis added, "Send a delegation back to tell them that we'll send boats to bring them over for council in the morning. Now you men get busy and unload the two pirogues there so we can offer decent portage to our Indian friends. Take care to stack the goods where they can be guarded easily through the night." Then turning to Dorion and Pryor, Lewis continued, "Men, you've done a good job. This is exactly what we are here to do: meet natives in a peaceful setting. Pryor, have the men unloading the boats save out some tobacco, corn and a few kettles. Take it all over to them right away and explain that we will bring them all over here in the morning for council."

By 10:00 the next morning, the area looked like a military camp ready for inspection. The flag was up and the men were in full dress uniforms waiting to demonstrate precision drill. When the Indians arrived, the bow cannon was fired. The Yankton were also anxious for the meeting and were dressed in their finest ceremonial garb with four musicians preceding their chiefs. As they made their way into camp, the men greeted them by exchanging handshakes, then they sat down.

Dorion interpreted as Lewis gave the same Indian speech he had given to the Oto and Missouri. They were now children of the Great White Father who would learn of their needs and take care of them as they set up forts to trade goods. They must be peaceful to whites and their neighboring tribes.

The Yankton watched the men go through the precision drill exercise and were impressed. Like the Oto before them, there was nudging and whispering as they observed for the first time a unit of men marching as one. By the end of the demonstration, Lewis had chosen a mental favorite, a chief called Weuche.

Lewis declared, "Sergeant Ordway, bring me the gifts we selected last evening for our Indian guests."

Ordway immediately retrieved the materials and placed them on the ground next to Lewis.

Lewis said, "Mr. Dorion, please translate that these gifts for the chiefs are a sample of the materials we'll be able to provide their people for showing their peaceful intentions. There will be many more products after the United States builds trading posts. They must be loyal to the United States to receive the rewards of this trade." Then continuing as he looked at Weuche, "This coat, this hat and flag, should be worn proudly by a strong chief. When other whites see that you have these, they will know you are a chief. When other whites see this flag, they will know that your people are loyal to the United States."

The Sioux did not answer immediately as the Oto had done. They had Dorion translate, "We are a proud people. We must talk about your trade offering and about receiving a new father to care for our needs. We must talk of the value of becoming part of a new trade system. We are not sure of your words yet. We have seen other whites."

Lewis whispered to Clark, "Patience. I'll have to learn patience. Help me, my friend, I don't understand why they would not want to trade with the United States."

Clark replied, "Maybe they aren't impressed with our cloth, needles, fishhooks, beads and paint. They want more. I think they want guns, maybe whiskey. We need to make it clear that the military power of guns can only be given after they demonstrate peace and willingness to trade."

Lewis looked at Dorion and said, "You heard Captain Clark. Tell them no guns until they demonstrate they can be peaceful toward whites and their neighbors."

That evening the young Indian men offered a show of skill with their bows and arrows. The soldiers of the Corps of Discovery rewarded them with prizes of beads. There was social interchange between the Indians and the Corps of Discovery, helping to make the newly formed bond of trust stronger. Indians adorned with body paint jumped through the campfires and danced. Many of the Indians wanted to get close to York to touch his skin and hair. They were very much taken with a man who had dark skin and asked if he had spiritual powers. There were women who the men observed and they enjoyed trying to make conversation with them. The Yankton were also impressed with Seaman and many approached to pet him. York kept Seaman under control so no one would get bitten. Through it all, the sentries were maintained on full alert.

The next morning the Yankton gave a reply to the Corps of Discovery. Waiting and listening patiently were Dorion as translator, Lewis, Clark, Sergeants Pryor, Gass and Ordway and Drewyer.

Weuche, the chief selected by Lewis, was wearing the red-laced coat Lewis had given him. Dorion translated, "We're poor and have not powder or ball. Our rifles do not always work. Our women have not got enough clothes for the winter. But, to show peace, we have decided that if you will leave the man, Dorion, with us through the winter, in the spring we will go to Washington to meet with the Great White Father. We'll explain our need for trade and guns in our land. Dorion will stay to help us speak with our neighbors of the trading peace you say you bring."

Lewis smiled broadly, looked at Clark, clinched his fist and hit himself in the chest, "I hate leaving our translator here. We may need him upriver, but, damn, this is success. They'll go! I think we should leave him here like they want."

Then the other chiefs spoke and were translated in order, each of them asking for powder and ball, some for whiskey if possible. These things the expedition could not provide. It was not an option for consideration. Guns, powder and ball were needed for their own survival. The last chief to speak came forward slowly. He was the eldest and he said, "My name is Arcawechar, and I am a poor man that does not speak well. I think that our friend Dorion will be able to open the ears and hearts of other bands of Sioux, except those bands above us, who will not open their ears, and I fear you will not be able to open them."

Sergeant Ordway said to Pryor, "Teton." Pryor nodded.

That evening they celebrated again. The Indians played their instruments of deer hoof rattles and drums while Cruzatte played the fiddle and tambourine. York danced, and as he was already a favorite among the Indians, many would dance with him and try to emulate the dance steps. The Indians cheered when York followed the warriors in ceremony by jumping through the fire.

September 7, 1804
Boyd County, Nebraska

The Corps of Discovery is moving steadily northward; the surrounding land is changing to shorter grasses. Wildlife is abundant everywhere. Lewis busies himself daily, collecting and writing about different forms of plant and animal life, fulfilling his charter to document the different species encountered. Each day he makes scientific descriptions, the first ever recorded, of the animals and plants of the West. These descriptions are augmented by taxidermy of the smaller animals that are to be sent back to Jefferson when the keelboat returns to St. Louis in the spring. The men continue their practice of stopping to make large kills, cooking and drying the meat to enable them to travel several days without slowing to hunt again. With all the abundant food, they decide to have a feast.

"Here, have one of these," Clark said as he handed Lewis a plum. "These are the best plums I think I have ever tasted."

Lewis, biting into the fruit replied, "Hmmm, I don't usually have a taste for fruit, but I must admit, the fresh flavor of these is as good as any fruit I've ever eaten. Hey, come along with me to the prairie today. I want to explore part of the meadow along this stretch."

Clark replied, "Sure, I'll stretch my legs with ya, maybe even get away from some of these skeeters and gnats. They're heavier along the river."

The two captains left the boats and began walking along the shoreline. Soon they found themselves amidst a group of small animals that would stand up on their hind legs and squeak, only to turn and dart into tunnels dug in the ground. Pausing to look around, the small animals seemed to be everywhere, by the hundreds. They were curiously looking at the men and running and darting all about. Lewis stood amid them and laughed, "Just look at them, Bill. Did you ever see such a sight? They have a whole community here and they must be conversing back and forth with those little squeaks."

"They're cute. Do you think they could be domesticated?" Clark asked as he watched the animals looking back at him.

Lewis smiled broadly and said jokingly, "Now that is one of your better ideas, my friend. Until now, I have been shooting a sample of each species so I could examine it, stuff it and send it back to Jefferson. Wouldn't it just be dandy if we sent back a live specimen? Maybe he could tame it."

"Live?" Clark said with a puzzled look. "What you got in mind?"

Lewis was excited, "Just this: let's get back to *Discovery* and get some men and some bags. We'll catch one and send it back to Jefferson in the spring. Come on, this should be easy; they're everywhere."

The two captains went back to the boats and got a small detail to return with them.

Sergeant Gass was explaining to Joseph Field, "Capt'n wants us to catch one of those funny little animals. Labiche called em, '*petite chien.*' They are little dogs of the prairie, prairie dogs. I can make a cage for one, but keeping it alive after it's caught? Well, that might be a different matter."

Joseph Field replied, "What do you suppose they eat? We'll have to feed them."

Gass replied, "Just don't feed 'em your fingers tryin' to catch 'em. Grab 'em through the bag or blanket so's ya don't get bit. What do they eat ya ask; I ain't got a notion. Since they live out here in the grass and live underground, I would suppose they eat grass, maybe some roots or an insect now and again." Then shaking his head he continued, "We can start by feeding them grass and some roots and just watch to see what they eat and what they turn their noses up to."

Field laughed and said, "Travelin' with us, they'll probably develop an appetite for tobacco and whiskey."

"None of my supply," Gass replied.

They were approaching the central location of the prairie dog village. Captain Lewis who was in front, stopped and turned around, "Let's start digging at these holes here. I want to get one alive. When we dig one out or flush one, throw a bag over it and we'll take it back."

It sounded like a simple plan. The men circled a concentration of holes and began digging. Occasionally, a prairie dog from several yards away would come up, stand on its hind legs and scold the men with loud chirping sounds. The men kept digging, exposing holes and shafts underground, but no animal was to be seen or flushed. The trench was three feet deep, then four, then six, and still no success. They began running sticks down the holes to see if they bottomed out; the holes appeared endless.

"There seems to be no end to these tunnels. Let's get some water 'n flush 'em out," Joseph Field said.

"Good idea," Lewis said. "Go get barrels and start pouring water down. We'll flush them out into the bags."

Clark observed the activity for awhile and then sat down, laughed and pointed all around, "Merry, I ain't never seen anything like it. Just look, these little bastards are makin' fools of us. They must have a network of tunnels that go everywhere. Probably been working on it for years. Do you suppose we should try baiting a trap?"

Lewis sighed and smiled at his friend, "Nawh, we already have excavated a pretty good hole here, I think pouring water just might get them to flush."

The men stopped digging and went to the boats and got empty whiskey barrels and filled them with water. They carried them back and began pouring water down the holes. Others stood near selected holes, watching intently, waiting for drenched animals to emerge. They poured. Nothing happened. They went and got more water; still nothing. The site was turning into a quagmire. Not wanting to give up, they moved off to another group of holes and started pouring water anew. With the second effort, there was success; an animal was flushed and captured. Gass immediately set about building a cage to house it while the men attempted to feed the frightened creature.

Clark smiled and said jokingly to Lewis, "Are you going to write in your journal again tonight?"

"Sure," Lewis replied.

Clark nudged him in the side and said, "Well, I would, by God, write about this little episode in code for sure. I wouldn't want anyone to accidentally get your regular journal and read it and find out how these little thirty-ounce animals made fools of half the Corps of Discovery."

Lewis replied defiantly, "They didn't make fools of us. We got one, didn't we?"

Clark laughed and said, "Yeah, you got one for sure, but two hundred others got away, all of 'em chirping and dodging around, daring us to try to catch 'em. Excavated more dirt in two hours than in all the latrine digging we've done in a year."

Lewis smiled and replied, "Just got to rub it in. Well remember, it was your suggestion to see if we could make a pet out of one of them."

September 9, 1804

"How's the meat supply?" Clark asked Sergeant Ordway.

The sergeant looked in some of the kettles and said, "Could use some fresh. I think we got plenty of fruit but then it's always good to get more there too, if we can."

Clark picked up his rifle and walked across the camp to where Reubin Field was talking to York and Drewyer. Clark said, "Men, get your rifles and come with me. I want to go on a hunt today." Seeing Lewis across the camp, Clark motioned to him to come over. "We're getting low on fresh meat. Let's see if we can get a buffalo. That should provide some variety to our diet."

York inquired, "You want York to go along?"

Clark looked at him a quick moment and said, "Sure, why not? We issued you a fine government rifle. Let's see if you can use it in a hunt alongside Drewyer here."

York stood and silently looked at Clark for a moment and then nodded his head, "York's happy to go on a hunt."

Lewis joined the men and said, "A buffalo hunt today, sure thing."

The men proceeded out onto the prairie. They were not gone long until Lewis shot a buffalo. Drewyer shot three deer, one at considerable distance. York went to where Lewis had felled his buffalo and began looking around. Seeing another bull walking slowly near a creekbed, he took careful aim and fired. The bull dropped on its forelegs and then collapsed.

Reubin Field said, "Good shooting, York. You brought him down with a single shot. We gotta take you with us more."

Drewyer walked over and looked at the buffalo, as Clark was approaching he said to York, "Clean kill. You can be proud of that shot. An animal this size often takes a second or third shot."

York beamed and said, "York is proud, but it's hard to miss a buffalo this size."

Drewyer looked at York and said, "It was near a hundred fifty yards."

Clark arrived at the scene, looked at York a moment and then said, "Good work, York. Today's hunt should keep us fed for several days. Make sure you get a piece of the hump; it's the best part."

York looked at Clark intently. Having just been offered a prime part of the meat, an unusual offer for him, he smiled and looked at the others who were looking at him. The moment was his.

Clark said, "We should head back now and send a detail out to field dress the kill and bring back the meat. I'll have Ordway get the fires going to roast it up."

York said, "Capt'n, would it be all right if York worked with the detail to bring the meat back?"

Clark looked strangely at York a moment. Then said, "That's the first time you ever asked me for work to do. First time. Well, I think a man asking for work should get it. Sure, York. You can go with the detail that brings back the meat."

York stood tall and smiled as he looked at his fellow hunters. As the men began the trek back to join the others, Reubin Field said to York, "I didn't know you could shoot. Was that just a lucky shot or what?"

York replied, "York's practiced some. Hold steady just like I see you do at target practice. This rifle's good and that makes it easy."

Reubin asked, "Why the hell did you volunteer to work with the detail to carry the meat back to camp?"

York answered, "'Cause York ain't never provided food all on his own afore. York shot it an' York wants to dress it out and carry it back for the others to share. York will provide for the fellow travelers."

September 11, 1804

The Corps of Discovery is on the river moving around a curve in its flow, Labiche, in front, shouted, "There's a man ahead. Man on the riverbank."

Sergeant Pryor rushed to look, "It's Shannon! We've found him; he ain't dead." Producing a loud whistle followed by a loud shout, he hollered, "George, hey George, is that you?"

Seaman ran to the front of the boat and began barking loudly. Shannon, sitting on the riverbank, looked up and then waved with one arm as he rose to his feet. He picked up his rifle and began walking toward the approaching boats.

Clark was on the foredeck looking at the approaching Shannon. "How about that? It's Private Shannon. It's good to see you're alive, skinny as hell, but alive."

Sergeant Gass said, "Got yerself lost, huh? Good and lost, too, I might add. We sent parties to look for ya, thought we came close a time or two, but we didn't find ya. Hell, I gave ya up for dead."

Shannon replied in a weak tone, "Yeah, I was lost all right. Traveled all night one time to try to catch up. Didn't know I was in front all the while. I finally gave up and decided to wait here, hoping to meet up with some southbound fur traders."

Sergeant Pryor offered Shannon a hand up onto the boat, "Here, George, come on board and get something to eat. You look like a sick cat." Then turning to Ordway, he said, "Get George here something to eat. Let him sit and rest a spell."

Ordway replied, "Sure enough," and turned to go after food.

Clark said to Shannon, "George, we were worried. We could see your tracks every now and again. We could tell you thought you were behind. What's happened to you? You look half starved. Game out here is easy to get. Why are you so skinny?"

Sergeant Ordway handed Shannon some beef jerky which he took eagerly and began to eat. Speaking as he chewed he said, "Ran out of bullets and couldn't get any meat to eat. One time I put a stick down the muzzle and used it as a bullet, killed a rabbit with it, too, but never got it to work again. Caught a couple frogs but I been livin' on plums and grapes mostly."

Pryor said, "Well, we're sure glad to have you back alive. We need all the good men we can get. One thing, with your sense of direction, don't go off a wandering again without someone with ya."

Shannon, nodding his head and eating, replied, "Umm, hum. Don't you worry none. I am plenty tired of being alone out here. Even glad to see your ugly face. Got any whiskey? I must have missed out on my share more than once."

Clark said, "Get him a double share, but make sure he fills his belly first."

September 23, 1804

The day has been good, Discovery has logged over twenty miles against the current. They finally add the elusive coyote and a mule deer to the new animal species being carefully examined and cataloged by Lewis.

Seeing a grove of cottonwood trees ahead on a flat land bank, Clark ordered, "Let's put in here at this cottonwood grove for the evening. Sergeant Pryor, see to setting up camp. Gass, make sure the boats get moored and anchored properly. Ordway get some dinner going, we're all hungry tonight. We've made good progress for one day."

As the men were making camp, three young Teton boys observed the voyagers from the opposite bank. They pointed to the men, exchanged conversation briefly and then the three plunged into the river and began swimming toward the campsite. Lewis stood talking with Drewyer. The two watched as the three teens crossed the river.

"Can you see who they are?" Lewis asked. "Try and find if they have a camp nearby and how many of 'em there are."

"Sure. Can you instruct the sergeant to get some food or something to offer them while I talk?" Drewyer said. "Any little thing to offer should be fine. We'll show our peaceful intentions."

Lewis turned to signal both Clark and Sergeant Ordway to come to him. They acknowledged and walked toward him.

Lewis said, "We got ourselves some visitors, Sergeant, get some jerky and a couple carrots of tobacco. And could you get Cruzatte to come over here, too? Wouldn't hurt to have an extra interpreter around." Then turning to Clark as they watched the young Indians finishing their swim across the river, "What do you think, Teton, maybe Omaha?"

Clark answered, "Teton, gotta be Teton. We been making such good time the last two, three days, we must be in Teton country by now."

The youths stood on the river's edge until they were all together, then proceeded to walk toward the men. Drewyer said to Lewis, "I must admit, it takes sand for three young bucks to walk into a group of strangers like this."

Lewis replied, "Yes, it does. They must be fearless from growing up in a country ruled by Teton Sioux. They've grown accustomed to being in control of any situation, but I agree, they're brassy as hell. Tell them who we are and that we're friendly."

Drewyer proceeded to try to communicate with the three teens by employing speech in the Indian languages he knew, (which meant nothing to the Sioux) and by using sign language. Cruzatte joined the group and stood next to Drewyer. He listened to the young men to try to interpret or understand their meaning. There were moments where both sides looked at one another strangely but proceeded on. Often the three teens would put their heads together and talk in muffled tones. The conversation continued for several minutes. Both Drewyer and Cruzatte used hand signals and then spoke to one another in French. Finally, recognizing the angst of the waiting captains, Drewyer stepped back as Cruzatte continued and said, "They are scouting buffalo for a large group of warriors, I think eighty lodges camped at the mouth of the next river. They say there is another party close by that is also hunting further up the river. That one has sixty lodges. They want to know what we are doing in the land of the Sioux."

Lewis looked at Drewyer a moment and then said, "Tell them that we want to meet with their chiefs tomorrow. If they will come to the place up ahead where the rivers meet, we will talk with them. Tell them we come in peace to bring a message from the Great White Father. Tell them that if they are peaceful, we will trade with them, that we have presents for them."

They gave the boys two carrots of tobacco to show good faith.

The youths took the tobacco, tucked it into their waistbands and returned to the river.

"What do you think?" Clark asked as they walked from the meeting site back toward the main campsite. "Do you suppose they understood everything we wanted? I wish now we had kept old Dorion. At least he could speak Sioux."

Lewis looked at Clark and responded, "True, I've thought about that some and here's what I came up with." Clark looked with interest as his friend continued, "Meeting Dorion was not in our plans. Never was. He was just something extra, a bonus, from Providence if you will. He knew the language and the meeting with the Yankton went well because of it. But, Bill, when he said *they* wanted him to stay or else they wouldn't send Little Thief to meet Jefferson, well, did you believe all that?"

"I didn't have reason to question it. What are you getting to?" Clark asked.

Lewis continued, "Just this. We think the Yankton would only go to visit Jefferson if Dorion stayed with them. But that was Dorion's interpretation of what was said. How do we know that wasn't Dorion just feigning an interpretation of the Sioux? Bending the conversation to his favor. How do we know Dorion didn't want out and used the trip to Washington as an excuse not to go with us further?"

Clark rubbed his chin and looked, "I see your point. Could've been that way. But if you had an inkling that he was lying so he could stay there, why didn't you call him on it? Make him stay."

Lewis replied, "I had no proof, just suspicion, and besides, I did want to get Little Thief to go to Washington. That part was a success. So I went along with the deal. After all, he wasn't, he didn't, join the Army. If you force an interpreter against his will he could do more damage than good."

Clark reflected a moment and nodded, "Probably just as well to let him go than to make him come along against his will. Still, it would be mighty nice to have somebody that could speak the lingo."

Lewis replied, "We have what we set out with from the start. We have Drewyer and Cruzatte. And Cruzatte understands Sioux some. He can use signing for the rest. Drewyer's good at signing and he's good at the gut feel of the talks. I trust him more than an unwilling Dorion. Besides, like I said earlier, Dorion was a bonus from Providence. We should just be thankful for what use we did get out of him for the time."

Clark looked at his friend and said, "Suppose you're right, we'll have lots of Indians to meet and negotiate with after the Mandan. We got no way of knowing those languages, we'll simply proceed on."

September 24, 1804 Near Pierre, South Dakota

In the morning the expedition breaks camp and moves upriver toward the meeting point they had arranged the day before. They pass a two-mile island where Colter, acting as a scout and with the last horse of the expedition, had camped the night before. He has been successful in hunting elk and has hung the carcasses in the trees for them to pick up. As they are loading the meat, Colter comes up, saying that the Indians had stolen his horse. They finish loading the elk and Colter joins them on board. They proceed on upriver and soon Seaman begins to bark.

Looking intently, the captains see five Indians emerge from the brush along the river. Seeing the Indians, Clark orders Sergeant Pryor to get the boats anchored.

Clark said, "Cruzatte! Come here."

Cruzatte moved over quickly to the captain's side. "Yes, sir?"

Looking at the five Indians while he spoke Clark said, "Tell these men that we come in peace, but that we will not tolerate their stealing a horse from our man."

Cruzatte proceeded to make gestures augmented with some language. Drewyer joined him and observed. Soon Cruzatte turned to Clark with a look of expectation indicating he had completed the translation.

Clark continued, "Tell 'em we came in peace. We gave gifts to the three young men who visited us yesterday. There were no problems. We asked them only to carry back the message that we were peaceful. Yet they stole our horse. We are not squaws, we'll not let them steal from us and then sit with them to talk of trade."

Cruzatte began to gesture and speak as before. The Indians muttered between themselves and pointed back and forth. Again Cruzatte turned to Clark when he finished.

Clark added, "Tell them we do not fear the Teton or any Indian nation. We are strong men with guns. The horse that was stolen was to be a gift to their chief. Now it will embarrass us not to have a gift."

Interrupting Lewis said, "Tell them we will not meet with them unless they return the horse. We expect the horse to be at the meeting of the two rivers."

Drewyer used sign language. Cruzatte spoke. The combination seemed to work or reach some understanding as the men grunted a simultaneous signal, then turned and left.

Clark looked at Lewis, Drewyer and Cruzatte, "What do you think?"

Lewis responded, "We'll find out tomorrow. But no horse, no meeting. They cannot begin a relationship of trade by stealing from us before we sit down to meet."

Once back on *Discovery*, Clark said to Lewis in a low tone, "Ya lied, you know."

"What do you mean?" Lewis looked strangely at Clark.

Clark replied, "Just this, you said no horse, no talks. Now you know sure as you're standing there, that we are going to meet with the Teton Sioux. Why, they're only the largest Indian nation and military strength of the area as far as we know. Even Jefferson had heard of 'em before we left. We can't just refuse to talk because of a horse."

Lewis smiled and said, "That wasn't really a lie, it was politics. A political statement."

Clark laughed and said, "Just politics. Not a lie, what's the difference? You must've been in Washington too long. You were telling them something that wasn't so, just to influence them, weren't you now?"

Lewis responded, "I wanted them to think there would be consequences for their actions, that we wouldn't see them because of how they were behaving even before we met."

Clark smiled, "I agree with that, but it's still politics. Saying one thing and meaning another."

Lewis replied, "Well, I wasn't the only one, you lied too."

"What do you mean?" Clark asked.

Lewis replied, "That business of telling them the horse was to be a gift to one of their chiefs. Horse hockey, we wanted to keep that animal for shoreline expedition. Never was to be a gift."

Clark smiled, "You got me on that one I guess. Maybe I can pass it off as politicking, not a lie. Still, we have to meet these people. The terms we hammer out here may affect trade up and down this river for years to come."

Lewis nodded and said, "Quite right, we shouldn't let our emotions about a horse thief interfere. This is an important point in our expedition. Jefferson would want us to reach terms if possible. We cannot let the stealing ways of four or five of them keep us from one of our prime objectives." Then looking off upriver he continued, "Still, stealing a horse from people you're about to negotiate with, why, even these savages have to know it would put the meeting on edge. Not a smart thing at all."

The men held the three boats in closer formation than heretofore as they moved on upriver. Sergeant Pryor ordered that all the men check their rifles to make sure they were in good working order and loaded.

Later that afternoon they reached the mouth of the river they had discussed with the teens the day before. Clark ordered the boats anchored several feet off the bank in the water, providing a natural water barrier for defense. Then he put the men on full alert. He ordered two-thirds to stay on board and one-third to make camp. All were to be on guard and alert. They would not take chances with the notorious Teton Sioux.

September 25, 1804

Morning comes and the captains order the men to set up an awning and raise the flag. This is to be the meeting place for the council. At about 11:00 Seaman begins barking again. Alerted, the men all look in the direction of the smaller stream. Approaching are three chiefs leading a group of warriors into the area. They have a packhorse loaded with buffalo meat, which they offer the captains. The gift is accepted as each side takes measure of the other. Clark then orders Ordway to bring up some pork and an exchange is made.

Lewis looked at Drewyer, then Cruzatte, "It is time to talk."

Drewyer and Cruzatte seated themselves near the captains. There were hundreds of Sioux warriors on the perimeter of the camp as the main delegation moved in and sat in a semicircle facing the captains. Lewis began his speech he had given earlier, "Children, we have come from the east to bring you a message from the Great White Father. The seventeen nations of United States will now control the trade on the river. You will no longer need to trade with the French or British. We come in peace and wish to establish peaceful trading between the Teton Sioux and the other Indian nations."

There was an awkward moment as Cruzatte fumbled with the words. He looked at Drewyer who also was confused. It became immediately obvious that Cruzatte had only a minute ability to translate in Sioux. Sign language is successful for basic exchange of thoughts but has serious limitations with ideas as involved as those encompassed in Lewis' speech.

Drewyer stepped back and said to Lewis, "The words are too complex for sign language, I don't think they'll understand. I can't explain land ownership or a great father taking care of their needs. I believe that if we continue, we run a risk of their misunderstanding our meanings."

Lewis turned to Clark and Sergeant Pryor, "Damn, we're not going to be able to explain our purpose completely. We'll have to alter plans and cut our talks short." Then looking at Drewyer he continued, "What do you think, can you get the ideas of trade across to them?"

Drewyer nodded, "Yeah, I think so, trade has more symbols and is understood. Ideas of government have no hand signals."

Lewis looked around. The Indians were all looking at him. He knew the next move was his. "I think showing is better than telling in cases like this. Military might is something we can demonstrate, something they should respect." Lewis walked to Sergeants Pryor and Gass. He spoke in a low but firm tone, "Sergeant Pryor, Gass, give them the close-order drill demonstration with those men that are here on shore. Sergeant Ordway, go to the boats and get the Teton gifts we talked about on the way here. Bring my air rifle, too."

Cruzatte continued with some translations and explained that there were three chiefs, the obvious three in front. "Their names are 'Buffalo Medicine', 'Partisan' and 'Black Buffalo'."

Clark told Sergeant Pryor to execute the drill but not to fire the weapons as they had in the past. "Keep them loaded just in case." The close-order drill was precisely performed. The men went through the various marching maneuvers, which included handling the rifles with the pause and aim, but, as ordered, they did not fire. Next, Lewis demonstrated his air rifle. The Indians were impressed and talked with one another as the rifle was shot three times without using powder. Lewis ordered the preparation of gifts, then he demonstrated burning leaves by using sunlight and a magnifying glass to start a fire. The Sioux were quietly impressed as they sat patiently watching the performance.

Lewis then ordered, "Sergeant Gass, give these chiefs medals. The one on the left, Black Buffalo, give him a red coat and hat."

Gass obeyed without response, handing out the medals, the coat and hat, as ordered.

The chiefs were instantly upset. The rest of the delegation talked back and forth as the chiefs looked at one another, spoke loudly and gestured. They looked at the medals and fondled the coat and hat. Employing hand signals they communicated to Cruzatte who said, "They wanna know if that's all. These gifts are worthless to important chiefs."

Buffalo Medicine and Partisan were especially agitated. Partisan, the youngest chief of strong physical stature, began waving his arms in the air and pacing around the campsite making jerky, quick motions. He spat on the ground, kicked dust and made sounds of anger. Some of the many Indians surrounding the camp began to respond.

Clark recognized a situation in deterioration. He told Cruzatte to invite the three chiefs onto *Discovery* for some whiskey and further talks. Cruzatte and Drewyer both began communicating, Cruzatte using his broken Sioux and Drewyer augmenting with sign language. The chiefs watched and calmed down. As they were calmed, the hundreds of warriors watching also calmed.

Once on *Discovery*, Clark had Ordway pass out whiskey in cups to the guests. They drank and indicated an immediate liking for whiskey and wanted more. Partisan took his cup and shook it in Ordway's face, indicating his demand for more. Buffalo Medicine made gestures of drinking from an empty cup, smelled the cup and acted out pouring more.

The situation on board *Discovery* was no better than the previous scene on shore. The three chiefs were acting disgusted and becoming belligerent. Clark looked at Lewis, and without speaking Lewis nodded his approval of what Clark was about to do. Clark stood and assumed a rigid posture. His voice was loud and gruff. Without interpretation, his body language was letting the Indians know he had had enough. There would be no more whiskey. Clark immediately ordered a detail of seven men, including York, to help put the three chiefs into the red pirogue and take them back ashore. Black Buffalo stepped into the pirogue reluctantly and was making gestures. Buffalo Medicine pushed one of the soldiers trying to help him into the canoe and shook his fist in the air as he shouted to the men ashore. At the same time, Partisan was objecting vehemently. He began pushing the men and resisted their attempts to put him on the pirogue. York stepped up and firmly grabbed his arm. Partisan looked strangely at the black man. Their eyes met, and for a moment Partisan was silent. York moved with him, forcing him into the pirogue. This action caused the many observers on the high shore bank to mutter and point. Excitement was in the air.

When the pirogue had traveled the short distance to shore, three Teton warriors immediately waded out into the water and grabbed the bowline and began pulling back. Another warrior jumped on board and hugged the mast in protest. They were obviously seizing the pirogue and its load of cargo. They were following orders from the chiefs. The situation was serious; this pirogue contained about a quarter of the material the Corps of Discovery owned.

Partisan feigned drunkenness as he staggered against Clark and Reubin Field. Then he stepped ashore to address the warriors lined on the riverbank observing the situation. Partisan now had his audience and he began to shout. He waved his arms and stepped in long erratic steps.

Cruzatte was at Clark's side, translating as best he could. "He says he's treated like a begging dog by the whites. 'White dogs have removed powerful chiefs from their boat. These whites have boats full of materials, of goods, of stuff we need for the winter. They insult Partisan by not offering more. They insult all the Teton by not offering more. Perhaps Buffalo Medicine is pleased, but Partisan is not'."

Cruzatte said excitedly, "Captain, he is getting them in a lather here. He's goin' ta....." then interrupting himself he went back to translation. "He says 'we are only a few men led by fools or cowards. Dunno which'. Sumpthin' like that. The proud Teton people cannot let them pass through their land without paying a toll, making tribute or a gift. I think that's what he's a sayin. Sir, he wants to take the boat here!"

Clark could see the agitation from Partisan infecting the warriors. The Teton numbered in the hundreds and they had the high ground on the riverbank. He instinctively knew he would have to face off with Partisan before Partisan had a call to arms. Clark walked up the shore toward Partisan with Cruzatte immediately behind him. As Clark approached Partisan, he stopped his wild charades and stared hotly at Clark. Clark returned the stare without blinking. Not taking his eyes off Partisan for a moment, Clark shouted loudly. "Sergeant Pryor!"

"Yes, sir," Pryor replied.

"Who is our best man with a rifle?" Clark shouted.

"That would be Drewyer, sir," Pryor responded.

Not flinching, Clark continued to stare into Parisan's face as he shouted, "Drewyer."

Drewyer replied, "Sir?"

Clark barked out, "You see this wild-eyed, crazy bastard here. Take aim on his skull right now and hold it." As he was speaking, he drew his sword. His face was flushed and his knuckles white as he held his sword and glared at Partisan.

Partisan was further enraged. He looked at Drewyer's rifle muzzle on him and began swinging his arms and shouting. As he did, hundreds of warriors took arrows from quivers and knocked them to shoot. Partisan began to speak and Cruzatte translated excitedly to Clark, "He says if the whites do not offer more, the Teton Sioux will take it. He says he wants one full boat, the white pirogue there, as tribute for passage."

Clark unflinching, shouted to Drewyer, "If he makes a move to order his men to shoot, kill him! He'll be the first to die."

Drewyer held his aim as Lewis lit a taper and moved aft toward the cannon. The men all held their rifles and knelt to one knee near the locker covers that could serve as breastwork. *Discovery* was preparing for battle.

All the while Partisan was walking and talking, the muzzle of Drewyer's rifle traced his every move. Lewis looked at Clark and then ordered all the men, "Throw up the breastwork. Cock your rifles and take aim. Hold fire for my command."

It was almost one sound as the men took position, threw up the breastwork, aimed and cocked their rifles. Lewis, holding a lighted taper, grabbed the cannon and swung it around, taking aim at a large group of warriors on the upper bank. Seeing the cannon move, there was a wave of reaction through the Teton warriors as some dropped back. All had arrows out, ready to shoot. Sergeant Pryor and Gass moved quickly to the aft of *Discovery* and manned the two blunderbusses. The Corps of Discovery was poised and tense, waiting for a command from Clark.

Clark did not look at his translator or at the bustle of activity on *Discovery*; rather he kept his eyes on Partisan all the while. Sword still drawn and face red, he said sternly to Cruzatte, "He wants a full boat of goods? Tell him NO, even Hell NO if there's an Indian word for it."

Then, shifting his weight and looking briefly at the men, positioned and ready for battle, Clark turned back to fix his gaze on Partisan. "Tell him that we will make the river run red with Teton blood if they do not release our boat lines!"

Cruzatte translated as the audience fell silent listening to his words. Partisan stared as he listened. The air was tense, no one on either side showing weakness. Silence continued for a long moment which seemed like hours. Then the elder chief, Black Buffalo, pushed his way through some warriors toward Partisan and Clark, who were still glaring at one another. Drewyer's rifle was still fixed on Partisan's temple.

Black Buffalo tapped on the wrist of each of the three men holding the towline as he passed. As he did so, each released his grip. Then he motioned to the warrior holding the mast to step ashore. Looking back briefly as the warriors obeyed, he stepped in between Clark and Partisan, still glaring at one another.

Black Buffalo spoke to Partisan in a low tone. Cruzatte could not hear to attempt to translate. Partisan let out a breath of air and sulked back to join the other warriors. As he reached them he turned and said loudly, and Cruzatte translated, "If we do not take the pirogue of goods as passage, then we should make them turn around and go back the way they came."

Clark didn't answer but looked at Black Buffalo and awaited his response. Meanwhile Drewyer's rifle muzzle continued to track Partisan's movement.

The elder Black Buffalo looked directly at Partisan and spoke loudly with animated gestures. Cruzatte translated, "You want them to turn around? Look at them. Look closely. Do they look like they will turn around? Do you see fear in their eyes? I think many may die this day, but they will not turn around. Are you ready to die?" Looking at the many warriors, he continued, "Have your warriors put their arrows away."

With that speech from Black Buffalo, Partisan glared for a moment, then looked at *Discovery* and at Clark. He turned to his warriors and made a hand signal by moving his hand from shoulder level in a quick arc to his knee. All the warriors removed their arrows from their bows.

Seeing this, Clark turned to look at Drewyer and moved his hand from an upward position to down. Drewyer lowered his rifle. Clark motioned for him to come up and assist in translation. The tension of the moment was relieved.

Clark put his sword back in its scabbard. Drewyer came wading through the water to his side. Clark turned to Black Buffalo and said in a lower tone, "It is good to see a man of peace can take control. We came in peace but we are prepared to fight. Here and now we will reduce the Teton numbers if they do not let us continue up this river."

Clark waited while his translators communicated his message. When Cruzatte turned and looked at him indicating the translation was complete, he continued. "We're not squaws or children. We're men who are trained to fight if we need to. We have enough power in our boats to kill **twenty times** the number that are here. This expedition must, and will, go on." Then speaking to Drewyer he asked, "Do you think you can translate that, make them understand?"

Drewyer replied, "I think any man in any language could see that you are serious, that you're prepared to kill or die."

"Good, that's exactly what I want," Clark replied.

Cruzatte and Drewyer translated to the observing Sioux.

While Clark was talking to the Teton, Lewis motioned an order to the men on shore to bring the pirogue back to *Discovery*. Once there, he had a dozen more men jump into the boat and return to shore to join Clark. When the detail reached shore and reinforced Clark, some of the warriors backed up from the immediate vicinity and blended with the larger group farther away.

The three chiefs circled in conference. Buffalo Medicine was talking and pointing. Partisan spoke more loudly than the others and waved his arms and gestured as he spoke. Black Buffalo could be heard speaking in a calmer tone but dominating the conversation. Finally, he seemed to take charge of the meeting as he spoke for a longer time, and the others listened without interruption. They apparently had reached a decision.

When it seemed that the tribal conference was over, Clark moved toward them with his hand outstretched as a peace gesture. They refused to shake hands. Upset with the refusal, Clark turned on his heel and walked away.

"Come on men, back to the boats. Now!" Clark said sternly as he motioned with a hand for the men to join him. They waded out to the pirogue and as the men were picking up the oars, Black Buffalo, with two warriors, hurriedly caught up.

He motioned for them to stop. Cruzatte translated, "They say they never saw a boat this big. The three of them want to sleep on it with us tonight."

Clark looked at Lewis, "Did you hear that? He wants to spend the night with us, what a change of heart. Can you believe it? What do you think?"

Lewis shook his head, "I sure don't know what to make of it. Probably wouldn't hurt. In fact, it may insure a peaceful night if they know one of their chiefs is with us."

Clark said, "Yeah, you're right, they probably wouldn't attack if one of their chiefs could be killed." Then motioning to Cruzatte and Drewyer, "Tell them it will be alright. We'll let him sleep on the big boat."

With all on board the *Discovery*, Lewis issued an order, "Sergeant Gass, Pryor, move out. Let's leave this place and find an island suitable to spend the night. I want some water between us and shore."

Clark added, "Hear this all you men, we are still on full alert. I don't trust this situation at all, even with the chief among us. He could just be scouting our strength."

About a mile on upriver the Corps of Discovery came to an island. Clark ordered them to make camp. "I'll call this 'Bad Humored Island' as we're all in bad humor today."

Clark moved onto the island and was watching the men set up camp. As the men were making camp and preparing food, Lewis, with Cruzatte and Black Buffalo, noticed Clark talking with Drewyer. He turned to Sergeant Pryor and said, "Pryor, stay with Cruzatte here and keep our guests company. They've indicated some interest in seeing Seaman up close and they also wonder about York. Be sure they're attended to, that they get plenty to eat. And, Sergeant..."

"Yes, sir," Pryor responded.

"Relieve York of his regular duties and let him be with you when you're talking to our guests. Let them think he has special powers. I want to talk with Captain Clark for awhile. We'll be with you by the time everyone is ready to eat."

"Yes, sir," Pryor responded and moved off with Cruzatte, Black Buffalo and the Indians.

Lewis approached Clark and Drewyer and said, "This has been one hell of a day. I could use a little whiskey right now, besides we need to talk."

Clark motioned to Joseph Field to come over and said, "Tell Sergeant Ordway that I ordered each man a gill of whiskey for today's efforts. Bring three cups to us, we will be joining you all shortly before dinner."

Field nodded and left to tell Sergeant Ordway to get the whiskey for the men. He returned soon thereafter to deliver three cups of whiskey. "Here ya go, captains, sure was a rough moment out there, wasn't it?"

Lewis took his cup of whiskey and sipped a little and then looked at Clark as he sipped his. While the cup was still at Clark's lips, Lewis broke the silence and said, "Twenty times? You said we could kill twenty times their number. Bill, I don't know what you could see from where you were standing on the shore there, but from my vantage point on *Discovery*, there were about six hundred warriors out there."

Clark smiled as he swallowed his sip of whiskey and looked at Lewis, "Well, Merry, my blood was hot, I was pissed with the whole affair. I wanted them to know that we were not, absolutely not, afraid of them. That we would fight if we had to, and if we did fight, a lot of them would die. And that we had more military strength than they could imagine."

Lewis nodded smiling at his friend and said, "Yeah, I know. I was feeling the same, but twenty times their number? Bill, twenty times! It seems a little brash, don't you think?" He smiled and awaited Clark's reply.

Clark said, "I suppose I was playing a little poker with them and the situation. They didn't know our hand, how strong it was. And I could remember old Dan'l telling me that if we saw a bear to stand up to it and not run. Running would get us killed for sure."

Lewis smiled and said, "Yes, my friend, but he said to stand and face that bear, he didn't say to attack it!"

Observing the two leaders, Drewyer interrupted the banter with a comment. "I think that these Teton Sioux, these feared bullies of the Missouri, have more than met their match. When they looked at Captain Clark standing in front with his blade ready for blood, when they saw Captain Lewis holding the cannon on them, when they saw all the rifle muzzles pointed squarely at them, they knew they could not make cowards of real men. They had to back down. Now we see them for what they are." Pausing a moment he continued, "They are nothing more than common river beggars asking for a larger dole. I do not like them. I do not trust them. As for the power to kill twenty times, it does not matter anyway. I did not translate the twenty times. I only said many times."

Clark looked at Lewis, then they both looked at Drewyer and laughed; Clark smiled broadly and slapped Drewyer's shoulder, "You didn't translate twenty times, you said many? Why? Why the hell did you do that?"

Drewyer had a smile on his lips as he responded, "The moment was tense, I said many instead of twenty because," then he paused. He looked at his whiskey and then up at the two captains looking intently at him, he continued, "because I did not think they could do the math."

September 26, 1804

The Corps of Discovery sets out early. From the onset, there are Teton Sioux lined along the shore watching as the boats make their way up river. Black Buffalo, dressed in the coat and hat Lewis had given him, watches the shoreline as Discovery makes her way against the current. He repeatedly looks at, and seems impressed with, the multiple means of locomotion of the large keelboat. He observes the wind in the large sail, watches as the men row in unison. Finally, he nudges Cruzatte and begins to point.

Cruzatte interpreted, "He says his village is over there. He wants us to pull over and meet his people."

Lewis listened intently as Cruzatte spoke and then looked at the chief and said, "He has appeared peaceful so far. If he wants us to pull in and meet some different Teton people, let's do it. Our mission is to meet with his people, we can give it another chance. I think he may be of a mind to try to make up for things." Then looking at Cruzatte, he instructed him, "Tell him we will meet his people."

The boats pulled in and anchored slightly closer to shore than they had the day before. Lewis ordered Sergeants Pryor and Ordway to stay on ready alert. Then, at Black Buffalo's insistence, Lewis and Cruzatte moved on shore to greet this band of Teton. As he reconnoitered the Teton village, Lewis observed there were about a hundred tepees of buffalo skin and lodge pole construction. They were painted with symbols and appeared to be in good order. Across the land around the tepees, there were several small herds of horses with young teenage boys tending them.

Cruzatte listened to the chief and the warriors as they spoke and pointed around the camp. Cruzatte interpreted, "Chief says they are the Brule group of Teton. They seem real proud of some prisoners, at least I think he said prisoners, maybe slaves, dunno which. They are here because of a war or battle of some kind."

Lewis stopped walking and inquired, "What's he telling you? They have slaves? Who did they capture? Where was the battle?"

Cruzatte immediately turned to the chief and the attending warriors and began to sign and speak. The Indians looked puzzled as they tried to figure out what was being said. Then a look of understanding came over their faces, and many began to speak at once. Cruzatte raised a hand and moved it back and forth to signal them to stop all talking at once. Then he pointed to one man, apparently because he could understand him best, and the designated man spoke.

Cruzatte interpreted, "They say they had a battle with the Omahaars, that they had a great victory killing seventy-five Omahaars and only lost seven of their own. When the battle was over, they took forty-eight women and children as prisoners." Cruzatte paused a minute looking at the Indian who was speaking and then said to Lewis, "He says they got scalps, too." Then pausing and smiling broadly Cruzette said, "This is good news, Captain." Lewis looked at Cruzatte strangely and before he could say anything, Cruzatte continued, "I can speak Omahaar good. I can maybe get one of them that speaks Sioux and we can translate better."

Lewis had a pensive look on his face as he said in monotone, "That is good, Pierre. Go with this man and find the prisoners. Talk to the Omaha there and see what you can learn. It may profit us to know what happened from their perspective."

"Sure thing, Capt'n," Cruzatte said with a smile. "But the chief here has something to say."

Lewis turned to Black Buffalo and said, "What is it? What do you want to say?"

Cruzatte listened as Black Buffalo spoke and made hand signals. Finally, he turned and chuckled as he spoke, "Capt'n, he says he wants to give you a squaw, a young one, you can pick the one you want. Do ya want one, sir?"

As he was speaking Black Buffalo was motioning to some other Indians who immediately grabbed some of the young women in the crowd and pulled them forward.

Lewis stopped looking at Cruzatte and snapped his gaze around to look at Black Buffalo. "Tell him no."

Cruzatte responded, "Well sir, alright, I'll tell him no, but do ya mind if I..."

Lewis interrupted as he made a quick response, "No Private, I said no and that means no for you as well. Have you forgotten yesterday so soon? We cannot compromise ourselves having relations with women while we're still very possibly in harm's way."

Cruzatte lost his smile and responded, "Yes, sir, I guess so, but it wouldn't take long."

"I said no, Private, and that's the end of it," Lewis said sternly.

Cruzatte looked around a moment and then smiled and said, "Well then, can I go talk to the Omahaars?"

"Yes, that you can do," Lewis replied, "but not just yet. Stay with me awhile longer until Drewyer gets here. Then you can go. I can't be without an interpreter."

Black Buffalo reached out to touch Cruzatte's arm. He began to speak and Cruzatte interpreted. "We are invited to stay the night in his lodge or tepee. He wants to show the powerful white man leader, Capt'n Lewis, that he can be peaceful. He wants to show that they can be friendly. Friends, I think he said. He wants you not to hate or despise his people. That is why you should take a squaw tonight."

Lewis pointed his finger at Cruzatte and shook it lightly, "Tell him no, we'll not take the squaws. We will talk of peace, but we can make friendly talk without using the women. Tell him no women."

Cruzatte spoke to Black Buffalo who seemed to understand what was being said but he did not understand the refusal. Then he touched Cruzatte on the arm again and asked another question.

Cruzatte translated, "He wants to know if we can bring the large dark warrior for them to see. Capt'n, I don't think they ever saw a Negro afore. Just a minute, there's more, he's got more, another question."

Cruzatte listened as Black Buffalo spoke and signed. Then he turned to Lewis who was anxiously waiting and spoke, "He wants to know if you will trade the large black dog. He wants his people to see the large dog and the large black man. Can they come together? He would like to have his medicine man meet York. Sir, I think that he thinks York is somethin' powerful, mebbie a medicine man or magic. I don't know what he is sayin' fer sure. I just know he wants to show him off."

Lewis looked at Black Buffalo and then back toward *Discovery* anchored off shore. Turning back he said, "Tell him they can see the dog, but he's not for trade. As for York, yes, we'll have them bring the powerful black man to his lodge." Then pausing a moment and catching Cruzatte just before he could speak he added, "Say that the black warrior is powerful medicine and there are more like him. Tell him his people will see other races."

Cruzatte replied, "I can't say races, ain't no word for it in any Indian language I know. No sign either. I'll try with the other part. They understand dogs and trade. I hope I kin get the other part across."

Nodding his head Lewis replied, "I understand, Pierre. Just do your best. We seem to be getting along."

Lewis continued to walk around the village of tepees and observe. He would question the construction of tepees, which Cruzatte was unable to interpret. He asked about the horses and the only information he could get was that there were sixty-three horses, many of them stolen, a fact the Indians seemed to be proud of. He did not see their stolen horse in the group and did not ask.

Lewis stopped and asked, "Why are they so proud of admitting this herd is mostly stolen? Wouldn't they prefer to say they bred them? In fact, why don't they breed them?"

Cruzatte stopped and posed the question to Black Buffalo and four other warriors that had formed a semi-circle as they listened intently. As he finished, the Indians laughed and nudged one another. One raised a hand and let out a small "Eeiiiyyaa." Cruzatte then turned to Lewis and said, "Capt'n, they say anyone can breed horses, horses do that themselves, but only a skilled warrior can steal horses from an enemy. Don't hurt the horses, no, no let me get it right. Take horses without hurt, without getting hurt or killed. I think he said if he doesn't get noticed or seen, the theft is better. If a man steals horses and keeps them, he can become a chief or leader or get some kind of prestige. I, think that's it."

Lewis looked at the Indians and spoke to Cruzatte, "You mean they get rank or status from stealing?"

"Yep," Cruzatte said. "I think that's the idea. If'n they steal from another tribe it's better. And the more dangerous it is to steal, the better. I think that was it, Capt'n, near as I could tell anyways."

Lewis said, "Tell them that we have come to bring peace to all the Indian tribes. Tell him that peace will let them trade and they won't have to steal. Tell them that peace and, no, no, say they can't steal from neighbors and then later expect to have peace or trade with them. They will be better off if they do not steal. Say that we will trade with them only if they do not make war on their neighbors or steal from them."

Cruzatte said, "I'll try, sir." He began making sign language and talking at the same time. The Teton watched and listened intently and then began to mutter things back and forth while Cruzatte continued. The body language was turning negative.

"They don't like it none," Cruzatte said as he looked at Lewis. "I don't think they understand or maybe they don't want to understand why stealing is bad. One of 'em said to trade takes blankets or skins. To steal only takes a quiet step and a dark night."

Just then there was a distracting commotion and Lewis did not answer. Looking in the direction of the activity he saw Clark and a large group of men coming into the village. They were approaching from the west.

Clark, Drewyer and Sergeant Pryor moved through the crowd and spoke to Lewis. "Merry, we came in from the west side there. They seem to be holding prisoners. A wretched lot of humanity in terrible conditions. They were dirty, filthy dirty, and looked pitifully poor."

Lewis nodded, "Yeah, they're Omaha prisoners. They evidently had a battle not long ago. It must've been a lop-sided victory as they were very proud of it. Took the prisoners as slaves I think. How many were there?"

"Clark replied, "I don't know, couldn't tell. I was just appalled by the living conditions. I don't think they have a latrine or let em use one cause it stinks real bad over there."

Lewis said, "We may be in luck. Cruzatte here is fluent in the Omaha language, or so he says. I hope it's better than his ability to speak Sioux. Anyway, he wants to go talk to them, I told him he could go as soon as you showed up. Maybe we can learn more about how the battle came about."

Then turning to Cruzatte, Lewis continued as he tapped him on the shoulder, "Alright Pierre, go ahead and visit with the prisoners. See what you can learn from them and let us know tonight. See if there is anyone among them that can translate Sioux."

"Yes, sir, I'm on my way," Cruzette said as he moved off toward the west side of the village where the Omaha slaves were held.

At dusk Black Buffalo and some elders came to ask the captains to join them in a ceremony. The captains agreed and were placed on decorated buffalo robes and carried into a central part of the village. There was a large area obviously designated for dancing and ceremonious activities. It occupied a much larger clearing than the normal interval between tepees. They were greeted and sat down to talk. Food was shared, tobacco was shared, and the mood of the evening was less tense. Lewis used the newly designed smoking pipe/tomahawk combination, to smoke with them. This item was instantly popular with the Teton. During the meeting there were lengthy explanations by the Indians of how poor they were and how they wanted gifts from the traveling whites who had so much. The explanations of poverty were ignored even though it was explained over and over by Drewyer and other translators. York joined the meeting and the Indians all wanted him to smoke the pipe. They would take turns sitting next to him during the smoke.

The Teton then began their display of dancing, evidently to impress their white guests. As the intensity of the music increased, the fire was stoked, and the Teton began bringing out scalps on sticks and whooping and hollering as the pitch of dancing increased.

Colter nudged Sergeant Pryor and asked, "Ya don't suppose they're cannibals, do ya?" Sergeant Pryor shook his head as he continued to watch. Clark, overhearing the comment, turned to Lewis and said, "Now there's a concept for you. Did you hear Colter there, he wonders, hopefully in error, if they're cannibals."

Lewis replied, "I really doubt that. We heard all manner of reports about the Indians on the river. We never heard of one that was cannibalistic."

Clark laughed and responded, "Well now, Merry, maybe that's because anybody that could have reported anything has already been eaten."

Lewis, still somewhat serious said, "We heard of all the Indians, even the Teton, and never heard of any cannibals.

Besides game is plentiful. There is no need to eat human flesh."

The dancing continued and the Teton displayed several scalps of the Omaha they had killed in the previous battle. As the display continued, Clark spoke to Lewis and Sergeant Pryor. "This display indicates how they'll wait until night to attack an enemy when they're weakest and least expecting. I don't trust 'em, not an inch." Then leaning over so that Ordway and Pryor could hear him, he continued. "Sergeants, make sure the guard is doubled and on full alert, post one sentry at the cannon and keep a taper nearby ready to light. At the first sign of anything, fire a shot in the air and get all the men you can behind the breastwork."

Lewis listened intently while Clark spoke. He nodded and then added, "If it comes to that, push the boats out into the river where you can defend yourselves better, stay within rifle range of the shoreline so you can cover any of us on shore that have to swim out."

Pryor replied, "Done."

The dancing continued. The Americans would toss tobacco and beads to those providing a better performance. One warrior, upset that his reward was not big enough, became visibly upset. He threw a drum into the fire and then broke another on the ground before he stomped off into the night. The entertainment continued until late. Black Buffalo again asked if he and Partisan could spend the night on board *Discovery*.

Clark turned to Lewis, "I don't mind Black Buffalo, but that Partisan, well, he's a wild one. What do you think?"

Lewis said, "I agree, yes. I think Black Buffalo is alright, but if we turn Partisan down, he may mount an attack against us. At least on *Discovery*, we'll know where he is and can watch him. Let's just have one extra sentry on duty to watch only him."

Clark looked intently at his friend and said, "Yes, I think you're right, having the devil where you can watch him is best." Turning he said, "Drewyer, tell 'em it's alright to spend the night with us." Then he motioned for Sergeant Pryor, who, seeing the captain, leaned over to hear. "Sergeant, they're going to spend the night on *Discovery*. Make sure all the trade goods, and, well, everything for that matter; stays covered. I don't want them to see what we have and take inventory. Keep it all covered, make sure it's just like the first night we were here."

Pryor responded, "I think it's all mostly covered anyhow, sir, but I will check just for sure."

As the men were bedding down on *Discovery*, Cruzatte came to the captains with a report. "I been a talkin' to the Omahaars, the prisoners back there, an' they told me frightful things about the Teton. They said they heard 'em talkin' about waiting their chance later upriver to attack us and steal all our trade goods. They would show no outward knowledge of those intentions, but Capt'n, the next dance will have our scalps."

Clark whispered, "Thank you, Pierre. Are there any of the prisoners that could serve to interpret?"

Cruzatte replied, "No sir, them that can speak Sioux want to keep it a secret. They learn more that way, and they don't want to be separated out or kilt."

They spent a restless night on *Discovery*. The next day they were again entertained by the Teton. The chiefs repeated the offer of women to the captains. They were shown all the horses that the tribe owned. They were shown the construction methods of the tepees. It was obvious they wanted to impress the explorers.

Lewis said to Clark, "One night they cry and whine about how poor they are; the next day they exhibit their wealth. Do they think we are stupid?"

Clark replied, "Exactly right. In a land of plenty, where they rule, selling the idea they are poor is ludicrous. I wonder what they make from fur traders on river tolls alone."

Through the day York continued to be sought out by the Indians. Many of them wanted to touch him. Some of the more youthful Teton would laugh and run away after poking him or feeling his hair. Captain Clark started to say something to him, "York, it's just that they've never seen a Negro before."

York smiled that Clark had shown concern over his feelings as he replied, "York don' mind, Capt'n. York don' mind at all cause York ain't never seen Teton afore neither. York is pleased they think he be powerful medicine. Maybe touchin' my skin will keep things peaceful."

Clark nodded, and they continued walking through the village.

That evening there was another feast around the central campfire. As they finished eating, the Teton held another scalp dance. Evidently they thought this had entertained their guests or perhaps they were simply proud of their victory. By the time the dance started, the captains were growing weary from lack of sleep. They told Drewyer to inform the Teton that they were going to go back to the boat to retire. Partisan and one warrior accompanied them to the bank. As Clark climbed into the white pirogue, he said to Lewis, "As soon as I am ferried over to *Discovery*, I'll have them come back for you and the others."

"Sure thing." Lewis replied.

As the pirogue moved out young George Shannon was steering. In the darkness he momentarily lost control. The pirogue swung around, out of control, and pushed into *Discovery's* anchor line. There was a groan followed by a sharp snap as the line broke. *Discovery*, no longer anchored, began to swing around out of control.

Seeing this Clark shouted, "All hands up! Get up and man the oars!"

Immediately the men on *Discovery* sprang into action. There was a flurry of activity that evidently confused and alarmed the suspicious Partisan standing and observing from shore.

Partisan was wide-eyed as he witnessed the activity. He evidently thought that the whites were about to attack or that the avenging Omaha were nearby. He waved his arms and shouted out what apparently was a call to arms. In minutes the shoreline was lined with hundreds of Teton warriors with bows. Lewis still on shore, alone with only seven men, ordered them to prime and cock rifles and hold for his order.

Black Buffalo moved to the shoreline and Partisan joined him. The two exchanged words as they looked up and down the river in the darkness. The mishap of the broken anchor line soon became obvious as the cause for alarm. The chiefs pointed to it and then jointly made gestures to the warriors to return to their tepees. The moment was quickly defused.

Lewis ferried across in the pirogue to join the men on *Discovery*, now being held steady in the current. As he approached Clark asked, "What the hell do you suppose that was all about?"

Lewis answered, looking back over his shoulder at the shoreline, "Don't know for sure. I think they were surprised by the sudden activity when the anchor line broke. Still, did you see how quickly they mustered what must have been two hundred braves to the shore for battle? The peace here is fragile."

Sergeant Pryor responded, "Just goes to show you, they're edgy. I don't trust 'em none neither. I'll be glad when we're outta here."

Clark replied, "Quite right, Sergeant, let's move our craft to the nearest safe place to tie up for the rest of the night. I want to head out early in the morning."

Lewis, Pryor, Ordway and Clark began to talk. Ordway said, "That business about them attacking at night, what the Omahas said, what do you think?"

Pryor with hands moving as he spoke replied, "Possible, definitely possible with this bunch. You saw how they bragged about stealing from the neighboring tribes. Well, if that makes 'em proud, just you imagine what they would do to steal from the white men in the large boats."

Clark added, "I think President Jefferson's idea of peaceful trade arrangements got a kick in the butt with the Teton. These people scare the hell out of me. If there ever was any doubt, did you see how quick they came to the shoreline when the bowline snapped? This group is a lit fuse just waiting for a powder keg."

Lewis looked down and nodded, "I fear we must disobey the President's order of peacemaking. It would do no good to die with an olive branch in our hands. Our first directive is to live and to get through this. We still have a northwest passage to find and chart. We'll persevere against the Teton if we don't instigate a fight. I don't think they have the courage to muster an attack into our rifle muzzles."

Clark replied, "I think they'd want an edge before they'd attack. They respect us and we just can't give them that edge."

The men were nodding in agreement when Sergeant Gass hollered from the bow, "Sir, I think I see a tree leaning out over the river ahead, maybe we should tie up to it while we can."

Clark responded, "Good, Sergeant, I don't want to flounder around here in the darkness without an anchor or tie-up spot for long. Take whatever Providence is offering us for now. We'll tie in tight and keep watch. Only the oar men get to rest, the others stand guard. Until we're out of danger, I don't want to be a target. No one sleeps tonight."

The men all worked silently as a team to get the boats tied and secured to the shoreline. Once secured, they assumed positions of watch, covered themselves with voyager's grease and mosquito netting, and settled in for the rest of the night.

The next morning the men prepared to set out. As they were just starting to move out, hundreds of well-armed Teton warriors lined the shore. Black Buffalo came to the river's edge requesting to board *Discovery*.

Drewyer and Cruzatte interpreted, "He wants us to stay in their village one, two more days. Not to move on, he wants us to stay."

While Drewyer was translating to the captains, Black Buffalo made motions with his hands, and the warriors grabbed the tow lines and began pulling the boats toward the shore.

Immediately Clark stepped close to Black Buffalo's face, "Tell him this is not a peaceful thing, let go of our lines. Friends do not keep friends against their will. We are not Omaha prisoners."

As the interpretation concluded, Black Buffalo looked back and forth between Clark and Lewis. He then moved toward Lewis to plead his case, Cruzatte interpreted, "He wants something for passage, not much, only a little something, a token. He must show he has gotten something. Tobacco, he wants tobacco. Then he will let you pass."

Lewis' eyes narrowed. He did not like being held for ransom, even for a simple carrot of tobacco. His temper flared and he stomped toward Black Buffalo saying, "Tell him we are mighty warriors and will not be forced into anything. We have given things to them willingly but will not let them steal from us nor exact a toll from us." Lewis motioned Cruzatte with his hands and said, "Tell him, tell him."

While Cruzatte and Drewyer were translating, Lewis hastily ordered all hands to set sail and take positions at their oars. He ordered another man to loosen the tie line. As the man began to untie the line, several Teton warriors grabbed the line and began shouting. Partisan came near the warriors holding the bow line and shouted that he wanted a flag and some tobacco. Lewis, still enraged, turned to move toward Partisan to speak.

Clark immediately held up a hand and Lewis stopped. Turning to Partisan, Clark said as Drewyer translated, "You say you are a great chief, a great man of a great nation. Then you must have influence. Here, take this tobacco and show your influence to all who watch by having your warriors let go of our rope. You will not have to die today."

While the translation was being made, Clark took a carrot of tobacco and threw it onto the bank. At the same time the translation was concluding, Clark lit a taper and stepped toward the cannon. All the while he stared intently at Partisan.

This was a repeat of the earlier confrontation. Black Buffalo again stepped in front of Partisan and faced Clark. He spoke and was translated. "I am a chief and I am angry, too. Can the white man put so much importance into a small amount of tobacco?" He waved his hands across the white observers and turned to look at all the warriors on the shoreline. "Can you do all this for something that will soon just be smoke blowing in the wind?"

Lewis, hearing the translation, grabbed some more carrots of tobacco and threw them at the warriors holding the bowline. Black Buffalo, with his lips tight, looked at Lewis then at Clark, let out a grunting sound, then jerked the line from the warrior's hands. The boat was free.

With the line free, the men leaned into the oars and the boats began to move away. Clark shouted angrily at those observing from the shore. "We are able to defend ourselves if you are thinking of trying to stop us anywhere on this river. If you attack us, we will kill many Teton, a great many Teton."

That night they anchored the boats on a small sandbar in the middle of the river and spent the night in a position they could defend. They rested well and set out early the next day making twenty miles before coming to another sandbar.

"Here, this sandbar," Lewis said to Sergeant Gass. "Pull in and we'll camp here tonight." Looking skyward he said, "Look there, geese migrating, listen, you can hear them honking."

Gass replied, "Sure enough, sir, there is a nip in the air lately, and I noticed the days are getting a lot shorter now. Not much longer till it's winter."

Colter pointed to the sky as he spoke, "There'll be a lot of ducks and geese now, should get some for stew, they make good stew."

Sergeant Pryor added, "I'm so damn glad to have the Teton behind us. You do think they are behind us, don't you, Capt'n?"

Lewis looked back downriver momentarily and replied, "Yes, I think so. If they were still around, we'd have seen them or Seaman would have been barking. Seaman's been quiet, I think we're clear."

Clark, looking at Sergeant Gass, said, "You're right Sergeant, I've noticed some nip in the morning air. One good thing, we get a good hard frost, and we won't have to worry about mosquitoes any longer."

Gass nodded enthusiastically, "Gnats, neither."

Sergeant Pryor moved next to Lewis and spoke, "Capt'n, the men have had their whiskey ration cut ever since we came to Teton country. Do ya think we're far enough away from 'em now that we can have a gill?"

Lewis smiled broadly and looked at Clark who, hearing the comment, was also smiling, "Why, yes, Sergeant, whiskey is certainly in order. I, for one, could sure use one. We've all felt the strain of being on constant guard."

The men set up camp on the sandbar, a secure location, and had their first relaxed evening in a long while. Cruzatte played the fiddle. York and Shannon danced to the music and many of the men sang. They all exchanged stories about the Teton as they smoked pipes or cigars. The mood was light as they bedded down; the Teton Sioux were behind them.

October, 1804 South Dakota

The Corps of Discovery is making good progress each day through what is a land of plenty. Lewis takes advantage of the time to reconnoiter the prairie, always carrying his journal and specimen book to document new plants and animals. He covers ground with long strides, going inland several miles each day. Later, toward evening, he will meet the crew at the river's edge. Typically, he takes George Drewyer with him as he values Drewyer's innate skills of observation and his abilities as hunter and marksman. Collecting and documenting samples of new animal species is a high priority. The two men compliment each other in their ability to spot new or unusual things.

On one occasion while Lewis was gone, Clark noticed large bear tracks near the river's edge. He called out, "Sergeant Pryor, Gass, Colter, York, come here, just look at this. Ever see such a site? Just look at the size of these tracks."

Colter walked over and knelt down beside the imprint, "Hmmm, it must've weighed some, too. See how the pads are pushed into the ground, got to be some weight there. Look at these claw marks, they're big, and look how far apart they are. It's got a big stride, bigger than any bear I ever saw."

Sergeant Gass said, "The Indians said something about very powerful bears, but they exaggerate about a lot of things."

Pryor commented, "Sure as hell didn't exaggerate about the size of this animal, look at this print."

York asked, "Do you suppose they as mean as we heard? York hear that bear will attack anything, anytime, just plain mean. That's what York hear."

Gass replied, "Well, now, York, when you're the biggest bear around, you can be mean if'n you've a mind to, or you can be sweet if'n you've a mind to, ain't nobody gonna argue."

York nodded, "Ummhum, you're sure enough right about that."

Clark kept looking all around as the men were discussing the bear tracks. "I don't see anything, no kill, no bears. Keep an eye out anyway, maybe we'll see one of these big fellas."

Pryor added, "Keep your powder dry. Sure glad we got these 54-caliber rifles. Ain't no bear can argue with a 54-caliber ball."

The men moved on. The days were noticeably shorter. Frost had come during the evenings and lasted through the early morning. With the frost, there weren't as many mosquitoes. Along the shore and near tributaries, there were abandoned earthen huts. Some farming fields had squash left behind, not yet picked. There had been a rapid exodus. There were clothing and other signs of previous occupancy laying around.

Lewis, traveling inland a mile or so with Drewyer, stopped at one such settlement. "What do you suppose caused them to leave in such a hurry?" Lewis inquired.

Drewyer looked around and then leaned on his rifle. He spoke softly, "Pox. Must be the pox or something like it. They left this village without taking anything. They were trying to get away from illness. Maybe they think they can leave the cause of death behind. That's what this looks like."

Lewis frowned and kicked a squash on the ground. "I think you're right. This looks like abandonment, there's no sign of a struggle. They didn't suffer a battle. I think smallpox is likely. Let's get the hell out of here, it's spooky."

The men walked away from the buildings and looked back when they were a few hundred yards away. Drewyer spoke, "So many people, we've seen so many like this."

Lewis replied, "Yes, something's wrong around here for sure." Then looking at his companion, he said, "We must proceed on, maybe we'll find out what's going on from the next Indians we meet."

By the time they joined the rest of the crew it was late afternoon. Sergeant Ordway was beginning to roast meat over
the large campfires and was also making stew from fresh vegetables. As they walked into camp, there was a group of men
talking.

"Cruzatte shot it, said he hit it, too," Reubin Field said.

Joseph Field replied, "Yeah, but you know Cruzatte, he
stretches the truth some when he gets a chance. He's not the
best shot with a rifle. How do we know he hit a bear or even
shot at one for that matter? There's no dead bear."

Shannon said, "With one eye, he may not be able to see
good enough to hunt a bear, hell, it could've been a porcupine,
you know how discombobulated Pierre gets."

Joseph Field looked strange, "There you go again,
discom...what? Anyway, with only one eye and a bear as large
as a barn, that's most likely all he could see. He had to hit it."

Reubin added, "He said it was ferocious, well now, if it was
bigger than life and mean as the devil, why didn't it get him?
We still got Cruzatte." They all laughed.

Joseph Field laughed as he said, "Maybe because that bear
never saw anything as ugly or smelly as Cruzatte. Skinny as
Pierre is, why he wasn't even worth that bear a chasin'. So,
being a real smart bear, he just decided to leave these parts
afore Pierre here could get a chance to reload."

The men laughed and Reubin Field said, "That's it, Joe, that
bear figured one clean shot's all he would allow Pierre here,
one shot for one eye. Why, I bet that bear's out there
somewhere tellin' the other bears about how he stared down
Cruzatte and then decided he was to skinny to eat."

Lewis stopped momentarily, "Did Cruzatte get a shot at a
bear? Did anyone else see it?"

Reubin Field answered, "No Capt'n, nobody else saw
anything. Cruzatte was sure excited enough though. He was

going on and on about how big and fierce it looked. Said it had a shimmery coat and stood near nine feet when it raised up at him. Nine feet, can you imagine that? He's got to be stretching the truth some there. Maybe he didn't see one at all, maybe he just saw tracks."

Lewis listened intently and then moved on into camp. He approached Clark, "It looks like we made some good mileage today? About eighteen, maybe twenty?"

Clark smiled, "Twenty-four, this stretch of the river has mild current, and the wind was in our favor. Did you find any new animals for your ledger? Any Indian signs?"

Lewis looked down, "We did get a couple birds and a big-eared rabbit that could jump a good long way. But as for Indians, we've been seeing some strange evacuations. Villages with no signs of life, like they left in a hurry. Drewyer said he thought it was smallpox, I think he could be right."

Clark said seriously, "We sure don't need smallpox to contend with. By the way, we have a couple of guests with us tonight, some fur traders coming down from the Mandan."

Lewis perked up, "Really! Good fortune's with us. How much further is it to the Mandan? I was beginning to get worried that winter would set in before we reached it."

Clark smiled and replied, "That's because you like to worry, Merry. Well this time there is just no cause for it. They said they left Mandan about three weeks ago. They've been trapping some and not on the river all the time. So, I figure we'll be in Mandan by November, probably before a hard freeze sets in."

Lewis listened intently and replied, "It's been getting cold at night. Are there any other tribes before Mandan? All we see are vacated huts."

Clark answered, "Yep, they said there are Arikara on a three-mile island just up the river a ways. Should be there to-morrow."

Lewis interrupted his friend, "Are they peaceful? We sure don't need another encounter like the Teton back there."

Clark smiled, "The trappers said they're farmers. They trade produce and grain for buffalo blankets and meat."

Lewis sighed and shrugged his shoulders, "That's a relief, Arikara, huh? Do these men speak the language?"

Clark replied, "Yep, it's your lucky day, they said they can speak the language some, enough to trade and get us by. You better brush up on your Jefferson speech. The Arikara may just listen to you."

Lewis answered, "That'd be a welcome change. Where are they now?"

Clark pointed and said, "Sergeant Ordway is showing them around our camp and *Discovery*. Seaman seems to like them, so they must be alright."

October 8, 1804

Discovery rounds a bend in the river where they see a long island in the river. The Indians on the island notice the boats and begin pointing and moving toward the shoreline talking loudly. Some of them run back to inform the others. The island seems to be lush farmland, fed by the river into a very fertile garden. The land is cultivated, and crops of corn are standing with yellow squash visible in the sun. Clark orders the boats to pull over on the left side of the river and tie up.

Lewis ordered, "Sergeant Pryor, get Colter and the two trappers and meet me on the white pirogue. We should go meet these Indians."

Sergeant Pryor walked over to Lewis and spoke in a low tone, "Captain, what about the smallpox? All those villages weren't abandoned for no reason, if we go over there, do you think we could catch the pox?"

Lewis paused a moment as he looked across the river at the Arikara Indians gathered on the shoreline looking back at him. "Thank you for your concern, Sergeant, but we are on a mission to meet all the natives that we can. We have a message to share with them. Keep an eye out for anyone over there that looks sickly or has spots. If you see any signs of smallpox, back off quickly and we'll leave."

Pryor came to Lewis, was silent a moment and then said, "Sir, we'll have the white pirogue ready in less than five minutes."

Clark ordered the men to post sentries along the shoreline, tie up the boats securely and be on full alert as they looked at the hundreds of Arikara lining the shoreline of the island. As the white pirogue approached the island, the Arikara seemed both curious and fearful. They displayed no weapons, but many of them were talking rapidly and moving back away from the water's edge.

As they drew near, a white man in buckskins moved through the Indians and waved. "Welcome," he shouted. "Name's Joe Gravelines. I live here with the Arikara. They're afraid of whites mostly because they were near wiped out by smallpox. This is all that's left of near thirty-five thousand. Are you all healthy?"

Sergeant Pryor shouted back, "Good to see a man that speaks English. No, none of us has smallpox. We get dirty as hell sometimes but nothing that won't wash off."

Gravelines replied, "Well, ain't nobody died here for awhile, they took to abandoning any village with smallpox. On this island they feel safe, nobody's been sick here."

Gravelines turned and spoke to the surrounding Indians who immediately began nodding and moving closer. "Well good, come ashore here. These are good people. I've been living here nigh on to thirteen year now. That's some boat you have there, biggest one I ever saw."

The white pirogue was nosing into the muddy sand on the shore as Lewis stood up. "I'm Captain Meriwether Lewis, and we are a military expedition, the Corps of Discovery. We were sent here by President Jefferson to explore the Louisiana Purchase and then on to find a passage to the Pacific." As he spoke he jumped out of the pirogue and extended his hand to Gravelines.

Gravelines, a tall slender man of about forty-five stepped forward and shook Lewis' hand, then extended his hand to Sergeant Pryor. "I haven't heard this much English in a long time. It sounds good to these ears, that's for sure."

Lewis replied, "We're fortunate to meet someone who can speak the native languages. We have a message from the United States to share with the natives."

Gravelines looked a little puzzled, "You said President Jefferson, ya mean Thomas Jefferson is president now? Well I'll be. He's a goodin' though. I came west to avoid British rule. Glad Jefferson and the others had the courage to stand up to 'em." Then motioning he grabbed Sergeant Pryor's shoulder and Lewis' arm and said, "Come on in to the main village here. Tell me about this Louisiana Purchase. What's that about? You say you're going to go to the Pacific. Well, I never heard of anybody going west of Mandan. The Pacific Ocean has got to be a long way off. Do you know how far?"

Lewis fell into the stride of his host and commented, "We have much to discuss. I'll fill you in on as much news from the United States as we know. We are seventeen states now and admitting new territories as they apply for statehood. The Louisiana Purchase added all the land in the Missouri River basin. Our charter is to explore it and meet the Indians that inhabit the area. Our mission is to continue on to find a passage to the Pacific, the United States will one day reach from Atlantic to Pacific."

"Gonna be lots of settlers," Gravelines stated.

Lewis replied, "Yes, part of our mission is to lay groundwork for trading with the Indians. We will establish U. S. sovereignty and promote trade as well as supporting immigration into the territory. This land is rich and should provide prosperous fur trading for the Indians. Modern trade goods should promote the Indians to establish trading posts. Those trading posts will attract settlements and the West will prosper. We've brought samples of trade goods in our boats there."

Gravelines commented. "Really? This is all so new, you got my head spinning. I see some French and English fur traders now and again. They usually are in groups of two to eight. Trade horses, gunpowder and ball for furs and blankets. This is the first I ever heard of settlements, nobody ever mentioned white settlements before."

They sat and talked for nearly three hours. As darkness was setting in Lewis rose and said, "Joseph, it's truly been a pleasure to meet you here. Providence has again smiled upon our expedition. Tomorrow please bring the chiefs and come visit our encampment on the shore. We'll be glad to have you join us."

Gravelines replied, "Of course, they'll all want to come. Now that they know there ain't no smallpox. They'll trade goods and listen to your talk of trading posts. Arikara have been good at trading, probably better than any people on this river."

Lewis answered, "We'll expect you in the morning. We'll show you our wares and demonstrate our technology to the people. It's a good show, quite a demonstration, if I do say so myself."

October 9, 1804

Lewis is up early and commands the three sergeants to ready the camp for guests. The men dress in their uniforms and clean their rifles in preparation for the Arikara visit. The weather turns stormy with winds creating large waves on the Missouri. Despite the obstacles of high wind and waves, a few of the Arikara come across in unique crafts they call bull boats. These are rounded bowl-shaped boats made of buffalo hides stretched over a willow frame. Each bull boat can hold six men with three squaws to paddle. The Arikara are comprised of three sub-tribes, each with its own chief. They also bring another white man, Pierre-Antoine Tabeau, who has established himself as a trader with the three Arikara villages. He can speak French, English, Sioux and Arikara. There are three chiefs representing each of the villages, Crow at Rest, Hawk's Feather and Chief Hay. Unfortunately, the stormy weather will not let up. The wind becomes so strong that it is impossible to hold a meeting or hold an orderly demonstration. Frustrated, Lewis calls the meeting off until the next day.

As the Arikara departed, Lewis sulked and walked toward the edge of camp and stood looking downriver. Sergeant Gass noticed him, went over and said, "Captain, Ordway will have some food in a little while, we can all relax until this storm dies down. We'll meet again with the Arikara tomorrow."

Lewis was in a bad mood, disappointed in the failure to meet with the Arikara. "Put the Arikara gifts back in *Discovery*," he ordered. "There'll be no meeting today. Get it out of my sight and leave me be." With that, he turned and walked to *Discovery* and entered his quarters on the keelboat.

Clark noticed Sergeant Gass looking strangely at Lewis as Lewis stomped over to *Discovery*. He approached Gass, and the sergeant said, "Capt'n Lewis is real angry. Must be disappointed over the weather."

Clark said, "Sergeant, prepare a couple plates for Captain Lewis and me. We'll eat on *Discovery*."

The sergeant nodded and started to walk away when Clark added, "Sergeant, a gill of whiskey for the men tonight."

Sergeant Gass perked up and replied, "Yes, sir!" and walked away.

Clark stood and looked at the keelboat for a moment. Knowing the moods of his companion he walked across the campground and boarded *Discovery*. Entering their quarters he said, "Merry, it's a good day, find the good in it."

Lewis looked up and replied, "What do you mean? Damned weather, we can't meet and we're about to lose another day. Winter won't delay just because we aren't ready for it."

Clark replied, "My good man, we're lucky. We got not one, but two, count 'em, two translators, that speak Arikara fluently. A lot better situation than we had with the Teton. They're friendly, no smallpox, and tomorrow, why, I just know that tomorrow we'll have good weather. This gives us more time to prepare a little feast for our guests."

Lewis looked a Clark, Clark looked at Lewis, they were silent for a moment and then a broad smile broke across Lewis' lips. "You bastard, you see right through me, don't you? You know me too well. I suppose I should thank you for that. Why hell's bells, you're right. I know you're right. Why should I question Providence if there's a storm today and we lose a day. I'm in good company and we have every reason to expect a good outcome."

"There ya go," Clark said as he hit his friend on the shoulder. "Ordway is bringing some supper to us. Did you see those Arikara? Three chiefs, I wonder which one is the big chief. I think this'll be a good council, don't you? Hey, while we're waiting, get out the instruments and we will fix this point on our maps. Windy as it is, the sky is clearing some."

Lewis looked at his friend, smiled and simply said, "Done."

October 10, 1804

The weather was calm, Pierre Tabeau crossed the river in a bull boat and watched as the other bull boats made their way across. Lewis and Clark joined him on the river's edge. Tabeau said as they watched the boats approach, "There's often some jealousy between these chiefs, especially when it comes to trading with whites. Each wants to be the better man at trading and showing that he's the better host."

At that time the bull boats were being pulled on shore by the Arikara. They proceeded up the riverbank toward the encampment. Gravelines approached Lewis and Clark. "We have quite a few that want to see the white soldier explorers. They're also very curious about the Negro you have with you." He looked around the camp and continued, "None of 'em ever saw a Negro before. Is he your slave?"

Clark replied, "His name is York, he came with me and should be over by my tent. He's bringing up some gifts we brought for the Arikara."

Gravelines answered, "Well, gifts will sure enough make you popular. Especially if they're things they don't have or never seen before."

Lewis said, "We've got sewing needles, razors, tomahawks and good knives, along with some other things that should be of interest."

Gravelines said, "Those items will be popular, out here they have twice the value they'd have in St. Louis. Maybe three times."

They moved to the central portion of the encampment where Lewis began his speech. Gravelines interpreted as Lewis spoke of the importance of peace between the Indian nations, to shun the Teton's warlike and thieving ways, and to trade with American merchants. The reward would be trading posts. They were invited to visit the Great White Father in Washington, chief of the seventeen nations.

When Lewis finished his speech, Sergeant Pryor had the men perform military precision drill, including rifle handling. At the conclusion they fired the cannon on *Discovery* three times, much to the amazement of the Indians who had never seen a cannon.

Clark motioned to York to bring out the gifts and lay them on display. As York moved through the Arikara, every eye was on him. As he passed they would nudge each other and whisper. Lewis was in a good mood. As they distributed their gifts the Arikara also brought forth gifts of food. Lewis asked Sergeant Gass to bring out some whiskey to share with the Indians.

As soon as this order was interpreted, Chief Crow-at-Rest spoke, "Why would you give us this to drink, it will only make fools of us. Would our Great White Father want us to be fools? No, we do not want."

Sergeant Gass looked at Lewis who, in turn, looked at Clark. Clark said, "He's got a point. I imagine sometime or other, some trader has liquored him up, took advantage and left him with a hangover."

Sergeant Gass added, "Well, sir, that just leaves more for us, now doesn't it?"

Apparently ignoring Tabeau's advice of Indian jealousy, Lewis made Crow-at-Rest the principal chief with Hawk's Feather and Chief Hay secondary chiefs. The presents were finally all disbursed and Lewis asked Shannon to bring him his air rifle. As before, the Indians were impressed with the gun that did not need powder. After the air rifle demonstration, the council broke up with the three chiefs in close conversation.

Gravelines interpreted, "They say they've seen much today. That they appreciate the gifts you've given them in good spirit. They've never seen close order drill and think the cannon on the large boat is very powerful. They think the whites are very powerful men. They have much to talk about. Much to tell their warriors when they return. They will hold council among themselves and talk more tomorrow."

They started to leave when Crow-at-Rest asked Gravelines a question, which he interpreted, "He wants to know more about York. Is he a man or a beast? Is he strong medicine? A spirit?"

Clark quickly answered, "Tell them he's not a spirit, he's a man."

York, overhearing this, looked at Clark intently and then smiled.

Gravelines added, "They've invited all the men to come over to visit the villages. Their women will be there, too. Arikara believe that their women, well," he paused and then said, "The men should enjoy the visit. Can you let York come, too? They want to see him for sure."

Lewis replied, "I think the men are due for a short leave. Sergeant, keep them in three separate groups. Only one group at a time visits the villages. We're still a military unit."

Sergeant Pryor immediately formed a contingent of men and took them to the red and white pirogues to embark on the trip to the island. Gravelines met the men at the shore while they were preparing to leave.

"Men, you should know about the Arikara people. They are a gentle, good-hearted race, and they have a belief that I am sure you will enjoy."

The men crowded around Gravelines as he spoke. Joseph Field inquired, "What? Do they have some religious thing we need to know about?"

Gravelines let out a raucous laugh and replied, "No, no, it ain't no religion. But you'll enjoy the concept I'm sure."

Every eye and ear was on Gravelines as he spoke, and he was dragging out the moment, knowing the men were anxious to hear his advice.

Gravelines continued, "It's just that the Arikara believe that if they share their women, that they'll get power from you that way. They'll open their tepees to you 'cause you already showed them your military might."

Joseph Field spoke, "Do they expect us to bring trade goods for the women? We got trade goods."

Gravelines laughed again, "No, young fella, they don't even want trade goods for the favors. They believe you'll leave part of your strength and power and they can then get your power the same way."

Colter spoke out, "Well now, that sure is rich. I don't know about the rest of you men, but John Colter sure has lots of power to share. Maybe even two or three squaws' worth." He laughed, and all the men joined him, nodding and talking among themselves.

Sergeant Pryor added, "Well now, men, I don't suppose there's a need to tell you to lean into those oars on the way over to the island now, is there?" The men laughed as they got into the boat.

Gravelines looked over the men and spotted York standing back with the others. "You there, York, make sure you come with the first group over."

York stepped up and replied, "York will go if Capt'n Clark and Sergeant Pryor says."

Pryor replied, "Why hell, man, you heard Gravelines here, the Arikara think you are big medicine, lots of power." Then turning to the others and laughing he continued, "Now don't a big man like you want to be generous and share all that power?"

York moved in closer and replied, "York will be glad to share his power some. York has lots of power, even more than Colter."

Colter laughed and said, "Now that's the kind of contest I like, I think we're both gonna be winners."

The men climbed into the boats along with Gravelines and began rowing to the island. As they approached, there was a large group of Indians to meet them.

October 11, 1804

In the morning, Crow-at-Rest, along with Gravelines and several warriors, came to meet with Lewis and Clark. They exchanged greetings and sat sharing breakfast. Crow-at-Rest spoke and Gravelines interpreted. "Our warriors are pleased to learn that we have a new Great White Father that will take care of us. I promise and pledge that our trails and rivers will always be open. No Arikara would dare to grab and hold the ropes of your boat. Not one would dare."

Clark replied, "Tell them this is good. We'll report that the Arikara are friendly to our expedition and the Great White Father will be pleased. Trading posts and forts will be built to help the Arikara prosper."

Lewis added, "When you make peace with our expedition, you are wise. We've been sent to make sure that all Indian nations should make peace with each other. Those that do not will have to answer to the power of the Great White Father."

Crow-at-Rest spoke, "We want peace. War does not bring us anything. We've already lost most of our people to the spotted death. We want you to help us make peace with the people upriver, with the Mandan and Hidatsa."

Lewis asked, "Where are the other chiefs, Chief Hay and Hawk's Feather?"

Gravelines interrupted, "I'm not sure, I can only guess, but I think they want you to visit them because they think you favor Crow-at-Rest. They want you to show them they are important by coming to their village."

Lewis looked at Clark, "What do you think, Bill? It's hard to know these cultures. Maybe they're insulted or just want to have a political show of power by having us come to them."

Clark replied, "Could be. They seemed all right yesterday. We did act as if Crow-at-Rest here were the main chief. Maybe he isn't. Maybe we should go see them, couldn't hurt none, they've been friendly."

Lewis turned to Gravelines, "What do you think? We will go to the island and visit the other chiefs. Our mission, our primary purpose, is to make peaceful contact and get support of all the tribal leaders for peace under our flag."

Gravelines responded, "I've lived here many a year and still find some of the things they do strange. I think they feel insulted or slighted somehow. If you go to see them, they'll be able to say that the powerful white leaders came to them. Couldn't hurt."

Lewis looked at Clark and back at Gravelines, "Alright, when you return, let them know we'll be over to meet the other chiefs. We want to know that all the Arikara accept peace."

Gravelines stood and shook Lewis' hand. "Done" he said and departed.

October 12, 1804

After breakfast the captains left with Gravelines, Drouillard, Sergeants Pryor and Gass, Colter, Shannon and York to seek out the other chiefs. They found Chief Hay surrounded by warriors and sat to talk.

Lewis asked, "We've come a long way to meet with you. We've given you our message of peace and of the Great White Father. You said you would give us your answer. We have come to hear you."

Chief Hay looked serious. He had listened intently to Lewis and now paused awhile before speaking. "My people and I have no hostility toward whites. We believe that whites can be our friends and bring us many good trade goods. We want peace with the Mandan and Minnetare. You have said you can make such a peace. I will go with you to hear the words. To know of the peace." He waited while the translation continued. When Gravelines stopped, Chief Hay continued, "I would be willing to go east to Washington to meet the Great White Father, but we fear that after you leave, many Indian people on the prairie will still want to make war against us. We want you and the Great White Father to stop this, stop their guns and prevent if possible. Finish."

Lewis, glad to hear the willingness of Hay to travel to Washington, smiled broadly and turned to Gravelines, "Tell him that we'll make peace with the Mandan. Tell him that he's welcome to travel with us and that he can later travel to Washington in the spring."

Finishing the talks, they rose to move on to find the third chief, Hawk's Feather. The meeting with Hawk's Feather's people was brief. The captains exchanged cordialities and listened as Hawk's Feather spoke. "Our people are peaceful and we're glad to have white men visit. We want peace with the Mandan and Minnetare, but we must know the truth. We do not believe the Mandan promises. Will they believe your words when you tell them of peace with the Arikara? Will you be able to send a Mandan chief to meet in peace with us?"

Lewis paused and answered, "Tell him that we'll bring the Arikara message of peace to the Mandan chiefs. We'll explain that the Arikara and Mandan should live in peace. Chief Hay will go with us and return to you with the message of peace that we will make."

The meeting ended on a friendly note, but clearly Hawk's Feather was skeptical.

October 14, 1804

The expedition sets out early taking Chief Hay and leaving the Arikara behind. Their next stop will be the Mandan, still several miles up river. The Mandan villages are the center of trade activity with many

*Indian tribes; Kiowa, Cheyenne, Crow, Assiniboine, Arapahoe, Sioux,
along with whites from the Hudson Bay Company, XY company and
North West Company. The captains and all the men are anxious to get
to the next major stop because it will be there that they would establish
themselves for the winter.*

October 24, 1804 Near Bismark, North Dakota

*The Corps of Discovery pushes onward and north along a continually
meandering river. As they round a curve in the river, Seaman begins
barking rapidly and looking ahead. Lewis knows by now to heed the
large dog's warnings.*

Lewis gave an immediate order, "Sergeant Gass, take three
men and go to the high point there on the riverbank. See what
Seaman's barking about."

The men jumped out of the boat and proceeded along the
shoreline. As the men left *Discovery*, Lewis, in anticipation of
meeting new Indians, issued an order, "Sergeant Pryor, get
Chief Hay and Gravelines. Form a small party of men and
we'll put ashore here. We should be ready to meet the Mandan
or any other group."

Looking northward the first group spotted the approaching
Indians; Sergeant Gass whistled loudly and waved at Lewis.
"Capt'n there's Indians coming, looks like a hunting party,
twenty or more, they're armed."

Lewis looked at Clark, their eyes met, and without a word
Clark nodded. Clark turned to the men and said, "Sergeant
Ordway, get a taper lit and man the cannon. The rest of you
men get your rifles ready and position yourselves by the
breastwork. Don't take aim, we want to appear friendly, but we
need to be prepared. Those of you on the pirogues go to the

middle of the river, drop anchor and wait." Obeying the order, the men moved in unison.

Lewis said to Gravelines, "Joe, you and Chief Hay come with me. We'll meet these men. From what we have learned, these people should be friendly."

The Indians heard Gass' whistle and began moving in his direction. They were waving and riding at a canter as they approached. Lewis held his rifle low in a non-threatening manner as he turned to Gravelines and instructed, "Tell them we're friendly, that we come in peace. Show them that we've brought Chief Hay of the Arikara tribe. Tell them the chief comes with us in peace and wants to offer peace with the Mandan and Minnetare people."

Gravelines raised his arms in the air and waved slowly, crossing his arms as he waved. The approaching Indians returned the signal as they slowed and began to dismount. This was a hunting party and peaceful. They did not carry their weapons with them as they dismounted. Lewis, seeing this, was pleased.

Gravelines began speaking to the Indians and then turned to Lewis. "This very large man on my left is Chief Big White. With him is his second chief, Little Raven. They're a hunting party and they're glad to see so many white men. They want to know if you have goods to trade. He says this is the season of trading and there are many people in his village with goods."

Lewis beamed. He strutted forward and extended a hand to Chief Big White. As he did so he said, "Tell them that we want to meet all the people of his village. We learned that many tribes come here in peace to trade. This is good. We want to meet all of them. Tell him that we will seek a site to make winter quarters. We will live as their neighbors and learn their ways. We'll stay with them until winter has passed."

As Gravelines began translating, Lewis motioned to Clark, still on board *Discovery*. Clark nodded and began ordering the men to tie anchor and come ashore. Clark and a small contingency joined Lewis, Gravelines and Chief Hay as they sat in a small conference. Clark brought a peace pipe and some tobacco, items that were immediately welcomed by the Mandan Indians. Chief Big White and Little Raven seemed cordial in their greeting to Chief Hay. Surprisingly, the moment when the rivals met face-to-face was not tense. Lewis was pleased that the meeting was peaceful and without a trace of hostility or animosity between the once opposing chiefs.

Lewis spoke to Gravelines, "Tell them we have trade goods to offer when we meet the main body of Mandan. We'll offer even more trade on a daily basis after we have established a winter fort and set up quarters."

Gravelines translated, "Chief Big White said he'd be honored if the Corps of Discovery would spend the winter near his camp. He said that there were two large Mandan villages of great importance to trade. His village was the most important to trading with whites and Indians. He said that there is a second Mandan village with a chief named Black Cat and a lesser chief called Raven Man Chief. The Mandan were the most important tribes to trade with and the white soldiers should trade with the Mandan first. I think he's giving you a sales pitch, sir."

Lewis and Clark listened intently as Big White spoke. Gravelines translated, "He says that there are also three Minnetare or Hidatsa villages in the area, one of forty lodges led by Chief Black Moccasin and a very large village of four hundred fifty lodges led by Chief One Eye, a chief with a wide reputation. Have you heard of him?"

Lewis said, "No, we haven't heard of him, but now that we know of him, we'll meet him. And when he's known to the Great White Father in Washington, all tribes will know of the Mandan and Hidatsa chiefs."

As they began to smoke, Lewis nudged Clark and said, "It's great, this will definitely be the largest village we have encountered so far, and they seem peaceful. We'll be able to winter here with ample time to explain our sovereignty, our mission to establish peace, and possibly set up the first city dedicated to promote our cause. It's simply poetic, historic, why, I couldn't ask for more."

Clark laughed and replied, "Merry, you are some piece of work. I must admit this seems a very welcome site to my travel-weary bones. It does seem to be fertile ground for establishing our policy. But whether or not it's going to be the St. Louis of the north, well, we still have a lot of other Indians to meet and interview. I must say I like your optimism. And I agree, things look good for now, and we should accept our good fortune with optimism."

Lewis smiled and said, "Accept good fortune, why this is a golden opportunity to promote it. Our mission will be supported here. With a city this large, we should be able to establish sovereignty firmly. Hell, Bill, even the Teton will have to recognize a city promoting trade and peace that's backed by the U. S. Government."

Clark smiled, "We should be able to meet with the English and French traders that are here. I think it will be important to let them know that this land is now part of the United States. It should be interesting to see their reaction to that fact and our flag. As for the Teton, I think they're powerful now, but they won't attack a settlement as large as Mandan. Yep, things look good for us now."

Lewis smiled and replied, "I think this is an extension of Jefferson's wisdom. He knew the Mandan trading center would host the British and French. Why, now that we have purchased Louisiana from the French, all the Frenchmen will have to honor the deal. It was made to benefit their country. And as for the damned British, well if they don't like the idea of our sovereignty, they'll have to accept the military might of not only the United States but now the combination of the French and U. S. forces. The British can be stupid, but they know a strong political alliance when they see one."

October 29, 1804 Mandan, North Dakota

The Mandan and Hidatsa chiefs assembled to hear Lewis' message from the Great White Father. As usual, the proceedings opened with the men performing close order drill and precision weapon handling. Midway through Lewis' speech, one of the older chiefs grew restless and began shifting around, then began side conversations with other Indians. Noticing this, one of the chiefs rose up and moved to the instigator and touched him on the shoulder. Words were exchanged, then all were silent and began listening again.

Clark observed the action and turned to whisper to Sergeant Pryor, "I see at least some of the Indians know what good manners are."

Pryor nodded in agreement.

When Lewis finished, Clark rose and motioned to Gravelines to rise. "Tell them we have brought Chief Hay of the Arikara. He has come with us to show that his people want peace with the Mandan. He has smoked the pipe to show he wants peace. He will now smoke again to show all the chiefs here in this meeting today that the Arikara want peace. Will all of you join him?"

As Gravelines was translating, the chiefs began to move closer and seat themselves in a large circle. Chief Hay looked around intently as he lifted the pipe. As he smoked he turned slowly to face all the men in the assembly. He then passed the pipe to his right for all to smoke.

Lewis moved over by Clark and Pryor and spoke, "This is good, they seem to accept him here in council as they did out on the river. It's as if there had never been conflict. Do you think our presence has made a difference this quickly? Do you think this is real?"

Pryor responded, "Sure do, Captain. These Indians would have slit his throat if he'd come here by himself. Now they treat him like a brother. Maybe they want to impress us to get themselves established as favored traders. To get that to happen, what's a small compromise of accepting the Arikara chief?"

Clark added, "I don't want to dampen the moment, but I'm not convinced these tribes know much of lasting peace or about regular councils to keep peace. This may just be a display to keep us content, maybe even to get more presents. I agree with Pryor."

Lewis looked at his friend a moment then replied, "You two could be right, of course, but I choose to accept this at face value. I think the spirit of all men, not just Indians, prefers peace. War is a breakdown of communication and trust. We can and will establish that communication link. All they have to do is provide the trust."

October 31, 1804

Several short expeditions have been conducted to select a site for the winter quarters. Finally, they agreed on the site about seven miles south of the Knife River. It is on the north side of the Missouri River just across from the Minnetare, one of the Mandan villages.

Two Minnetare warriors came to visit the Corps of Discovery. They first met with Sergeant Ordway and Pierre Cruzatte. Cruzatte immediately used sign language and some broken Mandan language. He turned to Ordway and said, "Sarge, can you send somebody to get Gravelines. We can find out what they want a lot quicker."

"Done," replied Ordway as he motioned to Joseph Field to come over. Field moved over and responded, "What's up, Sarge?"

Ordway spoke, "Go and find Gravelines or any interpreter you can right away. These two obviously have a message for the captains and we want to get it straight. While you are at it, have yer brother tell the captains that we have a couple visitors."

"Sure thing," Joseph Field replied as he moved off and gave his brother the instruction. The two Field brothers then moved off in opposite directions. In a very short time Clark came to where Ordway and the two warriors were standing.

"What's new, what have they got to say?" Clark inquired with a smile.

Cruzette replied, "I think they want to invite you and Captain Lewis somewhere. A meetin' of some kind but I'm not sure with who or exactly were or when. Sarge here has sent for Gravelines so we'll know soon."

Clark looked pleased as his eye caught Lewis and Gravelines approaching from a few yards off "Thank you, Private, here they come now."

As Lewis and Gravelines joined the group, Gravelines greeted the two Mandan warriors. After listening a moment, Gravelines turned to the captains and said, "They have come to invite you to a meeting with Black Cat, a powerful chief. They want to know if you can come now."

Lewis turned to Clark, "Just drop everything and go? Wouldn't you know it. We waited all these weeks for the opportunity to have serious talks, and when a golden opportunity presents itself, I have a conflicting meeting. I've already promised McCracken, the British trader, to sit and discuss the North West Company's presence along the river and the purpose of our expedition. I really don't want to miss this chance to learn from him. He said he came over 150 miles in nine days just to get here. Said he'd be leaving soon, maybe even tomorrow." Lewis looked disappointed as he looked at the two Indian messengers.

Clark, seeing the expression coming over Lewis' face, spoke, "Don't worry, that's why there are two of us. I'll go and visit with Black Cat and hear what he has to say. You go and learn what you can from McCracken about the British trading companies. We can do both."

"Of course, it's just that I didn't want to miss the exchange with Black Cat." Lewis had a serious look in his eye as he continued, "You know this meeting with the British fur traders is key. They have to know that the United States is now the owner of the Louisiana Territory. White influence on the Indian population will have to come from Americans from now on. I want to try to figure out if they have a problem with that. Jefferson will be interested in my read on their position. It may determine whether or not there'll be a war over parts of this new territory." Then pacing he turned to his friend and said, "You have to tell me everything that's said. Try to remember everything, I'll do the same. Then you write in your journal and I'll encode my exchange for the president."

Clark smiled as he replied, "Done, my friend, done. Rest easy, we'll be vigilant and make notes of our meeting. You concentrate on this business with the British and learn what you can. You should be good at interpreting their real purpose. You're experienced in politics."

Captain Clark, Sergeant Pryor, Gravelines, Cruzatte, Colter, the Field brothers and York go to meet with Chief Black Cat in council. A large, permanent, circular, earthen lodge constructed with wooden support members, typical of the Mandan villages, serves as the meeting place.

The men sat in a semicircle, the Corps of Discovery contingent facing the hosting Indians. The meeting began with an exchange of greetings as each man was introduced to the others. Then the council pipe was lit by one of the prominent Indians, possibly a medicine man, and passed to Black Cat. He looked around the room, lifted the pipe and smoked. Then, with a small nod, he passed the pipe to Clark.

Gravelines started to explain, "He wants you to...."

Clark cut him short, "I know."

Clark took the pipe and smoked it, then passed it to Sergeant Pryor who in turn smoked and passed it on. The last man was Reubin Field, who, upon smoking, passed the pipe to the Indian directly opposite him. The Indians then passed it around until the pipe was again returned to Black Cat.

Black Cat motioned to Clark as he spoke, "Where is the other white chief with the serious face? We invited him to council. Does he not want to meet with Black Cat?" Gravelines translated.

Clark straightened his back, looked at Gravelines and told him to translate exactly. "Captain Lewis must meet, even as we now talk, with the other whites that your people have established trade with for many years. They are from different nations, the British and Canadians, and now he must explain to them, as he has to you, that the United States is in charge of this region. He went to invite them to spend time with us, to share this great trading place in peace. He will explain to them that our Great White Father now will take charge of trade along the river."

Black Cat listened and seemed to understand the translation. Then he spoke, "The Mandan and Minnetare are pleased to have you as our guests, to have you live with us this winter. We will hunt with you and trade."

Clark motioned to Gravelines as he began to speak, "Tell him that we're pleased to be his guests. We've come a long way and are glad to be able to have our winter lodge next to the powerful Mandan and Minnetare people. We have selected the site for our winter camp; it is directly across from your lodges. Soon we will cut trees to make a fort for our men. We will name the place after your people. We will call it Fort Mandan."

Gravelines spoke, and Black Cat smiled and nodded and then smoked again as he passed the pipe back over to Clark. Clark took the pipe, puffed on it and passed it to Sergeant Pryor. He continued, "Black Cat and the other good chiefs have heard the words of Captain Lewis. You have seen the power of our cannon and how our men move as one. We have explained that we want peace. The peace we seek is not just between us and your people and not just for now." He waited while Gravelines translated, then continued, "The peace we want must live in your heart. It must be between Indians of all tribes. This peace must last forever. We want all of the Indian tribes to show peace to the whites traveling on the river. The peace will bring you more trade goods because all people will know they can trade freely and not fear attack." Again he waited while Gravelines translated. The peace pipe continued to move around the room. Clark continued, "War has brought nothing to the Indian tribes. Peace will allow all tribes to trade and receive goods, new materials of great value, from the white men who will follow. There will be new cities, stores for trade and your people will prosper."

Gravelines said, "Don't have a word for 'stores', Captain, I will say trading place."

Clark nodded and flicked his index finger as if to indicate to proceed. After the translation, Clark continued, "We'll begin to build our fort, we'll cut trees and make a lodging place. It will have a wall all around to mark what we will consider to be our area. We will guard this with soldiers. You and all Indian guests are invited to visit us through the day to trade for meat and grain. We will have our trade time only in the daytime. We must remain armed to protect ourselves from those Indians that are not friendly and may wish to steal from us while we sleep."

Gravelines translated and Clark remained silent as Black Cat listened. Then the chief spoke, first looking at all the men and then directly at Clark. "It will fill my heart with joy to have peace in this land. We would like to make peace between the Arikara and Mandan who for so long have stolen from each other. If there were peace, the men could hunt without fear, and our women could work in the fields without looking every moment to see if the enemy approaches," Gravelines translated. Black Cat continued, "I would be proud to have the men and guns of the Great White Father protect us from our enemies. Captain Lewis has asked me to travel to visit Washington village and see the Great White Father. This we will do. I will go when the river runs again," Gravelines translated. Then Black Cat raised a hand and the peace pipe stopped moving as he continued, "The Mandan people have heard of your coming and waited with excitement for you to come to our villages. Our men stopped hunting buffalo, elk, deer and beaver to come to see your men and your strange boats. Some came a long distance and all were expecting great presents from the powerful white men with boats full of gifts." Black Cat motioned with a hand to Gravelines to translate. After the translation, he continued, "Many of our people in the villages were disappointed with the small gifts they received. They complained that you were not just passing through but staying with us, and therefore, we expected more gifts, even guns and gunpowder. As chief, I was not so much disappointed. I told the people that the rewards of being good friends and trading with the white Americans would come when the Great White Father learned of how well we treated his people. I will make the long trip to visit the Great White Father."

Gravelines translated, and then Clark spoke, "Your decision to visit the Great White Father is good. It will do much to make your tribe stronger. You and your people will become known to him and the rewards for being peaceful will be great. There will be a large city here for trade. The flag which we have given you will be above the buildings to show all who come that the Great White Father is ready to protect his children that follow the word of peace." Gravelines translated, and then Clark continued, "As for our gifts, we have only room in our boats for small gifts, yet we share these with the Mandan and Minnetare. These presents, the metal fishhooks, sewing needles, steel knives and flannel material are but samples of what we can provide when you become a trading nation with the United States. The future will bring much more if you abide by the peace we ask. We cannot give more as we must have gifts for the other tribes we will meet as we move farther west." Then he paused and looked around. Gravelines translated and Clark continued, "Chief Black Cat, you are a wise man or you would not be chief. You, of all the men, must know that the real gift we bring is not what you were presented. The real gift is the knowledge that you are now part of the United States. That the Mandan will now be protected by Great White Father if you live in peace as he wishes. The peace among the Indian people will last much longer than the simple gifts we have given you. The peace will be enjoyed by all men, not just those favored by the small gifts."

Gravelines translated as Black Cat conferred with Little Raven and some other Indians. He spoke to them as he made gestures with his hands and all were nodding in agreement.

Then Black Cat spoke, "We have never seen a large black white man before. Word of his appearance has spread through our villages and many want to see him. Some of our chiefs believe that he is not truly black in skin but has covered himself with paint to gain power. Others think he is not a man, but a spirit being with great power. His hair is made of small circles. We do not understand how he does this. Many of our warriors have asked how he does this. They would like to have their hair as his. Can this be done?"

As Gravelines translated, York straightened his back and looked around. The men smiled and began nodding, and some whispered to one another. Captain Clark smiled and looked at York and spoke, "This man is York, he is of a different race of people. His people are all black in skin and have curly dark hair. It is not paint or grease; his skin is black all over his body."

Gravelines began to translate and then said, "Captain, I have no word for race."

Clark said, "Tell him that race means different. Just as the white man is different than the Indian. Tell him that some whites have blue eyes, some have wavy hair, I have red hair. All these features show that we are a different race. Tell him that York is simply of a different race. Tell him he is still a man, not a spirit being. As for his hair, there is no way to make your hair grow as his; that is part of his race."

Black Cat and all the Indian party listened intently to the translation. Then they spoke among one another briefly. Finally Little Raven spoke, "We would like to have York visit with us in our lodge and share buffalo and smoke. Our medicine man would like to see his skin. Some of our men want to share their wives with him so they can then share his power. Is this possible?"

York listened to the translation and smiled broadly. The men laughed and Clark raised a hand to quiet them as he spoke. "We'll meet with you this evening. Those chiefs and medicine men among you that have not seen a black man may come. They may touch his skin to see that he does not wear paint or grease. They'll see that he's a man. As for your women, if your warriors want to share their wives with York, that's for them to decide."

The men nodded and Reubin Field said to his brother, "I think we should get us some charcoal and voyager's grease. Maybe they'll give us their wives, too."

Colter looked at York and said, "Well now, York, it appears we got a real celebrity with us. What do you think of all this attention?"

York smiled as he looked at Clark and the men, then said, "York ain't never been so much a celebrity afore. York has noticed that all the tribes seem to like dis color. York don't mind. York don't mind at all. In fact, York is pleased to help make peace with the Indian 'cause they respects a man that is different."

Colter nudged Sergeant Pryor, "Respect hell, York, they are letting you have their wives. Now that's a little more than respect, right Sarge?"

Sergeant Pryor nodded and added, "It truly looks like York here is the benefactor of simply being different. Especially in a land where they ain't seen a black before."

York smiled and looked at his co-travelers, "Of course, York appreciates these Indians giving their wives for the night. York is also mighty proud to go meet the chiefs and let them azamin him all over. But mostly York is glad to hear Captain Clark tell them that York is not a spirit being." Then, looking at Colter, the Field brothers and Pryor, he added proudly, "An' that be the second time the capt'n said that York was a man."

Across the village, Lewis is meeting with Hugh McCracken.

Lewis walked with Sergeant Gass, Drewyer, Shannon and Seaman. They came to one of the lodges to meet with Hugh McCracken, a British representative of the powerful North West Company. They waited briefly and then noticed several teenage boys running toward them, ahead of McCracken.

McCracken immediately noticed the whites standing outside the lodge and waved a hand in the air as he shouted, "Hugh McCracken here, I've just come over 150 miles to meet Captain Lewis of the United States."

Lewis smiled and stepped forward with his hand outstretched, "I'm Meriwether Lewis. Captain of the Corps of Discovery. Pleased to meet you. This is Sergeant Gass, a good mess cook and a good carpenter. He's good at managing the men, too." Gass extended his hand and shook hands with McCracken as Lewis continued, "And this young man to my left is George Shannon, youngest member of our group but one of the best educated."

Shannon extended his hand and said, "Pleased to meet you, sir."

Lewis stepped back slightly and continued, "This man to my right is George Drewyer, not an Army regular but a damn good hunter and expert with a rifle, an all around good woodsman and translator." Then as Drewyer was exchanging handshakes with McCracken, Lewis added, "And of course, this is my dog, Seaman. He's a Newfoundland and lets us know when things aren't right." Pausing a moment, Lewis queried, "How long will you be here?"

McCracken smiled broadly and said, "I'll be here only a day. I have to move out northeast tomorrow, we have goods to get to the market." Then he looked at the men and continued, "A real pleasure to meet you, gentlemen, and you too, Seaman. You're the first Americans I've seen in a very long time."

The men stepped into the lodge and sat down. McCracken continued, "I'm with the North West Company. We merchandise beaver pelts mostly, but we also take any pelts of good quality. We meet here as often as possible with the Mandan. If we are not first, the damn XY or Hudson Bay traders will beat us to the best pelts."

Lewis looked at McCracken and spoke, "I have prepared a letter for you and your company officials. It explains our purpose for this expedition. We are a scientific expedition sent by President Thomas Jefferson to explore and map the Louisiana Territory, the entire watershed of the Mississippi/Missouri Rivers. We'll go west in the spring following the Missouri River and continue to map it as we have thus far. Those maps will be valuable as the land opens up. There will be more trappers, traders and eventually farmers and settlers in new cities along the river. I am also gathering samples of the flora and fauna. I prepare them to send back to Washington for scientific recording." Lewis handed a folded letter to McCracken who put it in a satchel.

McCracken spoke, "These are harsh lands and they're generous lands. There are many buffalo and beaver, and my company will pay top money for first right to examine any man's pelts or hides. My competition, as you know, is the XY Company and the Hudson Bay Company. I don't like them, especially Hudson Bay. They try to promote dissention between the natives and make alliances with Indians provided they favor Hudson Bay. While we provide some firearms for trade, Hudson Bay has provided arms to natives to the point where it has disrupted the natural balance of power in the region."

Sergeant Gass asked, "To the Teton?"

McCracken nodded and shook a finger in the air. "Exactly, Sergeant, the Teton or Lakota were not natural pirates here. Not the rogues you see today along the river. In actual fact, they were moving west away from the Chippewas to avoid confrontation. They weren't a military power until they began trading with Hudson Bay. They were given guns for beaver. They quickly found that they could get more beaver by exacting a toll on river traffic. Much easier than killing beaver themselves. Their large numbers, along with the guns Hudson

Bay has provided them, have made them successful, if you can call it that, in raiding river traffic for toll."

Lewis was listening intently and replied, "We met the Teton and found them to be deceitful and untrustworthy. They weren't pleased with the gifts we gave them and demanded more. When we refused, they threatened violence."

Shannon interrupted, "We stood up to 'em though; Captain Lewis and Captain Clark didn't flinch."

Lewis looked at Shannon and then continued, "The encounter was tense to say the least. We came as close as I would ever want to spilling a lot of blood."

"Were they there in large numbers?" McCracken asked.

Lewis nodded, "Yes, they had a large show of strength. At one point probably 500 or more. Most of the warriors had bows and arrows, but there were quite a few with firearms. The guns did look old and they wanted to trade with us to repair some of them."

McCracken said, "We have trade representatives coming here all the time under a British flag. XY will have men here frequently, and then there are the omnipresent Hudson Bay traders. Hudson Bay wants domination over the fur trade and, in my opinion, wants to divert the traffic northeast. They already have established trade routes to Europe and are profiting."

Lewis replied, "As I said, we are military men on a scientific expedition. We don't want to take sides between Canadian and British fur trading companies. We want to advise all those that trade here that the United States has sovereignty over the region now. Our sovereignty is recognized by the world powers from the Louisiana Purchase with Napoleon of France. The message from our government is to extend a welcome to our neighbors to the north and to the British traders. We'll be building a fort just across the river here, Fort Mandan. You and your men are welcome there anytime. We ask that all

buildings built by whites and occupied for trade or protection
fly an American flag. Any other flag would be considered a
challenge to our sovereignty. Now that the United States owns
all the watershed territory we must ask that no other treaties
be entered into with any Indian tribes."

McCracken smiled broadly, "Men, my interest and the
North West Company's interests are simple. We want to trade
for furs and hides, that's it. We are not politicians or government agents of any kind. We have no political interest and
will abide by the new sovereignty of the United States. Quite
frankly, I don't care *what* flag flies overhead as long as the
business is profitable. You'll get no trouble from our quarter.
We don't make treaties, only business deals, contracts for
goods at a good price."

Lewis looked pleased as he spoke, "I am glad to hear that,
but I have a word of caution for you and your company. Quite
simply, many of the white traders have not dealt fairly with the
natives. Prices are higher than a normal profit would dictate.
When the United States begins setting up trading centers, we'll
offer goods at fair prices for the furs and pelts. We won't abide
profits that are excessive or unfair."

McCracken looked at Lewis a long moment and almost
smiled before he became serious. "Captain, we do trade fairly.
The natives are not forced to take our goods for their furs.
Please realize that many of these items have to be transported
from Europe, stored and brought here. There are a lot of
freight costs and some losses that have to be reflected in our
trading structure."

Lewis started to speak, McCracken raised a finger and interrupted, "Captain, your point is well-taken. No one profits
in a trade arrangement if one side loses heavily. We want long-
term business here and we cannot establish that if we do not
trade equitably. I can't speak for XY or Hudson Bay, but as

for the North West Company, I will take your message back to our officials, and I promise we'll review our profits and our costs to bring goods this far west."

Lewis smiled and said, "If it needs review, it needs review. I've heard that all the white trading companies make large profits from the fur trade and offer little to the Indians. As part of President Jefferson's policy to deal fairly with the natives, we'll ensure equitable pricing as we establish trade centers." Pausing a moment, Lewis spoke again, "From your knowledge of the area, are there any maps available of the land west of here? We're headed west in the spring. What can you tell us? We'd like to know any scrap of information regarding terrain west of here or about Indian tribes."

McCracken paused and answered, "Captain, gentlemen, the North West Company will take goods from any region. Some of the furs probably do come from west of here from Indians or trappers, but to us, this is the western-most trade center. They bring their trade goods here; we don't go west of here to get them. No need to. Why risk going into harsh land when the Mandan are the magnet for all the goods in the area?" Then he looked around and continued, "I don't have maps of the area. I will ask around, maybe there is something for the land west of here. All I've ever seen myself is north, around Hudson Bay. I know nothing about lands up the Missouri."

Drewyer spoke, "And of the Indians, what have you heard of them?"

McCracken replied, "I hear names of tribes and meet some of their chiefs and braves, but only here in the Mandan, never west. There are Cheyenne, Crow, Assiniboine, Snake, Blackfoot, probably some others. I don't know anyone that can speak the languages, so we always rely on Mandan translators to make the trade deals. I don't know any that are as war-like as the Teton. Blackfeet may be hostile at times, but I have never confirmed that. I think that most native tribes are friendly, but you never know. I think any of them would steal a horse if they had the chance. Young warriors get praise and acknowledgment that way."

Lewis smiled briefly and then spoke, "As I said, we'll be moving west in the spring. In the meantime you and your trading neighbors are invited to visit our fort whenever you can. I know you can't stay long this trip, but when you return, please bring all the information you can regarding the Indians or terrain west of here. Some of what we hear is conflicting. And if you hear any news of the world, well it's been a year since we heard anything."

McCracken replied, "Sure thing, Captain, I'll try to bring you as much information as I can. How many men are you going to take with you when you move out in the spring?"

Lewis answered, "We are not exactly sure at this time. I have to send the keelboat back. We'll be sending back a lot of letters and notes. It'll be the first word our relatives have heard from us in a year. We'll also be sending samples of the flora and fauna we have taken so far. In fact, we have a live prairie dog and some birds that we captured. They will go back to Washington to show our countrymen evidence of our travels." Shifting his weight, he continued, "As far as how many, I estimate twelve to fifteen men will return in the spring, leaving about thirty to go west. Captain Clark and I are finalizing that decision later this winter."

"I understand," McCracken replied. "It's an important decision to make. I'd want to be sure I had the right men with me if I were going. It'll be taxing to say the least. Would you be interested in taking any of our men with you? I'm sure I could get volunteers. One man, Larocque, is the ambitious type; he'd go with you for sure."

Lewis looked quickly at Sergeant Gass and then at Drewyer. "Umm, no I don't think so. Our men are military and quite used to one another, and that took some doing.

There's a lot of work to do but I believe the sergeants have the workload under control."

The men continued to talk for awhile longer and then moved outside. McCracken looked at Seaman and said, "Now that is one fine animal you have there, Mr. Lewis. Where did you get him? Would you consider trading him?"

Lewis quickly replied, "He's not on the trading block. I got him in Pennsylvania before we started. You're not the first to offer to buy him." Reaching down to pat Seaman on the head, he continued, "He's my friend and you just don't sell your friends. Besides he's shown that we can depend on him to let us know when things aren't right."

McCracken responded, "Looks like a fine animal, seems to be well-tempered for a pure breed. Well sir, it was a pleasure talking with you today. I frequent this village often and I look forward to when I'll be back to visit. I must go, I have business to attend to." They shook hands and departed.

November 2, 1804

The men were busy cutting trees and moving lumber to a cleared area that would become Fort Mandan. They borrowed horses from the Indians and made harnesses to drag logs to the construction site. The plans for the fort were made. There would be two rows of huts with split plank floors covered with grass and clay. The captains would share a single cabin; the men would share the other seven. They would erect an eighteen-foot pointed pole fence with a large gate and sentry tower. Many Indians, mostly teenage boys, came to watch the construction. They found it interesting to see horses employed in such a manner.

During construction, a Frenchman of about 45 years, approached the area accompanied by two young Indian women. One of the women was pregnant.

As he approached he heard Cruzatte, Labiche and Drewyer speaking in French. He immediately moved toward them and said in French, "I'm a trader with years of experience dealing with Indians. I've heard you're going west in the spring. My wives are Shoshone or Snake Indians, native to the mountain area. We'd be able to translate for you if I could hire on."

Drewyer looked at the man for a moment as if taking his measure and then answered, "Yes we are, we will be, moving west in the spring." Drewyer looked around and motioned to Sergeant Pryor. Seeing Drewyer's summoning signal, Pryor moved to join them.

As Pryor approached, Cruzatte said, "Sergeant, these people, this man, is inquiring about us going west in the spring. He's French and his squaws can speak to the Indians west of here."

Pryor looked at the Frenchman and the squaws and said, "The captains will want to meet these people for sure. They've been interested in anyone that knows about the West. Does this man speak English?"

Drewyer turned to the Frenchman and asked, "Do you speak English? Our captains don't speak French."

The Frenchman replied, "No, only a little."

Drewyer told Sergeant Pryor, "Labiche and I can interpret. His English is poor."

Sergeant Pryor said, "I'll send for the captains; meanwhile, find out what you can about them." Then turning to Cruzatte he ordered, "Go and let the captains know we have visitors. See if we should bring them or if they will meet them here."

Cruzatte was gone in an instant and located the captains. Hearing the anxious Cruzatte, Clark said to Lewis, "I suppose we best go meet these people before Pierre here has a fit." As they walked toward the visitors, Clark continued, "Well now, Merry, Providence is looking out for us again. What do we need most of all before we head west? Translators! Well, translators have been brought to our doorstep. They are waiting for us right here, let's meet them."

The two captains walked across the grounds with bold strides, Cruzatte, half running, followed behind. As they approached the newcomers, Lewis extended his hand and said, "I'm Captain Meriwether Lewis, and this is Captain William Clark, we're pleased to meet you."

Labiche said, "He don't speak English very good, sir. This is Troussaint Charbonneau, a trader and interpreter. His two wives are Shoshone, from near the mountains."

Lewis asked Charbonneau, "Do you speak Shoshone?"

Labiche translated, "No, only Hidatsa, the women speak in Hidatsa."

Clark looked at Lewis and smiled as he spoke, "Well now, maybe I spoke out of turn about being lucky finding translators. If we hire this man and his wives to translate, it means that they'll speak to the Indians in Shoshone, translate to him in Hidatsa, then he'll tell one of our French speaking men who'll finally tell us in English! Makes me tired just thinking about that scene; we could lose a lot of meaning with that circular translation."

Lewis replied, "I couldn't have dreamt of a more complicated net of communication. Damn. But we haven't left yet and there's time to find another translator before spring. For now, this proposal is the best we've got, in fact, it's all we've got."

Clark replied, "I suppose you're right, some translation is better than no translation. Even this arrangement would have helped with the Teton." Then he laughed, "Can't you just see it, sitting around a fire at night; Shoshone chief speaks to Frenchman's wife, Frenchman's wife speaks to Frenchman, Frenchman speaks to Labiche, Labiche tells us what was said. My friend, it is going to take all night just to say 'Hello' or 'What's for dinner?'"

They talked a few moments and then agreed to offer Charbonneau the job of translator. Hearing this, Drewyer asked, "Captains, before the offer is translated, can I speak to you a moment?"

The captains looked quickly at one another and nodded in agreement. Drewyer took a deep breath and continued, "First, I think he'll want more pay than the rest of us. He keeps talking about how good he is and how much experience he has. Next, he has two wives to take with him. The men will respect a man with one wife and most likely say nothing. But a man with two wives, when there are no other women around? The trail is long; there could be problems."

Lewis replied, "Say no more, you have a good point." Turning to Clark he said, "We don't need trouble, that kind of trouble, on the trail. We've had enough discipline problems so far, I don't want to set the stage for more. What do you think?"

Clark rubbed his chin and said, "For now we can tell them we're interested. Tell him our accommodations may permit one woman but not two. Ask if he'll take only one of his wives."

Labiche translated and Charbonneau listened. He replied that he would think about this and let the captains know his decision later. He looked at the boats and left without saying anything further.

Later that evening, Chief Big White extended an invitation to council. Knowing it was a social event, the captains brought tobacco, smoked pork, vermilion paint, mirrors and fishhooks. At the council meeting, Big White's wife carried in an es- timated hundred pounds of buffalo meat for roasting on the central fire. There was an abundance of other food. The whites sat first. The Indians had a brief quarrel over their seating arrangements. Finally, the chiefs sat down.

There was a low drumbeat as the smoking pipe was lit and handed to Chief One Eye. He puffed the smoke, grunted approval and passed the pipe to Black Cat who in turn passed it to Clark. Clark smoked and passed it to Lewis. Lewis was about to hand the pipe to Colter when Black Cat and Big White waved their hands and made sounds of protestation. The men stopped and looked.

Gravelines interpreted, "The chiefs want the black white man to smoke next. Many have come a long way to see him. Many believe that this large black white man may have spirit power to make our next hunt large."

The captains motioned with their hands to give the pipe to York. Colter quickly handed it over. York stood as he took the pipe. He was grandstanding to an eager crowd. He looked around and drew deeply as he smoked the pipe, moving the pipe like a large wand. Pointing the pipe at the Indians, he exhaled the smoke in small rings to make the moment last as long as possible.

Sergeant Pryor leaned over and said to Clark, "Some showman that York, he has them all eating from his hand. I think he's enjoying this."

Clark replied, "Every minute of it, I'm sure."

Drewyer reached out and touched Clark on the shoulder, "I think the moment is ours. I'd have York take off his shirt to show he is black all over. Let's see where this goes."

Clark motioned to York and York came to his side. "York, these Indians are impressed with your color. We have all the important chiefs here and a medicine man. Go ahead, put on a show, take off your shirt and dance a little. Strip so they can see your body.

York smiled as he listened to Clark's instructions. "York will dance some, an' smoke some, and let the big chief see his skin all over. York will do it good." With that, York removed his shirt and moccasins. He danced with the pipe, handing it to

different Indians as he moved around. He removed his
trousers as he handed the pipe to Black Cat. Dancing with
only a loincloth, York moved and mixed with the Indians. One
of the elder Indians reached out and grabbed York by the
wrist. York stopped immediately as the elder man looked at
him closely. Then the elder wet two fingers in his mouth and
rubbed York's bare midriff. The elder rubbed a moment then
held the fingers to his nose and smelled them. Next, he tasted
his fingertips and finally raised his fingers over his head and let
out a long whining sound. The Indians all buzzed with conversation. The old man stepped back and as he did, others
lined up to touch York and feel his hair.

Finally, One Eye spoke loudly and everyone quickly found
seating.

Gravelines translated, "They now believe that he is a man,
but they still think that touching him will bring them good
fortune in the upcoming buffalo hunts. They have seen white
men with freckles, blue eyes and curly hair and even with no
hair, but none so strange as this man. They ask if there are
other races of men. Race is a new word for them. Are there
men with blue or green hair, what color of skin?"

Clark looked puzzled a moment and then said, "I suppose
that's a fair question. I never thought about it much though.
Tell the chief that it is wise to observe these differences and
imagine differences in unseen men. There are no men with
blue or green hair or skin."

The Indians were again buzzing with conversation, even
some laughter until One Eye spoke and the room fell silent.
Gravelines translated, "They want their buffalo hunts to be
successful. In winter, their lives depend on meat and hides.
Their custom is to have old men sleep with their wives to
transfer wisdom. They want the white powerful warriors to
transfer power through their squaws. Now they want the
black white man to transfer his spirit power to their squaws."

One Eye waited as Gravelines translated. As Gravelines finished, the men were smiling and nudging one another. George Shannon laughed as he said to Joseph Field, "This is tantamount to the Arikaras. We left some power with them. Do you men think we can muster up some power this winter to help them with the hunt?"

Field said, "Tanta what?"

Sergeant Pryor said, "Shut up, damn it men, they're still talking. Don't be rude." The men silenced and looked again at One Eye who was about to speak.

Gravelines translated, "The winter hunt is the most difficult and the most important. The days are short and the air is cold. Hunting is hard, sometimes men die, sometimes horses die. Often we come home without meat. If you cannot give us your guns, then give us your power by sharing our squaws before the hunt. If you do not despise us, you will share your power as is our custom with the old men and bravest among us."

Cruzatte spoke, "Capt'n Lewis, Capt'n Clark, there ain't none of us despises these Indians. Especially we don't despise their squaws none. Can we volunteer? We are a corps of volunteers, ain't we?"

Clark spoke, "The men are free to spend their evening time however they see fit. I'm sure they'll not despise our Indian friends. The black man also does not despise your people." Looking back over his shoulder, he gave a wink at the men, "Tell him that the buffalo hunt will have the power of the white men to help them."

Lewis added, "Tell them if they will provide horses, we'll join them in the hunt and use our rifles to make it successful. We also need meat for the winter."

As Gravelines translated, both sides were pleased. The food was ready and the squaws began passing the food around. The first portions were given to Big White and One Eye, then to Lewis and Clark. Chief One Eye began looking at Pierre Cruzatte, also with one eye. Cruzatte had an extra eye patch with him and offered it to the chief. This was an immediate success as the chief beamed with pride.

One Eye spoke and Gravelines translated, "He wants Cruzatte to be his friend with one eye." Gravelines then said, "There's more. He wants him to share buffalo and to share the squaw that handed him food." One Eye sat motionless waiting for the translation.

Cruzatte fidgeted as he looked at One Eye, then the squaw, and then the captains. "Can I take him up on his offer, Capt'n? We wouldn't want to let him be turned down."

Clark looked at Cruzatte and said, "Well now, Pierre, it looks like you have made a powerful friend and most certainly have come out on the better end of the trade. Make sure you adjust his eye patch for him before you enjoy the fruits of his offer."

The rest of the room had turned into a buzz of conversation. The captains formed a smaller circle with the leading chiefs while the others were in smaller groups making small talk. Lewis, forever inquisitive, asked Black Cat what he might expect in the lands to the west.

Black Cat spoke slowly, "The river is mighty and travels a great distance before you notice it getting smaller. In the spring you will see buffalo that have fallen through the ice and drowned. The tribes you will meet are Crow, Assiniboine, Blackfoot and Snake. Sometimes there are Cheyenne hunting parties. All of these people should treat you friendly as you are white and have no horses to steal. Your boats are safe on the river. They will not attack such well-armed boats on the water."

Lewis listened almost without blinking. He focused intently as the chief spoke and waited anxiously for the interpretation.

He asked, "Do any of these tribes have guns? Are you at peace with them?"

Black Cat looked at his guests and again spoke slowly, "Mandan prefer peace with all tribes. During the winter you may see chiefs and braves from all tribes as they come here in peace to Black Cat, Big White and One Eye for trade. The Blackfeet have the most guns. They trade pelts with the English for guns. If they lived closer, they may try to make war on us like the Teton, but they are distant. We do not like the Teton." He paused as he took a bite of roasted buffalo and continued talking with his mouth partially full. "Mandan do not want war, only peace, but when others bring war we must respond and not be weak." Then he added, "Crow will steal horses at night. They are not so brave as to try this in the daylight. Snake people live in the mountains and the Minnetare make war on them often. Not Mandan, we do not make war so much."

Clark leaned over to Lewis, "To hear his side, he is a saint. I think this is a politician. He's saying what he knows we want to hear. There's more to this story than we're hearing."

Lewis replied, "I think so, but he isn't lying about the guns or not liking the Teton. Maybe we'll learn more as winter progresses." Then speaking to the chiefs he asked, "What of the animals of the West, what can you tell us?"

Raven Man Chief spoke, "There are plenty buffalo, plenty elk, plenty deer and plenty beaver. We will be on a winter buffalo hunt soon. We want you to come with us. Our scouts look each day for the herd."

Colter pointed to a necklace of claws and asked, "Those claws you have, that necklace, are they from the great bear you call the white bear?"

Raven Man Chief beamed with pride as he lifted the necklace of bear claws. "These are the claws of the great bear. It is the white man that named it the 'white bear'. Whites were familiar with a smaller bear that was black and they knew these were not black bear. From not being black bear, they were called white bear." He laughed at his explanation. "To see the bear, it has a shiny brown coat and moves fast."

Colter said, "We will hunt the bear when we hunt buffalo. I will have a necklace like the one you wear."

As this was translated, the Indian chiefs looked at one another; whispered a few things, and then Raven Man Chief spoke again. "The large bear will not wait for you to hunt it. It will hunt you." He paused a moment and then said, "Even the brave among us do not hunt this bear unless we are in numbers. When it is hit with an arrow, it will attack the hunter. If there are not many hunters to shoot straight and fast, it will kill them."

Drewyer asked, "Some of you have guns. Have you shot the bear with guns?"

Black Cat spoke, "Yes, we have shot the white bear with guns and arrows. It does not die easily. It is not a buffalo. Always many shots before it will die. During this time all who hunt must be careful. The great bear is swift and will kill them. It can kill a man with one stroke." Then he spoke to the other chiefs briefly, they grunted in agreement as he continued, "Every one knows of the great spirit that lives within the bear. All men know of its power. Each of us here knows of friends and brothers that have been killed by the bear. Make no mistake, do not hunt the great bear alone. It will kill you even though you shoot it. It is a great honor to have the claw of this bear."

Colter said to the captains, "Well now, from the sound of this animal, I think the Corps of Discovery will have to see what a 54-caliber ball under a full charge will do to this bear's attitude. Our guns should fare better than the old 40-caliber muskets I've seen. Certainly far better than arrows."

Clark said, "I think you're right, our guns are better. I'm just not sure how much of the story we've just heard was just to impress us and how much is fact. Maybe they want to exaggerate the strength of the bear so that those who wear the claws are more powerful. Still, I believe there's good reason not to hunt alone. Too much can happen."

Drewyer said, "I don't know. I don't think they were stretching the truth all that much. We've seen the tracks. This is a big animal and most predators are hard to bring down. This bear will take a well-placed shot. That's what I think."

Lewis said, "Captain Clark is correct, we should be careful on hunting trips and stay within rifle range of our hunting companions."

The room settled into buzzing conversation and the ceremonial pipe was again lit and passed around. The meeting lasted well into the evening.

November 30, 1804 Fort Mandan

The fort was completed and secure. It was morning, the sentry at the gate tower shouted to those below, "Rider coming in fast. Single rider."

Sergeant Ordway, hearing the announcement, shouted back, "Open the gate and let him in." Turning around, he hollered, "Labiche, go get Gravelines and the captains, we have an incoming Indian with something to say."

As the men reacted to the command, the fort came alive. The captains, having heard the shout, were coming out of their hut before Labiche could reach them. Labiche went on to Gravelines' hut and emerged with him a few moments later. Meanwhile, the rider had entered the fort and the gate closed behind him. He dismounted and seemed out of breath while the soldiers closed around him.

The rider began to talk to the Americans, "There's been an attack, the Teton and Arikara have attacked us. They killed our people and stole their horses. We were only a small hunting party."

Lewis was in disbelief. "Did he say Teton AND Arikara?"

Gravelines said, "Yes, that's what he said."

Lewis motioned with his hands and said, "Well, damn it. Ask him again. Is he sure there were Arikara with the Teton?"

Gravelines turned and translated while they all waited anxiously.

The rider said, "Many Arikara, many Sioux. They came up fast, very fast. The Arikara were in front and we did not believe they would make war. We believed in the new peace, the peace we have just made with them. When they got closer to us they began screaming out war cries, whooping and shouting, making much noise. They have killed Walking Quiet and wounded others. It was confusing. We fled in many directions, leaving our deer and elk meat for them. They captured all of our horses. Today, Walking Quiet is dead, two other of our people are wounded bad. Nine of our horses are gone and they took our deer and elk. Our chief said to tell Captains Lewis and Clark that their peace does not hold."

Lewis spoke to Ordway, "Sergeant, take this man inside. Get him something to drink and some food. Find out whatever else you can learn." Then turning to Clark he said, "I think we should talk." They walked away toward the captains' quarters.

Clark, following behind, entered their quarters and said, "I don't believe my ears, how can this be happening?"

Lewis flashed back, "I don't know, the Arikara and the Sioux. What the hell happened to the peace promises that were made? Do you think it was, could it have been, a renegade band of Arikaras? Just a few outlaws linking up with the Sioux or what?"

Clark paced and replied in a slow exhausted tone, "I don't know, Merry. I'm at a loss to explain this behavior. I think you must be right. It's got to be a small group of discontents running off to join their old allies for a little raid on the Mandan." He paced as Lewis listened, "They could be, do you think they could be, doing all this knowing that we'd learn of it? Is this a test? Some kind of a stupid test? A test of our resolve, our will to stand and enforce peace treaties? A Goddamn test to see what we'll do about their attacking our friends?"

Lewis replied, "Not sure, I'm just not sure. I do think that they must have realized that we would quickly learn of it. If there are Arikara that do not agree with our peace initiative, what better way to destroy the peace than staging an attack on a small hunting party? I still believe in peace. Maybe I just want to believe that Chief Hay and the other Arikara chiefs were sincere, that they really wanted peace." Then looking out the door he added, "As for the Teton, we were right about them all along. They're not to be trusted. If we'd believed those half-baked overtures of peace, they would have set on us for sure. I'm glad we trusted our gut feeling about them. They're power hungry, they're testing to find our reaction. By God I think we should let them see the kind of support the United States Army can provide. What do you think?"

Clark replied, "This whole thing has my head spinning. Of course it's a test, but I think we should make sure it's not a trap, too. No doubt about it, the Teton want to show their dislike of our befriending the Mandan. As for the Arikara, well, I'm not sure. Could be, I hope, just a small group of political mavericks. I'm with you, I think their leadership was sincere. We can't be that far off from reality, can we? Both of us can't completely misjudge a situation and misread the leader's intentions. One thing is sure, these western natives are not anything like the eastern natives."

Lewis was upset as he began pacing, "I'm sure they want to see what we'll do. Ya know, this could be a good thing for us. We can show the Mandan that the Americans are not just talk. We'll put our rifle barrels where our promises are. At the same time, we'll show the Teton that we support our friends and allies. Not by providing guns as they may think. We'll send our men to counterattack. But I agree it could be a trap. We have to be careful here. What about this? We'll send out Drewyer, Colter and Labiche as scouts to see if there are large numbers of them out there. Meanwhile, we should get the men ready to ride out."

Clark said, "Merry, what if they want us all to go chasing them? Leave the fort undermanned and weak. Then they can come in and take what they will."

Lewis snapped his fingers and replied, "Just so. I believe you're right. We cannot react in a predictable manner and leave our fort unprotected. Let's do this. We'll get the scouting report. I'll go meet the Mandan leaders with a small contingent. Let 'em know that we're there to support them, not with words alone, but with men and guns. We'll go and get the horses back, and if the Teton put up resistance, I'll kill their leaders. Meanwhile, you stay here and keep the fort on full alert. We'll double the guard and keep watch twenty-four hours."

Clark said, "Merry, I'm pissed at this turn of events, too, but I think you've got your Virginia blood up a little more than I do. The Mandan should see a cooler head. I think I should go and only take a few men. I'll take twenty men and leave right away. Twenty should be enough to show force and defend themselves. You and the rest of the men stay here and defend the fort."

Lewis stopped pacing and listened to his friend. Then he walked to the door and looked out across the courtyard. Turning to Clark he said, "I think that's good. I may very well have trouble holding my temper when I learn the details and confront the Arikara. You're cooler under fire, well, most times anyway. I do recall a mad redhead when you were dealing with the Teton chief." He paused and looked at his friend and said, " Yes, it's probably better that you go. Done."

Clark replied, "Done."

The scouts were briefed and left on horseback. Orders were not to engage but reconnoiter only and report back as soon as possible. They were to be back within two to three hours.

Meanwhile, Clark mustered twenty men and left the fort, marching across the frozen river to meet with the Mandan. They took the Indian rider with them to lead them to the party.

They reached the Mandan where they found an aroused and angered Chief Raven Man. The Indian leader spoke, "You see what has happened? Do you know what has happened?" He paced and shook a war lance as he continued, "Walking Quiet is dead. He believed in the white peace. Two others who were only hunting were wounded and left for dead. Is this the white peace with the Arikara?"

Clark replied, "We're disappointed to learn of this attack. We think that a few Arikara have not agreed with their chiefs and have left to join the Sioux. I've brought men to support your raid. Your counterattack on the Sioux will have our men and guns for support. We'll get your horses back."

Raven Man was still very irritated as he shrugged, "Hummph, these are the Arikara that I have always known. No change unless the white soldiers bribe them with presents. When you leave, so does the promise. They are liars, hear me, **liars**!"

Clark spoke firmly, "Chief, we are ready to fight to protect your people and preserve the peace. We believe that the Arikara in this raid were not the same as all Arikara. In every tribe, as the wise among you know, there are bad men. Those bad men should not make the image for all the men. Is this not true?"

Chief Raven Man replied, "It is good to see your swift reply when we have been attacked. Your numbers show us that you support your words. Now the snow is deep, and our elders say it will be cold soon, maybe tonight. They say cold will kill our men just as the enemy. As much as we would like to see Arikara blood on the snow and Sioux scalps on my lodge pole, we will not go. We will attack them later."

Clark countered, "Chief, peace is worth working for. Let us find the men that did this. We'll find out if they have acted alone."

Chief Raven Man let out a grunt and walked away; he would not discuss the matter further. He turned back toward the main village.

December 7, 1804

The tower sentry called out, "Riders coming."

Lewis, Clark and the sergeants were just finishing breakfast. They rose and walked toward the gate as it was opened to admit the guests. It was Chief Black Cat with a few others.

Lewis advanced and said, "It's good to see our friend Black Cat today. Welcome."

Black Cat waited for his men to surround him then spoke. "Our riders have told us there are many buffalo nearby. We'll be leaving soon to hunt. There will be fresh meat and new robes for the winter. You and your men have spoken of hunting with us. Today will be a good day. We must hunt early, before the cold."

Lewis replied, "Yes, we'll hunt with you. As soon as you provide horses. We'll get a group of men to go with you."

Black Cat questioned, "How many men will go?"

Clark replied, "How many horses do you have?"

Black Cat smiled, waved his arm horizontally and said, "We have more horses than you have men. How many will join us?"

Lewis replied, "I'll have fifteen men ready in as many minutes. It's cold and we want to get going soon. Can you provide extra horses to bring back the meat?"

Black Cat replied, "Horses are no problem. There are always horses ready for a buffalo hunt. There will be many squaws waiting for our return. They will make roasts and prepare the hides." Pausing, he turned to his men as one of them said something. Returning to Lewis he said, "Our people say we must move quickly. Our medicine men have warned us that it will be cold tonight."

Joseph Field said aloud, "Cold tonight! What the hell does he think it has been so far? It's been cold enough to freeze a bucket of water in a few hours. Why does he warn us now about cold? Hell, it's already cold now." They laughed, and all the men nodded in agreement.

The hunt was very successful. The Americans added to the success by killing eleven buffalo. They watched their Indian companions closely and were impressed with the agility of the Indian hunters on horseback. They effortlessly guided their mounts using their knees, freeing their hands to launch arrows. The horse and rider were as one. Their bows had enough power to put a well-placed arrow entirely through a buffalo. The Indian squaws would follow along to field dress the animals and pack the horses with meat. A lot of the women would carry the meat on their backs.

Sergeant Pryor said to Lewis, "Sir, the low clouds have broken; the sky is mostly clear now except for a ridge of clouds coming in from the northwest. See 'em, they are real high. Indians said it would bring the cold. What do you think?"

Lewis looked at Pryor and replied, "I don't know, Sergeant. It seems cold enough for me now, but the weather does look like a change. We should make sure we have firewood and blankets. It could get colder just as they say."

They concluded the hunt early in the afternoon and headed back to their villages to celebrate and cook. That night it became bitterly cold. In the morning the mercury showed the temperature had fallen to forty-five degrees below zero. That was the coldest night they would ever face.

Sergeant Pryor came to the captains' quarters and pounded on the door. Clark opened the door and a very cold Pryor entered. He shook lightly as he brushed his arms and said, "Forty-five degrees below zero sir. Forty-five! That's damn cold in anybody's book."

Lewis inquired, "Did you check the reading on all three thermometers?"

Pryor, blowing on his hands to warm them, replied, "Oh Yes, sir, I did, but I didn't have trouble believing it. All you gotta do to believe is go out there for twenty minutes."

Clark added, "Sergeant, this is too cold for the men to stand normal sentry duty. Put them on half-hour rotation, starting immediately."

Pryor replied, "Thank you, sir. I was going to ask for twenty-minute rotations, it gets awful cold out there."

Clark said, "Twenty minutes after the sun goes down, thirty daytime."

Lewis said, "Sergeant, make sure that you have a good fire going and that each man, upon returning from duty, is given priority at the hearth. The next man to go out should warm his breeches and blouse before putting his outer cover on. Maybe they can stay warm a little longer. Have them warm some stones by the fire to carry with them."

Pryor acknowledged, "Thank you, captains, I'll change the rotation immediately. I already told them to keep moving in tight circles and bundle up as much as possible."

Clark said, "Sergeant, leave that as a standing order until the mercury rises to at least ten degrees above zero."

Pryor nodded, "Done."

York entered the captains' quarters, as was his custom each morning, to find out what Clark may want him to do. York said to Clark, "York didn know it was possible to be this cold. York's been cold in Virginia afore, but this cold goes through clothes like they ain't nothing on."

Pryor said to the captains, "Did you hear the Indians? They predicted this. How did they know?"

Lewis said, "As I have said before, they live here. They are used to this climate. It is not unreasonable to think they can predict the changes. But I must agree, I have never known it to be this cold. The scary part is, this is early December! What will January bring?"

Pryor replied. "What bothers me is how do these people stay warm? I've seen them dressed in little more than a buffalo robe and elk skin. A normal body would freeze solid in a minute. How do they keep from freezing?"

Lewis replied, "I don't know. I have noted that very thing myself. I'm sure that they must have a high incidence of frostbite and people freezing to death."

Clark added, "I, for one, would like cotton underwear and a warm comforter. As for the natives, the customs of these people cause them to bear more cold than I thought it possible to endure."

January 1, 1805

"Did ya hear that?" John Colter said to Joseph Field. "York's complaining to Sergeant Ordway. Thinks he's got frostbite on his pecker. If that don't beat all. Ordway sent him to see the captains. Good thing. We can't treat him none here. Especially for that."

Field snickered and replied as he elbowed Colter, "Frostbit pecker, huh, well, no wonder. It's been colder than hell here and besides, he don't keep it in his pants much. Always out givin' away his black power to help the buffalo hunts."

Colter added, "Lord knows that's true. It's cold enough ta freeze almost any part left out very long. Just be glad you got loincloth to wear to keep your Johnny from freezin'. That was probably York's problem. No clean loincloth, so he went without. This weather's brutal, I don't ever remember it being this cold, ever."

Shannon smiled and said agreeing, "Sure is, I know I won't go out without a scarf over my ears and nose. Ever notice the natives? They don't wear hardly enough to keep a body warm. I honestly don't know how they keep from freezing their asses off. Then you take York, being black and all. If there's any such thing as geographic adaptation by race that these Indians use to keep from freezing, well, it would work the opposite for York. This is a long way from the African equator."

Joseph Field said, "Say what you will. Cold is cold, and damn cold is damn cold. It just don't matter what color your skin is. These natives have red blood just like we do and it will freeze just like ours will. I'll wager they lose people every winter to the cold."

Reubin Field said, "All I know is, it's cold. Is it cold enough to freeze York's Johnny? Well, I don't know, don't care, but all of us have had to have our toes, fingers, ears and private parts warmed up by the fireside after only twenty minutes on guard duty."

Shannon turned to Sergeant Ordway and asked, "How's the project with the boats going? They're frozen solid in the river, could be damaged some. I don't think we can get them out. Are we going to wait for better weather before we try to break 'em free?"

Ordway took a twist of tobacco from his mouth and replied, "Well George, them boats is froze in good. That's for sure. Ever time we try to get them chipped free, seems like we run into water. No one wants water on their feet in this climate. We've made some progress though and I think we'll continue to try every day the weather permits."

Colter replied, "I sure wish we had moved them boats when the river was running. Now, even with the winch, I don't think we've got the power to pull 'em out. Ropes will probably break when we apply force."

Ordway said, "Face it, we were too busy getting the fort built and set up. That had first priority. Nobody thought the river would freeze up that deep, that fast. Can't fault the captains there. This is one hell of a winter. Came on sudden, too. Who would've known? Anyway men, like any winter, there will be breaks in the cold. We'll use those to chip the ice and get her free."

Shannon inquired, "Sarge, how's the little prairie dog doing? I would bet it's not used to this cold either. I'd hate to see the little critter die after all the work we went through to get it here."

Ordway replied, "Mostly York takes care of it. He's good with animals. Big man with gentle hands, the animals seem to notice that and respond to him. He checks on it all the time even though it hibernates a lot. He has the birds eating from his hand. He cleans the cage up and gives 'em water. Like I said, York has a way with animals."

Colter said, "Good thing, too, I wouldn't know the first thing about caring for a critter. Especially one I never run across before. Do you think those prairie dogs could ever be domesticated? Can't ya just see it, kids playing with prairie dogs. I bet that would be some sight to see." Then looking back at Ordway, he continued, "I do agree with you, Sarge, about York. Ever notice Seaman? Why next to Capt'n Lewis himself, York's the one the dog prefers."

Joseph Field said, "Say what you will, York earns his keep. He works the towlines on the boats with all the rest. Works side by side with us then does extra duty as Captain Clark's servant."

Shannon laughed and replied, "An' the strange part is he still has enough energy left over to dance around the fire at night and sing to Cruzatte's fiddle. Then to top it all off, he donates his power on a regular basis."

Joseph Field added, "An' how about you, young George Shannon. Weren't it you that donated his power four times in one evening?" They all laughed. "Gotta say they did get buffalo the next day. Keep up the good work there, George, you're doing just fine."

Across the fort in the captains' quarters York had been examined and found that he did not have frostbite. He was relieved and promised to wear his loincloth at all times. As he was leaving, Sergeant Gass came in with Privates Labiche and Cruzatte. He directed his speech toward the captains as he stomped his feet and seemed to brush the cold off of his clothes. "The chiefs have sent an invite for us to join 'em. They know that today is a big day for us. They would like to hear the tambourine and Cruzatte here on the fiddle."

The excitable Cruzatte added, "an' Captains, it's important. Ol' Cruzatte here has heard that some of the French have new music for me to learn. I can teach 'em my tunes and they can show me some new ones. Wouldn't you want to hear some new tunes? I may even get a new bow for my fiddle. It's gonna be a good party to go…"

Lewis interrupted Cruzatte, "Yes, we'll go. We'll all join in celebrating 1805 with the traders and our Indian friends. And yes, we would like to hear these new tunes and give you time to master them, words and all." Then smiling as he looked around the room he continued, "An excellent idea, Sergeant, get with the other sergeants and decide which men will stay at the fort. We should enjoy this time. We'll go as soon as we can ready ourselves."

Gass inquired, "How big of contingent should stay in the fort, sir?"

Lewis replied, "Fifteen should be enough. We'll rotate the leave with the others so each will have an opportunity to visit the celebration festivities."

The men went across the frozen river to the Mandan villages to a large communal earthen lodge. The Indian chiefs were pleased to see the Americans. Big White spoke, "It is a good way to start the new white man year by celebrating with our white friends."

The Frenchmen in the group moved to converse with the French traders who had already been there awhile. They exchanged greetings and the musicians among them examined one another's instruments. After a few minutes of discussion, Big White rose and spoke. "We would like to hear your fiddle and tambourine. We do not have white man music and we enjoy it much."

When the translation was complete, the men struck up the music, and soon it was in full swing. The music reached a good rhythm and the men began to dance. One Frenchman, skilled in gymnastics, began to dance on his hands. He moved about the room with his feet in the air as he moved close to one Indian and then another. This brought a lot of OOOHHs and AAHs from the Indians who nudged one another and pointed at him and laughed.

Lewis was sitting with Clark, Pryor, Colter and Bratton. He looked around the room and then turned to Clark and said, "Our supplies will hold up, I think. We don't have to trade goods for food. We've been able to trade medical treatments and advice for grain and squash. I like that, keeps our supplies the same."

Sergeant Pryor added, "Have you seen our blacksmith shop? Bratton and Willard have set up shop in the fort that would rival anything I ever saw back East. Every day the Indians are bringing things they got from the British that need repairs or sharpening: hoes, knives, tomahawks and the like. Those two have a forge and bellows set up that work real good." Then, motioning to Bratton, Pryor asked, "Do you have one of those crazy tomahawks you made? Show the captains, they gotta see the damn thing."

Bratton beamed as he pulled a tomahawk from his waistband. "Kind of an ugly thing, not practical either, but it seems to be what they want. I get more goods for these than anything. Eight gallons of corn for each one. Now I think that's a good price. I don't know why they're so willing to pay so much. Maybe it's 'cause they're unusual, more of a collection piece than anything practical."

Clark looked amused as he examined the strange tomahawk, "Well, go figure. How many of these have you made?"

Bratton replied, "Seventeen so far, sir. They bring me old pots and I make these things. I'm getting better at it now, I can make two in the time it took me to make the first one."

Sergeant Pryor commented, "Just because it takes you less time and your production is up and all, don't take less for them. In fact, I'd raise the price."

Lewis said quickly, "No, that's not a good idea. We don't want to be like the Hudson Bay or North West Company, making exorbitant profits. That kind of word spreads fast. One man tells another what he pays for a thing, and the second or third man will quickly know we've changed our prices. Before long they'll either not trade at all or raise their prices too. No, keep your price the same, eight gallons of corn is fair, keep it there. If you are becoming more efficient in making them, well, that's your extra profit."

Sergeant Pryor inquired, "What if they offer different things? They don't always offer corn and squash."

Lewis nodded, "Do what is fair. If you're offered moccasins or something else other than corn, make a fair trade, equivalent to the corn."

Clark spoke up, "Men, we're here to be friendly neighbors. We want to show the natives that we are **not** like the British and French traders that they are accustomed to dealing with. We want them to support our concept of trading posts, peace and U. S. trading partners. The best way to do that is to make a fair deal. They'll ultimately know if the trade is fair or not. We want to make friends, not profits. Let us establish the idea of fair trade along with peace, we are ambassadors, too."

Lewis patted Clark on the shoulder, "I could not have said it better. Men, we are not the first whites these Indians have seen, but we are the first American soldiers representing the U. S. government. Each of us sends a message with what we do and how we treat these natives. Be fair and we won't have to worry about accounting for our actions later."

Private Bratton listened intently as the two captains spoke, then he simply replied, "Done."

January 26, 1805

Sergeant Gass came to the captains' quarters, "Captain Lewis, the woman that carried all that grain in to trade for medical services for her boy's frozen feet. Well, she's back, and he don't look none better neither."

Lewis rose and walked over to his doorway. Concern was on his face as he said, "Go get the lad, Sergeant, and let's see what is going on."

Gass disappeared and soon returned carrying the boy, his mother following close behind. "She told the interpreter, she don't have very much grain this time, maybe a half gallon. She carried all she could the first time. Wants to know if you will help him for what she has. She said that it's all she has."

Lewis replied, "All she's got? Why, that's more than anyone's ever paid me before. If she's willing to give everything, everything she has, we need to see what can be done."

He saw the worried look in the mother's eyes. He knew that severe frostbite would mean eventual gangrene, and, untreated, the boy would die. He looked at the boy who was obviously scared, moved to a table and leaned over a moment, exhaled and spoke. "Bring him here. Sergeant, get me some hot water and clean cloth. White if you can. Get some whiskey and some laudanum. Go to Bratton and get me a sharp, I mean sharp, knife. Get his sharpest saw too and bring it over."

The sergeant started to leave when Lewis said, "Oh Sergeant." Gass turned around. "Ask one of the men to get Captain Clark to help me here. I'm going to need help."

Gass looked at the captain and said, "Gonna cut 'em off, sir?"

Lewis looked at him a moment and nodded. Gass turned and disappeared as the fearful mother stood holding her boy and looking at his swollen, black toes. There were maroon-colored lines running to his ankle from the toes.

Lewis approached the woman and motioned for her to bring the boy over to the table. She obeyed quietly. He took the boy from her arms and gently set him on the table. Then, reaching over to a cot, he took a pillow and placed it under the boy's head. "Are you going to be brave here young fella? I sure hope someone told you that this is necessary. That you'd die for sure if I didn't cut these toes off. Sure wish we could have saved them the first time. Just froze too bad." Then he looked at the boy and placed a hand on his shoulder and said, "I'll try the best I can young man. It's just that this kind of surgery isn't certain, there's risk. Way out here, away from proper hospitals and bandages, well, I'll do the best I can."

The mother and son looked intently at Lewis as he spoke. They did not understand the language, but they could sense the concern and genuine feeling in his manner. Clark entered the room and looked at Lewis who simply glanced at the boy's feet.

Clark stepped over and lifted the foot up by the heel as he examined the toes. "I've seen this before. There ain't no choice here. It doesn't get any better, could get gangrene. Are you going to take them off?"

Lewis replied, "I don't have a choice. Bill, this little guy is going to die if we don't get rid of the gangrene."

"I suppose you're right. I don't see any other way either," Clark responded.

At that time Sergeant Gass entered with the materials Lewis had requested. Lewis ordered in a quiet tone, "Give him some laudanum, then a little whiskey. Save some whiskey to pour over his toes."

The boy took the medication and lay back. Clark bound his leg and foot to the table to hold it secure. "Ready when you are, Merry," Clark said in a hushed tone.

"I'm going to wait a few minutes for the whiskey and laudanum to take effect."

The boy went into a half-dazed slumber as his mother held his hands. Lewis moved quickly as he removed the blackened flesh, cut through the tendons and removed the toes. During it all, the boy did not scream out in pain. When it was over, the mother carried the boy outside. His father came and put him in a sleigh and they left without saying anything.

February 11, 1805

Sergeant Gass came to Lewis' quarters with a Frenchman, Jessaume, an Indian interpreter. "Capt'n, that Charbonneau feller's squaw, Sacajawea. Well, sir, it's her time. She's in labor and her husband asked Labiche to have you help. Did ya ever deliver a baby, sir?"

Lewis looked up and moved quickly to get his coat. "Get me some water, a sharp knife and something to use as a bandage. Did they say how long she's been in labor?"

Gass replied as Jessaume and Lewis walked through the door toward the hut, "Naw, nobody said how long. Must be awhile though because her husband announced that she was having trouble and would need help. He wanted Cruzatte to get an Indian midwife to help."

Lewis replied, "I've never delivered a baby, but I probably know more about medicine than the native squaws." Then he added reflectively, "Still, maybe it's not a bad idea to have a squaw here as a midwife. Tell Cruzatte to go get help."

Jessaume spoke with a French accent, "I can speak her language and ask how long she has been having pain. I can help you ask questions and let her know what you want to know."

"Good, Jessaume," Lewis said with a smile. "Having a new baby has got to be a better medical experience than just about anything. Sure beats treating tumors and diarrhea."

As the men approached the hut, Sacajawea's moans could be heard. Lewis entered first with Gass and Jessaume closely behind. Charbonneau saw the men come in and his eyes lit up as he spoke to Jessaume in French. "Tell them that she has been in labor for a long time, several hours. I do not want to lose the baby or the wife. I have said many prayers. She is brave but now, after so long, she just moans in pain."

Lewis knelt beside the young Sacajawea. He brushed her hair back from her sweaty brow as he took her pulse. He checked to see if he could see the baby and then looked up at Charbonneau and shook his head. "Tell him, 'no baby yet'. She must bear down with the labor pain. Tell him to tell her to bear down when she has pain. That should help the baby's head come out. From there on it is easy, the birth goes quickly after the head."

Jessaume translated for Lewis as Charbonneau listened and nodded. Then Jessaume said to Lewis, "I've heard the Indians say when a woman cannot bear a child that a potion of warm water and rattlesnake rattles will bring the child. They swear this will work. Do you want to try it? She's been in labor quite awhile."

Lewis looked at him strangely and repeated as if a question, "A potion of warm water with rattlesnake rattles?" Lewis looked at Gass and Charbonneau and then at the painful face of Sacajawea. "Sergeant, go to my quarters. Near my writing table is a small sack with some rattlesnake rattles. Bring them here. What the hell, let's try it. It sure can't hurt."

Gass was gone in an instant and quickly returned with the rattlesnake rattles. "Here ya go, sir. Although I don't see how any good can come from a critter as mean as a rattler."

Lewis took the rattles and ground them to powder with the heel of a cup. Then he pushed the granulated material into the cup and added water and stirred. He gave it to Sacajawea and said, "Here, drink."

She seemed to understand Lewis' command. As she grasped the cup, she looked at her husband. He nodded and motioned with his hands to proceed. Lewis looked at Gass and said, "Well Sergeant, I guess we'll see if there's any truth to this remedy. I've heard a lot of things that the natives practice as medicinal. A lot of it don't make sense, but some of it works. Let's see what happens."

Gass nodded as they heard footsteps approaching. It was Cruzatte. He spoke to Jessaume and Charbonneau in French. "There are two squaws coming to help, two midwives. They'll be here real soon."

A few moments passed. Sacajawea had a couple of labor contractions, but nothing happened. Then, in less than ten minutes from the time she had drunk the potion, she let out another moan as contraction pain gripped her body. She groaned and strained as she pushed. Lewis looked and reached down as he said, "Here it comes. I can see a baby's head! That's good. Push again. You're doing good. Just a little more, it's almost over. This is good."

Sacajawea did not understand the words, but instinct had her pushing again. With her last push the baby's head came out. Lewis cupped the baby's head in his hands and gently pulled as the baby's torso followed.

"It's a boy!" Lewis said as he tied a cloth around the umbilical cord. At that moment the two Indian midwives came into the hut. They looked at one another and then laughed.

Charbonneau beamed. "A boy, a son, this is my first child. My first and it is a boy! I'm happy today. I'm going to name him Jean Baptiste."

Lewis looked at Gass and said, "It hasn't been ten minutes since she drank the rattlesnake potion and here's the baby. I'll be damned. Some would say it's coincidence. Others would say it's too much of a coincidence. I'll have to think a bit on that one myself and reserve judgment until later. Maybe see the results in a second circumstance."

Gass replied, "It sure is a coincidence. Why that potion barely had time to work; it must be powerful. The baby had a smooth delivery after the head started. As if there had been no trouble at all until then."

Cruzatte turned to Gass and Lewis and asked, "Does this call for a little celebration? This is our first baby. Can we toast this new baby with a gill of whiskey?"

Lewis looked at Gass and nodded, "A gill of whiskey is certainly in order. Go ahead. Spread the word to the rest of the men that there's a celebration. But Pierre, be sure you tell them there's a new baby boy **before** you tell them there'll be a gill of whiskey."

Cruzatte replied, "Oh sir, Yes, sir. I'll shout about the new baby and whisper about the gill of whiskey."

March 12, 1805

The interpreter and guide, Troussaint Charbonneau, accompanied by Labiche and Drewyer, comes to visit the captains. The latter are along because of their ability to speak French and English. The Charbonneau family has been staying with the Corps of Discovery. It is assumed that they will be going with the expedition when it departs in the spring.

Labiche spoke, "Capt'ns, our interpreter has been talking with us. I think there is a problem. There's a big difference between what we've heard he'd be doing with us and what he's now saying he's willing to do."

Lewis frowned as he slammed down his compass and a group of papers on a table. He looked at Labiche, then at Charbonneau, and finally at Drewyer. There was silence as Lewis stared at the men.

Before Lewis could ask a question, Drewyer spoke, "I think he has changed his position because the time now grows near when we'll depart west, and he knows that we'll need his services. I think he believes we cannot now get anyone else to perform the work. Now he wants to talk again. Capt'n, he wants a new deal."

Lewis hesitated while the men seated themselves, then he looked at Charbonneau as he spoke to Labiche. "Francois, will you handle the translation? George, I want you to let me know when you think he's lying. Let me know what is being implied with his words."

The men nodded in agreement as Lewis continued with Labiche acting as translator. Lewis opened with a cordial question. "Mr. Charbonneau, how is your new baby boy? It's been a month now; is your wife doing well?"

Hearing this, Charbonneau smiled and replied, "Yes, the baby, Jean Baptiste, is doing well. Already he is bigger and stronger. Sacajawea seems to be a natural mother. The baby does not cry much before she has him calmed and happy."

"Good, that's good to hear, with such a small one about to make a big trip, it's good that he's healthy." Lewis then changed the subject to that at hand, "The men tell me you have something you wish to discuss with us. We do not have a written agreement yet, but we plan on adding you and your family to our expedition. We know we'll need horses to help us cross the mountains. Sacajawea's people have the horses and we'll need an interpreter to make trading arrangements for us."

Charbonneau listened and then replied, "Sacajawea is a Snake Indian. She'll be able to translate to the Snake you need for horses and help arrange the trade terms. She will speak to me in Hidatsa and I in French to any of your men. We are both needed for you to make this trade and the translation to take place." Then looking at the men he added, "I gave up my other wife to join this expedition. She will be left behind. That is a big sacrifice for me. I will take Sacajawea because she has my son. Because of my sacrifice, I want to be compensated for my loss."

Lewis was upset as he anticipated the new terms would not be favorable. Clark, seeing his friend becoming tense, spoke, "It would not be wise for one man to have two wives in a strange land where there are only men. Our men recognize and honor your wife and child as a family. They would have a problem with your having two women when they have none.

Surely you can understand this. To avoid problems it's good that you have not asked to bring both wives. That would not be wise. As far as compensation for not bringing a second wife, well, our pay offer will not be changed. Your personal circumstances were of your own doing and do not require compensation."

Charbonneau listened to the translation and stiffened his posture as he replied, using his hands as he spoke, "My wife is a translator, but it is me, Charbonneau, that is able to translate her words to French." He looked nervously at the captains as he continued, "I am important to you. You cannot get horses to cross the mountains without me. Because I am giving up much, I ask that you give me special treatment." Then he sat quietly during the translation and observed faces.

Lewis, now tense, said in a slightly louder tone, "Special treatment, what special treatment? What exactly is it that you think should be changed? What the hell do you want here?" His knuckles were white as he made a fist and pressed it against the table.

Charbonneau replied, "As an important translator, valuable to the success of your mission, and because I sacrifice to join your expedition, I must have the following conditions and terms: I will not work on the boats, nor will I do menial work around the campsites. I will not stand sentry duty at night. I will be with my wife and new baby. I will not stand guard over any supplies, nor will I be expected to lift heavy loads and handle supplies. If I have any disagreement with any man, any man, then I will be given a canoe and be able to return back down the river to the Mandan. Because I have a wife and baby, I will be given first choice of the available supplies. Should I leave, I will be given as many supplies as I will be able to carry at the time."

Hearing the translation, Lewis was furious. He slammed his fist on the table and did not listen as Labiche continued to finish the last of the translation. "Delusions of grandeur!" he said through his teeth as he rose up and motioned to Drewyer to join him outside.

Drewyer quickly joined him away from the others. Lewis looked at Drewyer and said through his teeth in a loud, almost hissing, tone, "Who the hell does he think he is, that arrogant bastard? He can't tell me what he will or will not do on the river. Let's get out of here before I lose it completely."

Clark shook his head as he listened to the translation and watched as Lewis stomped out of the hut. The moment was confusing and he held his hand out level as he spoke, "Calm down men, calm." He then looked directly at Charbonneau as he spoke, "On the river the demands on each man are the same. Physical demands do not change or discriminate because one man happens to speak Hidatsa, French or any other language. The work must be shared or you will not be respected. If you don't work, you will not eat. It's that simple. You will eat when we eat, work when we work, dance and sing when we dance and sing. As a commander I have never granted special conditions to any man under my command. I will not start now." Clark waited as Labiche translated, then he continued, "It is a sad day that you bring us word that you now have these demands. We cannot, will not, meet them. If this is your position, we'll not have you join our group. We are not without resources. We'll find another interpreter or make do. We have men among us that are skilled in sign language. It may be difficult, but we will prevail. Mr. Charbonneau, what we cannot do is let one man, regardless of his special talent or contribution to our progress, refuse to contribute, as required, to his full ability. Your demand is, frankly, ridiculous. Please leave our fort as soon as you can get your things together. Your proposal is inadmissible. You are no longer welcome here. Good day, sir."

With his final comment, Clark stood and addressed Labiche, "After you translate, escort this man and his family out of the fort. Have a small detail of yourself and three others escort him to the gate."

Clark walked out, just as Lewis had earlier and met his co-captain outside still talking with Drewyer.

Lewis turned to Clark and said, "That insolent bastard, he has wasted my time. He tries to change terms at the last minute when he thinks we can't do anything. This is, at the least, inconsiderate. It's self-serving and absolutely won't work. Why, the men would get mutinous and beat or kill him if he had special privilege. He thinks we're out of options. Our deal was fair. Verbal only, but fair. Where I come from a deal doesn't have to be in writing. A deal is a deal, a handshake is all that's needed."

Drewyer added, "This arrogant man, he has his head in his ass. He will think this over and realize he is stupid. Stupid. I'll immediately let the others in the trading villages know we're looking for a Shoshone translator. We should also ask the Minnetare if any of them knows the language and could come with us as translator."

Lewis responded, "Interesting idea. The Minnetare have contact with the Shoshone, true enough, but hostile contact. Maybe some of them speak the language and perhaps one would act as translator."

Clark said, "I hate to think of losing this opportunity. Replacing Charbonneau with Minnetare could have problems. Especially since their history with them has been so hostile. The Shoshone would be suspicious. We may be better off with sign language than hostilities."

Lewis looked at Clark a moment and replied, "This is all too new. I'd like to sleep on it and then discuss our options with Drewyer and the sergeants later. We could even ask Black Cat and the other chiefs if there are translators we could use. Let's not make a decision now." He turned to walk away, then stopped and said, "A man should stick to his word. Charbonneau is an ass."

March 17, 1805

It was nearly noon when Drewyer came to Lewis and said, "Capt'n, the interpreter Charbonneau is at the gate. He wants to talk to you. He said he has seen his foolishness and wishes to talk to you about re-joining the expedition. Do ya want to see him?"

Lewis looked from Drewyer toward the gates of the fort as he replied, "Well, I'll be damned. I'm in a good mood today. Tell him I'll see him. Ask one of the men to get Captain Clark and meet in our quarters. Get Labiche to join us. Same as before, you stay too. We'll hear what he has to say."

Lewis arrived in his quarters only a few moments before Clark entered. Clark had a huge grin on his face, "He's back huh? Well, I should hope he has come to his senses. I didn't want to use Minnetare translators, there's bad blood out there."

Lewis replied, "Even a fool would see the position he took the other day was ludicrous. He must be used to dealing with squaws. He has got to know that real men don't deal that way. I wonder how long it took him before he realized his stupidity?"

"I'll wager he wasn't even out of the gates yet," Clark said. "It's just taken him this long to get courage up to apologize."

The footsteps of the approaching men stopped the conversation. As they waited, Drewyer, Labiche and Charbonneau entered and were seated. Charbonneau spoke to Labiche a few moments and then looked at the captains and spoke. "I am tired of being a fool. I've come to you now to say that my demands were made without thinking. I've seen military groups before. I should have known there would be no way to accomplish the demands. In fact, I believe now that those demands would have, as the good Captain Clark pointed out, led to disruption in the men and caused them to hate me. Out there on the river, I should not want to be hated." He looked back and forth as Labiche translated, then he added, "I have been the fool, I apologize. I ask that you permit me to re-join and serve in any way you need. Charbonneau, the good interpreter, will do whatever the captains wish him to do."

Lewis rubbed his chin as he listened to the translation. He nodded slowly and then responded. "Mr. Charbonneau seems to have realized the error of his ways. Today we are forgiving, our original offer still stands. You'll be paid as originally agreed. You must realize you'll also share in the work, whatever the work may be at the time. Each man will help the others. There is no other way."

Charbonneau listened as the words were translated, then replied, "I will work as one of the men. You may use me where needed the most. I should point out that you may find I have some talents as a cook, a needed service with so many hungry men. My wife may be able to help me prepare food. We will work with your cook if that is acceptable to you."

Clark smiled and said, "Now we are getting somewhere, a definite change in attitude. I don't know how a French chef can do much with only elk, buffalo, venison and beaver to work with, but that, my friends, is what a French cook is good at doing."

The translation was made, and all the men laughed. Lewis stood first, followed by the others. "It is done then, you and your wife will join us as translators. Until we reach the mountains and the Shoshone, you will work when called upon and serve in any capacity that Captain Clark, the sergeants or I deem necessary."

Charbonneau listened intently to the translation and was nodding as it was concluded. Clark extended his hand to shake and said, "It is done then?"

Charbonneau replied in English, "Done, Captain."

April 7, 1805

The day is beautiful, the sun shining warm and brightly. There is a gentle southwest breeze as the men are all outside working on loading the boats in preparation for departure. The ice has been breaking up on the river more and more each day. Large chunks of ice are floating downstream, bumping into each other, creating swirls and whitewater waves. Other chunks slam against the shoreline, catching momentarily on the shallow waters and dislodging sections of the riverbank. The Indians walk out across the ice floats to snare drowned buffalo that are floating downstream to recover the hides.

The Corps of Discovery has completed construction of six canoes using tree trunks. They have them lined up next to the red and white pirogues at the water's edge, awaiting loading instructions. The large keelboat, Discovery, is being prepared to go back downstream to St. Louis. Every man that can write has written letters to his family and loved ones. Lewis has several scientific journals on the flora, fauna and mineral discoveries he has made. There are carefully prepared specimens, each laid out with accompanying detailed explanations. Lewis has written encoded letters to Jefferson regarding the Indian tribes and the white trading establishments. Lewis also includes personal, non-encoded letters to the president. He also has several others to his mother and family. Clark includes volumes of maps of the river and its tributaries, the first accurate maps of their kind. He also has letters to his brother and to his girlfriend Judith, who is waiting back home for him.

Included with the outbound mail are papers from their British friends in the North West Company. These are principally letters to Jefferson regarding acknowledgment of U. S. sovereignty over the area and promises of fair trading practices. Lewis and Clark have spent a great deal of time impressing on them what they must do. They insist on continual acknowledgment of U. S. sovereignty, including display of the flag. They must exercise fair dealings with the natives. Failure to do so or failure to pursue peace among the natives will force the United States to establish competing trading posts.

Discovery has Corporal Warfington in charge along with the returning members of the crew. Also leaving are Gravelines and some French traders going as far as the Arikara villages. The men that had been separated from the main body for disciplinary actions are also being returned. On board are the live specimens of the magpie and the prairie dog, animals kept alive by York all winter. These animals go with personal instructions from Lewis in a letter to Jefferson regarding their care.

The men are all working arduously but happily; this is a labor of high anticipation. They are now preparing for the true expedition. It's what they have waited the long, cold and boring winter for. It is what they have spent the previous year toiling to achieve. They are about to embark on a venture into the unknown, into lands where no white man has ever been. This is the Corps of Discovery.

Lewis and Clark sat having a late lunch as they watched the men loading the boats and executing their orders to prepare for departure. Clark said, "I have to hand it to Newman, he did try his best to repent for his actions on the way up. He was always there to do any difficult task. I think he really was sincere in repenting."

Lewis replied, "I know, but conditions at the fort were under control and predictable most of the time. Newman had shown insubordination earlier, and that is more a character fault than any specific act of defiance. Yes, I agree, he did bust his butt to show he was sorry about the insubordination. If I were at a post back East, I would reinstate him fully. But that's not the case. I'm not willing to bet the morale or success of the Corps of Discovery on a man that has demonstrated weakness under fire."

Clark who was nodding slowly all the while replied, "I know you're right. I thought this over several times and came to the same conclusion. He's a good man, and yes, given the right circumstances, at a fort back East or a post with adequate exposure to frequent trade, he would probably continue to be all right. But, that ain't where we're going. I never thought of it as a character fault, but I think you are right. He may have difficulty out in the unknown elements. We'll have plenty to overcome without bringing along a potential problem that we already know about."

Lewis answered, "I wrote out instructions to pay him half the pay the others are entitled to. I think that's fair, especially since he won't have to face the rigors of the trail."

Clark quipped, "I agree, he had extra baggage that wouldn't show up until the wrong time. We couldn't take him no matter what."

Lewis reflected a moment and then asked, "Do you think we did any good here? Were our peace efforts effective? Sometimes I think I may as well have been talking to cattle. The Indians seem all too willing to go on raids to steal horses. Their hostilities against one another are longstanding and deep."

Clark joined, "And counterattacks, reprisals and raids of their own. I don't know, Merry, peace isn't easy. War is easy. You've got to work at peace. It doesn't just happen the first time it's tried. I think that with time the Indians will recognize the fruits of peace. Some of them seem to be reasonable men. Perhaps after we have established trading posts in a few years, peace will follow."

Lewis added, "Yes, I think so, when we get trading posts, forts and civilized cities out here, their petty raids and battles will give way to peace. I have to believe that. Jefferson knows democracy and peace are the best way for humanity to survive."

Clark asked, "You seemed to get along well with Hugh McCracken. I thought that our efforts with the British and French traders were successful. How do you read the British? Do you think they're sincere?"

Lewis leaned back in his seat as he spoke. "McCracken is a good man even though he is British. I think we got the message across that the only flag to fly is ours, and he understands that means all that goes with it. Really, Bill, these merchant traders over here are a long way from the Crown. I believe they see things differently. Their motives are monetary. McCracken said so himself, his short-term goals are to make money for the North West Company. They're smart enough to see the political change of the purchase. They'll keep our flag overhead, and they should practice fair trade with the Indians."

Clark added, "They should support the peace efforts we have tried to establish. After all, there is more profit for them if all the Indian tribes can bring their furs and hides to trade without worrying about being raided by a neighboring tribe. Peace makes good business sense, and like you said, for them it's just a business."

Lewis nodding said, "I think so. They aren't concerned about sovereignty and won't be a problem that way. McCracken sent quite a few letters back to the President to reassure him that they are here only to conduct business."

Clark said, "I think of all of them, McCracken's group is the most trustworthy. But the basic philosophy is true for XY and Hudson Bay companies, too. They'll support the government in power as long as they can continue to conduct business. They know that the current power is ours. I think they believe they must begin to employ fair trade practices or suffer the consequences as the territory gets settled."

Lewis said, "If, my friend, they have long-term foresight. All too often they're blinded by short-term profits. We can check on them to see if they are taking fair profits on our return."

They sat and watched as the final touches were being put on *Discovery*.

After a moment of silence, Lewis spoke, "Bill, I've got a small favor to ask."

Clark turned toward his friend, "What?"

Lewis continued, "When we head out, I don't want to leave in the boats. I'd like to just walk along the riverbank. I've got so much pent up energy from spending the winter here that I really need to work it off with a good walk. Besides I can resume my studies of flora and fauna. I'll take Drewyer with me for an extra gun."

Clark nodded and replied, "Sure thing, I could recognize your mood a mile away. Fussing and looking for your traveling plant press, fiddling with the compass, pacing while the men were loading the canoes. Yes, Merry, I'd say you're ready to go for a long walk."

Lewis smiled and said, "Thanks." Then looking out at the river's edge he added, "Bill, just look at our little fleet there. Six handcrafted canoes and two pirogues. They hold everything we've calculated to make the journey across the unknown. Everything we'll need to subsist or to defend ourselves. I don't know about you, but I'm proud of them. As proud as ever Columbus or Captain Cook could have been of their craft. I'm sure we have a better crew than they did. The men are all in good health and almost as eager as I to get underway. I can say without reservation that this truly is the best day of my life."

Clark smiled as he listened to his friend describe the pride he felt in the small fleet of river craft. "And proud you should be, Merry, you've spent years preparing for this, physically and mentally. Those little craft hold more than just our provisions, they hold our dreams."

"At least ten years' worth," Lewis replied, "I've had this in my mind since, well, I don't rightly know. It's been my darling project as well as Jefferson's. Seems like I always wanted to explore the West." Then he looked westward and continued, "We are now on the brink of it, heading into country at least two thousand miles in breadth, upon which the foot of civilized man has yet to trod. I see the future as challenging, even threatening, but very bright. Hard work but pleasing as we uncover new sights and record new discoveries."

Clark added, "Ya know, Jefferson sure knew what he was doing. This will create a great nation as people move behind us to settle these lands."

Lewis replied, "And unity, we now have a goal that will unite the country just as it unites these men. The people will no longer think of themselves as thirteen or fifteen or even seventeen states of the East. We'll have it in the minds of the populace that we are an ocean-to-ocean country. They'll depend on our reports to lead the way."

Clark stood and said, "Quite right my friend. It's important, and I think we better get to it. Let's go see how the cargo is stowed and how close we are to shoving off."

As they walked over to where *Discovery* was being prepared to return, Sergeant Pryor was talking to Corporal Warfington. "When you get to St. Louis, make sure the captain's letters to the president get sent back right away, special dispatch if you have to. The other letters and packages to the families get second priority. Be careful going through Teton territory. Keep her in the middle of the river, keep a guard out and try to run at night. Only anchor at sandbars, never on shore. Stay quiet, and you may be able to sneak through unnoticed."

Clark spoke up, "Good advice, Sergeant, but I would not assume that your passage will go unnoticed. Keep all guns loaded. Maintain watch at full alert until you are well past them. Don't go ashore for any reason. You'll have the current at your back so you should be able to make good time. They won't know your strength and probably won't risk attack. They've seen our guns."

Warfington replied, "I'll keep everyone quiet, sir, you bet. I don't want a run-in with the Teton. We've got enough provisions to float past them without need to hunt or discharge our weapons. No need to tell us stay on full alert, we all want to keep our scalps."

Lewis looked solemn as he stepped close to Warfington, faced him and grabbed his elbow. "Corporal, listen well to the advice you have been given. You carry the results of a year's work with you. People back East will be anxious to learn of our first year's activity. Take care of all the mail and mind what Sergeant Pryor told you. Keep her in the middle of the river where the current is swift and out of harm's way. We're proud of you, Corporal; this is an important mission." With that he released Warfington's elbow and stepped back.

With this final word, the men leaving for St. Louis shook hands with those proceeding on. Captain Lewis watched as the keelboat he had designed and brought all the way from Pittsburgh slipped into the river's current and floated around the first bend in the river and out of sight. He took a deep breath, exhaled and turned to look at his crew. Clark, observing his friend, gave his orders, "Alright men, load the boats. We're ready to push off." He motioned to Sergeants Ordway and Gass.

The sergeants, in turn, gave their orders. Ordway spoke, "Get the Charbonneau family in the red pirogue, Labiche take the white pirogue, Cruzatte take the lead in the red. Everyone push off together. Men, we are **underway**!"

There was a loud and simultaneous cheer from the men as they moved toward the boats. Several of the Mandan were gathering along the river's edge to watch as the boats departed. Many teenage boys were running along the riverbank following the boats as they moved onto the river. The boats moved in unison as they sought the less swift water near the edge and moved against the current upstream.

Lewis stood for a moment, Seaman at his side, then picked up his rifle and satchel. "Come on, Seaman, we've got a long way to go. There's a whole continent waiting for us out there." Turning to Drewyer he commented, "George, I will be walking with Seaman here. Stay next to me or at least within rifle range. We'll be in the unknown again."

With long strides Lewis moved out as they walked along the river floodplain. They would meet with the men again closer to evening. Lewis, ever the observer, would collect specimens of the newly budding plant life for recording. The wind was gentle and continued from the southwest. Lewis raised his eyes to the horizon and walked away from Fort Mandan. As they walked the sounds of the men singing and chatting on the river faded in the distance.

April 13, 1805

The white pirogue would be the flagship of the small fleet. She was slightly smaller at thirty-seven feet, against the forty-one of the red pirogue. Yet she was a more stable craft, especially when under sail. The pirogues were flat-bottomed boats and required good helmsmen to navigate smoothly against river currents and crosswinds. Due to their larger size and available cargo space, the pirogues were loaded with the more valued goods of the expedition: gunpowder and shot, the writing paper and ink, as well as the laptop writing desks used by the captains for regular journal entries. On board were astronomical instruments, compasses, thermometers, the gift packages for the Indians, as well as the three men that could not swim, along with Charbonneau, Sacajawea and the infant, Jean Baptiste. By prior arrangement, only one of the captains would be on the water in the pirogue at any given time. The other would supervise the pulling shore crew and make observations. The cottonwood canoes were round-bottomed craft and held only three oarsmen, food and camping gear.

"The damned things are back," Clark said loudly as he swatted a mosquito on the back of his hand. "I wonder how long it will be until there are swarms of 'em."

Sergeant Gass added, "Those little monsters, I was hoping it would be a few more weeks before they started in."

Cruzatte hearing the captain replied, "Yes, sir, they're here, I saw one earlier today. The wind is good today; that usually keeps them away."

Clark acknowledged with a nod and added, "It's still early, only about nine, there's a favorable wind coming up. Let's take advantage of that and hoist all sails. Pierre, let's see if we can make some good time today." Clark turned to the other boatsmen and shouted orders. "Sergeant, hoist the sail on the pirogue and catch this wind. We are going to put some miles behind us today. You canoe men, stay close to the shoreline and keep up with the sailing craft. Today is going to be a good day."

Lewis, on the shore, nodded in agreement and waved a hand westward as the men moved out. The shore crew consisted of eight men, Lewis and Seaman. They would hunt for fresh game to provide for the evening meal. Continuing the practice employed on the trip from St. Louis, they would stop to eat only the evening meal. The midday meals were taken enroute in the form of pre-cooked meat and corn.

In the afternoon the steady gentle wind turned into a sudden gust or squall. The wind was strong enough to turn the white pirogue sideways in the river. Charbonneau, at the helm, lost control of the craft and let out a cry in French, "What is happening? The boat, the boat, I cannot steer!" Just then, a second gust of wind caught the sails of the boat, now in the worst possible position, being broadside to the wind, nearly tipped her over. The boat was leaning sideways in a precarious position for a few moments while Charbonneau cried out, "Oh my God, I cannot swim good, save me, save me!"

The same wind that had gusted briefly and laid the boat on her side, suddenly calmed. Lewis, observing the action of the inept Charbonneau, shouted a command to Drewyer, "George, take charge there! Take the helm from him and get

her under control." Instantly Drewyer moved into action. He reached out with his right hand and grabbed Charbonneau's shirt over the right shoulder. With a powerful pull he pulled himself forward while jerking Charbonneau down, putting him on his hands and knees.

Charbonneau cried out in French, "What are you doing? ...o ashore."

...vered through his teeth, "Shut up, you coward ...and stay out of my way or I will throw you ...ish, Drewyer commanded, "Take the sails ...wind won't capsize us. If we don't right ...lay her on her side, and we'll take on ...had been leaning over the side to use their weight to keep the boat afloat responded quickly, and the pirogue was again righted and smooth on the water. With the pirogue now upright and calm, Drewyer ordered, "Reset the sails, if we keep her attitude right with the wind, we'll be all right."

Lewis observing from shore shouted, "Is everything all right over there? Did you take on water? Do you need to come ashore or can you bail?"

Shannon responded, "It's alright now, Capt'n, she's steady now with Drewyer in control. It might not be a bad idea to go ashore and make sure some of this stuff isn't too wet. Some waves splashed in on us."

Lewis looked around and then replied, "George, see that bend in the river ahead, just past the sandbar. Pull in there. We'll make camp and check the goods for damage."

The boats pulled in one by one, and the men pulled the noses part way onto the land to secure them. They unloaded to make camp. Clark, who had been on the red pirogue at the time, came over and inquired, "What happened out there, Merry? I could hear shouting but couldn't make out much. I saw the white nearly on her side."

Lewis shook his head and looked down momentarily as he responded, "That squall caught the white unprepared. Charbonneau didn't know what to do. He steered exactly the opposite of what he should have. He turned her sideways into the wind and nearly laid her over. If the wind hadn't calmed momentarily, she would have capsized. He would have been better to let go completely than to steer sideways the way he did." With a disgusted look on his face he looked at Charbonneau and continued, "That man is simply stupid. He began praying when he should have taken action. Good thing Drewyer was there. He took over and got her righted." Then he looked around as he watched the men unloading the cargo and checking for water damage. "Bill, maybe this was a good lesson. I had all the papers, the instruments and all the valuable cargo in one boat. That was stupid on my part. Going forward we'll split it up. If bad fortune befalls one boat, at least we won't lose everything."

Clark, listening intently to his friend, replied, "Right. We can ill afford to lose it all with one mishap. They're unloading it anyway to check for water damage. I'll have them reload in different boats. Good idea, we should have done that sooner." Then looking at the plant press Lewis was carrying, he asked, "How was the investigation on the shore today? See anything worth mentioning?"

Lewis replied, "As a matter of fact I did. I collected some plants. Colter put them in my press for me. I think there'll be even more specimens as we advance upriver. Do you want to see them?" Clark nodded as Lewis paused a moment to open the plant press.

Clark commented as he looked at the plants, "We saw several buffalo carcasses along the river's edge earlier this morning. Apparently victims of drowning. Probably fell through the ice last winter and are just now being exposed as the spring melt continues. I think the wolves and bears have

</br>
</br>
/tl

hi.

ie"

un all

hunt

good

Indians

hunt in

ath as many
tracks as I saw today, it won't be long before we encounter this
legend of a bear." Then with a smile he added, "Got any of
that lovely paint we brought for the Indians? They said they put
it on for a bear hunt just like for a war party. It's quite a deal
for them to hunt these bears."

Just then Sergeant Ordway came up and said "Excuse me,
captains, but the Indian woman, Sacawaga, well, whatever her
name is. She has some vegetables for us. Did you notice her
out there with a baby on her back, hunting for vegetables?
Uncanny how she seems to know where to look. We sure have
plenty of artichokes to add to the evening meal because of
her."

Clark said, "Well, I'll be. How about that? I think it would
do us all good to have a few vegetables to go along with the
meat each day. It's good to add variety, and these artichokes
will make our supply of corn and squash last longer."

Ordway asked, "That Charbonneau fellow, he claims to be
able to cook, should we let him?"

Clark replied, "Sure, why not? He has to be a better cook
than he is a boatsman. Stay with him and make sure he does all
right. We should encourage his talent. The trail is long, and we
need to identify strong points of anyone whenever we can."

Ordway looked at Lewis and inquired, "See any new animals today, sir?"

Lewis replied whimsically, "I did see two new types of mosquitoes that I had never seen before. I have some plants drying in the press, but that's all."

"New mosquitoes!" Ordway replied in horror. "That's all we need to complete the day. Wait till the men hear about that. Maybe now they'll fight over which ones get to suck us dry. Were they bigger than the others? Maybe we can stuff one and send it back East with the other specimens."

Lewis smiled and said, "No, not bigger, they were just of a different marking, but they seem to all be endowed with the same willingness to bite."

Ordway replied, "Well, I for one, don't look forward to meeting those newly discovered friends. There's been no shortage of the old kind."

Lewis changed the subject and inquired, "The Indian squaw, Sacajawea, how did she get those artichokes?"

Ordway said, "I think she looked for caches of the mice and small rodents. How she found those, I don't know. The rodents dig little holes and put the food they gather in there. She was walking along the riverbank over there with a stick. Pokin' it in the ground back and forth, and then she would stop, take a knife and dig. Sure enough, there'd be artichokes and grain in the hole, all ready and wait'n. She found quite a few of 'em too, and all the while carrying the baby on her back. Quite a little woman, that one."

Clark looked at Lewis and inquired, "What was the lay of the land out there? We couldn't see much from the water."

Lewis replied, "The land is mostly level and stretches for miles in all directions. The soil is uniformly fertile, mostly a dark loam intermixed with fine sand. The most common vegetation is grass; I didn't see trees except near the river's edge."

Clark replied with a laugh and smiling said, "Your answer sounds more like a report in your scientific journal than a re-

Clark paused and then replied, "That's a good theory, but I think there is so much grassland here that it must simply be a natural plain. All the grazing animals could be a factor, too. Just like the fires, the little trees don't get a chance to sprout up before they get nibbled off."

The conversation ended and they walked toward the camp where the men were laying out goods from the pirogues. Others were making fires for cooking dinner, and some were pitching tents for the evening. Lewis and Clark shared a large tent made of buffalo skins with the Charbonneau family. Drewyer also stayed in their tent and provided the communication link as interpreter. This camping arrangement would continue throughout the trip. It separated the only woman, with her husband, from any temptation the men may have had.

Ordway said to the men that were pitching tents, "Make sure you get the mosquito netting out. They're starting early this year, and Captain Lewis said he discovered a couple new kinds."

The men simply nodded and continued working.

Lewis turned to Colter and said, "That coal we found in the outcropping back there. Put some in the fire, and let's see how it burns."

Colter replied, "Sure thing, Capt'n. Do you suppose we can use the coal instead of firewood? There sure is a scarcity of trees in these parts."

Lewis answered, "Well the answer is in the test. If it works, we can collect some as we go along and use it for cooking and night fires."

They proceeded to settle in for the camp. Lewis made celestial observations to fix his longitude and latitude and wrote them in the journal. Cruzatte played the fiddle and used some of the new tunes he had learned. York and Shannon danced, and the men were in good spirits.

Lewis said to Clark and Sergeant Pryor, "I think we're getting close to the mouth of the Yellowstone. If the Indian descriptions are correct, we should see it soon. Tomorrow I'll advance along the larboard side and see if we can find the Yellowstone."

Pryor inquired, "Who do you want to go with you, sir?"

Lewis reflected momentarily and then answered, "Drewyer, the Field brothers and Colter. Let them know; they'll appreciate not having to row."

Pryor replied, "I'll let the men know."

Clark said, "Colter told me you had a friend today. A buffalo calf followed you?"

Lewis smiled, "I was going to get to that. Strange thing, I was walking along, and this little buffalo calf chose to follow me. He went along beside me for quite awhile, couple miles I'd say. Probably its mother had been killed by wolves."

Clark asked, "What happened to it? Did it simply quit following you, or did Seaman chase it off?"

Lewis responded, "Seaman didn't chase it. In fact, I think the calf thought Seaman was a relative. Probably figured if Seaman could walk along with me, so could he. Then later I chased after something. You men spread the word. If Seaman comes back to camp this evening, let me know. Wake me if he comes in."

Dratton responded, "Sure, Captain, we'll all look for him. Maybe with the smell of the cookin' he'll come in by hisself."

Lewis repeated, "Remember, wake me no matter what time it is."

Dratton nodded said, "Done, sir. We'll look for him in the morning.

Lewis spent a restless night. Drewyer, a light sleeper, noticed the restless Lewis and whispered, "Captain, we will most likely find the dog tomorrow. We have a strong scent for him to find. Don't worry; this dog can handle himself." Lewis nodded and tried to sleep.

In the morning, the camp began to awaken and get ready to depart. Everyone knew Seaman was missing, and everyone kept an eye out for him as they proceeded with their chores of preparing for departure. The morning was cold, so cold that there was ice forming on the oars and boat hulls. Clark prepared to leave with the river crew. The small crew Lewis had selected earlier prepared for the day's march in search of the confluence of the Missouri and Yellowstone. York, who had been at the edge of the campsite looking downriver, suddenly turned and came over to Clark's side and said, "York sees something moving out there in the haze, comin' toward us it is. York thinks it's Seaman comin' back ta join us."

Clark immediately looked in the direction York indicated. "By golly, I think you are right. Run and fetch Captain Lewis. Tell him Seaman is coming back."

York ran across the campsite to where Lewis was watching the men folding up his tent and packing it into the red pirogue. "Captain, York seed ol' Seaman coming in this morning. Just moving through the tall grass and dew like he had no worry about nothin'."

Lewis looked at York and gave a quick nod, "Thanks, York."

With that, he immediately ran across camp to where Seaman was now clearly in view, walking slowly in from the downriver direction. Lewis said as he knelt to give the dog a hug, "Seaman, hey, ol' boy. Where you been all night? Don't you know that out here that's desertion? What you been doing all night? Did you go looking for our friend the buffalo calf?"

The large dog simply wagged his tail and licked Lewis and was joyful in the reunion.

April 26, 1805

Lewis ascended and stood atop a hill near the confluence of the Yellowstone and Missouri Rivers. Joseph Field and John Colter were the first to join him.

Lewis said, "Just look around men. Have you ever seen such a beautiful land? Out there you can see the Yellowstone meandering toward its confluence with the Missouri. They seem happy to greet one another, these two rivers, lined with trees and feeding this fertile valley."

suppose, are more comfortable grazing in the open."

As the men watched and talked to the others, Drewyer and Reubin Field joined them. Reubin Field said to the others, "I could hardly believe it. We were walking down there where all those animals were grazing on the grass, and none of them were afraid of us. It was like the Biblical Garden of Eden. The animals were so close we could have shoved them out of the way. Some of them, antelope especially, seemed to recognize that we were different but were not afraid. In fact, they would follow us along, just being curious. Strangest damn thing I ever saw."

Lewis nodded and said, "I know it, men, Reubin has it right, this is a sort of Eden. I think that as this country is settled, these animals will adopt a more fearful respect of man. The trappers, farmers and traders will harvest these animals to where they'll develop a respect for hunting they don't have now. This moment in time, this place, these animals, is a rare moment. I don't think it will last long."

Joseph Field replied, "These great plains, why, any farmer should be able to raise large herds here with little effort."

Lewis answered, "Yes, those who follow after us will have the wealth of the fur trade followed by the natural wealth of these fertile prairies."

Just then they heard the sound of distant gunfire. It came from downriver. Drewyer looked in the direction of the shots and said, "We'll have fresh buffalo meat this evening."

Lewis smiled and began walking downhill, "That's good enough for me. I'm hungry now. By the time we reach Captain Clark and the others, I'll be more than willing to have some fresh buffalo."

Joseph Field joined in, "Me too, all this walking and fresh air, sure works up an appetite."

Lewis walked with a steady stride, and the men fell in with him as they moved downhill to meet the others. Lewis continued, "Tomorrow, Joe, I want you and Reubin to go up the Yellowstone as far as you can and still be able to return in one day. I want a report on the river itself; width, depth, riverbank composition, vegetation on both sides. Keep particular watch for signs of Indians, where they may have built fires, camps and such. If you meet with any Indians, let them know where we are and that we would like to talk with them. If you see any unusual plants, take a sample and bring it back. Meet us back here."

Joseph Field replied, "With pleasure, sir. Reubin and I used to hike all over Kentucky as kids and then tell our folks about it that evening at supper. This is more of the same."

Reubin said, "Well, not exactly the same, brother; this is all new, all different. It'll take both of us just to tell everything we see tomorrow."

Lewis smiled and added, "You men know how important documenting is to me. You see me writing in the journals all the time. When we get back, people will depend on our descriptions to be able to learn what's here."

Colter spoke up saying, "I'm going to enjoy listening to Pierre playing his fiddle and tambourine tonight. Just being out here makes a man want to dance around a fire."

others entering the camp. He shouted at Lewis, "How did it go today? How far up the Yellowstone did you get?"

Lewis laid his rifle down as he looked his friend in the eye with a broad smile. "It's beautiful out there. Joe Field had it right. It's like a biblical Garden of Eden. We saw game so close we were nearly brushing against them. They were un-afraid and would even follow us. We looked down at the river valleys from some hilltops; could see for miles. Tomorrow I'm dispatching the Field brothers to explore the Yellowstone as far as one day's travel will take 'em. I'd like to know if it differs much from the Missouri."

Clark, listening intently, nodded and responded, "Well, I measured the rivers at the confluence. The Yellowstone has the broader bank-to-bank measurement at eight hundred fifty-eight yards, but that includes sandbars and all. Depth was twelve feet."

Lewis said, "The Mandan said it was navigable all the way to the mountains, it's no doubt a respectable tributary."

Clark continued, "The Missouri measures five hundred twenty yards bank to bank, with the water measuring three-thirty. That's slightly wider than the Yellowstone at two ninety-seven. Seems like the Yellowstone is wider in its bed, maybe meanders a little more than the Missouri, but she's not as deep or swift. Has cleaner water though."

Lewis said, "Now it's you that sounds like a journal entry. The Missouri has more muddy water. Probably has more tributaries and a larger drainage basin." Then he looked around at the area and said. "We are lucky to see all this first. Like it is now. I have a lot to write about tonight. Did you see any Indians?"

Clark shook his head, "No, and that surprises me a little. I've seen some older campsites and evidence, nothing fresh though."

"I'm in a good mood. This land won't tolerate any other mood," Lewis said with a smile. "I think tonight we'll have whiskey for the men and listen to Pierre's fiddle. Maybe even some extra tobacco for the men, they deserve it. They've worked hard and made good miles considering the current."

Clark replied, "I couldn't agree more. A little whiskey, a lot of music, a good way to wind up the day." Then pointing at Charbonneau he added, "Look over there. Charbonneau is making a meat mixture that he's putting into the intestines after he cleans 'em out. He says it makes into lengths that can be cooked up with the artichokes. Sounds good to me."

Lewis nodded in agreement, "It's good to see him productive. If he can add a new food, it will help him keep the respect of the men."

April 29, 1805

The men were going out to hunt for game. It should be an easy hunt as there was a lot of wildlife. They would go with a lead group of five men: Lewis, Drewyer, Colter, Shannon and John Shields. A second group: the Field brothers, Bratton and brown object in the distance. It was a grizzly bear. The men drew together, and Lewis issued orders. "Stay downwind. I don't think it's seen us yet. Let's move in where we can get a good shot. I want to get him for voyager's groups. Remember men, the Indians say this animal is difficult to bring down, so take careful aim."

Colter said, "Just look at it, captain, that is some bear. See that hump on its shoulders. The fur there seems grizzled and not as shiny as the rest. Look how the fur shimmers as it moves along. It sure seems to have a lot of confidence."

Drewyer added, "It may take all of us to carry it back to camp; it looks big from here."

The men nodded in agreement as they fanned out and moved toward the large bear. When they were within an average of about seventy five yards, Drewyer gave a signal and they all knelt down. Espontoons in place, they took careful aim.

The grizzly had been watching the buffalo herd and did not notice the men moving in closer. The men waited, watching Lewis for a signal. Lewis took aim and motioned to the men to fire when he fired. There was a sudden 'pitt cratoowh' issuing from each of the five flintlock rifles firing in rapid succession.

The large bear flinched and moved sideways slightly. Then it rose and stood on its back legs, looking toward the gunsmoke and the hunters. It let out a roaring growl and began to charge in their direction. At first its motion was fluid and swift, as if it had not been wounded. It covered ground swiftly at first then began to slow, the wounds taking their toll. Still, it was coming at them, an unexpected maneuver as most wild game ran in the opposite direction once wounded. As the great bear moved over the ground on its charge toward the hunters, its breathing in a heavy panting noise could be heard. 'Hunh, Hunh, hunh, hunh'. The men, firing in a group, fully expected to kill the bear instantly and were not prepared to see it rise and move toward them in attack. They were rattled. As they were trying to reload, they began to fall back in retreat. The other hunters in the second group heard the shots and witnessed their companions' falling back. Seeing the charging bear, the supporting four moved in and took aim. Again the sound of flint striking and powder flashing, 'pitt cratoowh', as four rifles spoke in rapid succession.

The great bear flinched again and wheeled and redirected its charge toward the gunsmoke of the last volley of shots fired. By now the men who had fired first were reloading and running along to try to get to a position where they would have a clear second shot at the bear. More excited now, they did not rest their rifles on espontoons. They ran up, stopped, aimed and fired. With each report of a rifle the wounded and confused bear would turn in rage and charge the closest man. The second group of four began running back toward the river as they attempted to recharge their rifles.

Finally, the bear was closing in very near to William Bratton, who had not yet reloaded his rifle. As the large animal drew closer it rose up to attack Bratton. Running up on the slight ridge, Lewis, Drewyer and Colter quickly took aim and

Colter added, "We hit it, it just rose up to right round. . . . admire that. Just like the Indians said, the bear is powerful, not easy to kill. Did you see how it moved toward the gunfire?"

Drouillard replied in an excited tone, "What do you mean did I see it move toward gunfire? Hell, man, I could smell it! I could see its eyes and teeth. Any closer and its breath would have been on my neck."

Lewis said, "How many of you fired twice? I want to know how many shots were made."

The men nodded and quickly looked around as each held up fingers indicating how many shots each had fired.

Lewis stepped forward, "Alright, nine men, fifteen shots. Let's see how many hit the mark." Then turning to Shannon, Lewis said, "Let's get some measurements on this animal. I want to record its size in my journal. I have never seen such aggression."

Drewyer commented, "Out here, this bear is the top of the food chain. It knows this, and it does not die easily. It will fight."

Joseph Field said, "You got that right for sure, George. I've killed bear before but none like this one. This animal is huge, bigger than any bear I ever saw. And no animal I ever saw came after the shooter, unless it was rabid."

Bratton knelt beside the fallen grizzly and lifted a front paw
to expose the large claws. "Look Capt'n, ever see such claws
on a bear? I saw those that the Indians collected back at
Mandan, but somehow they just look bigger and meaner when
they're attached to the bear."

Shannon added, "Especially to you, Bill. It damn near got
ya."

Bratton looked around and replied, "Would have, too, if it
weren't for the Capt'n and Drewyer there. Just look at these
teeth, its mouth's a lot bigger than any black bear I ever saw."

Reubin inquired, "Look at the fur. A lot longer and thicker
than any black I ever saw, and it has lighter tips on the guard
hair."

Colter, who had been quietly kneeling and examining the
fallen bear, rose slowly and said, "Capt'n, I got bad news for
ya."

The men fell silent as Lewis looked at Colter in apre-
hension.

Colter knew he had everyone's attention, and he spoke
quietly, "This'n here's a female."

The men stood silent for a moment, then Joseph Field bent
down and picked up his rifle and spoke, "Well then, that explains it. That's why this'n was so gentle and easy to put down.
I just can't wait to meet one of them full grown nasty males
with an attitude, so we can test its mettle."

The men laughed. Lewis looked around at the men who all
had puzzled looks on their faces. He spoke with a serious tone,
"We will always hunt in pairs, preferably in groups of four but
a minimum of pairs." Then turning to Joseph Field he spoke,
"Joe, you're the fastest runner here. Go back and tell the
others we got our first grizzly bear. Have them send a detail to
bring it in. We can use all the voyager's grease we can get.
Tonight we'll taste of the large bear's meat."

Drewyer and Colter had been kneeling over the carcass looking at the number of wounds. Drewyer stood and looked at Lewis. Lewis, catching his eye, waited for the quiet man's comment. Drewyer said, "Twelve hits. There were only three misses. Twelve hits to kill one animal."

Joe Fields nodded, picked up his rifle and left in the direction of the river. He repeated to himself as he shook his head, "Twelve hits to bring down one animal."

Lewis said to the others, "Let's continue on the hunt. If we see another bear, we'll take it, but we're after buffalo now."

The hunting party continued on toward the last sighting of the buffalo herd.

May 5, 1805

It was morning and the camp was waking to brisk, cold air. Sergeant Ordway was moving over to read the thermometer outside the tents. Colter stepped out of his tent and shook briefly in the cold air as he rubbed his hands together and put a hat on his head. The steam from his breath carried as he spoke, "Damn, it's cold. What does the thermometer read, Sergeant?"

Sergeant Ordway looked at the thermometer and replied, "Says twenty-eight degrees. That's cold."

Colter replied, "I could feel it was below freezin'. Look there at the bucket; it's got ice on top."

Cruzatte stood looking at the two men and remarked, "Sergeant, this is May, is it not? Our calendars are right, aren't they?"

Ordway replied with a puzzled look, "Yes, Pierre, it is May, but it's a cold May. Remember we're farther north than you're accustomed to. Spring must come later in these parts."

Cruzatte responded shaking his head, "A whole lot later. It's May, a person's got a right to expect better weather than this. Why, look out there on the prairie. See them flowers? See the green grass? See the new leaves on the trees there? Why, how, what makes it so cold? It ain't natural I tell you. Just ain't natural."

Colter replied, "Look at the good side of it, Pierre. If this little cold snap lasts, it'll kill off some skeeters. Maybe before they get a chance to breed and fill the air every night."

Cruzatte shook his head and pointed around, "It just looks strange to this one eye of mine to see snow an inch deep on flowers. To see any kind of snow at all in May."

Ordway said firmly, "Well it is not expected, I'll give you that. But we will do what we always have done since we first began encountering difficulty on this trail."

Cruzatte queried, "What's that?"

Ordway said, "We will proceed on."

Colter reflected a moment and then nodded in agreement said, "Yeah, I remember, that was Sergeant Floyd's favorite saying when we all were complaining, sweating, fightin' boils or whatever. We proceed on. We proceed on, that's all we can do. Turning back or staying here is simply not an option. Besides, you've seen all the changes in the land we have discovered so far. Cold or not, ain't you curious what tomorrow or next week will bring? What's waiting for us around the next bend in the river? Nobody knows, but I for one am curious."

Cruzatte nodded, and the men moved to where the others were loading the boats to proceed upriver. The wind was strong, making the air seem even colder.

Sergeant Pryor was coming back from the red pirogue. Labiche and Bratton were walking with him. He saw Sergeant Ordway approaching and announced, "The rudder broke on the red. It may have caught in the sand or on a rock last night. I think she twisted a little in the current, not enough to break free but enough to break the rudder. I'm going to inform the captains that we'll be delayed. I've got some men pulling her up out of the water so's Bratton kin have a good look to see what it'll take to fix her."

After hearing of the delay, the captains decided to make use of the repair time by adding meat to their supply. Later that day, Clark took Drewyer and York and went upriver to explore the river's edge and hunt buffalo. After they had been gone awhile, gunshots were heard back at the main camp where the boat rudder was being repaired.

Sergeant Gass said to Sergeant Ordway, "What do you think, deer, elk or buffalo?"

Ordway responded, "Well now, I'll bet you a twist of tobacco that the first game shot was beaver. Captain Clark likes beaver. He would even let a deer go by just to get a shot at a beaver."

Gass smiled broadly and answered, "Done. The odds are in my favor. There are a lot more herd animals out there than beaver. Capt'n C is a prudent man with gunpowder. He'll go for quantity of meat instead of the best tasting."

Bratton joined in, "A twist of tobacco, heh? Is that bet open to all takers? Cuz I'm with Ordway. There's plenty beaver on this river, and Capt'n C would rather bring in beaver than buffalo. How about it, Sarge, a twist here too?"

Sergeant Gass smiled and said, "Winning two twists of tobacco is better than one. Done."

The men returned to repairing the boat. Later, Clark, with Drewyer and York came back into camp. York was excited as he moved ahead of the other two men to speak to the group of men in the camp. "York ain't never seed nothin' like it. Nothin' like it at all. Mister George spotted a grizzly bear, big one, too. Bigger'n any bear York ever saw."

At the mention of a grizzly bear the men stopped what they were doing and moved in closer to hear about the hunt. Lewis, who had been looking at some plant specimens, folded his collection book up and walked over to meet the three re-turning men.

York, seeing he had the men's attention, continued using his hands as he talked. "Da bear was out in the river, fishin' or somethin', when Mister George spotted him. The bear moved on the sandbar like he didn't have a care in the world. Capt'n and Mister George just lifted their rifles kinda slow like. York raised his, too. Then we all let go, all three at once. Dat bear, he just raised up and looked around, like we all missed the mark or somethin'. York could see he been hit. Hit square, too. He was bleedin', but not even noticin' it or anything. He jus' raise up and let out with a horrible roar. He was looking for us he was. He come back down on all fours and started to move along the sandbar there when George, den the Captain, put another one in him. He flinched a little that time but not so's we could tell much. York was glad there was a river between dat bear and the closest ground." York smiled broadly and looked around at the others.

Clark stepped closer and put his rifle butt on the ground and held the muzzle as he spoke, "We finally brought it down, but York's got it right. That bear was a fearsome monster. Died hard, real hard. It's still on the sandbar where it fell. We should be able to get a lot of meat and voyager's grease out of that bear."

Lewis said, "It'll be dark in a couple of hours, let's get a detail together and go get it. Sergeant Pryor, bring my in-struments. I would like to measure this creature to put the details in my journal."

Pryor nodded as he went for the instruments.

Sergeant Gass looked at Ordway and said, "Looks like the bet's off. A bear's not an elk nor a buffalo, and a long way from a beaver."

Gass nodded and said, "Who'd of thought he would have kilt a bear." Then after a short pause he added, "Let's get that detail together, clean out the canoe and we'll go dress it out and bring it in."

Upon arrival at the sandbar, Lewis was the first out of the boat with Clark and York close behind. Lewis walked quickly, then slowed dramatically just as he approached the large bear.

Clark said, "Merry, I never saw a bear this large before, for that matter, any carnivore this big. This one is a male, and just look at him; he's huge."

Lewis had been standing looking at the bear as his friend spoke. When Clark finished talking, Lewis knelt and picked up a front paw. Anticipating the next order, Sergeant Pryor handed Lewis the ruler to measure the claws. Lewis looked up briefly at Pryor as he took the ruler and then measured the animal's claws.

Lewis spoke aloud as he examined the bear. "Five talons, four and three-eighths inches long." Then measuring around the animal's neck he stated, "Three feet eleven inches at the neck." Then he motioned for the men to take a string to measure the chest and height. As the men were taking the measurements, Lewis turned to Clark and said, "York is right. I've never seen a bear this size. What do you think, six hundred pounds?"

Clark replied, "An easy five hundred for sure, six is easily possible. We got no way of knowing for sure, but no reasonable man would argue with your estimate at six hundred. You should have been here, Merry, it just would **not** go down. Whirling and roaring all the while until the final shot brought him down. Had the river not been there to separate us, I'm confident he would have charged and possibly reached one of us."

Just then, the men measuring gave Lewis the string from around the animal's chest. Lewis took the measurement, "Five feet ten and one-half inches. This animal is considerable," he said in a low, serious tone. Just then the string from the animal's height was handed to the captain. Lewis measured and spoke again, "Eight feet seven and one-half inches. Now that must have been a formidable sight to behold. This bear rising up on his hind legs and roaring at his attackers." Then shaking his head he said, "Over eight and a half feet tall. This is tremendous. It's so large that it seems not even to be a relative to the black."

Sergeant Pryor looked at the animal and added, "Gentlemen, can you imagine what a Virginia farmer would say if he saw one of these? After being used to seeing an occasional black, this would be a nightmare."

The men proceeded to prepare the carcass for transport back to the camp where it could be cooked for the meat and grease. All of the men in the camp were in awe at the size of the bear.

Charbonneau was busy preparing what he called *boudin blanc* or a type of sausage made by use of the buffalo intestine and a mix of the various meats the hunters would provide. This particular dish was an immediate favorite among the men who were accustomed to eating primarily roasted meat or jerky. Sacajawea also helped in the preparation as she added the vegetables and roots that she collected along the river. She busied herself with the preparation of the vegetable portion of the meals.

As the evening meal was being consumed, all the conversation was about the grizzly bear. Lewis commented, "I have never seen, nor has Captain Clark ever seen, nor have any of you ever seen, an animal as impressive in size and ferocity as this bear. I think it's safe to say that our curiosity with regard to this animal has been very well-satisfied."

The men nodded in agreement as Clark added, "When we hunt game we should avoid this bear if possible. I have the distinct feeling that we'll still be killing this animal in self-defense."

Hearing the conversation, Labiche asked Charbonneau to find out what Sacajawea knew of this animal.

Sacajawea listened as Charbonneau spoke to her and then paused a moment to respond. As she spoke Charbonneau translated to French and Labiche translated to English. She spoke in a soft, almost submissive tone. "This is the great bear of the plains, it is considered a Great Spirit by our people. The bear follows the buffalo herds just as we do. It does not fear the largest of the male buffalo. It does not fear the wolves, even when they are in great numbers. It has no fear. My people and all Indian people believe this strength and lack of fear come from the Great Spirit."

The men listened intently as she spoke, then they asked questions. Sergeant Ordway inquired, "Do these bears live all along this river, all the way to the mountains? Do they live in the mountains?"

Many of the men nodded in agreement as Charbonneau translated to Sacajawea, and again she spoke, "These bears live all along the river and all over the prairie. They feed on the herds mostly, but they will also eat anything people will eat. They are in great numbers in the land. They do not live in the mountains because there are no buffalo in the mountains. This bear goes where it wants to and does what it wants to."

As the words were translated, the men laughed at the young Indian mother. Joseph Fields nudged Colter and Shannon, "She sure got that right, that bear can go where it wants to. Who's going to argue with it?"

Sergeant Gass went over to the captains and knelt down and asked a question. Lewis nodded his head and Clark smiled broadly and said yes as he waved a hand, pointing to all the men. Gass rose up quickly and announced in a loud voice, "Captains said we had a good day killin' that monster bear and all. Another good job too in getting the rudder fixed on the pirogue today. Want to know what that means? Whiskey! A whiskey for all that wants it."

Immediately the men began to follow Gass to the boats where they could get their gill of whiskey. On the way back Bratton shouted at Cruzatte, "Hey, Pierre, get your fiddle. The night is young, and we could celebrate with a little music to go along with this whiskey."

Cruzatte shouted back, "Wouldn't be a celebration without whiskey and some music. I'll play if you'll dance with York."

Bratton responded, "Done, my little friend. Play it good and fast. Come on, York, show me a step or two, and I'll be try'n to keep up."

The men were in good spirits and enjoyed the evening dancing and singing.

May 8, 1805 Milk River, Montana

The Corps of Discovery comes to the mouth of a large river. Its water is colored slightly white, and there is a considerable discharge of water. Lewis decides to go upstream a few miles and investigate its navigability. Clark goes to the opposite shore from the river's mouth and ascends a large hill to make observations.

Later, when Lewis returned, Clark asked, "How far up did you go? What'd you think of that river? Sure was wide enough. Do ya think it is the one the Indians called the River That Scolds All Others?"

Lewis walked near his companion, laid his rifle down, sat down and looked back upstream. "You sure got a lot of questions. I went up about three, maybe three and a half miles. Don't know for sure if this is the river, Bill. I can say it is definitely navigable with boats and canoes. It could be the Scolding River, I just can't be sure. They didn't say anything about the color of the waters. I would have thought they would mention the color of the water. It's such a distinguishing feature."

Clark nodded as he listened to Lewis, "Sure didn't. I would have remembered any comments about a milky river. Looks like tea with some milk in it. Think I'll call it that on my charts, Milk River."

Lewis asked, "Could you see much from the hillside over there?"

Clark responded, "Yeah, in this prairie land, a man can see for miles from almost any rise. That hill is high enough, I suppose I could see fifty or sixty miles. The river bears northwest for about twelve or fifteen miles; then it apparently forks, in one direction almost due north and the other west to northwest. You know, I could've sworn I could see a column of smoke at a great distance on the north fork. Maybe there's an Indian village out there."

Lewis looked at his friend, "Really? Well, I don't want to go that far upriver to seek out a new tribe. By the time we get there, they could have moved anyway. By the time we visit with them and get back..., awhh, just too much time." Then he took his telescope and looked north. As he looked, he spoke, "I wonder if this river joins the Saskatchewan further north. I'll bet it does. This river may define the northern territory. The Saskatchewan will define Canada's southern territory. Could be important."

Clark responded, "That's good material for the next expedition. I agree with you that we really can't afford the time to go check things out. What should we name this river? I'll mark the charts."

Lewis said, "You already said it's the Milk River. If you said so, then it's the Milk River. That's explorer's rights. We get to name all the major objects we find and map."

Clark smiled, "Good enough for me; Milk River it is."

Lewis remarked, "Bill, ya know I saw some new vegetation on the short trip up the Milk. I'd suppose that we could find more of the same and possibly even some others today. Would you go with me today and explore a little?"

Clark replied, "I'll put Pryor, LaBiche and Cruzatte in charge of leading the boats. I'll join you today. After all, according to our charter, we're the Corps of Discovery. We're charged with recording all new species. Today we'll look for new plants and animals."

Lewis smiled broadly, picked up his rifle and his flora press, and said, "Done," and headed upstream.

As the day continued, the two captains walked, took samples of plants and made idle conversation. Lewis' eyes, always on the horizon, noticed clouds building again and motioned to his friend. "Let's get closer to the riverbank. I want to wave the boats in, in case this storm produces troublesome weather."

The two moved nearer the river's edge as the sky blackened. As they looked out over the river, they could see the small fleet with the white pirogue following behind the red and two canoes. Charbonneau was at the helm of the white, and Pierre Cruzatte was adjusting the sails. The two pirogues, by necessity, held the wherewithal of the expedition. The white, being the more stable of the two, held the larger share of the valuable items. Seeing the sky blackening and noticing Charbonneau at the rudder, Lewis was immediately concerned.

Lewis stood tall and focused on the river. Then he spoke in a low serious tone, "Bill, look, damn it, look at that. The white has Charbonneau at the rudder. Didn't we learn about him? Hell, he's no kind of river man. He can't even swim."

Clark, looking at the boats on the water, leaned on his rifle as his eyes scanned the water and the small craft on the river. "You're right, that's Charbonneau. At least Cruzatte is working the sail, and he is a good river man. Still, with the sky turning ugly, we should get them in."

Lewis interrupted, "And quick." He began waving his arms and then shouted loudly, "Pull in the sail, damn it. Pull in the sail. Cut the halyards. You're going to lose her. Cruzatte, take control! Take control! Don't let her go sideways in the wind."

As the sudden squall turned the river into choppy waves, the wind hit the pirogue's sails at a ninety-degree angle. The force of the gust was strong enough to tip the pirogue. Charbonneau, lacking experience, turned the white pirogue across the wind instead of correctly steering against it, a repeat of his earlier mistake. The wind took over. Its force pulled the brace of the square sail out of the hand of the man attending it. This immediately turned the pirogue on its side, and it would have gone over had it not been for the sail lying flat on the water to resist further capsizing. The wind was causing waves to wash water into the craft. Lewis' eyes were filled with desperation. He looked at Clark who also had concern on his face as he studied the situation and waved his arms. In the same moment, without speaking a word of what to do next, the two captains took their rifles, held them up, and fired in an attempt to attract the attention of the men in the boats. Unfortunately, the boats were at least three hundred yards distant, and the men on the river could not hear the plaintiff shouting of the captains. They could not even hear the gunfire against the rising wind.

Charbonneau at the rudder of the troubled vessel, released control instead of steering correctly The troubled boat wrenched sideways in the water, rolled and began taking on water with each wave. Charbonneau began to scream in a chant to God to save him, "Oh God, Oh Jesus, Oh Mary Holy Mother of God, please save me. Save me; I cannot swim. God save me; I do not want to die in this horrible river. Blessed Virgin, save me!"

This display of weak character was too much for Cruzatte, an experienced river man. Cruzatte grabbed his rifle and pushed its muzzle under Charbonneau's chin. Charbonneau, with a crazed look on his face, immediately quit his chant to God and looked at Cruzatte. Cruzatte speaking French, shouted as he cocked the hammer on the rifle, "Get hold of yourself, man! Take hold of the rudder and steer this boat into the wind, or I will kill you right now! You want Jesus? You will meet him before your heart beats again if you do not take the rudder and steer into the wind!" Cruzatte had wind and mist in his face. His hair blew wildly in the wind, and his face was stern as his one eye, unblinking, focused on Charbonneau. "Do it!"

Charbonneau regained his senses and moved to control the rudder as ordered. Cruzatte immediately instructed the men, "Bail, damn it, bail! Don't look up, just bail until I tell you to quit or you will drown! Today you will drown if you are not quick about it!" The pirogue was filling with water and articles were beginning to float away.

While all of this bustle was going on, Sacajawea, with her baby at her side, remained calm. She looked briefly at her husband and Cruzatte and then began carefully pulling in the boat's precious cargo as it floated past her. She caught the captain's writing desk and some of the journal books as they were beginning to float by. Fortunately, she was located in the boat such that as the materials went overboard, they floated directly past her outstretched hands. She methodically continued to pick things up, item by item, and put them next to herself along the dry side.

Seeing the boat in such desperate condition, Lewis stopped shouting and immediately began taking off his jacket. He was preparing to plunge into the river in an attempt to assist in the rescue. Clark, seeing his friend taking clothes off, grabbed him firmly by the arm. "Merry, are you crazy? You can't go! It's too far. You'll drown for sure." Then he looked at the scene and back into his friend's eyes, "It's got to be three hundred yards to them. There's nothing we can do from here."

"I can swim. I'm a powerful swimmer," Lewis retorted.

Clark shouted in his friend's face, "Swim? That water's cold! Too damn cold to swim in. You'd die from the cold water alone, even if you can swim! What the hell were you thinking? By the time you got to them you wouldn't have enough left in you to help."

Lewis replied, "I want to save our journals. It's too much work. This mission, my life's work..."

Clark shook Lewis, "Journals! The damn journals! Damn the journals! You would die for those journals? Merry, look, there, the Indian woman, she's pulling in things out there. She's saving things. At least whatever floats. If Providence wants our journals to be saved, they will be saved. This is no time for you to risk your life. Why, hell man, by the time you could swim out there, the journals would be all over the river or sunk. Now that's the truth of it. Get your coat back on, and let's try to help them get ashore."

Lewis, still wild-eyed, did not speak but nodded in agreement and put his jacket back on as the men proceeded toward the river's edge to meet the approaching boats.

Pierre Cruzatte was in control. He had two men bailing with kettles. Sacajawea was still shepherding articles around her in the boat while Cruzatte and two other men were arduously rowing toward shore. The other boats, recognizing the distress of the white pirogue, were all heading toward shore where the captains were waving to them. As the white pirogue's bow touched the river's edge, Lewis was on board in an instant.

He gave orders immediately as he proceeded toward Sacajawea and the items she had resting near her. "Pierre, you and the men get this boat pulled up and secured on shore here. Then get back here and help me with the wet stuff. I want to get it laid out near the fire tonight to dry. I'll need an inventory of the instruments. I need a.."

Clark interrupted in a loud voice, "Merry, relax before you explode. Pierre, do what the captain said. The rest of you men in the other boats there, get over here. We need all the cargo unloaded quickly and dried out. Each man take material and lay it out to dry. Sergeant, start the inventory. Have the men tie up all the boats, anchor them and we'll make camp here."

The men acted as one. Further orders were not necessary. They pulled in the remaining boats and tied them securely. Others, well-trained to the drill, were setting up the tents and making camp. Clark looked around a moment and then asked, "How far behind are the other two canoes? Were they going on a hunt?"

Sergent Gass replied, "It shouldn't be long now. They're behind us and were going to get some fresh meat. We heard shots so I reckon they were successful."

Sergeant Ordway stepped over and said, "We'll be getting supper ready soon, Capt'n. The others should be here any time now."

York, with Seaman beside him, was looking out over the river. Seaman barked and York pointed as he spoke. "York sees 'em. Here they come. Look, there they come round the bend yonder."

Sergeant Ordway said, "Sure enough, York, here they come."

The men in the campground were efficient in making fires and establishing a campground. The captains' buffalo hide tent was the first one up. The others were quickly set up as the last two canoes pulled in and tied next to the other boats.

Sergeant Pryor was first off the boat. He walked up to where Clark and the other two sergeants were talking. "Did we ever have some excitement. Those damn bears, I never saw anything like those damn bears."

Sergeant Gass inquired, "What happened? Did ya see another grizzly?"

Pryor continued, "See one! That's an understatement. I ain't never seen anything like what happened back there. Still don't believe it all, and I was there!"

Reubin Field added, "Those bears just keep getting harder and harder to kill. It had us all scurrying around like ants. If it weren't for Colter here, one would have kilt Whitehouse. It had him for sure."

Clark said, "Come with me, men. I want Captain Lewis and the others to hear of your escapade. Then we'll tell you ours. It's really been quite the day, quite a day for sure."

The men all began walking toward the main encampment. Lewis was watching over the men as they inventoried the materials Sacajawea had previously saved from the river. Clark spoke, "Gather round men. I do believe the men have another grizzly story to tell."

George Shannon spoke, "You bet we got a story to tell."

Sergeant Pryor, with hand outstretched and moving downward, motioned for the men to sit. He looked around and then began to speak, "Captains, we had an experience that was almost beyond belief. The six of us went hunting. We saw a grizzly bear and decided to take it. There was a small hill on the prairie that we took advantage of in order to creep as close as we could before shooting. By plan, four of us were in front and the other two stayed back, acting as reserve. We fired on that monster, and it immediately charged, just like the other one did. Here it came, mouth open and roaring, right at Shannon. The other two men fired and one struck it square. Broke a shoulder bone I think, least ways the monster slowed some. Good for Shannon, too, 'cause it gave him some time to run into the willows and hide. There we were, trying to recharge our rifles and running away from this monster at the same time. Me and Colter hid in the willows next to the river while we worked our ramrods quick as we could. Meanwhile that bear was after Whitehouse and Hall." Pryor paused a moment and looked around. All eyes were on him as he told the tale of adventure. "It seems humorous now 'cause we are lookin' back on it. Anyhow there we were, next to a cliff of about twenty feet on one side and a chargin' grizzly on the other. The men fired one more time, and when that didn't seem to slow it none, they all three jumped over the cliff into the river. Well, there they were, going through the air into the water, hollering all the way down. That bear, he didn't stop. He went right in after them. Plungin' in right where the men had just broke water. It came up closest to Shannon there. Shannon began swimming away, and that bear was right after him. Just then Colter got to the riverbank. Cool as an icicle, he took careful aim and shot that bear through the skull. It was not far from George there; real close it was. Colter got him all right, straight through the skull. Probably the only shot that will kill one of those monsters."

George Shannon looked at John Colter, "I owe you, John. That bear was closer than I ever want to get."

Lewis, listening to the men, remarked, "Mark me well, men. This bear is nothing to be taken lightly. If you see one and you are not in strength of numbers, don't shoot it. Don't shoot it unless it charges at you. Leave it be, and it may leave you alone and go its own way. One shot will probably not kill this bear. From what we've seen, it takes several shots to bring down a grizzly. If you must shoot, aim for the head. A shot through the lungs won't kill it. I don't want to lose a man to one of these bears. This story is a repeat of a few days ago. Far, far too close, too close."

Whitehouse said to Sergeant Pryor, "Well, I didn't rightly want to jump over that ledge into the river, but at the time, there wasn't much choice."

Pryor replied to Whitehouse, "Tomorrow we will go back and get it. We should get several gallons of voyager's grease from that one. You can take the claws to trade with the Indians. After all, they have value."

Shannon spoke up, "Those claws are mine. They were damn near into my backside."

Lewis looked at Clark, and both smiled as Lewis spoke, "This has been a considerable day. Remarkable, truly remarkable for sure, but not a day worth repeating. We almost lost a man to a bear and almost lost our most valuable notes and instruments to the river."

Sergeant Pryor looked quickly back and forth at the captains, "You had trouble on the river? What happened? Is that why everything is all spread out over there?"

Clark nodding replied, "We'll tell you our story over dinner this evening. It seems that the details of each of our tales will be enough to entertain us all night. Just say it is fortunate that we have our instruments, papers and numerous other items Sacajawea was pulling things in as fast as they were being washed overboard. If it weren't for her, we'd have lost a lot. Everyone else was too far away to attempt any real rescue at all. If it weren't for her, we'd have lost a lot."

Colter remarked, "Sacajawea saved all that stuff? How'd she do it with the baby and all?"

Clark responded, "I don't know. I only watched as she stayed calm and grabbed the items that were being washed over. Captain Lewis and I have spent a lot of time on that material."

Lewis added, "Time is not all of it. If she had not saved those materials, I seriously would have considered not going on further. I have a lot of my energy in those journals, and the instruments are not replaceable."

Colter remarked, "Ya know, some of us have trouble with her name, SAH-KOG-A WEA. Can we name her a more English sounding name so the men can remember it and get it right?"

"Sure," Clark answered, "Let's call her Janey."

Sergeant Ordway came over to the small group and said, "I think that our dinner is about ready. Charbonneau and his wife been workin' on it since we got the fire goin'."

Sergeant Pryor said, "Janey, Sergeant, we are going to call her Janey now. She seems to be able to rescue our materials and fix our appetites in the same day. We've decided to give her a more English sounding name."

Ordway looked at the men and stood silent a moment and then said, "Janey, huh? Well, I like it. Works for me. What does she think?"

Clark smiled and replied, "Well, Sergeant, we haven't told her yet. We just came up with the name this minute. Let's go see if her husband has any problem with the idea. After all, she's his wife, and he should agree before we just do a thing like that."

The men moved to where the dinner was being prepared. Drewyer spoke to Charbonneau on behalf of the men. "The men are grateful for the things your wife, Sacajawea, has done today. The captains especially want to thank her for saving their writing desks and papers."

Charbonneau nodded and smiled, "It's good that she could collect these items from the river."

Drewyer continued, "There's more. The men would like to call your wife Janey. Seems they get their tongues twisted trying to say Sacajawea. Would that be a problem?"

Charbonneau, pleased that he was not being shunned for his part in the boating incident, wanted to cooperate. "I have no problem with this trail name for her. Let me tell her so she will recognize it when she is spoken to."

As Charbonneau spoke to Sacajawea, she listened intently and looked around at the men. When he explained that they had given her a new name, her face lit up and she nodded with a broad smile. She then spoke back to Troussaint in a mild tone.

Charbonneau turned to the men and explained, "She is glad to have the name Janey. It is the Indian way to be given a name by the tribe for something notable, something recognizable. She wants to know what 'Janey' means so she can tell her people."

The men looked at each other a moment and then laughed. Clark spoke and Drewyer translated, "Tell her that we are pleased that she saved our materials today on the river. But tell her that the name 'Janey' has nothing to do with what she did. The name has no particular meaning in English. Janey is the name of a young girl only. White men do not have meanings to their names as the Indians do."

As the translation was made to Charbonneau and then to Sacajawea, she looked puzzled for a moment and then smiled and nodded. She spoke back to all the men that were looking at her as Charbonneau and Drewyer translated. "She said she is pleased with having a new name even if it has no meaning. She will listen for it."

Later that evening the men were exchanging comments regarding the narrow escape from the river accident and the close encounter with the grizzly. Everyone was in good spirits, everyone but Lewis. Clark noticed his friend sulking and then moving toward the tent. Clark rose to follow him.

Lewis went in the tent and closed the outer flap. Clark followed shortly after. "Merry," he said. "What's the problem? We should be grateful that Providence has spared us from not one but two encounters today."

Lewis, looking down, spoke, "I almost went into the river after it. Would have too if you hadn't stopped me. I was a fool and no kind of leader."

Clark replied in a calm tone, "We both were emotional. We both were watching helplessly from the shore. They couldn't hear us even when we fired. Like you, I felt helpless, but it turned out all right."

Lewis remarked, "Bill, everything I depend on was in that pirogue. If it had been lost I would have had serious doubts about going on. I almost wish Cruzatte had shot Charbonneau, blown his damn head off. A leader shouldn't feel that way. I now know that it was wrong. But Bill, at the time I didn't, couldn't think straight."

Clark nodded and looked Lewis in the eye. "A leader should care about his crew; a leader should care about his critical supplies. You were no different than any man in your position would have been. As for trying to swim out there to attempt a rescue, "(changing his voice he continued), "now that **was** stupid. Merry, I don't think you would have gone very far before you realized the folly of it. The cold water would have brought you to your senses quickly. You and I are still the ones they all look to for leadership. None of them saw you. None."

Lewis glanced quickly into Clark's eyes. "Maybe I would have come to my senses when the water hit my face, but I know I was willing to make the attempt at the time." Lewis turned and sat down and looked at Clark. Changing the subject, he said, "The grizzly. That's the second time we have had the almost identical story with that animal. How many times can we expect to avoid disaster with that beast? *Ursus Horribleus.* That's what I am going to name it - the horrible bear."

Clark sat down facing Lewis and spoke calmly, "That bear is a fact of life on this prairie. But ya know, I don't think the natural prey of the grizzly is man; it's buffalo and the other animals natural to the land. Your advice to the men out there was right on the mark. Don't hunt them. Don't shoot them unless we know we can make a kill. Always go for a killing head shot. Merry, that was sound advice of a leader. The men took it, and it was good. I think we'll have future encounters with grizzlies, but we've learned, and we'll be smarter about how to kill them when we have to."

May 17, 1805

Today they have made only a few miles against the current and the meandering river. Progress against the current is most successful by pulling the craft, walking along the riverbank or wading in the shallow portion of the river, pulling with rope cords made of elk hides. This method of movement has been employed instead of rowing or poling because it yields more progress for the amount of effort expended. Occasionally, they set the sails if the winds are favorable.

Evening comes, and they decide to make camp in a wooded area. The hunters have killed fresh meat to feed the crew, and the men have built large fires. The region is very dry, and the evening campfire is built from dry wood found around the campsite. Tents are set up, and the men relax in idle conversation.

Sergeant Gass said to Drewyer and Colter, "This country, for the last several days, has been like a desert, very dry. The only water around these parts is the Missouri itself. Did you notice how many dry creekbeds there were emptying into the river? Probably only see water a few times a year."

Drewyer remarked, "It's good that there is a lot of timber along the river or we wouldn't have firewood at all. I wouldn't want to scour the riverbank for driftwood to make an evening fire. Dry as it is, there still seems to be plenty of herd animals though. I grant you not as many as below, but ample to support our needs."

Colter agreed saying, "Dry as I ever did see. This is not a simple drought. Least ways, I don't think so. I don't think this is a drought of missing a few weeks of rain. I think this is a natural desert. I think it must be dry around here most the time. Look at all the prickly pear. Cactus like that prospers best in dry land."

Sergeant Gass nodded saying, "I heard Capt'n Lewis complaining just yesterday about the dry weather. Said it was so dry he was having trouble with the ink and writing in his journal."

Drewyer said, "Yes, it's dry, but it doesn't seem to stop the mosquitoes; no shortage of 'em around here. I remember last year there were so many that I had trouble taking aim on elk. So many in my face I couldn't get my sights set."

Sergeant Gass quickly added, "I think those devils will be with us all the way to the ocean. Gnats too. Have you noticed all the flies? A lot of blow flies lately. Why do ya think they're all over?"

Drewyer answered, "The flies. I think they're here because of the way the Indians kill buffalo. Indians select a few men to dress in buffalo robes. Then, disguised, they mingle with the herd and lead the animals near the edge of a cliff. Then the others begin whooping and chasing them. Those in the buffalo robes jump over the cliff edge and hold on. The rest of the buffalo follow blindly and fall to their death trying to escape. The buffalo jump is easy for them to start, but not so easy to stop. More buffalo die than they can deal with at one time. The carcasses draw flies and they breed quickly. When the wind is right you can smell the stench for miles."

Colter replied, "I don't know whether to be grateful for the wind or not. It does keep the skeeters away, and the flies, but the sand. The wind drives the sand everwhere. I never saw sand so fine as out here. It gets in my eyes and my ears. I wrapped my rifle and it still gets in there. Sergeant, I'd tell all the men to clean their rifles every night, fired or not, 'cause that sand will sure enough get in the action and ruin a fine rifle."

On another side of the camp, Clark was showing York a rattlesnake skin. "Look here York. I killed this one today. It's a rattler all right, but not like the eastern breed. These out here seem to be smaller. Look at these markings. Captain Lewis will have plenty to write about on this one."

York looked at it and said, "York is glad to see the skin all by itself. York don' want to see that skin with the snake inside, no sir. I don't care if it's smaller than back East. Ain't nothin' sayin' it is better tempered. If it's a snake, York don't like it."

The conversation continued about the difficulty negotiating the boats around sandbars using cording. Cruzatte and Labiche warned the men to take the boats through any dangerous rapids in single file. Labiche said, "Watch carefully because if a rope broke and a boat went sideways, it could hit a rock and capsize for sure."

Lewis overhearing Labiche, spoke up loudly, "Men, mark those words well. We cannot be too cautious in the rapids on this river. Single file through the rapids. To give all our attention to each boat is an excellent practice. Make that an order. We don't want to risk a boat if we can avoid it."

Later, Lewis and Clark were watching the campground as the men were beginning to retire for the evening. Clark spoke, "No Indians. I thought sure we would have seen some by now. We have seen evidence of a few campsites here and there, but I am surprised that we have not met a local tribe."

Lewis nodded, "Well, it is part of our mission to contact the natives. But, Bill, I got to be honest here. I, for one, am glad that we haven't seen Indians. We're not making good time - some days only eight or ten miles; our best day was twenty some. Slow by my expectation, too damn slow. It's like we have a curse on our mission."

Clark nodded in agreement, "Meeting natives would only cause us to lose time. Three days minimum to meet and greet, present gifts, explain our mission, and that's if they're friendly."

Lewis added, "I agree. The men are tired enough each day from pulling the boats upriver. If we had to add the extra burden of increasing our guard every night, it would be troublesome to say the least. Tired and weary men do not make good sentries."

Clark looked around and saw that the Charbonneau family had already moved inside the tent. Drewyer and York had also gone in. Except for the night sentry, they were alone. Without saying anything, he and Lewis stood and moved inside the tent. Their tent was located under the overhang of a large tree branch that was leaning out over the campsite.

Later that evening, the Sergeant Ordway woke them up. "Captains, excuse me but there's a problem here."

"What is it, Sergeant?" Clark inquired.

"Well, the wind has picked up some and blown hot embers up into the dry branches of that tree overhead. They've caught fire, and I'm afraid that they could drop out and set fire to your tent. The wind is picking up too. That tree is making noises, and I don't like it. Cracking and groaning like it was possessed. Some of the smaller twigs and leaves have already been blown out. The next ones could land on your tent. I know it's late and you're bedded down and all, but I think you better move. I don't feel good about this."

Clark stepped outside the tent with Lewis and Drewyer behind him. They looked up at the tree smoldering and burning, "You're right, Sergeant, let's move."

They awakened the Charbonneau family and moved them. York and Drewyer proceeded to move the tent out from under the large tree. As they were resetting the tent in a safe location about fifty feet from its previous spot, a strong wind moved through the campground. Twisting in a violent noise, the main section and several of the large tree branches cracked and broke. Branches of the burning tree came crashing down onto the spot where just moments before they had been sleeping.

York looked at Clark with wide eyes and pointed. As he started to speak, "York don't believe his eyes. That tree's smashed down right where we was sleepin'!"

Clark looked at Lewis then spoke, "You're right, York. We all got to be thankful the sergeant got us up and out of there."

The noise of the fallen tree was horrendous. Charbonneau was visibly shaking as he looked at the huge branches that had fallen on the spot where they had been sleeping only moments before. He immediately raised his eyes and began a prayer chant to God. "Thank you, Blessed Virgin, for saving me. I could have been killed by this devil tree. The fire is from Satan, but you saved me. Oh God, thank you for saving me."

Drewyer looked at him disgustedly and said, "God didn't save you; Sergeant Ordway did. And what of your infant son and wife, aren't you thankful they were saved?"

The campsite was immediately alive with action as everyone came out of their tents to see what had caused the commotion. The fire was still burning in the smaller branches. Hot coals had been blown all over the campground causing small fires. Many of the tents, including Lewis and Clark's, required extinguishing the hot ashes. All the men were engaged in swatting embers with their clothing and blankets.

"What the hell happened?" Sergeant Pryor shouted.

Clark responded, "It seems our tent was beneath a leaning tree that could not withstand one more stiff wind. If it had not been for the vigilant eye of Sergeant Ordway, I fear we would have perished."

Lewis was standing and observing, looking at the burning tree in the place where, moments before, he had lain. Finally, he spoke slowly, "I think we must get some rest this evening. Let's get what rest we can before the morning finds us exhausted."

As the camp was retiring for the second time, again Lewis and Clark were the last to enter the tents. Lewis said, "Bill, I wonder sometimes if we do not have an evil genie with us. This accident seems so unnatural, unlikely, even weird."

Clark smiled as he replied, "Merry, don't look at the dark side of things. An evil genie? Why man, you don't recognize good fortune when it's staring you in the face. Yeah, that tree falling could have killed us, but the point is it didn't. Hardly a curse my friend; I think you're blessed. You have a guardian angel looking out for ya, not an evil genie after you. That's what I think."

Lewis looked at his friend a moment without speaking and then nodded and proceeded toward the tent for the evening. The evening passed quickly, and in the morning the weather was calm. The camp arose and moved out. After they were underway, Cruzatte saw a beaver moving along the water's edge. He quickly picked up his rifle and fired. The shot was ill placed and only wounded the beaver which took to the water and began to float downstream. Seaman saw the beaver and immediately jumped into the water in pursuit of it. He swam rapidly after the floating beaver and soon was upon it. As the large dog was about to take the beaver in his mouth, the beaver suddenly revived, turned and bit him on the left front leg. Seaman let out a loud "Yelp" and turned away as the beaver disappeared beneath the water.

Captain Lewis saw Seaman swimming back toward the shore. He was bleeding profusely and yelping and whining as he swam. Lewis met his dog on the shoreline, "Come here, boy. Let me look at you."

Seaman limped as he came out of the water. Blood was squirting from his foreleg, just above his paw. The bite had apparently severed an artery.

Cruzatte pulled the boat in quickly and was followed by the white pirogue with Clark, York and Sacajawea. Having observed the incident, everyone was concerned about Seaman's condition; he was obviously in pain.

Lewis was gripping the dog's front leg and looking at the wound. "Beaver got him. Bit his front leg here. It looks pretty bad."

York got out of the white pirogue, and Sacajawea followed. Clark delayed a moment as he grabbed some of the medical packages stored on the pirogue and followed the others.

Clark spoke, "I've got some bandage material here. If you wrap it tight, it'll stop the bleeding."

York joined Lewis and spoke to the dog in a comforting tone, "It's goin' to be all right, Seaman. We goin' take care of you." He stroked him as Seaman lay down to permit treatment.

Clark handed some elk skins to Lewis, "Here, wrap it tight and tie it off. Not too tight; don't want to stop circulation."

Meanwhile, Sacajawea had begun to gather some leaves. As Lewis was preparing to place the elk skin bandage over the dog's leg, she interrupted. She nudged his shoulder as she handed him the leaves and motioned to put them on the wound and wrap it.

Charbonneau spoke as Cruzatte translated, "She wants you to put the leaves on next to the wound, then the wrap. She said it will stop the bleeding. Make it heal."

Lewis looked at Sacajawea and nodded, "Thanks, Janey."

York also nodded as he continued to comfort the dog as the bandage was being applied. When it was completed, York asked, "Capt'n Lewis, can York put Seaman in the boat with him so he don't got to walk none? Maybe a few days he be good again. Right now, Seaman shouldn't walk 'cause he'll bleed. Seaman needs some rest."

Lewis looked at York and Clark and nodded as he spoke, "Sure York, get him on the white. Ol' Seaman deserves a little rest here. I think the bleeding will stop pretty soon. He's pretty tough."

Lewis looked at Clark and asked, "Would you take shore duty for awhile? I would like to ride along with Seaman. I want him to stay calm until I'm sure the heavy bleeding has stopped."

Unknown to the Corps of Discovery, Cruzatte's rifle shot had drawn attention. They were being watched. There was a small group of eight Crow warriors watching them.

"Who are they? Why are they in our land? Shall we go for more warriors and attack them?" one warrior asked of the leader.

The leader paused a moment and then replied, "No, we should let them pass without notice. This is not a war party. They do not come to raid for horses, women or food. See, in the front boat, there is a woman, a woman with a baby. This is not a war party. No war party would have a woman and baby with them. We will not raid them."

A third warrior spoke, "You're right. A woman with an infant is not the mark of a war party. I believe they could be peaceful. But look, they seem to have many guns in the boats."

The leader nodded and replied, "More reason not to attack them. They have no horses for us to capture. We do not want the boats. They have a woman with them and many guns. We would lose many Crow in a raid. We should go back to our village and see if the other chiefs want us to attempt trade with them."

The first Crow said. "I agree, they are not worth any Crow blood to try to take boats we do not need. They're moving toward the Blackfeet, maybe the Blackfeet will try to take boats they do not need. Crow are smarter than that."

That evening the men around the campsite were concerned about Seaman. The large dog had become the best sentry in the expedition. The men knew to be alert when Seaman barked.

Under the care of Lewis, Sacajawea and York, Seamen healed quickly and was walking without a limp in a week.

Sacajawea had busied herself in the collection of plants to supplement the evening meal.

"What is this stuff?" Reubin Field asked as he looked at the wild onions, artichokes, wild licorice and white apple root.

Sacajawea proceeded to take the vegetables and cook them. As she prepared the foodstuff she said, "Good food. You must eat more than meat. This food will keep you strong."

Reubin stood patiently while Charbonneau translated her words to Labiche, who, in turn, explained to him. Reubin laughed and said to his brother Joseph, "Would you listen to this? Janey here sounds just like our Ma. Eat your vegetables now or you don't get any puddin'."

Lewis, hearing the conversation, commented, "I must admit the apple root is an insipid food. As tasteless as anything I have ever eaten. But taken with our meat, it may fill our innards so as to prevent diarrhea. It does not hurt to add some variety to our diets. Janey here has spent a lot of time collecting these foods, and we'll all eat 'em. I think they'll be good for us even if they are short on flavor."

May 26, 1805 East of White Cliffs, Montana

It is late May and still cold enough in the mornings to have ice on the oars from the overnight chill. Camp breaks as usual, and the Corps of Discovery moves upriver, pulling the boats by means of the cords.

Clark looked ahead to some rather steep hills along the river. "Continue on. I think I'll go up those hills and have a look see. High as they are, I should be able to see where the river turns and what's ahead. I'll be back shortly."

Lewis nodded his agreement as he proceeded to walk along the shoreline examining plants. The men strained as they pulled the boats along with the lengthy elk skin cords. Soon Seaman barked and ran forward. Clark was coming back toward the group. Lewis smiled and said, "Well, what did you see? Any Indian camps or signals?"

"No, Indian camps," Clark said. "But I could see mountains. Mountains on both sides of the river. There are some others running irregular and look like they're about fifty miles out."

Lewis perked up and inquired, "Mountains? Which way are they running?"

Clark replied, "Looks like they run mostly northwest." Then pointing back toward the hills he added, "Merry, you want to see mountains? Go ahead, have a look, they ain't going anywhere. By the way, I saw another one of those long-eared, long-legged rabbits. It can run, zig and zag just like something was after it."

Lewis said, "Yeah, I have already got a specimen. I think I'll climb one of the hills a little further upriver. No need to get the same view you did. Maybe those hills ahead will give us a different perspective."

As they walked on Lewis said, "Those mountain sheep, sure are unusual aren't they? I never would have thought an animal that size would have such large horns. Its head resembles an ordinary sheep except for those horns."

Clark replied, "They are unusual all right. I expect we will see a lot more of them as we get into the mountains. Did you see how easy they move over the rocks and up the slopes? Being so agile, I really don't think they would have natural enemies. Wolves or bears couldn't catch one."

Lewis said, "Maybe a panther could get one if it laid in ambush or snuck up on it at night. But I'm with you, I don't think any predator could catch one in an open chase."

As they moved further up the river Lewis pointed ahead and said, "See that group of hills on the starboard side? I think I'll use them as a vantage point and have a look."

Clark said, "You taking anyone with you?"

Lewis replied, "Just Seaman. I'll have you all in sight most of the way. There won't be any bears up there."

Sergeant Pryor said, "Here, Capt'n, don't forget your telescope."

Lewis took the telescope and said, "Thanks, Sergeant. I'll be back in an hour."

In a few moments Lewis was at the bottom of the hill and began his ascent. The hillside was steep in places. He put his rifle over his back and grabbed rocks to pull himself up. There were several ruts and obstacles on the way. Finally, after a great deal of effort, he reached the summit.

"How about this, Seaman? Great view, huh?" Then he took his telescope and looked westward. There, in the west, were the majestic Rocky Mountains. Lewis alternately looked with his telescope and with his naked eye. "Well now Seaman, this climb, tough as it was, was worth it. Just look. There's the Rocky Mountains ahead."

After looking in all directions and taking measurements with a compass of the degree of the mountain range, Lewis put his telescope in his satchel and proceeded back to meet the advancing boats.

Clark spoke as Lewis came near, "Did you see the mountains? I thought I could see the beginnings of the range. I definitely saw mountains on both sides of the river ahead."

"They're there, mountains stretching toward the northwest, Lewis replied. "They have snow on them. They're actually quite scenic, even from this distance."

Clark reported, "I had Drewyer and Colter go on ahead to look for a good campsite for the evening. They came back with both good news and bad news. They found a couple of good spots for a campsite, plenty of firewood and in a spot on the river where the river is calm and riverbank is gentle. On the darker side, they said there were some strong rapids between here and there. I don't know about you, but I would just as soon get that bad stretch behind us before settling in for the evening."

Lewis nodded in agreement as he spoke, "I couldn't agree more. Let's get any possible danger behind us before nightfall. Tomorrow will have its own set of problems. Besides, there's time to make some miles before evening. How far did Drewyer say the campsite would be?"

Clark said, "A few hours away. He said the river looked better after that."

As they advanced, they approached the rapid section of water. They put the boats in single file and the elk skin ropes strained as they pulled the canoes against the stretch of rapids into the calmer waters. Seeing the problem, Sergeant Ordway, Sergeant Gass and Francois Labiche conferred as to the best strategy.

Ordway walked away from the small huddle nodding. He approached Clark and said, "Capt'n, we just finished taking the small boats through these rapids. I don't mind telling you, it was a strain. Sergeant Gass an' me talked it over with Labiche. He's a good river man. He said we should pull all the smaller boats first and then take all the lines to pull the red and white through."

Clark looked at the sergeants a moment and then at Lewis, "Good idea, Sergeant. Let's do it."

Following the plan, the men advanced the red pirogue into the rapid current. The elk skin ropes strained as the men leaned into the work. Suddenly, one of the elk skin ropes snapped. The load now uneven, caused the boat to swing around in the water. The men quickly grabbed the other ropes and pulled. Cruzatte, the best boatsman on the red pirogue, was in charge. He immediately barked out orders to have the men paddle to align the boat with the tow lines. The red pirogue swung slightly sideways for a moment and struck a large, partially submerged tree. Cruzatte and Drewyer, working in unison with paddles employed as rudders, managed to get the boat re-aligned to the tow ropes.

Seeing the boat back in line from the brief near disaster, Joseph Field shouted, "Way to go. Give her hell, Pierre, George. Ain't no little bit o' rapids going to get the better of the Corps of Discovery."

All the men simultaneously cheered as they redoubled their efforts and leaned into the remaining tow lines. The red pirogue sliced through the water and into calmer water where the men finally let up on the ropes as they pulled her toward the smaller resting canoes.

Clark shouted, "Get her pulled into the calm water and anchored. Good job men; good job."

Sergeant Ordway shouted, "Let's do it. Only one more to go. The white should be nothin' compared to this one. Hell, with one line broke, that just gives us more men to pull on the other ones. Let's go get her; make her move like one of the canoes."

The men were in high spirits after overcoming the threat of the rapid section of the river. They quickly disconnected the ropes and moved out at a quick pace, back downriver to retrieve the white pirogue. Lewis, waiting with the white, was a little surprised to see the men running back as a group, rope lines in hand, to bring up the last of the fleet. The men moved in unison as they tied the lines; again Cruzatte and Drewyer jumped into the white pirogue and took positions. The men heaved to, the lines pulled tight and the boat began to move out.

That evening, the mood around the campfire was jubilant. Sergeant Ordway asked Captain Lewis if they could have a gill of whiskey after the meal to celebrate seeing the mountains and getting over the rapids.

"Of course, Sergeant," Lewis replied smiling. "In fact, when the men have their whiskey, I would like to tell them something."

Hurriedly Ordway nodded in agreement as he said, "Thanks Capt'n, its been a hard day. The men will want to celebrate some." He quickly left Lewis and moved back across the campsite to mingle with the other men.

Clark looked at Lewis and inquired, "What's up?"

Lewis replied, "Have you noticed the men, especially today? They're becoming every commander's dream. They're a unit. They moved in to get the white pirogue like it had been a drill they had practiced for months. Very little was said. Each man knew what to do. It was a beautiful thing."

Clark nodded in agreement, "Yeah, I saw the same thing upstream when the line broke on the red. They were not confused by it, they scarcely missed a beat. Like you said, it looked as though they had practiced it over and over."

Lewis, looking over the campsite at the men said, "I just want to tell them I am proud of them. That's all."

Clark responded, "Good idea. With all that work a little encouragement never hurt a thing."

When the men finished eating, each got a gill of whiskey and moved to the center of the campfire where Lewis was waiting for them.

Lewis rose up, drink in hand, and announced, "Men, today I witnessed every commander's dream - men responding in crisis without need of individual orders. I watched you with a great sense of pride. We are now, more than ever, the Corps of Discovery. A toast to you, to each of you, the Corps of Discovery."

The men all raised their whiskey in toast to themselves and drank. Lewis again raised his voice to speak. "Men, today both Captain Clark and I ascended high points to survey. Captain Clark was first to report that he could see mountains on each side of the river ahead. But, more importantly, he said he could see even more distant mountains. He believed them to be the Rockies."

The men let out a cheer, and Lewis raised a hand to calm them as he continued to speak. "I also climbed a second hill. It was a very difficult climb, but I also could see the mountains on the river, just as Captain Clark reported, both starboard and larboard sides. Then as I looked to the northwest, I saw a range of large and distant mountains, beautiful mountains, covered with snow. Those, gentlemen, are the Rockies. I must tell you that there was a sense of accomplishment in just seeing those mountains and knowing that within the mountains would be the fountainhead of the heretofore boundless Missouri."

With that, Lewis raised his cup, and the men mimicked his move. "To the Rocky Mountains."

"To the Rocky Mountains," all the men said in chorus.

Lewis continued, "Those distant mountains mean we have reached a milestone in our journey, a significant milestone. Soon we'll be close to finding and recording the Northwest Passage, the passage that President Jefferson sent us to find. Our goal is clear, fixed and dead ahead. I must admit that while seeing those mountains gave me a great sense of joy in accomplishment, I also realized that those same mountains, so high as to have snow on them at this time of year, will present a problem in crossing. But I must say, I have optimism and until proven otherwise, I believe that we will overcome any obstacle. Seeing our men work as a unit today let me know that we have every ability to overcome whatever difficulties or obstacles those mountains may present." He paused a moment and then looked for Pierre Cruzatte. "Pierre, could you play some tunes for us this night?"

May 28, 1805 Judith River, Montana

The daylight lingers until late evening. Lewis waits for the skies to produce stars and then takes measurements to try to determine latitude and longitude. Afterward, both he and Clark sit in their tent making journal entries. Lewis also is documenting new plants he has discovered along the river's edge.

Sergeant Pryor asked Drewyer, "Did ya see the large poles the Indians used? Had to be Indians. They seem to be all over around here. Funny thing, those poles out here where there are so few trees."

Drewyer replied, "They take the poles with them when they can. The shortage of trees forces them to haul the poles too, not just the tents and blankets. Only reason they would leave them behind is they probably killed enough buffalo they couldn't afford to take the extra weight of the poles."

Pryor responded, "They could have used the poles to load the buffalo meat and hides, strange to leave so many. Maybe their scouts said they could get more on ahead. Hell, who knows? I just wonder why we haven't seen any Indians."

Just then Reubin and Joseph Field approached. Joseph inquired, "Hey Drewyer, did you get a shot at a big-horned sheep today? I thought I saw you shoot."

Drewyer smiled and replied, "Yeah, it was me you saw shooting."

Joseph asked, "Was it you that got him?"

Drewyer looked up and replied, "It was a clean shot. It paused to look back at us. That was its mistake and our supper."

Reubin nudged his brother and added, "Ya didn't have to ask if Drewyer got the big horn or not, just whether or not it was him that got off the shot."

Joseph nodded and said, "Yeah, you're right. Those sure are odd looking animals. They can move over the rocks and cliffs as easy as a deer moves over the prairie. Ain't never seen anything like it. I just like to watch them run. I'll bet we see more of them when we get in the mountains."

The men continued small talk and then, one by one, began to retire for the evening, knowing they would have another day of cording and pulling the boats upriver. The stars shone brightly; evening settled in. As usual with the Corps of Discovery, only the night sentry remained awake.

Across the river a large bull buffalo had been grazing earlier and had wandered away from the rest of the herd. This type of mistake is what wolves look for. A large pack encircled the lone buffalo and began to nip at its back legs. The buffalo, instinctively knowing the wolves would kill him if he did not get away, panicked and began running wildly. Through the night the bull ran, wolves in close pursuit, until it came to the river. Immediately he turned, snorted and headed into the water, his instincts telling him that the wolves would have difficulty attacking him in shoulder-deep water.

On the opposite shore, with boats tied and anchored, lay an exhausted and sleeping Corps of Discovery. When the bull plunged into the water, the wolves stopped at the river's edge and watched as the fear-crazed bull swam away. Seaman, always alert, heard the wolves pursuing the buffalo. He growled low in his throat and moved from Lewis' side toward the opening in the tent where he looked out into the darkness. Everyone slept.

As the bull swam away from the wolves, he left behind one kind of fear only to realize he was trapped in the river current. Seeing the campfire, the only light, he swam toward it. The white pirogue was anchored and pulled one-third onto the riverbank. Stored inside the craft was much of the valuable merchandise of the expedition. The bull came to the shallow water near the shoreline and raised himself out of the water. He began running toward the campfire and as he did so, stepped inside the white pirogue.

There was a loud noise as his hooves struck the wood of the boat and materials were kicked about. As the buffalo climbed across the white pirogue, the craft took on water and writhed beneath the weight. One rifle was stepped on and its stock cracked loudly as the bull clamored across the pirogue. As the frightened animal was attempting to leave the water and the pirogue behind, it stepped on one of the blunderbuss shotguns stored on board and crushed it into splinters. Parts and shards of the stock went flying about.

The evening sentry heard the noise and saw the large animal moving into the campground. The bull was completely panicked. It was stomping and running haphazardly. As it moved, its hooves narrowly missed one man's head and another's legs or arms. The calamity continued as the marauding beast nearly missed first one man and then another.

The sentry raised his rifle above his head and ran shouting loudly at the buffalo in an attempt to distract it and save his companions from the thundering hooves. Twisting and turning, the frightened buffalo ran first one direction and then another. Finally, the buffalo turned and moved toward the tent where Lewis, Clark, York, Drewyer and the Charbonneau family lay sleeping. Seaman rushed out of the tent quickly and barked loudly as he launched a counterattack against the raging buffalo. Nipping at its front hooves the bull stopped, snorted loudly and then ran as fast as it could off into the darkness.

The campground was immediately alive with men rising from their slumber. Colter shouted, "What the hell's going on? What was that?"

Shannon and Goodrich both looked and pointed in unison as Shannon exclaimed, "Buffalo! There it goes, did ya see that? A buffalo came straight through camp!"

William Bratton, the sentry, said, "It was a large bull. It came right up out of the river. Looked like it was climbing out of the white. There was a lot of noise and commotion and then suddenly there it was, right in the middle of the campground. A campfire on every side of it, it was scared or stunned. I ran at it to try to scare it off. It looked like it was trampling everyone. All I could see was buffalo hooves and bodies on the ground rolling around. Is anybody hurt?"

By this time Lewis was out of his tent and approaching the men as they were buzzing with what happened and "Did you see this or that?" On his approach Lewis had overheard Bratton's remarks. He quickly apprased the situation and asked, "Is anyone hurt, trampled? Is anyone not moving?"

The men were all standing by now and they looked around. No one was down, and Sergeant Pryor replied, "No sir, everyone seems to be alright. Hell of a big buffalo though. What do you suppose spooked it like that?"

Lewis looked around as he replied, "I don't know, Sergeant. Could have been anything."

Clark who had also joined the group said, "I think we better get another sentry to join Bratton here. It could have been Indians that caused that buffalo to run through here at night. Buffalo aren't normally active at night. It's too unnatural to suit me. Sergeant, select another sentry to finish off the night."

Lewis added, "Bratton here said the buffalo came up from the river, right over the top of the white. Let's get it pulled the rest of the way out of the water and check it out. I hope there's no real damage. I don't want anything to get water soaked."

Sergeant Pryor waved a hand toward the white pirogue and pointed toward some of the men. In addition to the few he had selected, twelve more men moved in unison to get the tow lines and pulled the boat out of the water.

Bratton moved over to Lewis and said, "Capt'n, you should have seen Seaman. I was whistling and shouting to try to get that buffalo to run out. Then ol' Seaman came out of the tent like a shot. Black as he is, I don't think that buffalo even saw him. There he was, barkin', growlin' and nippin' at that buffalo. The damn thing outweighed him twenty times over, but that didn't scare Seaman. He kept after it like he had a mission. Maybe he did too - saving all you in the tent."

Lewis turned and looked at Seaman then knelt down and grabbed the big dog by the neck and shook him gently. "Good boy, Seaman. You sure know how to stay on guard. That buffalo didn't scare you, huh boy?"

About this time Sergeant Pryor and Clark came back to the campfire circle. Pryor was carrying some of the pieces of the blunderbuss. "Look at this blunderbuss. That buffalo broke it like it was a dry twig. Powerful animal, powerful."

Clark had a damaged rifle in his hand and said to York who was standing near Seaman, "This is the rifle I gave you, isn't it, York?"

York, seeing the rifle, nodded and said, "Yes, sir, that's York's rifle. I must have left it in the white when we were getting firewood for the campfire."

Clark looked at York with a stern face, "York, this rifle must be with you at all times. A man never leaves his rifle anywhere, any time, for **any** reason. You got that?"

York looked ashamed and down at his feet as he replied, "Yes, Capt'n, York got that."

Clark continued, "An Indian will kill to get a rifle, not even a question or second thought about stealing one left on a boat overnight. Rifles like these are expensive, and out here, there is just no replacing one. When it's gone, it's gone. The whole expedition is now down by one rifle. I don't like being down one rifle. Don't like it at all." He looked at York with a stern eye, York knew better than to reply. Clark continued, "Tomorrow, you get all the pieces of this rifle, all of them, even the splinters, and take them to Willard. He's good with the rifles. See if he can fix it. Ain't no excuse, York, for being stupid with a rifle. It's life and death out here."

York never lifted his eyes from the ground as he turned slowly and walked toward the white pirogue to get the fragmented rifle.

Lewis turned and said, "Men, this has been truly exciting. We're fortunate that none of you were trampled or killed. Be that as it may, tomorrow morning will still come on time. We'll check for damage and dampness in the morning."

The men returned to their original sleeping positions. There were now two sentries on guard the rest of the night.

Morning came and the camp arose. Attention was immediately directed toward the white pirogue. There had been no damage to it structurally, but it had a small amount of water in it. Other than a few small articles, the cargo and instruments remained undamaged.

Clark smiled as he said to Sergeant Ordway and Lewis, "After all that commotion last night, I feel very fortunate that we have not sustained any greater damage than this. Very lucky indeed."

Ordway nodded in agreement, "Yep, it sure is amazing how so much happened without anything more getting ruined. I think we should get loaded and get this place behind us."

Lewis said, "Now that, Sergeant, is a good idea. Let's get upriver."

They moved out again by pulling ropes to advance the boats upstream. Later in the morning they came across a clear water river. The captains decided to examine the river a short way up from the Missouri.

After a few miles Clark turned to Lewis and said, "This river has unusually clear water. If it maintains its beauty and clarity further up, I think I'll name it Judith's River."

Lewis looked at Clark a brief moment and then smiled broadly, "Judith's River it will be then. What a shame that your romantic gesture will not be recognized for such a while. I do believe you must be serious about Miss Hancock. Excellent choice, Bill, you picked the finest river we have seen so far to name after the apple of your eye. Here we are in a wilderness, and you show your romantic side. Romantic for sure, but I like it. You're not all business after all."

Later that day they proceeded on up the Missouri where they passed a large pile of dead buffalo carcasses. Lewis looked at Drewyer, Colter and Sergeant Pryor and said rhetorically, "A pishkin*?"

Drewyer and Colter both nodded as Drewyer said, "Nothing else could account for so many dead animals. That cliff has at least a hundred fifty foot drop."

Lewis said, "Let's get past this place. The stench is terrible, the flies are too thick. Some day these Indians that kill buffalo so wantonly will see the waste of their ways."

Sergeant Pryor said, "I think they don't aim to kill so many. It's just that they can't stop it once it gets going."

Lewis said, "I don't like it. Let's get it behind us and look for a place to camp for the night. Look at that sky. There's rain in those clouds; we could be in for a rough evening."

May 31, 1805 White Cliffs, Montana

The two pirogues are in the lead. It has rained all morning. They continually encounter rock obstructions in the river, obstructions they have learned they cannot ignore. The only way to prevent the boats from

---

* A place where Indians made buffalo fall over a cliff.

*striking the rocks and turning sideways to the current is to put men in the
river, pulling and guiding the small fleet through the rough waters. This
means the men are often up to their chests in cold water for long periods of
time. When they seek relief from the water by pulling their ropes from
along the shore, the mud is slippery, and they cannot wear moccasins.
Wading in the river, they are pulling the burden of the canoes against the
current. They frequently suffer from stepping on sharp rock fragments
that have fallen from the cliffs along the river's edge. Lewis and Clark
are walking with Sergeant Pryor along the shoreline just in front of the
men. To lighten the load of pulling, no one rides in the boats. Upstream
progress is entirely by means of pulling on elk skin ropes.*

After watching for a moment, Clark spoke, "Look at them.
That work has got to be the most difficult I've ever seen or
hope to administer. Cold water, slippery mud, yet they
continue without any negative comment whatsoever. In fact,
quite the contrary, they are in good spirits and even sing.
Simply incredible."

Lewis looked stoically at the men for a moment and then
replied, "I know. I have often wondered how I would rekindle
their morale should they lose faith in the mission. Watching
them would inspire anyone. Their attitude is laudable and up
lifting indeed."

Sergeant Pryor, listening to the captains added, "These men
are the best I've ever worked with. They require little direction. Why most times they seem to anticipate an order and
just do the necessary thing. I think they're all feeling the excitement of new discovery and that holds them together."

Clark stared at the men and said, "Family, that's what it is.
These men have become a family. No one man will slack in
pulling his share because he knows that his brother will have
to do more. If we had any worries or doubts arising from
those disgruntled few we sent back to St. Louis, this should
belay all doubts. These men are family as close as any I ever
saw."

"I couldn't agree more," Lewis replied. "The expedition, the land we see each day, does offer challenge and excitement. None of us knows what may lie beyond the next riverbend or what tomorrow will bring. Yet these men, more than any I have ever commanded, work as one. Their very spirit seems to have melted into one and I am proud to say that spirit reflects the vision that the president had in sending us here."

As they stood watching the men move the boats upriver, straining at each turn, Sacajawea, her baby on her back, proceeded to move past the men from a rearward position. She stepped past the men one by one and sometimes gripped plants on the riverbank to steady her pace. As she passed the men and moved out to the front, Reubin Field shouted out, "Hey fellas, lookie there. Janey just passed us all up and she's got a baby on her back. Now if a young squaw can not only keep up with us, but pass us carrying a baby on her back, all the while picking up plants for supper along the way, well I think we got no room to say our work's too hard."

George Shannon shouted out, "Let's keep up with Janey. Any pace she sets, we gotta match."

Sacajawea, hearing the name 'Janey' knew the men were talking about her. She turned and looked at them for a moment.

Shields motioned with his hands for her to continue as he said, "Keep it up, Janey. You got the Corps of Discovery behind you every step."

Sacajawea smiled and seeing Shield's hand motion to move on, turned and proceeded upriver, all the while carrying her baby and continuing to gather plants for supper. Uplifted by the brief incident, the men continued on.

Later in the day, as they moved further west, there were vistas of perpendicular white cliffs of amazing beauty. Each had an appearance of having been sculpted. There were white rock ledges rising straight up for three hundred feet or more, some with caps that looked as if a large hand had delicately balanced them atop one another.

Shields said, "Look at those cliffs. They look like pillars. How did they get that way? I never saw anything like it. Some of them actually look like some sort of construction of man. They seem to be the same width at the top as they are at the bottom. What do you think, Captain?"

Lewis replied, "These vistas are truly remarkable. While some of the more spectacular, those with rocks apparently balanced on top, seem to have been constructed, I can assure you they are not. This is a natural process which has worked over many thousands of years, a product of the river and the wind and rain. The softer rock was washed away, leaving behind these scenes of visionary enchantment that seem to go on without end."

George Shannon said, "Look. Some of them look like building pillars. That one over there has a peaked top, real sharp looking, all of them so white. I sure wish I could send a painting of these back home because nobody there will believe me. My credibility would be gone."

Joseph Fields said, "There he goes again. What is credibility?"

Lewis smiled and replied, "It is his ability to tell the truth."

Fields rebutted, "Well, I wish he would just say that."

They proceeded on through the white cliffs, all the while observing the surroundings. As evening was only a few hours off, Lewis ordered a hunting detail. They walked inland a short distance and killed two deer and six elk that would be used both for food and hides for moccasins and rope.

As they returned, Charbonneau said, "I'll try to make sausages from elk. I don't think it will be as good as the buffalo, but everyone likes the sausages and gravy so much. My wife has collected some vegetables and roots for the sauce. This should be a good evening to cook up all the meat."

Drewyer replied, "Yes, it will be a good evening to cook. Your specialty will be enjoyed more because we have not stopped for a midday meal. We need to get plenty of jerky prepared so we can keep moving. There are simply not any good places to stop during the day. Jerky, onions and artichokes make a good traveler's meal."

Charbonneau asked, "I think we should ask the captains for some whiskey tonight. What do you..." Just then, interrupting his speech, a grizzly bear came out of the grasses by the river. It was possibly attracted by the smell of the fresh meat. Immediately Charbonneau screamed, "A bear, a demon bear!"

The bear was closer to Drewyer than Charbonneau. Drewyer didn't have time to get his rifle to his shoulder to shoot. He reacted instinctively and started to run with his rifle still slung over his back. As he ran away from the bear, it began to close in after him. Drewyer ran in a zigzag pattern, but the bear was closing quickly and was very near to striking him with its large claws.

Charbonneau, still frightened, had his rifle in hand, but instead of shooting at the bear, he began running toward the river and long willow weeds along the shore. As he ran he shouted, "Oh Mary, oh God save me, your deserving servant." As he ran away his finger accidentally closed around the trigger. It fired wildly into the air. The bear, which had been charging after Drewyer, heard the shot, immediately stopped, swung around and focused on Charbonneau. With a roar it rotated instantly and took after him. Charbonneau, seeing the bear now coming toward him, moved to try and hide himself in the thick willows along the river.

The large bear moved swiftly to close the ground and stopped suddenly for a moment at the edge of the tall willows. The bear snorted and began to paw the ground. It then began moving straight toward the shivering Charbonneau, now kneeling in fetal position. Meanwhile, Drewyer, who had been spared, gripped his rifle securely and ran back toward the bear and Charbonneau. The bear was now within a few feet of Charbonneau; Drewyer, seeing that there was no time to spare, raised his rifle and fired. The bullet went through the bear's skull, killing it instantly.

Charbonneau, hearing the bear fall and exhale a last huge breath of air, looked up from behind his hands. "Oh God, you have spared me. Thank you! Thank you for the willows to hide! Thank you for guiding Drewyer's shot to spare me!"

Drewyer came closer to the scene, looked at the dead bear and then at the shivering Charbonneau. "Reload your rifle," he said in a stern command and turned and walked away.

Charbonneau was immediately on his feet and ran to Drewyer's side. "You killed this beast with one shot; this has never been done. God saved me. Tonight I will fix you a special meal of sausage. I will cook it in bear grease. I will do whatever you want me to."

Hearing his statement, Drewyer stopped walking and turned to look at Charbonneau. "Then leave me alone. Go and get help to dress out the meat and load it into canoes. It was not God that fired the rifle; it was George Drewyer." With that, Drewyer turned and walked toward the men who were now coming toward them from the boats.

That night the men celebrated having fresh meat by having a large roast and feast. The bear was used both for its meat and for preparation of voyager's grease as mosquito control. Bear grease was also used in cooking for flavor. As they were around the campfire, the men talked about the scenery, the river, and wondered why they had not seen Indians.

Clark, sitting with Lewis, the three sergeants and York, said, "Did you see when Janey came from behind and passed the men up? Did you see how that lifted them up and made them go."

Sergeant Gass said, "I don't think they wanted a young Indian mother to pass them up; it was a challenge. She has grit that one. She's been walking right along with the men. They respect that."

Sergeant Ordway said, "It gave them something to do, a goal. Anything to break the monotony of the steady pulling of boats. Janey came along just at the right time, and the men were inspired."

Lewis said, "Inspired. Good choice of words, Sergeant. I believe that a competitive spirit in them was awakened, that, along with respect for her effort, caused them to redouble their efforts."

Clark added, "It's the mark of good men. They're easily inspired to greatness. Pretty as the scenery has been lately, I'll be glad to leave this section of the river behind us."

Lewis said, "I look forward to the falls the Indians had told us about. We should be coming to them soon. That'll let us know we're close to the mountain crossing. That milestone will give me an uplift."

Sergeant Gass said, "We should be seeing Janey's people after that, too. Isn't that right? Snake Indian territory ahead?"

Clark said, "That's what they said; just after the falls we'll be in Shoshone territory and they have horses. Won't that be wonderful? Moving out of the river and making some real progress."

Lewis said calmly, "As I look upon those mountains ahead, I have mixed feelings. I am pleased to know that we are so close to the head of this great river, yet seeing that they are still covered with snow makes me wonder what terrible difficulty may lie in front of us. Still, I believe in the ability of our small group to overcome any obstacle and will continue that attitude until it is impossible to hold."

June 3, 1805 Maria's River Fork, Montana

It is midmorning, the Corps of Discovery has been underway only a few hours when they come upon a fork of two great rivers.

Drewyer, who had been walking in front with Lewis and Seaman said, "Captain, there's two rivers here. See how they twist and turn as they become one. It's as if they cannot agree upon where they should merge."

"I see, I see," Lewis replied. "Which one is the Missouri? Both rivers seem to have equal strength, yet one moves northward toward the mountains and the other southward." Then he stood there in silence for a long moment and said, "I'm going back to get Captain Clark. There's a great deal to discuss." With that statement, he turned and walked back toward the river where the boats were moving forward. Drewyer stood for a moment looking at the rivers and then turned and walked back.

At the river Clark was in the lead pirogue. "What did you find?" he shouted at Lewis.

Lewis shaking his head replied, "A mess, a real quandary. There's a fork ahead. One river's coming from the north and one from the south. Hard to say which is the Missouri. Let's find a good place to camp here. I want to be as certain as I can be with this decision. If we take the wrong river we could lose weeks, not to mention a lot of effort."

Clark, listening intently to his friend, said, "Quite right Merry. I don't remember any of the Mandan saying anything about a large river junction." Then turning in the boat he shouted, "Sergeants Gass, Ordway, Pryor, bring the boats around and we'll set up camp. As soon as that is done, I want to see the three of you. Labiche, Cruzatte, meet me and the captain."

He proceeded to get out of the pirogue, when he was on land he added, "By the way, bring Charbonneau and Janey. She may just be able to recognize something. We should be getting close to where she's from. Meet Captain Lewis and me atop that bluff over yonder."

With Clark's orders the men set into action. They pulled the canoes and the red pirogue to a convenient spot and set anchors. They began unloading the tents and proceeded with the familiar routine of setting up a campground.

Lewis and Clark stood to one side as the men worked. Clark asked, "What did you see, two rivers? Why didn't the Mandan tell us of a confluence of two rivers?"

"I don't know. Perhaps this is really the 'River that Scolds All Others' that they talked of," Lewis replied. "And as for the one lower down, well, maybe we were mistaken." Lewis looked off into the distance with a grimace on his face. He was troubled, "Come Bill, let's go have a look see." With the statement they set off to the west.

Soon the two captains were standing on a high bluff overlooking the confluence of the two rivers. Lewis pointed as he spoke, "Look, the southern river is clear, clear enough to see rocks and cobblestones on the bottom. Its surface waters are swift but seem calm and even flowing from shore to shore. Over there, the northward river is less wide but it has the familiar look of the Missouri that we've known. Its waters are muddy and turbulent, in the same rolling and boiling manner that has characterized the Missouri."

Clark stroked his chin as he looked at the rivers. Then he pointed as he spoke, "Look at the south fork, the range of mountains stretching there from southeast to northwest. Behind them there looks like a second range of mountains which looks even higher stretching to the northwest. The southern fork must issue from some point in those mountains."

Lewis had his telescope to his eye as he followed Clark's conversation. When Clark finished his sentence, Lewis added, "Yeah, just look. The whole range is perfectly covered with snow." He handed his telescope to Clark who also looked at the distant lofty mountain ranges. Lewis continued, "Looks cold, got to be cold and high to have snow like that. Go ahead. See if you can spot the river's direction. I lost it in the prairie and can't see evidence of it with the telescope."

Clark replied, "Yep, the prairie swallows it up. This telescope don't help much here." He handed the instrument back to Lewis. "What about the other?"

Lewis said, "Well, there are some mountains off that way in the distance, but with all the soil this river carries, I would think it must travel a great distance over the prairies. Maybe this one goes to the headwaters of the Saskatchewan. I doubt it comes immediately from the mountains. It's just too dirty to be fresh from the mountains."

Clark looked at the northern fork and let out a "Hummm." He did not say anything more as at that moment, the group he had requested approached.

Sergeant Pryor said, "Just look at the view from this bluff. Green prairie as far as I can see. More buffalo than a man can count. I can hardly believe all the buffalo."

The small group gathered around the captains. Clark spoke, "Labiche, ask Charbonneau to find out if Janey can tell us anything about this place. The joining of these two rivers must be a significant landmark for her people. See what she knows."

Labiche turned to Charbonneau who had an expectant look on his face, "Ask your wife if this, any of this, looks familiar to her. Captain said these landmarks might be something she'd remember." Charbonneau spoke to Sacajawea and she listened intently. Then she answered pointing in one direction and then another.

Finally, the translation was made to Labiche who turned to the captains who were riveted on the translation process. "No sir," Labiche said. "She said she don't remember this place. She said that when she was captured, her captors moved at night frequently, and she doesn't remember this place. Maybe they came through here at night."

"Damn," Lewis said, and he kicked at the dirt in disgust. "I thought that she would be of value here. Damn, send them back to the camp." Then he turned to Labiche and Cruzatte, and he spoke in a lowered tone. "Pierre, Francois, you are our best river men. I want you to study these two rivers in detail and let me know which one you think is the Missouri. Don't rush. Take your time. In fact, I don't want your answer right away. I want you to go up both rivers with a detail tomorrow and then give me your opinion. You must understand; we want to be careful here. We have to know where we're going."

The two men listened intently as Lewis spoke. Then Cruzatte said, "Yes, sir, we'll study 'em both. Me and Francois here, we know our rivers. That's for sure."

Lewis said, "Good men. I'll await your opinion."

Clark turned to the sergeants, "Men, we've heard the Indians. There's a waterfall on the true Missouri. We cannot tell to a certainty which of these two rivers is the Missouri. We're not going to proceed further until we are certain we're going the right way. As soon as the campsite is set, gather two details. We're going to advance up both of these rivers as far as we can and still allow time to return by nightfall. Be observant. What you see and report will weigh in our decision."

Sergeant Ordway replied, "Yes, sir," and he and the other two sergeants turned to walk back to the campground.

Drewyer said, "With so many buffalo nearby, it will be a simple matter to get meat for the evening, I'll take a small party to bring in meat for supper and jerky."

Lewis replied, "Fine, George, go ahead."

As Drewyer left, the captains were again alone on the bluff. Both were silent for a moment. Finally Clark spoke, "Merry, we'll make this decision just as we have made all the others thus far. Meanwhile, we should enjoy this little piece of Eden. Look at the prairie. I have never seen so many animals."

Lewis looked around and replied, "I think so. I must continue to believe that Fate will deal with us fairly." Then he looked out over the prairie to the east and commented, "I truly believe that if I wrote I could see ten thousand buffalo within an area of three miles, it would be accurate. The question is, do you think anyone not seeing this site would believe it?"

Clark laughed and replied, "Merry, if you write it, it's true. Jefferson knows that as well as he knows the back of his hand. This land has produced many remarkable scenes, truly remarkable scenes. If I had not witnessed them myself, I would have difficulty believing everything we have seen."

Lewis started to walk back toward the camp. As he walked, he said, "We'll advance up both rivers until we can be sure. Right now I think the south fork is the Missouri, as it quite possibly issues from those mountains. But we have to be sure."

Clark said, "We have some good and experienced men with us. Let's make use of their counsel along with our investigations of these two rivers before we move."

Lewis asked, "Yes, but Bill, if we make a mistake and choose the wrong fork, we could lose weeks of travel backtracking. And we still have those snowy mountains to cross. If we lose too much time, the mission itself may be at risk. I don't know what we'd do if we chose the wrong fork."

Clark interrupted his friend, "What we would do? My friend, we would do what we always have done, we would proceed on."

Lewis stopped and looked at Clark and said, "Done."

That day the men took measurements of the two rivers. The southern fork was three hundred seventy-two yards wide with swift, clear, smooth water. The north fork had a muddy bottom and measured two hundred yards across. Its waters were turbulent and deeper than the clear river. A group moved up the north fork and found a small tributary about a mile and a half upstream with well-wooded bottom land. They brought some of the wood back to the campsite for the fires.

That evening around the fires and over their supper, the men talked about the two rivers and which one they thought could be the true Missouri. That evening before retiring Lewis and Clark made an announcement to the men.

Clark said, "Men, as you know, we have a puzzle to unravel. From your conversations this evening, I believe that many of you think the north fork is the Missouri. Captain Lewis and I are not so sure. Either way, we must try to make our best decision. We have chosen the following men to explore the rivers until we have enough evidence to make a decision. Reubin and Joseph Fields, Sergeant Gass, George Shannon and York will go with me up the south fork. Sergeant Pryor, Drewyer, Shields, Windsor, Cruzatte and LaPage will go with Captain Lewis up the north fork. Again I repeat, we'll proceed upriver and reconnoiter the land until we can decide one way or another. We'll expect to meet back here in three days and decide which way to go. Meanwhile, those of you remaining in camp will work with Sergeant Ordway to prepare jerky and dry skins for clothing, moccasins and rope. Have a good night's rest; we'll leave in the morning."

The men retired early, in the morning Clark and his contingent headed south up the clear river while Lewis and his contingent moved north.

Clark advanced his men up the river for two days. They observed snow-capped mountains reaching toward the south and west. Seeing a high ridge, Clark ordered that they advance to its summit to make observations. He spoke to the men, "Seeing these mountains stretching so majestically south and west, I believe that this clear river is the Missouri. Its source will prove to come from these mountains, and from that source I believe we'll cross the divide and find the small rivulets that will eventually form the Columbia. What do you think, Sergeant?"

Sergeant Gass looked toward the southwest. "Could be. I am sure of one thing. The water certainly comes from those mountains. It's as cold as any river I ever saw. I sure hope we find those falls and the passage to the mountains soon. Ain't one of us goin' to be sorry to put the Missouri behind us and float down the Columbia for awhile."

Clark said, "I think I've seen enough. Let's return to camp and find out what Captain Lewis and his men have discovered. I hope they're back by the time we get there. One thing sure, we want to find the most direct way to the fabled Northwest Passage, and we can't keep burning daylight trying to make a decision."

As they moved back toward the river, they came across a grove of cottonwood trees. Clark stopped and said, "I think I will carve my name here while we close camp and get ready to move out."

Reubin Field said, "Just think, fellas, it took us two days to get here, going back will be easy as pie. We just sit back and ride the rapids."

George Shannon said, "Ride the rapids? Now you've got to love that. One oarsman to do a little steering to keep us in the current and the rest of us ride in ecstacy."

The men were in high spirits as they made ready to return back downriver to meet the others.

June 7, 1805

It was morning and the small camp was rising for the day.
"Sergeant Pryor," Lewis said as he looked up the river. "I want
you to take Windsor and go on ahead until you find a
prominent ridge to make observations. Take my octant and
make measurements of latitude and longitude. Let me know
the bearing of this river as far as you can make it out."

"Yes, sir," Pryor replied. "Were you able to make any
reading yesterday?"

Lewis shook his head, "No, too much cloud cover. I'm rea-
sonably sure this river makes its course through the prairies to
the north. That's why its filled with so much soil. Every observation shows it heading northward, not a favorable
direction for us this far west to still be able to meet with the
Columbia. I just don't feel right about it."

Drewyer said, "Well now, isn't that what we are here for?
To make doubly sure that we know."

The two men selected headed out as ordered. Lewis and
the others went hunting for elk, both for food and to make
hides for Lewis' metal-framed boat. The boat frame had been
brought all the way from Pittsburgh for use in shallow waters.
They also set to making rafts for their descent back down the
river, hoping to make better time by employing the river's
current than traveling overland. The rafts would also allow
them to take cargo.

Just after noon, Sergeant Pryor and Windsor returned.
They had reached a summit where they saw the river going
slightly west for a few miles and then turning north as far as
they could see.

"How far do you think you could see?" Lewis queried.

Pryor replied, "We got up on the ridge. We could see
pretty good, maybe fifteen miles or more. The river is definitely north as far as we could see."

Lewis looked at the two men and replied, "Thanks men, that's what I imagined you would find. I think we should head back now. While you were out, we made a couple of rafts. How about it? Would you like to float back to camp?"

Windsor said, "Oh, hell yes. Let's get started."

Pryor spoke, "We don't have much stuff, but let's load the rafts and get underway."

They had not been on the turbulent river very long when they realized that the rafts would not be river worthy. Cruzatte told Lewis, "Capt'n, the load just shifted, and I near lost my rifle over the side. These little craft are just no good. We'd be better off walking. If we don't put up soon, we'll be swimming for sure."

Lewis looked at the small rafts and replied, "I won't argue with that, Pierre. These rafts are too slender, just too small. No need to put ourselves in danger needlessly. Let's put in here as quickly as possible or we may regret this adventure. This is folly. We'd be fools to continue with it."

They put in to shore as quickly as they could and abandoned the makeshift rafts in the weeds along the river's edge. Thick clouds were forming, causing the evening to set in early. The men bedded down on the ground without benefit of tents and attempted to spend the night. Then rain started lightly, ruining any possibility of getting a restful night. The rain continued steadily all night. Not being able to sleep, the small group was up and out of the watery beds at first light.

John Shields rose and picked up his rifle, "Well now, that was a peaceful night's rest, wasn't it?"

Pryor said, as he rose, "Cut the nonsense. We need to get this place behind us and back to the main camp to dry out or we'll all get pneumonia."

Lewis stood looking at the stormy sky for a moment. Rain in his face, he said, "Horrible weather, but this rain may break up within a few hours. Who knows? The sun may even break through. With this much wind, these rain clouds may blow over. None of us knows what Captain Clark has found. I, for one, am very interested in his report. I'm sure he is also keen to hear from us. We've already spent more time than planned on this adventure. We're late in returning to the camp. Let's put some miles away."

Cruzatte said, "Well, maybe the capt'n has it right. This rain may break up midday and give us some sunlight. The wind could blow these clouds away."

Drewyer said, "We'd all welcome that. This ground is wet and slippery, your wet moccasins would slide easily. That'll make the trip back seem longer. I don't recommend trying to retrace our steps. Some of the slopes will be too slick."

Lewis said, "This reminds me of frozen ground in Virginia when it gets partially thawed and turns slippery. This soil has a lot of clay and it's hard to keep your feet under you. Use your espontoons as walking sticks if you need."

They walked along slowly but steadily through the wind and rain. The landscape presented frequent bluffs along the river's path. Rather than increase their distance by going around them, they proceeded to walk near the river's edge close to steep bluffs. Passing along the edge of one of these bluffs, Lewis was in the lead. There was a narrow passageway about thirty yards in length. Lewis inched along slowly, his back to the bluff as he sidestepped his way along the narrow ledge.

Suddenly, his wet moccasin slipped on the ledge. He held his rifle in his left hand and espontoon in his right. He swung the rifle out as a balancing pole as he automatically plunged the espontoon into the ground to stabilize himself. As he teetered on the ledge momentarily, he looked down to see a sheer drop of nearly ninety feet over rocks and bushes to the river below. He took a deep breath and let it out slowly as he said to himself. "Careful Meriwether, don't want a broken bone or worse. Got to lead these men."

Lewis continued to sidestep along the ledge to a point where he could get a stable stance and feel secure. He was about to turn and shout out a warning to the men following him when he heard a voice crying out, "God, God Capt'n, what shall I do!"

Turning and looking, Lewis saw Windsor, soaked and muddy, lying on his belly from a fall. He was in a precarious situation where the small supporting ledge could crumble or he could slip on the wet clay and tumble to the river below. He had his right arm and leg over the ledge and was holding on with only his left foot and arm. His face was white with fear as his left hand and fingernails clawed at the muddy ledge to try and hold on.

Lewis looked at the man and was alarmed for his safety. Knowing he could see the man cascading over the ledge at any moment, Lewis gathered his wits, kneeled down and spoke calmly but firmly to Windsor. "Private Windsor, you are going to be all right. I just came across, and you'll be alright. Now then, just listen to me. Don't look down. Listen carefully. I want you to do exactly what I tell you. Do it slowly, no need to rush here. You're going to be all right."

Windsor, lips thin, eyes wide with fear, replied, "Yes, sir, alright sir, just tell me what to do!"

Lewis said calmly, "Alright, now with your right hand move slowly and take your knife out of your belt. I can see your knife and it's on your backside on your right. Alright, do it now, slowly, slowly. You're going to be all right in no time." As Lewis spoke, Windsor followed the instructions.

"Alright, sir, I got it!" Windsor said in a trembling voice.

Lewis, still calm, continued, "Good, very good. Now we're going to work on making you a way out of there. Take the knife and dig a hole with it in the bank there in front of you.

Make it big enough to put the toe of your moccasin into it. You'll find that the damp ground is only on the top, it's dry underneath. Dig it out dry all the way."

Windsor proceeded obediently and said, "Yes, sir. Oh God, it's working, sir. It **is** dry under the surface just like you said."

Lewis said, "Of course it's dry. You're going to be alright. Didn't I tell you you'd be all right? We didn't bring you all this way out here to see you fall over a stupid ledge. Now put your right foot into the notch you just made."

Windsor sounding calmer, "I got it. My foot's in the notch."

Lewis continued, "Good, good. Now I want you to move slowly to pull yourself up on your knees. Use your knife, stab it into the ground and pull yourself up. Pull steady and slow in case the knife slips out. Do it now."

Windsor accomplished the movement, and Lewis continued the instruction, "Now that you're on the ledge, take off those moccasins, no need to slip again. Come toward me on your hands and knees."

Holding his rifle in one hand and his knife in the other, the obedient Windsor, hanging on Lewis' every word, followed the instructions until he was able to reach a place where he could stand back up without danger. Windsor erected himself and took a deep breath as he looked back at the ledge. Then he looked Lewis in the eye, "Thank you, Capt'n. I'd have fell over the edge for sure if you hadn't been there to tell me what to do." He extended his hand to clasp Lewis' hand.

As they shook hands Lewis looked back at the path. The others were coming into view. Lewis immediately released the clasp, stepped forward and shouted. "Drewyer, Pryor, all you men, listen up here! Windsor and I both damn near fell here. Go back down to where you can enter the river. Come down in the river. Stay as close to this edge as you can. Keep your rifles up and dry."

The men reversed their direction and soon reappeared in the river below. When the entire contingent was together again, they proceeded downriver by walking along the riverbank whenever possible. Where there was no bank, they had to wade in water breast deep on occasions where there was no place to wade or walk along the shoreline. In these places they had to use their knives to cut handhold grips in the steep bluffs to maneuver past hand over hand while their bodies were in the water. Thus, they continued for eighteen miles until evening when they came upon the remains of an abandoned Indian village.

Lewis looked at the site and announced, "We'll stay here tonight. Drewyer, Shields, get us a deer or something for supper. Sergeant Pryor, the rain has stopped. Prepare a dry spot and build a fire. Cruzatte, LaPage, Windsor gather firewood for the evening. We'll have meat for supper, and we all need to dry out. This is a welcome little shelter and we'll make good use of it."

Fortune in their favor, the hunters quickly killed a deer. The venison was prepared for roasting just as the fire was beginning to get large enough to accomplish both roasting the meat and drying out.

Sergeant Pryor said, "What a day. Hey, Windsor, this is a day I'll bet you'll not want to soon repeat."

Windsor nodded and said, "No doubt about that, a day from hell for sure. I must confess to you all that I was completely panicked back there. I thought for sure that I was a goner. Capt'n saved me. Just kept talkin' and telling me what to do, one thing at a time."

Lewis spoke, "Any one of you would have done the same for another. I was just the closest one, that's all. Let's all have a hearty meal, dry out and get a good night's rest." Then smiling with a wry smile he said, "I don't know about you men but this is the first food I've had all day. Nothing like a full belly and a dry place to sleep to make a good night's rest for a weary traveler."

Sergeant Pryor said, "None of us got any sleep last night. Tonight we'll sleep. Tomorrow we should be back with the others."

June 8, 1805

Lewis and his small contingent, weary from traveling all day, were uplifted at the sight of their fellow travelers as they saw the main campsite ahead. Pierre Cruzatte fired his rifle in the air, whistled, then shouted, "Hello there. Is that the Corps of Discovery?"

Turning as they heard the shot and Cruzatte's call, the campsite came alive, "They're back. Hurrah!" as the men moved in unison toward their returning friends. All the men welcomed one another with handshakes and each began telling stories and all talking at once.

Clark and Ordway approached Lewis simultaneously. Both were smiling broadly as Ordway spoke. "Good to see you, Capt'n. We were expecting you no later than yesterday. We were getting worried. Capt'n Clark had us prepare a big meal, a regular feast for when you came in. We got buffalo tongue and hump, beaver, almost anything you want. Charbonneau has made up some of his special sausages. Janey has been collecting food up and down the river, leastways until day before yesterday. She stayed in camp today. I guess she's not feeling too good."

As Ordway finished his oration, Clark stood and smiled at Lewis. He extended his hand and said, "Welcome back, Captain. Ordway has it right. We planned a real feast for your return and a celebration of which river to take. Everyone's anxious to get on with the expedition."

Lewis smiled broadly and said, "Glad to be back. We spent some hellish time out there, and we're glad to be back. I had to go upriver farther than I had originally thought I would have to. I wanted to get to where I could make a reasonable decision."

Clark said, "Sergeant Ordway was right. We were getting worried. In fact, we were going to send a detail upriver to look for you in the morning. Damn glad to see you back. You look a little frazzled. A good meal should help you out."

Lewis nodded as he replied, "Could use a good meal, the comfort of friendly faces and a dry campground. Let's eat, I'm anxious to exchange opinions with you as to which of these two rivers is the true Missouri."

"A hot meal's coming right up," Sergeant Ordway said as he turned and walked back toward the campfires.

As the men were mingling again and comparing stories of what each of them had learned, Sergeant Ordway said to Cruzatte, "Pierre, we're glad to have you back in camp. I didn't know we'd miss your music so much. After dinner would you pleasure us with a few tunes?"

Cruzatte smiled and looked around the campsite at all the men looking at him. "Sure enough, I'll play tonight. I've missed playing my fiddle, too. Ol' Pierre will give you all a treat tonight."

Windsor had everyone's attention as he told of how he nearly perished on the slippery slopes in the rain. He was animated as he made gestures to demonstrate to the others about how he had hung on to the ledge and then later how they had to cut handholds along the river's edge to come downstream. Lewis and Clark sat together and away from the main body. As they ate they talked of the two rivers.

Clark said, "We actually started back earlier than I thought we would. Even though the water is clear, I think the south river is the Missouri. I'm sure enough of it that I didn't see the need to pursue it further. We saw the mountain ranges apparently converging with the river. It does bother me some that it heads south as far as we could see. I didn't see the falls the Indians said were there. That bothered me, but you know, those falls could be just another day away from where we turned back. What did you see? What do you think?"

Lewis sat riveted to every word as Clark spoke. He was nodding with a piece of roast buffalo meat in his hand. He stopped eating and said "Bill, I'm so glad to hear you have reached that conclusion. I agree completely. We went up river quite a way. There were several high bluffs that provided a vantage point for observation and I took advantage of many of them. Each one added to my conviction that the northern river was not the Missouri. It moves through the plains, across the prairies and continues north. At the farthest point we traveled, I had Pryor and Windsor go out to make a last observation. When they returned, they confirmed my analysis. The river turns from the mountains and proceeds north through the plains. I think it will ultimately form the northernmost boundary of the Purchase. On our return trip, I plan to investigate it further. There may be possible disputes with Canada or Great Britain over this drainage basin if it continues as far north as I suspect. I think we can discount the maps we were given. The Canadian rivers do not headwater this far south."

Clark, who had also been concentrating on Lewis' words, replied with a smile, "So we agree. Independently we have come to the same conclusion?"

Lewis said, "Yes, I believe it enough that I am ready to pursue the clear river as the Missouri. But I'm anxious to hear what the men have to say. We've some experienced men with us. We should benefit from their counsel on this. We have to consider everything. There's simply too much riding on it."

Clark looking puzzled for a moment asked, "Why do you suppose the Indians never told us about this one?"

"I've been thinking a lot about that, Bill," Lewis said. "I think maybe they did; this must be the River That Scolds All Others. The one lower down that we thought was it, well, we were just mistaken. Maybe we were too anxious."

Clark said, "Any way you look at it, the Mandan weren't too clear on that one, now were they? It confused both of us all the while. Well, if the south fork is the Missouri as we both believe, what are you going to name the north fork? You explored it, you get to name it."

Lewis said, "I've given it some thought. I think I'll name it Maria's River."

Clark said, "After your cousin, Maria Wood?"

Lewis acknowledged, "Yeah, although the river is rough and turbulent and unlike her personality, it is a large and prominent river, and it will be an important tributary for trade. The land around it is beautiful and fertile. It seems to be well-populated with fur bearing animals. This river, even though it does not lead to our sought after Northwest Passage will, nonetheless, be important to future commerce. Because of its importance, I will name it after Maria."

Clark added, "Well Merry, I've already added the river to the charts. I had time to work on them some while waiting for your return. Everything's there but the name. Maria's River it will be."

At this time Sergeant Gass came over and said, "Pardon me, captains, but before we have Pierre start playin' the fiddle tonight, we'd like to know where we're headin' in the morning."

Lewis said, "Excellent question, Sergeant, gather all the men around; we're going to have an open forum."

Clark added, "I know that all you men have been talking about these two rivers. Now that you're all together, let's have only two of you give the opinion of which river is the Missouri. One of you speaking for the south fork and one for the north fork. Captain Lewis and I have our opinion, but we very much would like to hear what you men think before we say anything or make a final choice."

Gass said, "No need for two of us to speak, sir. Everyone, to the man, thinks the north river is the Missouri."

Lewis rubbed his chin and said, "Very well, Sergeant. Then two of you can present the case for the north fork being the Missouri. We're interested in your observations."

Sergeant Gass said, "Good, sir, I think Cruzatte and I can do it. Let's get all the men to shut up and move in close so we can talk this over."

They moved to form a semi-circle in front of the captains.

Clark said, "Men, we are literally at a fork in the road. Which one we take will ultimately be the decision of me and Captain Lewis. Still, we want to hear your arguments for why you would select the northern river. Your opinion will be considered. When we hear the arguments, we will consider them and then we'll tell you our decision."

Lewis added, "We want to be sure that we're making the right choice and going the right way. You all know if we make a mistake here, we could lose so much time that we would not make it over the mountains before winter."

Sergeant Gass spoke, "I went with Captain Clark up the southern river. It's clear water and flows real smooth all the way. It probably gets its volume from those snow-capped mountains. We don't think the Northwest Passage lies south of here on a clear water river. The Missouri we've been working against is a muddy water river, turbulent and wide. It looks like the north river." He sat down.

Clark said, "Pierre."

Cruzatte stood and looked around. He watched as Sergeant Gass sat down then turned to focus on the captains. He brushed his hands against his sides and then spoke, "Captains, I been a river man all my life. I've seen big rivers and the tributaries leadin' into 'em. I followed many of those tributaries till they were no more than little creeks. The main river always has a flavor, a character of its own, like a personality. Yup, a river has a personality." He fidgeted slightly, looked around and then continued. "I went up the north river with Capt'n Lewis. It had some tributaries to it, all little ones. That river looks and smells like the Missouri we been working all these months. The Missouri has been heading north and west all the while we been on it. That river there goes north. It cuts through prairie, just like below. The personality seems the same all the way. The water is rough and turbulent, just like below. I think it's the main river and that it'll turn and go into the mountains, and we'll find the Northwest Passage there. I don't think the Missouri turns south, just not its character. The north river has the turbulent, muddy waters that we all know as the Missouri." Finishing his statement, Cruzatte nodded a thank-you gesture toward the captains and sat down.

Clark stood and looked at the men. "You've given us much to think about. We've just finished a handsome meal and are now ready to listen to music and retire. Captain Lewis and I will discuss your point of view, and we will let you know our decision in the morning. Meanwhile, a gill of whiskey to each of you."

The men returned to their discussions. Windsor was still talking about his episode on the slippery cliff. All the men were holding their cups of whiskey as Cruzatte began to play the fiddle.

In the morning the men were up and about early, anxious to get underway. Captain Clark gathered them together and spoke, "Thank you men, for your opinions of last evening. Captain Lewis has studied the science of geology and I have also become familiar with it. We have spent time discussing the principles of that science. I must agree that your arguments for the north river are strong, convincing and made with conviction. Captain Lewis and I have both said nearly identical things to one another. We believe that the north river has its headwaters to the far north. But we concluded that it does not go into the mountains to form our sought after Northwest Passage. Our gut feeling says south."

The men turned and looked at one another, some murmuring comments. Then Sergeant Pryor stepped forward and said, "Captain Clark, Captain Lewis, we men have followed your lead into this unknown land with every unexpected turn of the river. Without question you have shown us leadership. We are proud to serve under your command on this great venture no matter what the outcome. While we do not agree that the south river is the true Missouri, we will all follow your lead, without question, up the south river until we find the falls and the passage or until we perish in the attempt."

Lewis looked at Clark, and they stared at one another for a moment and then both looked at the men. Lewis spoke, "Thank you men, for the vote of confidence in our decision. Because of the lack of a positive certainty regarding this river, I will take a small detachment and head out in front of the rest of the group with the purpose either to find the falls or a passage through the mountains. So that we do not lose time, the rest of you will follow with Captain Clark. Before we move out, I believe that we should bury the red here along with a cache of goods for use on our return trip. Leave the heavy things, some of the blacksmith tools and such. First repair all rifles." Then as an afterthought, "Please look at my air rifle. I want it in operating condition when we move out. The Indians have all been taken with that technology."

June 11, 1805 South of Maria's River to Great Falls

"It's all finished, sir," Sergeant Gass said, reporting to Lewis. "The red's buried and all the cargo has been tied down. We kept out some blacksmith tools, buried only the heavy ones. I put some gunpowder and lead in and included a little tobacco, too. Covered it all with oil cloth."

Lewis replied, "Did you mark some trees for location?"

"We'll get that done too, sir, sure enough," Gass answered.

Lewis looked at the area and seemed pleased. Then he turned to seek out Drewyer. He walked over to him and said, "George, get Gibson, Joe Field and Goodrich. We'll head out as soon as they're ready. I'm going to get my pack and put writing materials in my portable desk. I'll be ready to head out in ten minutes."

Drewyer nodded and went to tell the others to get ready.

Lewis went to the tent and found Clark outside. "I'm going to head out now. How soon do you think you'll be able to break camp and follow?"

Clark replied, "We should be ready in about an hour or two. The boats are being loaded now. Everyone is ready to go." Then pausing slightly he added, "Except Jancy, she's been ill the last few days. Last night Labiche came over and said Charbonneau was asking for help. I went over and bled her. Then I gave her some hot soup made of bone marrow. She had a fever and didn't respond. I'll see how she's doing this morning. If she isn't up to walking, I'll have her ride in the canoe. I don't want her to lose her milk. The baby needs her and that takes her energy."

Lewis looked concerned, hands on his hips, he looked in the direction of the Charbonneau tent, "Well, keep a close eye on her. Without her, the baby would be in trouble, too. We'll soon be near the Shoshone, we'll need her to interpret to trade for horses. She's been a real trooper. I hope she gets better soon."

Clark said, "Ahead you'll see where I carved my name in a tree by the river to mark how far I'd gone. From it you can see the high point where I looked to make my final decision as to whether or not this was the Missouri."

Lewis replied, "Good idea. I'm sure we won't miss it. As soon as we find the falls or determine that we've made the wrong choice, we'll come back to join you."

Clark looked at his friend, extended his hand, and as they shook hands he said, "I look forward to meeting you again at the falls."

June 13, 1805 Great Falls, Montana

Lewis and his small party moved out of the river channel and began walking over the prairies, headed southwest. There, stretching before them was a beautiful, level plain that seemed to stretch on for fifty to sixty miles.

Silas Goodrich said, "Look ahead there, Capt'n. Ever see so many buffalo?"

Lewis paused as he let his eye pan the expanse of prairie in front, "No Silas, I have not. Every time I see herds of buffalo in this land, I am in awe. It seems they go on without end. Even with the predation of wolves, grizzly and native Indians, they prosper like no other herd animal I have known. Look at the beauty of this place, the river, the prairie and the mountains. Those two yellow clay mountains look as if their tops have been scraped flat. The enchanted views that we behold are magnificent. I hope that my journal entries will do them justice so those who read them later will believe and understand what it is we are seeing."

Goodrich replied, "Seems like every week we see something new. It's been hard work getting the boats this far, but none of us regret that. We're proud to be part of discovering this new country."

Lewis looked at him a moment and said, "I know the feeling." Then he looked at the other men coming up from behind. "Drewyer, you, Gibson and Field go off and hunt near the river bottom; get us some meat for supper and we'll meet you later upriver tonight. Goodrich and I will go on ahead due south."

Drewyer nodded, and the men split up. Lewis continued to walk southward, and his long, steady stride was beginning to leave Goodrich behind. All the while he was walking, his eye was ever vigilant, surveying all about him, looking for new plants to document or potential danger. Lewis slowed his stride slightly to allow Goodrich to catch up. In slowing, the sounds of his own walk diminished, the rustle of his buckskins against the plants, his footfall on the grass. Suddenly he heard a noise and perked up. He stopped still in his tracks, turned his head toward the south and listened intently.

"Yieeee haaaa!" Lewis shouted. "Goodrich, come here! Hurry, listen. Listen good. Tell me what you hear."

Goodrich quickened his step to catch up to Lewis. The impatient Lewis continued to walk on forward, motioning with his arm to Goodrich to catch up. Then he stopped, pointed and spoke excitedly as Goodrich caught up. "Look. Look there. See that column of smoke? Hear that sound? Well, that is the Missouri Falls! And that is not smoke. It's spray, water spray. By God, Silas, we've found the falls. This is the true Missouri!"

Goodrich, slightly winded, smiled broadly and replied, "I hear it; I see it! There it is. It's gotta be the falls! You were right all along, sir, that's gotta be the falls!"

Lewis said, "Silas, go back and join the hunters. Hurry up now. Tell them we have found the falls. The Falls of the Missouri River! Tell them to come with all haste. Bring whatever meat they have forward. If they don't have anything yet, tell them to come on ahead without. We'll hunt closer to the falls. Tonight, we're going to eat near the spray of the falls."

"Yes, sir." Goodrich said, as he turned and walked back toward the river.

Lewis shouldered his rifle and proceeded directly toward the falls. The longer he walked, the louder and more pronounced was the sound of cascading water. He could see the spray lifting high into the air. It was near midday as he reached a point where he first beheld the river and the falls. He climbed onto some rocks directly opposite the tumbling falls and stood there in awe observing the falls. Lewis said to himself, "I wish President Jefferson could see this. I wish my mother and family could witness the beauty of this place. This is the most beautiful sight I have ever beheld."

He stood and looked left and right and then back left again. He moved over to seat himself near some cottonwood trees and took out his writing desk and began to write. As he wrote, his pen raced across the paper. Almost frantically he dipped into the ink and wrote, dipped and wrote, dipped and wrote. Finally, he stopped, "Oh, damn, I don't think I have the ability to capture in words what my eyes are witnessing." He almost tore up the paper in order to begin writing anew. Then he paused, looked at the falls and back at his paper. "I don't think I can improve on it. This scene needs the talents of a painter. My writing skill will not improve. I'll leave this description as I have set it down."

Lewis set his writing desk down and began looking around for the best place to set up camp and wait for Clark and the others. About this time, Drewyer and Goodrich came into view.

Goodrich shouted, "Captain, I found them easy. When I thought I should be getting close, I just fired my rifle. They heard me and fired back."

As they closed the distance between them, Lewis asked, "Get any buffalo?"

Drewyer replied, "Yes, three good and fat cows. And the good news is they are only about three-quarter mile downriver from here. Fact is, we could hear the falls from there. We should have a good supper tonight."

Joseph Field said, "Just look at this. Cliffs must go up two hundred feet, straight up. Look at that foam. It just stretches out and continues downriver even after it leaves the falls. This is incredible."

Drewyer smiled and looked at Lewis, "Well now, Capt'n, this proves you were right all along. These falls are a very convincing argument that this is the Missouri."

Lewis smiled and replied, "We all won this argument. Being on the right course means we won't have to double back. More than feeling vindicated, I'm relieved that we've made good progress today."

They began setting up camp for the evening. A campfire was made of cottonwood limbs, and the men brought meat in for roasting. As they were eating, Lewis said, "What a feast we have for such a small assembly. This is a meal fit for the entire crew: buffalo tongue, hump and marrow. Goodrich not only knows how to catch fish, he knows how to prepare it and make it rival buffalo. Well done, men; well done, indeed."

Goodrich said, "Well, sir, we're all hungry enough, ain't none of us ate a single bite all day."

Lewis smiled and replied, "I have always said, Silas, that a good appetite is as much a part of a feast as any of the food. It's a luxury to appease a keen hunger in such a manner and a good appetite just adds to the flavor."

Joseph Field, mouth full and chewing replied, "You betcha, sir. I sure enough brought an appetite to this meal. Don't think it'll stick around long though, not with all this roast."

All the men nodded and then Lewis said, "Joe, you are one of the fastest men on foot we have. Tomorrow I want you to set out early and take this note back to Captain Clark. It simply says we await his arrival at the Falls of the Missouri River."

Field replied, "My pleasure, sir. I'll bet Capt'n Clark and the others are gonna be glad to know we are on the Missouri."

June 14, 1805 Great Falls of the Missouri

Lewis was up early and anxious to explore around the falls. He told Drewyer, Gibson and Goodrich, "Men, I am going to reconnoiter these falls. I want to explore for the best route around. Beautiful as they are, they're an obstacle, and one that we'll have to deal with. These sheer, steep walls must have a passage. If I'm not back by nightfall, don't worry. I'll build a fire and be back not later than midday tomorrow."

Drewyer said, "Good enough. We'll make some more moccasins from the hides, and extra jerky is always good. Which side you going up? I may explore the other if I have time."

Lewis replied, "I'm going on the south side. If you have time to explore the other side, that'd be good. One thing sure, we'll have to portage around these falls, and we can save time by finding the best route before the others get here."

Lewis left to explore the upper falls, and by midday, at a steady pace, he was quite a few miles upriver. He learned that there was not just one set of falls but five, stair stepping their way up the river. His exploration took him farther than expected. Time passed and he resolved to spend the night under some cottonwood trees near the river. There was plenty of driftwood available and he decided he would make a fire for the evening. Buffalo were abundant in the area and he had no trouble selecting a small cow, which would be his evening meal. He took careful aim and fired. The animal dropped and was expiring as Lewis approached. For some reason, he failed to recharge his rifle, a practice that was nearly automatic for all frontiersmen, especially Lewis.

The sound of the rifle fire caused a patrolling grizzly to stop, turn around and proceed toward the unsuspecting Lewis. Its sense of smell is keen and it could already smell the blood from the dying buffalo. It saw Lewis and began to move slowly, silently, steadily toward him.

As Lewis approached the fallen buffalo, the large grizzly suddenly emerged from the tall weeds. It was within twenty paces of Lewis. It raised up on its hind legs and snarled as it waved its front paws threateningly. Momentarily Lewis froze as he recognized the bear and how close it was to him. Lewis raised his rifle to shoot but realized that it was not charged and that he had no time to reload with the grizzly so close. Quickly, he scanned the situation for a tree to climb or some brush in which he could hide. There was nothing, just the grizzly, an unloaded rifle, the dead buffalo and Lewis. With nowhere to go, Lewis decided to try to reach the river for safety. The river could possibly give him some advantage and perhaps the bear would not follow. He slowly started to back up, toward the sloping riverbank, hoping the water would slow the bear's advance.

No sooner had he turned to walk toward the river when the bear growled, mouth open wide, and pitched himself toward Lewis. Lewis ran about eighty yards, zigzagging toward the river. The bear, in control, was gaining on him very fast. He could hear the large paws hitting the ground and hear its heavy breathing as it closed the gap between them.

Lewis ran into the water. Then he decided that retreat was not the best course of action with an animal faster than any human. He stopped, turned to face the bear, raised and pointed his espontoon to defend himself.

At that moment the bear had come to the water's edge and was within twenty feet of the frightened explorer. The bear, seeing Lewis in the river, espontoon pointed directly at him, paused, raked the ground several times with his claws, snorted and raised himself up on his hind legs and roared. Then, as if the bear had decided not to fight in the water, suddenly it wheeled around and ran, as if frightened, in the opposite direction.

Lewis stood in the water a moment and watched the great bear running away. He let out a breath of air and then slowly advanced toward shore. At the shoreline, he immediately charged his rifle and looked at the bear, now at some distance and still running away. He said to himself, "Close one, Meriwether. What made it run?"

Lewis began moving back toward the area where he had killed the buffalo earlier. Then he noticed an animal about two hundred yards distant with brownish yellow fur. It was about the size of a small wolf. The animal was near a burrow, and, wanting a specimen of the unusual animal, Lewis rested his rifle on his espontoon and took aim. He fired and it disappeared into its burrow. Examining the hole he could see it had long claws but he could not determine whether or not he had killed it. He recharged his rifle and, after a while of waiting, decided to move on.

He had not proceeded more than three hundred yards further on his course when three bull buffalo separated themselves from the herd and ran directly toward him at full speed. Knowing he could not outdistance them, and recalling that the bear had retreated when confronted, Lewis paused a moment and then moved directly toward the three charging buffalo bulls. When the animals were within one hundred yards, they suddenly set their hooves and came to an abrupt halt. The three stood silent for a moment looking at Lewis, and Lewis returned the stare. Then the three turned and trotted back to join the main herd.

Lewis said to himself, "With these three curious and unusual signals, back to back, I don't think it prudent to stay the night here alone. Better join the men lower down." He turned his stride downriver as night began to close in around him. He walked on, through the night with an occasional lance of pain from the ever-present prickly pear cactus. Finally, he saw a campfire ahead and joined his companions at the falls.

Meanwhile, Clark is moving upriver with difficulties of his own.

"How is she?" Clark asked Labiche as he pointed to the listless Sacajawea. Labiche, in turn, asked Charbonneau, who leaned over and spoke softly to his wife. Hearing his voice, she moaned, turned her head slightly and looked at Clark with half opened eyes. Clark was holding the baby who was resting quietly. Sacajawea motioned that she wanted the child.

Clark said, "Tell her we have given him some soup of marrow bone and wild onion." As the translation was completed, Sacajawea nodded and again motioned to have her child.

Clark nodded as he said, "She wants the little guy. There's no arguing with a mother's ability to care for a child. Go get Ordway and Pryor. I want to talk about our situation."

Labiche moved off as Clark looked down at Sacajawea in the canoe with the infant in her arms. Soon the two sergeants came over. "Yeah, Capt'n, what can we do for ya?"

Clark sighed and said in a low tone, "It's Janey. She's getting weaker all the time. I don't know how she gets the strength to care for the child when she is so weak herself. She hasn't eaten anything and she's got a fever. She is complaining of pain in her lower abdomen and I don't know what to do for her. Either of you got any ideas?"

Pryor looked serious as he replied, "She looks like Floyd did last year. He was the same just at the end." Then he turned and looked at Ordway, "You know of any poultice or anything we can do?"

Ordway looked at Sacajawea and then at Clark, "Did ya bleed her?"

Clark said, "Yeah, but it didn't help. I want to try something that will perk her up. Can you make her some soup from marrow bones and a little meat? If we lose her out here, we'll have to feed the child, and that may be a problem at his age."

Ordway continued, "How long has she been this sick?"

Clark replied, "Four days that she's been down with it. Don't know how long she may have been feeling bad before she complained."

Ordway nodded and then said, "I have some bark and some spices. I could make a hot wrap for her to apply. I think maybe a little whiskey might just help her, too. What you think, sir?"

Clark nodded as he spoke, "Sure, go ahead; try it. Try anything you can. It might work; sure couldn't hurt any. If any of the men knows of any remedy, no matter how strange, let me know. I'll listen, and if it is plausible, I may try it."

Pryor said, "We could start a fire and get some green wood to make a lot of smoke. If we can get some Indians to come here, maybe they'll have a remedy. At least if she dies, they could find a wet nurse for the child."

Clark said, "Good idea, but I ain't seen any Indians for a long time. We really can't stop and wait. They may never come. Besides, her people should be in this area, maybe just past the falls. If we're on the right river, we could be finding her own people soon. They'd be able to help her. I don't think stopping to try to signal for Indian help is the thing to do."

Pryor replied, "Just a thought."

Clark changed the subject as he looked at the river and said, "The current has been fast. How are the men doing?"

Ordway replied, "Well sir, we have taken on water a couple of times in the small canoes. Hard not to with this current strong like it is. There's been lots of times when they've had to pull while wading in the river. They slip on the rocks, sometimes cut their feet. They would pull from the shore, but there's a lot of rattlesnakes around, lots of 'em. I think they'd rather be in the river than watching out for snakes all the time. The river is hard going sure enough, but the men seem to be in good spirits. They been pulling like hell all day."

Just then there was a shout from Reubin Field, "Hey everybody. Hey Capt'n, it's Joe, my brother. He's comin'. See him comin' there."

Clark looked up as all the men were waving at the approaching Field. As he drew near all the men said, "Good to see ya. Did you find anything? See the falls?"

Field moved quickly toward Clark as he retrieved a paper from his waist. "Here ya go, Capt'n. It's a message from Capt'n Lewis." He looked around at all the men gathered to hear what he had to say, "We made it, sir. We found it. Capt'n Lewis sent this message to ya from the Falls of the Missouri River."

Clark beamed as he unfolded and read the message, "This is good, real good. Hey, everybody, it's from Captain Lewis. He wrote us from the Falls of the Missouri River." Clark held the note up high for all to see.

A chorus of cheers went up.

Clark asked Field, "How far upriver?"

Field said, "Ain't more than twenty miles, sir. You'll hear it long before that though. See the mist, too. First you can hear them a good way off; then you'll see the mist rising up in the sky. Prettiest sight you ever want to see."

Clark replied, "Did you hear that, men? Twenty miles to the falls. What are you waiting for?"

With that the men all turned, the ropes on the boats tightened, the boats jerked and once again sliced through the water. The men were cheerful as they moved out at a steady pace upriver.

June 16, 1805 Great Falls, Montana

It was nearing midday when Lewis heard men approaching. One of them was shouting, "Hello there, Capt'n Lewis, is this your camp?" It was Sergeant Gass and a small party.

Lewis and the others immediately ran toward the approaching men. They greeted one another. Sergeant Gass said, "We're just downriver a ways, sir. We only left Capt'n Clark about two hours ago."

Lewis said, "You're really close. Could you hear the falls from there?" Gass nodded and the excited Lewis continued, "We have been drying out some buffalo. Must be six hundred pounds or better here. Got some fish, too, thanks to Goodrich. He even dried some for later. We should have a good welcome feast tonight. We've made some thick-soled moccasins from the buffalo hides. I hope they fare better against the prickly pear. As you can see, we had some time on our hands just waiting here. We were beginning to wonder what was taking you so long."

Sergeant Gass said, "We sure enough could hear the falls. When Joe joined us we were all excited. It's been hard work on this river and we're sure glad it's the right one. That roar of water was reassuring to us all."

The men talked briefly and then Lewis looked at his timepiece a moment. Then he looked around and said, "Drewyer, you, Goodrich and Windsor stay here with the food. I don't want any bears or wolves to get to it; keep a fire going. I'm going back to meet with the others."

Sergeant Gass asked, "Captain, do you want me to go with you or stay here?"

"Come back with me; the others can stay here. Let me know more of the trip upriver." Lewis picked up his rifle as he and Gass headed out to meet the main contingent and reunite with Clark. Within two hours he saw the laboring Corps of Discovery working its way upriver. The captains exchanged greetings as Lewis looked the crew over.

Lewis said, "Hard work. This has got to be terribly hard work. Have the ropes held up?"

Clark replied, "Only broke one, day before yesterday, they've all held. It ain't for a lack of tugging on 'em; the workload has been, all too frequently, severe. These men maintain their energy though. We've been using the cord all the way; against this current, there's just no other way. When we can, we pull from the land, but all too often they have to pull in the water, sometimes up to their chests."

Lewis looked around and said, "Impressive, the way they work, this dedication. They seem to do it naturally."

Clark said, "They know we're making good progress. After Field got here with news of the falls, they all perked up. Everyone knows we're on the right river now. Oh, there's been a lot of talk about these mountains to the west. Hot as it's been down here, all that snow up there, they know there's more work ahead. I think they want to get to them as soon possible. They're looking forward to riding the Columbia down to the sea."

Lewis said, "I'll bet they are tired. Good thing they're all healthy as oxen. We'll have plenty more work getting around the falls."

Clark's face suddenly drooped as he spoke, "Not all of us are healthy. Janey has been sick, real sick, for several days now."

Lewis' face showed immediate concern, "She wasn't feeling too well when I left for the falls. Still none better, huh? What do you suppose it is?"

"Not sure," Clark replied. "I was worried that it might be the same thing that took Floyd. She complains of being sick in her lower abdomen, maybe some bowel infirmity."

Lewis looked puzzled and asked, "What have you done for her? Has she responded to any treatment?"

"We've tried everything we could think of. I bled her, but she didn't respond." Clark continued, "Ordway got some bark and leaves. He ground them up, heated it all up in a warm water poultice and laid it on her. That seemed to relieve her some, but she's stayed pretty weak. We gave her a sip of whiskey, which also only had a temporary effect. The laudanum and bark seem to work the best at relieving her pain. Whatever it is, it's resistant to treatment. Nothing seems to provide a cure. Whatever it is, it just hangs on. I must admit, I also worry considerable about the baby. If she dies, I don't think we could keep him alive on soup and bone marrow. Probably have to leave him with the first Indians we meet."

Lewis said, "I'd like to see her." He walked back to the canoe where the young Indian mother was lying, covered with blankets. Charbonneau was there, standing with York. York was holding Jean Baptiste.

As Lewis approached he kneeled down and put his hand on her forehead and felt her fever. Then he felt her wrist for a pulse.

Sacajawea looked up at Lewis and with a weak smile said in English, "Hello Cap-Tan Lew-Us, Cap-Tan Cla-Lark, how are you?"

Lewis looked at Clark, put his hand on her forehead as he inquired, "She has a fever and hardly any pulse. Hey, when did she learn English? That was pretty good."

Clark said, "She has heard enough of it, day after day on the trail. I don't know exactly where she learned it. I think York and Cruzatte have probably worked with her some. She just knows a few words, some sentences. She's been waiting to show off what little she knows to you. York and Charbonneau have been taking care of her, feeding her and holding the baby so she can rest."

Lewis rose and walked away slowly with Clark walking at his side. He spoke softly, "This is serious. It could be the same as Floyd. I'd hate to lose her. She has kept up the hard pace right along with all of us and has been so strong for such a young mother. What would we do with the baby?" Then he snapped his fingers and looked at Clark. Clark stopped in anticipation, knowing that Lewis had an idea. Lewis said, "Ya know what? There is a sulfur spring near the falls; I remember one of the doctors back in Philadelphia saying that sulfur had medicinal properties. Good for skin problems, stomach problems and general good health. What the hell, I think I'll try it with her."

Clark said, "I don't think we have a lot of time to waste here. We have to get her treated quickly. She is not getting better. In fact, I think she's just barely holding on. I'll send some men ahead to get the sulfur water so you can treat her right away."

Lewis nodded and said, "Sure thing. I'd like to try the leaves and bark at the same time, the poultice that Ordway made up. You said it worked some. Get me the laudanum, too. It'll relieve the pain and lower her fever. We'll treat her with everything we have." Then he looked downriver and said, "I'd like to send some men to look for chokecherry bushes, too. A few days back I got terrible sick in the stomach and abdomen. I made up some tea with them and drank two cups about two hours apart. I was up and running by the evening. Whatever was in it seemed to work fine on me. If we can find some chokecherry, I'd try it on her, too."

Clark dispatched six men to find the sulfur spring and return with some of the water and firewood that Lewis said could be found in the area. He sent three others back downriver to look for chokecherry bushes. He told the rest of the men to continue on upriver. They would camp where Lewis had established a spot, near the falls.

The three sergeants and Clark walked with Lewis as they discussed the falls. Lewis, now talking about the falls, was encouraged, "Listen, you can hear them from here. It's a beautiful sight, a beautiful place. It's a rugged kind of beauty though, powerful. There's lots of buffalo around there, too." Then he took on a serious look as his eyes narrowed, "One thing is sure, it's not going to be easy portaging around those falls. I went up them. There's actually four sets of falls, stretched out over a distance of about sixteen miles. Rugged terrain the whole way. A lot of it is impassible, and where you can walk in a narrow path, it's steep and loaded with prickly pear."

Sergeant Pryor smiled and replied, "Gee, Capt'n, from that description, I can't wait to get there." Then he said seriously, "As difficult as they sound, those falls are a major milestone. We will have to portage 'round 'em. Without horses, that's gonna be a chore."

Sergeant Gass added, "If it stands between us and the Pacific, we'll just go around like we have everything up to now. We can prepare at the base of the falls. Get all the buffalo jerky and drag these canoes behind us over the land. The white pirogue will be something else. It's big and heavy. From what you say, we may be better off caching it like we did the red."

Lewis said, "Don't worry about the jerky. We got plenty, six hundred weight at least. As steep and rough as the climbing will be, we'll use all those moccasins you made back at the Maria. We may need more ropes."

Clark asked, "Trees? Are there any good trees there to make wheels? Gass is right. We should bury the white. It's too big to haul, but we could use her mast to make axles and slices of tree trunks for wheels."

Lewis said, "Not many trees there, mostly cottonwood. We'll have to search a little to find one big enough to make wheels. But rope, we'll need to double the thickness or they'll pop like glass."

Sergeant Ordway asked, "Your iron boat? Is this the place to use her?"

Lewis replied, "I think the place has chosen us more than the other way around. She's come all the way from Harper's Ferry for the moment. As soon as we clear the last of the falls and the river levels out, we'll put her in. It'll take everything we had in the white. We'll have plenty of hides to sew together. It's the tar pitch that we may be short of. I didn't see any pine. When we get there, we can fan out and look for pine to make tar. Somewhere in the distance from the first falls to the top, there's got to be some pine trees for tar."

"Which side of the falls is the best to go around?" Pryor asked.

Lewis looked upstream and replied, "I think the south side, but I want to wait until we're all there. We'll explore both sides for the best route then. That, for sure, is a decision that we'll want to make after we reconnoiter a bit more."

The men continued to talk about the trip, the rattlesnakes and prickly pear on the shore and the swiftness of the current. They marveled at the beauty of the land and the majesty of the ever-present snowcapped mountains. They knew they were headed into the mountains; they just didn't know where.

About two hours passed. The men that had been dispatched earlier returned with the sulfur water. Reubin Field said, "Here ya are, Capt'n. I hope this stuff helps her; it sure 'nuff smells like medicine."

They stopped and pulled the white pirogue in to shore where they could administer to Sacajawea. Lewis took the sulfur water and went to where Sacajawea was resting. York came over, took the baby and began gently rocking him. Labiche was with Charbonneau, and Lewis asked, "Ask him if she has stirred or asked for anything. Where does she feel the pain?"

Labiche turned to Charbonneau and asked. He, in turn, asked Sacajawea.

She opened her eyes again and reached for her son as York returned the child to her. She pointed to her naval and made a circular motion.

She seemed to understand as Lewis handed her a cup of the sulfur water. She drank it without hesitation. Lewis then put the poultice on her abdomen and gave her a dose of laudanum. He turned to Labiche and inquired, "Did the men find any chokecherry?"

Labiche shook his head, "No sir, they didn't, but they ain't back yet. They'd a been here if they found any. Everybody's worried about Janey making it."

Lewis rose up and spoke to Clark, Labiche, Charbonneau and York. "We've got nothing to do but wait it out with her. That sulfur water may do it. Maybe the men will find some chokecherry. The pain being low on her makes me wonder if it's a female problem, something with her menstrual period. I never studied anything about females; never thought we'd have a woman with us when we left. I think we've done all we can for her. Let's wait and see." Looking upriver Lewis pointed as he spoke, "We'll be at the campsite near the falls soon. She can bed down there. She can rest and gain strength while we calculate the best way around the falls."

June 17, 1805

The men were up earl, and Clark set out with five men to explore the falls for the best possible portage route. Lewis looked at Sacajawea to see how she was doing after the night. To everyone's surprise, her condition was greatly improved. She spoke again in English, "Good mor-ning Cap-Tan Lew-Us. I feel gooder."

Lewis told Charbonneau and York to feed her soup of boiled buffalo meat seasoned well with salt and pepper. York welcomed the opportunity to tend to her and the baby. He said, "York will take care of the little mother and baby Jean Baptiste. York will take good care, for sure, Capt'n. York will do anything Mister Charbo want; keep little Janey warm and fed, too."

Lewis replied, "Good, York; I think that now that her fever is gone and she seems to be responding to this treatment, we'll continue the sulfur water medication, and if you and her husband can keep the baby from crying, she'll be able to get better. As I said, keep giving her sulfur water from time to time. I'm pleased that she is responding well to it."

Clark was busy as he set six men to work converting the boats. "Men, we'll make carts of the smaller canoes. Let's take the white and bury it here. I think we can use the mast for the wheel axles. Least way it is the best we have for now."

Just then Willard came up and said, "Capt'n, we found a fairly large cottonwood down by the mouth of a small creek."

"Is it big enough for wheels?" Clark asked.

"It's the only one around here. All the rest are saplings and not more than ten — twelve inches diameter. This one is the granddaddy. I think we should cut it down and use it."

Clark ordered, "Sergeant Ordway, get some men and go with Willard here. See if you can make some wheels. We're going to need wheels to make carts."

Drewyer said, "We can save the sail, use it when there is a good wind; it may help our labor some."

Joseph Field said, "A sail on a cart? How about that? Why, we can call ourselves land sailors."

George Shannon added, "A lot better than tugging all the time. If a fortuitous zephyr chooses to help us, who would argue?"

Joseph Field, hearing Shannon use large words, looked at Lewis. Lewis, seeing the inquiring glance, replied, "A lucky gentle breeze." Field simply nodded.

Drewyer added, "The sail can be used as shade or rain shield just like when we were on the river. Right now we need to make some harnesses for ourselves. There's going to be a lot of weight, a lot a pulling."

That evening they talked around the campfire about the best way to portage the falls. Clark sat next to Lewis as they talked about the coming effort.

"One thing sure," Clark said, "the Indians were wrong about these falls. I don't think we'll be able to go around them in one day."

Lewis replied, "I'm afraid you're right. We won't find any smooth or easy way around these falls. The land on either side is steep and there's just too many ravines. We'll be going over very rough terrain. I think the south side will be our best route, and even it is going to be tough."

Clark said, "Yeah, and the men know it, too. But you know, Merry, even though they all know that we'll have trouble portaging these falls, and the promise of even more troubles in those snow-covered mountains, they all, to the man, seem to have made up their minds to succeed in this expedition or perish in the attempt."

Lewis smiled as he nodded in agreement, "That's what they said back at the Maria's. Ya know, Bill, since we sent back those few men from Fort Mandan, we've had no hint of discipline problems. They work together like they were of one mind, one man. The sergeants give few orders; they all know the routine." Then looking at the falls he continued, "From what I've seen, this could be the roughest portion of our trip so far. God, we really need horses. Without horses this portage is going to be extremely difficult."

Clark listened and then said, "I've had second thoughts about sending some men back to St. Louis. I know we talked about it last winter, but now that we are here at the falls, I don't know who we would select to return."

Lewis agreeing said, "Not only that, I think we will need every last man going forward. Besides Bill, these men have put so much effort into getting this far. I don't think any one of them would want to turn back now. They've earned the right to proceed. Every man wants to get over those mountains and ride the Columbia."

Clark replied, "That's for sure. I have heard them talking about that a lot since we left the fork of Maria's River. I don't think it would be wise to break up this team. It's one of those things where the whole crew is greater than the sum of its parts."

"Much greater," Lewis concurred. "As much as I wanted to send letters and news of our progress back to St. Louis, I think that in the interest of succeeding and keeping our crew intact, we should abandon the idea of a boat to St. Louis."

Clark said, "The men didn't know we were ever considering sending a boat back. Let's keep it that way."

Lewis said, "Done."

June 26, 1805

The Corps of Discovery is working on the problem of portage around the falls. Travel is extremely difficult due to the rough terrain. There are several deep, dry gorges formed by water rushing down slopes to join the Missouri. In addition to the difficulties of the topography itself, there is the constant irritation of their three incessant pests: mosquitoes, eye gnats and a blanket of prickly pear that injures their feet with needles of pain. Buffalo tracks, left in mud, have dried into hardened sharp ridges. These produce unavoidable obstacles that injure their feet.

The portage of the falls, which they had been told would take one day, will obviously take much longer. Lewis is worried about time. Knowing that it is already late June and they have yet to find the headwaters of the river, cross the snowcapped mountains, and find the Columbia. He knows they need horses desperately. He is coming to the realization that there will be no way to accomplish all this travel and return as far as the Mandan by winter.

Lewis advances to an upper camp at the top of the falls while Clark is preparing the lower camp to be ready to depart. At the upper camp, Lewis prepares to employ his invention, the metal-framed boat. The skeletal iron frame will first be covered with hides, sealed for leaks and then set afloat. The boat is capable, per calculations, of carrying four tons of cargo. From the lower camp they have six canoes laden with materials and dried meat. All this material will have to be drug over rough terrain by pulling on elk skin ropes. Decisions are made regarding what materials to leave behind in safely located caches for recovery on the return trip.

In the morning Lewis rose up and looked back downriver to where Clark and the others would be coming. He moved over to where Joseph Field and Drewyer were talking. "You men go on upriver. Take one of the canoes. Get us as many elk as you can. I want the hides for the iron boat hull. Frazer, I want you to begin sewing the hides we have already. Make them as tight as you can. Any leftover odd pieces, use for moccasins or liners for moccasins. Sergeant Gass, you and Shields go on over to the wooded bottoms and bring back as much timber and bark as you can. If you see any pine trees, let me know how many and where. We'll need pine tar to seal the seams."

Drewyer replied, "I'll get some powder and ball and we'll be on our way."

Joseph Field said, "I'll make sure the tow ropes are sound and tied securely before we get the canoe underway. It's empty now, isn't it?"

Sergeant Gass said, "Yes, it's empty. I took everything out the other day to make sure it could dry out." Then turning to Shields he continued, "Make sure we take an extra axe head and some handles. We've been breaking handles below."

Shields replied, "Got it covered. I already thought of that."

Lewis observed the men leaving and said, "I'll take on the chores of being the cook for you this evening. Be back before it's too late. I plan on having boiled buffalo and suet dumplings if I can get it all to turn out right."

Joseph Field said, "Well now, sir, with you as the cook, ain't nothing for me to do but go out and work up an appetite."

Drewyer smiled and said, "We'll bring back elk hides and as much meat as we can load. Capt'n, I'd like to reserve two of those dumplings, one for my Canadian half and one for my Indian half."

Lewis laughed and said, "I'll work on it. Remember, there'll be some men here from the lower camp, too. I'd bet my sore feet that they'll have worked up quite an appetite."

Joseph Field said, "Well, it looks like we'll all be in for a treat tonight. I'll bet there won't be any dumplin's left over for Seaman."

Lewis said, "Don't worry about Seaman. He'll get his share. I've got to have someone sample my cooking, don't I?"

Frazer came up and said, "Look Captain. All I have is this larger needle to sew the hides. When we pull 'em tight over the hull, do you think they'll leak?"

Lewis looked at the work completed so far and at the needle being employed. "Make the stitches a little closer together. Like these here." He showed a sample to Frazer, "We don't have any smaller needles. That will have to do."

Frazer said, "I'll sew all these up. Then I'll have to make some more rawhide thread and let it dry. We have some buffalo hides, too. Do you want me to use 'em?"

Lewis said, "I prefer elk, but we may have to use buffalo. I was planning on using buffalo hides for moccasins and leggings. Are there any more kettles? I thought there was another one."

Frazer said, "There's another one. I think I saw it over there by the hides."

At about four o'clock Gass and Shields returned with firewood and bark. Gass reported, "We couldn't find much, sir. This may be enough to cook with. We did see some buffalo near the wood down there, took seven of them. Brought the better parts of the meat and all the hides in case you could use them instead of elk."

"Excellent, Sergeant," Lewis said beaming. "This is more wood than I anticipated and just in time, too. My supply here was running out. Only really had enough to get it started. This'll keep the fire going under those dumplings. Put the buffalo meat over there. We'll start roasting as soon as the fire gets up."

As the evening began to set in, Sergeant Gass asked, "Do you think Drewyer and Field had any trouble? If they are not back soon, maybe we should go up and find 'em."

Lewis looked pensive for a moment and then said, "Drewyer's an excellent woodsman, and Field knows his way around, too. I'm not worried. They probably just have more meat than they can handle and skinning elk isn't easy. They'll be in tomorrow I'm sure."

Just then two canoes, laden with cargo, came in with very exhausted crewmen. Whitehouse, his face flushed, asked for water. He stood and drank heartily, the water coming out around the edges of the cup as he gulped water as fast as he could.

Lewis said to the new arrivals, "Welcome men. You must all be hungry and exhausted from the long pull. I have cooked up some buffalo stew and suet dumplings."

One man replied, "Well now, Capt'n, I don't know if I am more tired or more hungry. Whatever you got sure smells good. Hungry as we all are, we would probably eat a polecat if it was cooked up an' ready."

Colter said, "We were lucky several times on the way up. A good stiff breeze came up and we hoisted the sail. Hell, it was like having three more men pullin'. All we had to do was keep her steering straight."

Reubin Field added, "That breeze sure enough was welcome. Not only did it take the load off of pullin' so hard, it cooled us down some and took away the skeeters and face flies. If I could put in a request right now, it would be for more breezes like that one."

Colter said, "Breeze did help, and we were becoming good land sailors. We used it when we could, but those ravines are steep with slippery rock and prickly pear. This haul is no picnic. Just look at Whitehouse there. Talk about tuckered out. He was panting pretty hard there at the end."

Lewis said, "I made extra, thinking you would be here. Go ahead and help yourselves. You've all certainly earned a good meal fixed by your captain." Then he looked across the campground at Whitehouse who was leaning over holding his stomach. "What's wrong?" Lewis asked concerned. "Got a gas pain?"

Whitehouse had a dazed look in his eye as he replied, "Don't know, sir. I was powerful thirsty and I drank down all that water. Cold as it was, maybe that upset me. Being in such a lather, I shouldn't of drank so much."

Lewis walked over to Whitehouse who was sitting and said, "Wasn't how much you drank. It was how fast. A body can't take that much all at once. You should take your time with thirst like that in the future. Here let me take your pulse."

Lewis looked at the suddenly ailing Whitehouse. He took the pulse and looked into his eyes. Then he said, "Your pulse is strong enough, but your face doesn't have good color. I think if I bled you, you would feel a little better."

Sergeant Gass, hearing the last remark said, "No need for that, Capt'n. The mosquitoes been bleeding us all day."

Lewis had a quick glance at Gass and then softened his look at Whitehouse as he spoke, "I only have my pen knife. If you'll give me a vein on your arm there, I think we can make you feel a little better. We're going to need you tomorrow. Don't want you being sick and infirm on us now."

Whitehouse nodded in silent agreement as Lewis made a small cut on a vein in his arm and let it bleed. As he was finishing the treatment the wind from the southwest began to pick up.

Sergeant Gass remarked, "Well now, this wind may keep the skeeters away from us tonight. We could use a good night's rest."

In the morning a brief storm blew over with rain and hail. It didn't last long and soon it was over. Drewyer and Joseph Field returned with their canoe full of hides and meat. They had taken nine elk and three bear. Whitehouse, still not feeling well, was put to work with Frazer. They were sewing hides together to cover the iron-framed boat. Shields and Gass were working on wooden horizontal cross-members for the boat. They were having problems with the wood because much of it was too crooked for use.

Joseph Field let out a "Whoop te haaay" as their canoe approached the campsite. Lewis, who had been roasting meat for later use, stopped what he was doing and walked over to greet the hunters. "Glad to see you two. Sergeant Gass was worried you had some kind of misfortune. I assured him it was just the labor of getting meat and hides ready for us. From the look of it, you did quite well."

Drewyer nodded and pointed toward the canoe, "Yes, nine elk hides and the better part of the meat. We also got three grizzlies."

Joseph Field interrupted with a broad smile as he added, "Yeah, you could say we got three grizzlies. Then again, you could say they nearly got George and me."

Always anxious to hear a good hunting story involving grizzly bears, the men moved in closer to Field as he continued. "We were hunting along the river's edge. When we came across this thick brushy bottom land where there were bear tracks going into the bush. We figured that the bear were using the place to hide and get close to the elk when they came by. George spotted a large tree with leaning branches that would make a good observation point. From there we could look down on the brush and see if there were bears or not. I figured it was a lot better than just walking into the brush after 'em. I agreed with George to climb that leaning tree. Well, we got up there, maybe twenty – twenty-five feet above the ground. Soon as we were secure in the branches, George gave me a signal. We both whooped it up and hollered real loud. Then we shut up on his signal and waited. Didn't wait long neither. Here he come, bigger 'n life. A bear. There it was, biggest grizzly I ever saw, an' I was looking down on him. Well this monster bear just kept coming toward us, snortin' and rakin' the ground with its claws. When he saw us in the tree, he raised up on his hind legs and let out a growl. I looked over at George and there he was cool as ever, cocking his rifle and getting ready to take aim. Just before he aimed he said, 'These bears are too big to climb trees'. Well, I swung my rifle around, cocked it and was waiting for George to say 'fire' or something. I kept waitin', but no, all I hear is the 'pitt cratoowh' of his rifle. I didn't have to shoot at all. George's fifty-four split that bear's skull wide open and it fell in a heap."

Drewyer said, "It was a large bear, big, and I was glad to have Joe here for back-up, even in the tree."

Field laughed as he continued, " Large, take a look at the hide we brought back. That bear was…"

George Shannon interrupted, "Leviathan?"

Field looked at Shannon and said, "Yeah, it was leviathan, big enough to be the granddaddy of bears. Tell 'em George. You measured its paws."

Drewyer said, "The front paw was nine inches across, and the rear paw was eleven and three-quarter long."

Field excitedly added, "And that measurement don't even include the claws. George here is being modest."

Drewyer said, "We have the hide here. I think it may be the largest bear so far."

Lewis who had been listening added, "Just last night we had a bear come very close to our camp. It got about thirty pounds of suet and meat that we had tied up on a pole. Snapped the pole right off. These bears are not to be ignored. We already know that only a head shot will kill it quickly. Any other shot will permit it to pursue the shooter. Keep your rifles charged at all times and avoid ambushes. These bear, as large as they are, can rush a man quickly."

June 29, 1805

At the lower camp they had cached material and prepared to move on up to meet the others. Clark looked around and said "I'm glad that shower's blown over. Still, the open prairie looks too wet to navigate. The clay out there is so slippery it makes travel impossible. I think our best bet is to stay close to the river." He turned and gave orders, "Sergeant Pryor, you and the others continue to load the boats and give one last check on the cache. Make sure it's covered with oil cloth for winter and marked so we can find it." Then he turned to York and said, "Go help Charbonneau and his family get ready. We'll head out as soon as they're ready."

York nodded and moved away.

Soon they were on their way toward the upper falls. The sky suddenly turned black again, and it began to rain lightly. Clark looked around for shelter. He told York, "Go look around for a shelter not facing the river. The wind can be strong on those small ledges. I want a shelter out of the wind where a body can stand firm."

York nodded that he understood and set out to look in the ravines for an undercut section that could provide shelter. Clark looked ahead and saw a deep ravine with shale rock eroded in such a manner that it made a small cut-out shelter. He motioned with his arms as he hollered, "York, I see a cliff cut upriver about a quarter mile. Come on. Let's get up there before the rain sets in."

York immediately stopped his search and turned to join the others. "Yes, Mister William, York's comin'. Just listen to them clouds, we don't have much time to get there dry."

York moved quickly to join Clark and the Charbonneau family. They moved to the shelter near the river that Clark had spotted just as the rains began to fall heavily. Clark turned and handed his rifle to York, then said to Charbonneau, "Here, give me your guns. Take my compass, put them on that small shelf above. That should be safe from the rain."

Charbonneau did not clearly understand the English but he instinctively knew what the order was as he handed his rifle to

York. York took the rifle, along with Clark's and his own and laid them where Clark directed. Then he placed the powderhorns alongside them.

Clark said, "This rain shouldn't last long. The wind is strong, but we should be all right here. We can wait it out. With this wind it'll be gone soon."

The rain turned to torrents in less than a minute. There were sheets of rain mixed with hail. It was so heavy they couldn't see across the river. Charbonneau and Sacajawea were silent but apprehensive as they looked at Clark for the next signal of what to do.

Just then York said, "Just listen, Capt'n. York hears something. It sounds terrible strong."

Clark looked up the ravine which had been dry when they crossed a few minutes earlier. He pointed as he exclaimed, "My God, look! There's a wall of water coming this way. Mud and rock moving with it. We got no time here. Let's head for higher ground! York, get the rifles and shot, we're moving up!"

York responded instantly as Clark grabbed the terrified Charbonneau and Sacajawea and pushed them forward. Charbonneau quickly reached the next level and reached back for Sacajawea and the child. Because she held the child, she could only reach up with one arm. He was failing in the attempt to pull them up, partly because he did not want to over-extend his reach and tumble into the raging water below. He made repeated attempts to reach her, but each lacked the distance to secure the grasp. Seeing the problem, Clark took the young mother's leg and foot and with a lunge, hoisted her as high as he could. Charbonneau, taking advantage of the thrust, pulled her as he fell backward. Sacajawea, her baby still in her arms, landed on top of him. The raging torrent of floodwater was rising quickly. By the time Clark finished giving the lifting thrust to Sacajawea, he was in water up to his waist. As he pulled himself up from the rising water and onto the higher ground he looked back to the position where he had just exited. The swirling muddy water was now ten feet over where he had previously stood only moments before. As the party scrambled on up to the top of the hill, they looked back. The raging floodwater was now fifteen feet above the point where they had been standing.

With slippery footing, Clark cautiously reached the top. The rain and hail were pounding down. He stood and looked around. There, about a hundred feet away, was York, running around looking over the edge and hollering, "Capt'n, Capt'n" over and over.

"Here, York," Clark shouted and whistled. Hearing him, York immediately lowered his arms, turned and ran to join his soggy companions.

As he approached Clark, York grabbed him by the arms and said, "York was terrible worried; terrible, dreadful, afeared that you all be washed away. Soon as York was up he looked 'round. All 'round. Couldn't see nobody. Nobody at all. Just all that water down there, muddy with sticks in it. Roaring and churning an' smashin' through. If York'd seen ya, Capt'n, he'd jumped in after ya to help. But York couldn't see nothin'. Nothin' at all."

Clark looked at him a moment and replied, "I know you would have, York. You're a powerful swimmer. But I think that water would have claimed even the best swimmer." Then he looked around at Charbonneau, Sacajawea and the child. They were all shivering in the rain, waiting for direction from him. He ordered, "Let's move out as quick as we can. York, you take the lead." Then he grabbed Charbonneau and turned him toward York. He gave him a slight shove as York began to move. "We gotta move as fast as we can back to the camp. The baby's got no clothes, and Janey is wet. If she don't get dry quick, she may have a relapse." The party was already moving as he finished his command.

When they reached the camp Clark immediately put Sacajawea and her child in a tent. He turned to Labiche and the others who were approaching. "Get some dry clothes for the baby and Janey right away. Give them to Charbonneau here."

The men moved in response to the order. The rain had stopped, and the skies were already beginning to clear as the storm front moved on past. Sergeant Pryor said, "Get a fire going. We need to dry out some."

Clark said, "Sergeant, get me a little whiskey for the Charbonneau family. That and some hot food."

Pryor moved to obey the order. As he handed the whiskey to Charbonneau, the men from another party that had been caught in the storm without shelter began coming into the campsite. All the men were talking excitedly, and some were helping others who had blood streaming from their heads. Sergeant Pryor shouted to Clark, "Look Capt'n! Just look! Those men look like they've been beaten with clubs."

Clark looked in astonishment at the returning men. There they were, bleeding from scalp wounds caused by hailstones. Some were bleeding from their knees where they had fallen. All were limping with sore feet caused by the prickly pear. Those less injured were supporting the others as they all came into camp.

Looking at the bedraggled sight, Clark said, "Sergeant, get more wood on the fire. As soon as these men get into dry clothes, give them a grog. They look like they were beaten in Mother Nature's woodshed."

"Done, sir," Pryor said, as he moved toward the incoming detachment.

As the men changed into dry clothing, they sat by the larger fire and talked about the storm, how suddenly it came up, the size of the hailstones and how quickly it was gone again.

The camp was buzzing with this talk when Clark spoke to the men. "Janey lost her pack and cradle for the baby. We'll have to make her another. New clothes for the baby, too. We've got plenty of hides. Make up some new clothes for the little guy. I lost my large compass, the only big one we had. Looks like the storm claimed my tomahawk, shot pouch and powderhorn, too. When this river goes down some, I want to send a small party on both sides to see if we can find anything, especially the compass."

July 4, 1805

The men have been toiling heavily for days pulling and pushing wheeled canoes, laden with materials, up and down over steep ravines through terrain blanketed with prickly pear. They are constantly assailed by mosquitoes, and their feet are punctured by cactus needles. The pull ropes cut painfully into their hands and shoulders as they labor. So tiring is their labor that whenever Clark calls for a short break, they fall asleep leaning on the canoes or lie down where they have stood. Yet the men remain in good spirits. When called back to duty, each one does so without hesitation.

Late this evening they finally arrive at the upper camp, pulling in the last of the six canoes. As evening falls, the men eat roast elk, buffalo and duck. Tired as they are, spirits are light as they celebrate reaching the upper camp. The long arduous portage of the Falls of Missouri is now complete. Lewis and Clark sit together as they observe the campground. Lewis has a serious look on his face as he stares over the campground at the crew of men.

"Something wrong, Merry?" Clark inquired.

Lewis was silent for a moment, then spoke in a low serious tone, "Such men. Where did we find such men as these? I have watched them toil against nearly impossible odds in moving our cargo of goods around these falls. Everything seemed to be against them: gnats, mosquitoes, prickly pear, the burden of ropes cutting into their flesh as they pulled. Even the weather was not kind. Yet ever onward they toiled, always in good spirits. I tell you, they are an elite group like none other the Army has ever enlisted. When the load seems too heavy to bear, they bear it. When there is nothing left to push them on except a **will** to go on, they go on. When their physical strength has left them, they reach inside themselves, I don't know where, and find the power. I think they do it, as you once aptly said, 'to not fail one another in this joint effort'."

Clark stared at the men as he added, "You're right, absolutely right. They are the elite of our Army, even of our country. Possibly the best and most elite ever assembled anywhere. I do believe that they get their strength through honor and respect. Each man pulls or pushes as hard as he can, knowing that his brother in this chore is also pulling and pushing as hard as he can. To give up or even to slack a trifle in the effort would mean that the other man, his brother, would have to pull harder or longer. They respect and honor one another so much that without saying it, their actions say loud and clear: 'If you can pull, I won't let you down. I will pull also. If you can make it to the next ridge, I will make it with you. I will not let you down. Your burden is not going to be made more difficult because of me.' These men, this work, it's a privilege to witness. That's what I think."

Lewis looked at his friend as he spoke and nodded in agreement. "I couldn't agree more. In this joint effort they have built pride in themselves and in one another. No one of them, left to his own devices, could demonstrate that kind of strength and stamina. Here we see the whole being much greater than the sum of its parts. These are real men. Yes, the elite of the Army and the best it has ever assembled. For sure the **first** such group ever assembled. If our young nation is to be populated with these kind of men, men with a 'won't quit' character and spirit, then Jefferson is right. We **will be** a mighty nation from sea to sea."

Clark changed from the more serious tone and said, "Speaking of our mentor, Mr. Jefferson. Today is the Fourth of July. We cannot simply let it pass without notice. We should celebrate. Our little affair will mark the farthest west celebration ever held in the country. How much whiskey do we have left?"

Lewis smiled broadly as he looked at Clark. Then he motioned to Sergeant Ordway. "Sergeant, get the keg of whiskey. Today is the Fourth of July, and we are going to raise a flag, salute it and share in the last of the Kentucky blend."

Ordway smiled as he turned to obey the order, "Yes, sir, the Fourth of July on the Missouri River Falls." Then he shouted at the others, "Hey men. We're going to celebrate! Captains said to break out the whiskey and raise the flag. We'll fire off a salute and dance. Let's fill our bellies with buffalo roast and listen to Pierre on the fiddle. It's the Fourth of July!"

After the men had raised the flag and finished eating, the whiskey was doled out. York was given a share along with the others. Before he started to dance, Lewis rose to speak. The men fell silent, "Men, in case you didn't know it, this is the last of the whiskey. I think that it is proper to share the last of our spirits on such a grand occasion. We have conquered the Falls of the Missouri." Everyone cheered and applauded. Lewis held his hand out, and they quieted as he continued, "Captain Clark and I were talking earlier about the admirable spirit we have witnessed in you men during this endeavor of portaging these beautiful, yet terrible falls. We agreed upon one sure and solid fact. A fact that is obvious, we are in command of a very elite and steadfast group of men. You are the **Corps of Discovery**. We are very proud to be in command of the Corps of Discovery."

Then he looked around and spotted George Shannon in the group and continued. "Ya know, young George Shannon here has been using big fancy words on all of you all since we left. Sometimes you come to me to find out what the devil he's saying. Sometimes I don't know either. And remember, I have spent time with Washington politicians. But let me tell you this. There is one word that neither George nor any of you seem to know. That word is **QUIT**. There is just no quit in any of you. It is inspiring to know that. As we move forward, not knowing what the next day will bring, as we look at these lofty and terrible mountains, I know, Captain Clark knows, that men who don't know what quit means will take us to the sea."

The men all cheered in chorus and then buzzed with conversation. York laughed as he engaged in the conversation with the other men.

July 9, 1805

"Get around her and lift on my command," Lewis said as five men positioned themselves around the iron-framed boat, now covered with hides. "Heave," Lewis ordered as they all lifted the long boat and walked into the water and set her down.

"Lookie there, Capt'n, she floats real good," Sergeant Gass exclaimed.

Lewis said, "Well now, Sergeant, get the seats fitted and the oarlocks positioned. Soon as that's done we can load her up. Sergeant Pryor, have some men bring the bundled cargo over. We'll load her hand over hand."

Sergeant Gass set to putting in the seats in place and preparing the oarlocks. The other men were loading the other canoes in preparation to depart upriver. As the work was proceeding, a storm began to blow in. The storm front was swift and powerful. Soon it was obvious that the canoes would have to be unloaded again due to the rising waves on the river. The men, unquestioning, removed the cargo and moved it back to the campsite to avoid wetting the contents.

As the storm developed, wind was high and fires were not possible. Sergeant Gass went to check on the boats to ensure that they would remain anchored properly. He returned and approached Lewis with a look of angst as he said, "Capt'n, our sentry just reported the iron boat is…, well, sir, she's takin' on water. Seems the wind and water have caused the skins on the hull to separate. She's leakin' bad, sir."

Lewis immediately ran to the river's edge. He stood there, wind in his hair, his eyes narrow and lips tight. His face was a picture of disappointment. He stepped into the water near the boat and pushed down on the separating protective hides. "Shit!" he exclaimed as he picked up a bundle of material and slung it to the aft section of the boat. He stood for a moment and looked at the partially submerged fore section of the boat. Then he turned and walked back to camp staring at the ground.

Clark noticed his friend coming back into camp and approached him. Lewis seeing him draw near said, "She's gone. We had no pitch. We can get no pitch. There is no damned pitch! It couldn't be sealed. She's gone, simply not worth any further effort."

With that comment, the disgruntled Lewis brushed past Clark and proceeded to his tent. He entered the tent and closed the flap behind him.

Clark stood silent a moment and then asked Gass, "Was it the seams?"

Gass replied, "Mostly, yeah. I think if we had tar pitch she would have held. The framed boat was a good idea. There was no way of knowing that there would be no pine in these parts. No way at all."

"Did you get all the cargo out of her?" Clark asked.

Gass nodded and said, "Yeah. Some got a little damp but no worse than the stuff in the canoes. We got it all moved up to camp. It'll air out tomorrow. Funny thing, Capt'n, the buffalo hides we used; they seemed like they held. We only used them 'cause we didn't have elk skins. Maybe if we had enough buffalo hide she would have held."

Clark looked at the river edge and the aft section of the iron boat. "No pitch. No way to get any, not in these parts. Buffalo, well, in case you didn't notice, there haven't been any around in awhile. Pine tar pitch is what we really needed. There was just no way to know that when we needed it, there wouldn't be any. It's a sad situation. Too damn bad we can't do something about it."

Gass nodded and replied, "Do you think we should try to pull her out for Capt'n Lewis?"

Clark shook his head and replied, "No Sergeant, leave Captain Lewis alone for now. He's disappointed. He needs to be by himself awhile. He brought that thing all the way from Harper's Ferry. That's a hell of a long way to push, pull and tug on a boat that sinks when it's needed. He had his hopes and part of his personality in that boat. That's really what sank here. What you can do is select some more cottonwood trees for canoes. With the iron boat down, we'll need at least three or four to replace it."

Clark moved over with the other men to explain what had happened. The mood in camp was somber because they had put a lot of effort into the iron-framed boat and because they commiserated with the disappointment of their captain.

July 19, 1805 Gates of the Rocky Mountains

Clark set out overland with Joseph Field, Potts and York in search of game and any sign of the Snake Indians. Sacajawea tells them that this is the country where her people used to hunt in the summer.

Lewis and the rest of the Corps proceed to follow the river, which is now more rapid and getting more narrow than before. They come across signs of several small campsites. The campsites are judged to be about two weeks old, probably Indian hunting parties. The captains frequently dispatch small groups to seek Indian contact; those attempts are to no avail. They surmise the Indians had heard their gunfire during hunting sessions and then assumed they were hostile and fled. They also discover one large campsite. There are remnants of a lodge nearly sixty feet in diameter. However, the lodge appears old and is presumed to have been abandoned for over a year.

The scenery all around them is spectacular. The prickly pear and sunflowers are in full bloom. There are many kinds of berries ripening along the river's edge which Sacajawea continually gathers and adds to the evening fare. Nearly two weeks from the falls, they are now beginning to see pine trees along the river's edge. The mountains are more pronounced, and the river knifes through sometimes nearly vertical rock outcroppings. Mountain sheep are frequently seen and admired for their agility to cross the rock faces.

Labor continues to be difficult in the high July temperatures. They marvel how they can be in such heat while the mountains around them are covered with snow. As evening approaches, they enter a section where the rocks are abruptly rising from the water, nearly perpendicular to heights of 1200 feet or more. The rock face is black near the river and light yellowish-brown higher up. Due to the time of day, the cliffs seemed to threaten that they will tumble rock down. The river is now about 150 yards wide. Due to the sheer cliffs, there is no shoreline to enable them to employ cording. Fortunately, they can make progress by rowing.

As they move across the river toward the opposite side, Lewis looks upriver. There, before him, the perpendicular cliff faces give the illusion of gates opening as his canoe moves from right to left across the river.

Lewis pointed and said, "Look there, those cliffs. As we move, they look like gates slowly opening. Just one name for this place: I think I will call it the 'Gates of the Rocky Mountains'."

Sergeant Ordway said, "Sure does look like gates opening to me, sir. I just hope this means we'll get to the headwaters soon."

About that time Labiche shouted from the lead boat, "Capt'n, there's a clearing ahead. It's getting dark. I think we better take it."

Lewis replied, "Good eye. Yes, let's pull in and make camp. It's dark in this canyon, and I don't want to continue without a place to rest. It's dangerous enough in the light of day. Cross back over the river and we'll settle in."

Sergeant Pryor said, "We're in luck. Looks like there might be some driftwood around and a few trees. Men, gather some kindling for a fire. We'll set up camp here."

Meanwhile, Clark and his group had been walking along, away from the river, along an old Indian path. They saw a herd of elk and were able to take one for their supper. There was no wood around to build a fire to roast the meat.

Joseph Field said, "Capt'n, I'm hungry enough to eat this meat raw. Don't want to though. Should we carry some to the river an' see if we can find driftwood for a fire?"

Potts replied, "Back at Mandan, I heard the Indians say they sometimes used dried buffalo dung when they couldn't get wood."

York said, "York has seen plenty buffalo dung. Lots of it. All dried out."

Clark said, "Good, York. You and Potts go gather some up, and we'll make a fire and cook this meat."

Field replied, "Now that ought to be something real new. We used to hickory smoke beef and pork all the time back home. That made it taste real good. We never tried dung flavor though."

Clark said, "Now it wasn't more than half a minute ago I heard you say you were thinking of eating this meat raw. A buffalo dung fire sounds a lot better to me than eating raw meat. Besides how we gonna carry any with us tomorrow unless we roast it up tonight?"

July 24, 1805

Lewis stood with Sergeants Pryor and Ordway talking about the river and surrounding country. Finally, Lewis said to Ordway, "Go and ask Janey. Her people hunt these areas in the summer. She may have been somewhere around these parts. Let's try her again, maybe she'll recognize some of the landmarks."

Ordway replied, "Yes, sir, I'll get Labiche to translate."

Lewis shook his finger at the horizon as he said, "These nearby mountains conceal the more distant snow-covered peaks. I'm concerned there will be more falls. A river cannot simply run flat through such rough terrain. If we encounter more falls without horses to help in the portage, well, I just don't know."

Sergeant Pryor looked at Lewis and said, "Cheer up, sir, we should meet up with the Shoshone soon. We've been seeing signs right along. Fact is, that grass fire we saw a few days back, that was just the Indians making some kind of signal to one another. When we do find them, they'll have horses. We'll be able to head out straight across the mountains." Then, pointing he said, "Here come Labiche and the Charbonneau's now."

Labiche said, "Capt'n, Sergeant said you wanted to talk to Janey so I got them to come over."

Lewis said, "I just want to ask her if she recognizes any of the landmarks around here. The river, the mountain peaks, anything at all that will let us know where we are and how far we have to go."

Labiche spoke to Charbonneau who in turn spoke to Sacajawea. The men waited patiently while the translations took place. Sacajawea's face lit up as she began to understand the questions. She began to point to the river and talk.

The translation again moved back to Labiche. "Captain, she said that there are no more falls. We've passed the falls, and the river stays the same to the mountains. She said there is a joining of rivers soon. Three rivers come together. That's the place where she lost her people." Labiche turned and said, "I think that is where she was taken by the Minnetare. She said she remembers the split rivers and the attack. But for the river, she says there are no more falls. That's it, sir."

Lewis said, "Thank you, Private, and thank the Charbonneau's for the information. And Private, spread the word among the men, Janey knows we are close to the three forks. We'll soon find the headwaters of this river."

Labiche smiled broadly and said, "Yes, SIR, you bet. We'll all be glad to see the headwaters of this river."

Lewis added, "Private, have Janey show the men where those small onions we have been seeing are to be found. I want to gather as many of them as we can. They add greatly to the flavor of our evening meals. Those we don't eat now we'll dry out and add to the fare later. Give all you get to Ordway. Urge the men to continue to collect all the ripe berries we can get. I think these things break the monotony of meat for every meal, and they're probably healthy, too."

The men moved the canoes out onto the river, where Lewis, wanting to share in the labor, assisted by using the pole on the boat while others pulled ropes from the shoreline. They continued on until later in the evening when they arrived at Clark's forward camp on the right side of the river.

Clark shouted as the canoes pulled in near. "Don't unload here, there's a small island just up ahead that's a better campsite. We've got some venison and elk to load up."

As the men moved to load the canoes, Clark stepped on board with Lewis. "My feet are killing me. Damn prickly pear has made meatloaf out of 'em. It'll feel good to ride awhile. I'm real tired. Exhausted. I think I'll retire after supper."

Lewis had concern on his face as he looked at Clark's moccasins. He moved toward his friend and said, "Let me take those off and see what condition your feet are in." As he lifted Clark's foot up he winced as he saw cactus thistles sticking out of the moccasin. "I'm going to pull these."

Clark simply leaned back, looked up at the ridge of mountains and let out a "Huummmmmmph."

Lewis proceeded to remove cactus thistles from his friend's moccasins and then removed the moccasins. He wrinkled his lips as he pulled even more thistles from Clark's swollen feet. Neither man spoke. Finally, Lewis said, "There you go, Bill. When we get to camp I'll heat some water up and wash them off for you. Tomorrow, I'll take the duties of land exploration. You ride in the canoes."

Clark raised up, shaking his head as he looked Lewis in the eye. "No, I'll go. Thanks, Merry, for the foot treatment. It really felt good. I'll take you up on the offer for a hot water treatment later, but tomorrow I'll go out with Frazer and the Field brothers. Charbonneau can come with us in case we meet any Indians and need an interpreter."

Lewis looked at Clark and said, "Bill, your feet. You should…"

"Never mind," Clark interrupted "I'll go. These men, you, everyone suffers from prickly pear and mosquitoes. I'm no better than any man here. I'll be out there tomorrow just like the others. I'll not be an invalid when I'm needed."

Lewis looked at Clark a moment and replied, "All right. Have it your way. I'd go in your place in a minute. You don't need to prove anything to me, you know that, don't you?"

Clark answered, "Maybe it's the spirit of these men. Maybe I got it, too. Come tomorrow, I will be heading the land expedition."

Lewis looked at him a moment and then replied, "Done."

July 27, 1805 Three Forks of the Missouri

It was about 3:00 P.M. when Lewis and the men reached the three forks of the Missouri River. They took measurements of each of the three rivers and recorded them. Shannon came running toward Lewis, "Capt'n, I see Capt'n Clark and the others coming in. Capt'n don't look too good. York and Reubin are walking with him. Joe and Charbonneau are behind."

Lewis looked up with concern. When Clark came close, Lewis asked, "What's wrong, Bill? You look disheveled, don't you feel well?"

Clark sighed and responded, "I'm wrung out. I've had a fever two days now, can't seem to shake it. I did manage to get to a high point and make some good observations."

Lewis said, "Come. Sit down and relax." Looking at Ordway, Lewis commanded, "Sergeant, get some food and refreshment for the captain. Prepare some of that fruit. Get the roast venison and onions. We need to feed these men. They all look fatigued."

Ordway moved off to prepare food and Lewis explained to Clark, "There's three forks here. From here we know the first river, the smaller one, joins in a little further down. These two larger ones have me in a quandary. I walked down both of them and I honestly cannot satisfy myself which is the larger stream of the two. In fact, they appear the same. There is no difference in character or size. To call either of these rivers the Missouri would be giving it a preference which its size does not warrant. One is no larger than the other. It reminds me of the Maria's back there. By the way, what did you see out there?"

Clark, who had been stretching out and relaxing, looked at Lewis and said, "We went to that high peak over there. Had one a hell of a time just getting up it. Tuckered us all out, that little point. From it, I could see the north fork for about ten miles. No signs of Indians at all. Nothing fresh enough to stand out anyway. I got a good look up the smaller river and the middle one, too. Couldn't tell which was the Missouri, but I would choose the southwest fork over the middle one. I think it will lead to the mountains first. We've been up the middle fork ten to twelve miles. It stays pretty much the same. The river is strong though, there's a lot of volume and current, just like the southwest one. Damn near lost Charbonneau out there." Lewis looked up in concern as Clark continued, "Yeah, wouldn't you know, the one man that would slip on the rocks crossing the river would be Charbonneau. Good old 'I can't swim a lick' Charbonneau. There he was gasping, gurgling and flailing away at the water. Splashing like a fish on a line. It would've been funny had we not been alone out there. I found the strength to go after him and he clung to me like a leach. He could have pulled me under too, the way he hung on. He wouldn't let go until we reached waist deep water. It took him half an hour to calm down. Enough of that adventure. What do you think of the river fork? Want to take the southwest?"

Lewis listened and said, "These forks are a puzzle, no doubt. Neither river seems to dominate, so I don't know which to call the Missouri. But as far as which one to follow from here, I agree with your observation. I'd choose the southwest fork. As for the name of the river, I don't think we have to choose, Bill. At this point, so far up the river, we can name each river individually as its own entity. The Missouri simply starts here. At the forks."

Clark nodded as he scanned the rivers, "You're right. There's nothing I can see that would say one is the Missouri and the other is not. I do think that the southwest river will lead to a mountain pass before the middle fork. I have no problem calling this point the headwaters of the Missouri and naming these three separately. Got any names in mind?"

Lewis answered excitedly, "Yes, Bill, I do. I've been thinking while waiting on your return. The lesser one I would name the Gallitin, after our Secretary of the Treasury. It is slightly more narrow than the others, but it has a considerable volume of water and moves quickly. The middle fork I would name the Madison, after the Secretary of State. The right fork, the one which we agree we will pursue..."

Clark interrupted, "We will call the Jefferson. I can read your mind, Merry. You are Jefferson's man. Good choices! I'll enter those names on the charts this evening."

Lewis beamed and replied, "Yes, the Jefferson. The author of this enterprise. He would be proud to have this stream, the probable Missouri, and the one we have chosen to follow, named after him. I can just see him with a big smile, nodding his approval."

Clark said wearily, "I think I'd like some rest. My illness won't leave me and perhaps a little rest will help. If I don't improve, tomorrow you should bleed me."

Lewis said, "I think I'll give you some of Dr. Rush's laxative pills. In these cases a good internal cleansing helps before bleeding. Who knows, maybe you'll feel better. Would you like a warm foot bath? That should help, too."

Clark replied, "Yes. But forgive me if I fall asleep."

Lewis got some hot water and soaked Clark's feet. Clark lay back with his feet in the kettle and closed his eyes.

Lewis said, "I am getting more concerned each day. We can't continue up this river pulling the canoes by cord. It's just too tough on the men. The river is so strong that the effort doesn't yield much progress. Bill, we need horses. We need them now."

Clark opened his eyes and replied, "I agree. This river cannot remain navigable much longer. We'd make a lot better progress with pack horses not having to follow the meandering of the river. Should we make a base camp here and set out with two or three contingents to find the Indians?"

Lewis said, "That's tempting. We need the horses, we'd make better progress without question. But without a sign of a campsite, I think we should wait a while yet. We can go on up the Jefferson until we see fresh signs, then we can look."

Clark said, "Makes sense to me. No sense looking unless there's a reasonable chance of finding."

Lewis said, "Today, Labiche translated for Janey. Seems like this is the place she was taken prisoner by the Minnetare. She said this place had the bad memories of her capture. She remembers details, too. When they first saw the Minnetare war party, they retreated about three miles up the Jefferson and hid in the woods. They were pursued and attacked. They lost four men, four women and some teenage boys. They captured four of the boys and all the young girls and women that didn't offer resistance. Strange thing was she told the story with a completely straight face. No emotion at all."

Clark replied, "She was young then. Would have been only eleven or so when that happened. Recalling the detail may have been difficult, but I'm sure that whatever she does recall is accurate. I think she hasn't shown emotion toward the land yet because she hasn't seen positive signs of her people. When we see signs of them, or better yet, when we meet them, I think she'll show emotion. Remember, Merry, she's been a slave and now the wife of Charbonneau. Not a great life or a lot of emotion for her lately."

August 6, 1805

The Corps of Discovery moves up the Jefferson. The river is now punctuated with sandbar islands alternately changing to sections of rapids and deeper water almost without notice. This repeats every three to four hundred yards. Crossing the shallow portions is difficult and requires several men to pull the cording ropes as the canoes drag bottom on the sand and rock. Then, reaching the deeper water, the canoes require ropes and cording to advance upstream.

During one such crossing, one of the canoes passes from a shallow sandy area to a section of deeper, more rapid water. The men are pulling on ropes while Private Whitehouse is in the canoe using a pole to push. Suddenly, one of the ropes snaps. Instantly the canoe swings around sharply, lurching as the remaining ropes pull tight. Whitehouse loses his balance and is thrown overboard into the rushing water. The canoe, still heavily laden with cargo, continues to swing around in the rapids and passes over his torso, pinning his legs to the bottom and against the rocks on the shallow side. His upper torso is then underwater in the deeper, rapidly moving water.

York, who was pulling on one of the ropes, immediately let go and rushed through the water toward the canoe where

Whitehouse was pinned beneath. First, he attempted to lift the canoe. Then he tried pushing to dislodge it. The rapid water was too strong for him as it continued to hold the boat over Whitehouse and against the sandbar. York's efforts could only make it rock. He looked down at Whitehouse, inches below the surface, submerged and struggling to break free for air.

York shouted, "He's goin' to drown! He's drownin' right here!" Then, York took a large breath of air, held on to the canoe and bent down under the rapids. He grabbed Whitehouse's head with his free hand. Lifting the trapped man's head, he put his mouth to his mouth and resuscitated him. Then he came up and repeated with another breath of air. Meanwhile, the other men were rushing to the accident scene. York came up, looked briefly at the rescue team, took another breath of air and went back down to Whitehouse.

Sergeant Pryor shouted, "Get on the front. Get on the shallow side and lift! Push her out! Now! Do it now!" Four men quickly waded through the rapids and positioned themselves at the front of the canoe. They lifted as two more men pulled from the opposite end. The canoe rocked but remained immovable. Meanwhile York continued to resuscitate Whitehouse. With a second lunging attempt, the canoe made a grinding sound as it pulled free from the shallow rocks and moved over Whitehouse's legs. Whitehouse, although submerged, shouted in pain as the laden canoe tipped over him and passed on downstream. Once cleared, he rose up out of the water, York pulling on his arm. He was screaming in pain as his head broke the surface of the water.

Pryor waded over to the injured man, "Whitehouse, you all right? Is your leg broke? Can you walk?"

Whitehouse replied, "Oh, God, it hurts like hell!" Then, as he tested his weight while leaning on York, he continued, "Don't think it's broke. My guts hurt, too. I really got smashed. What the hell happened?"

Pryor answered, "The rope snapped. The canoe swung round and pinned you under and against the rocks. York here made it to you first but couldn't move it himself. Took four men on the front and two on the back just to push it off the rocks against the current."

Whitehouse was still leaning on York. He pulled away and looked him in the eye. "Thanks, York, I coulda drown while they were tryin' to get that damn boat off my legs. Where did you learn to do that?"

York looked at him and replied, "York didn't learn it. York just saw you under the water there, not bein' able to get yerself up to air. York took some air to you, that's all."

Whitehouse replied, "That's all! York, I owe my life to your quick thinkin', for God's sake! These other men, I owe them for getting that canoe off my legs. But I would have drowned for sure while they were doin' it. Sure as hell would have drowned had it not been for you bringing me air like that." Then he limped over to the shore and sat down. Looking up at York he said in a low, serious tone, "York, I don't think any of the other men would have done what you just did. Don't think they would have thought of it. Thank you, man."

York looked at Whitehouse and said, "You're welcome. You best take good care of yerself. You could have hurt yerself bad. That leg don't look good. Some o' that hurt may not show up until later. Better watch for infection."

Pryor said, "York's right. You take it easy for awhile. We'll see if you're able to work tomorrow. For the rest of the day, don't do anything except rest up."

Whitehouse replied, "You don't need to repeat that order, Sergeant," as he leaned over and looked at his legs.

Pryor looked upstream and said, "Capt'n Lewis is up there, just ahead. Let's get up there and let him know what happened. Then we've got to get all this stuff out of the canoe and let it dry."

Seeing the confusion, Lewis was alert and approached. "What's wrong? What happened? How did everything get wet?"

Pryor responded, "We had an accident, sir. The canoe tipped on Whitehouse and pinned him under. It took six of us to dislodge it an' set him loose. Everything got pretty wet in all the splashing."

Lewis looked at the cargo in the canoe and stood silent for a moment as he surveyed the surroundings. Then he ordered, "There on the left side is a gravely sandbar. It appears to be high and out of the water. Let's get over there and make camp for the day. Get the campfires going and everything out of this canoe to dry. I want an inventory of what's damaged. The air here is dry, if we act quickly the goods may dry out without damage. Sergeant, give me a damage report after supper."

That evening Lewis sat with Clark as they ate elk the hunters had killed while camp was being set. Sergeant Pryor came to report the damage from the earlier accident.

"Capt'n," Pryor said as he approached, "seems like we lost a shot pouch and powder and all the implements for a rifle. Must have gone overboard without anyone noticing. Whitehouse has one leg hurt bad, it's all swole up. The other is just cut and bruised. He's complaining a lot but not much we can do for him. Lucky thing it didn't get broke." Then he looked around at the materials drying on the ground and continued, "We lost all the parched meal, some corn, a lot of the packaged Indian presents." Then he looked at Lewis and added, "Your air gun got banged around a bit, too, sir. Sights are off. Maybe you can look at it tomorrow. Lost some opened powder, too. About twenty pound or so got spoiled, but all the rest was packed in the lead canisters with cork and wax. It's all good, dry, and we still got plenty. Those canisters, sir, that is the only way to keep the powder. If it didn't get ruined after complete submersion in that spill back there, well, it's safe no matter what."

Clark replied, "Good, Sergeant. It was Captain Lewis that invented that means of stowing gunpowder." Then turning to Lewis he added, "Excellent design, Merry. I just hope we don't have to give it another submersion test." Looking at Pryor, he inquired, "Any sign of Shannon? Have you heard from Drewyer? If anyone can find him its Drewyer."

Pryor said, "Yes, sir. Drewyer came in just moments ago. He would have come over directly but the men were telling him all about the canoe accident today. He didn't find Shannon. He went several miles upriver without a sign of him. I think we should fire a volley tonight to give him direction in case he can hear."

Lewis looked at Clark and smiled as he said, "Good idea, Sergeant. Seems we have lost young Shannon again. If he doesn't respond to the volley, fire again in the morning. For a smart kid, he sure gets lost easy." Then looking across the camp he said, "I think I'll check on Whitehouse. I don't want infection to set in."

Lewis got up to join Pryor to check on Whitehouse. Clark rose to go with him, hobbling as he went. "Damn. My ankle's sore. This boil will give me no relief."

Lewis said, "Stay here, rest."

Clark responded, "No. We have a man down due to injury. We should see if we can give him something. He was hurt in the line of duty."

As the captains approached Whitehouse, his expression of pain momentarily disappeared as he smiled to greet the captains. "Good evening Captain Lewis, Clark."

Clark sat down next to him and asked, "How are ya? I heard you had some excitement today."

Whitehouse said, "Yeah. I fell out of the canoe like I was falling off a log. Somehow got pinned under it. Your man saw me there, under the water and kept bending down giving me air while the others moved it off.   I got to tell you, sir, I'd a died without York."

Clark replied, "I heard."

Whitehouse inquired, "Those two rivers we came past today. Shannon went hunting up one of them, didn't come back. Are we sending someone after him tomorrow?"

Lewis said, "We'll fire a volley of shots again in the morning to see if he can hear us. If we don't hear return fire, I'll send some men to look for him."

Pryor asked, "Those rivers we passed today, was there any question as to which was to be the Jefferson? How did you decide?"

Lewis looked at Clark and then replied, "Yes, at first there was a question. The one river seemed to have more volume, but its waters were colder. It also meandered more. I believe the one with slightly warmer water is the Jefferson. It's has more time to travel from the mountains. We did name them for Captain Clark's charts. The larger of the two I named Wisdom and the lesser one Philanthropy, after those cardinal virtues that President Jefferson so amply demonstrates."

Pryor said, "That sounds good enough to me." Then looking around at the materials on the ground, he continued, "With this dry air and everything spread out, we should be able to get underway tomorrow without delay."

Clark said, "It looks to me like we could do with one less canoe. Now that we have fewer materials, we should look at leaving one of the canoes here. Check it out tomorrow, Sergeant. If we can load everything in one less canoe, let's do it. That'll be one less to drag up this river."

August 8, 1805 Beaver's Head, Montana

Moving up the river is difficult. The men are not in good health as they are exhausted from the rigors of travel. They urge the captains frequently to go overland in order to cover more ground and avoid the work in the meandering river.

As they paused to make observations, Labiche approached the captains. "It's Janey, she's been pointing and talking. More than usual. She's got something to say to you."

Clark looked at Lewis and said, "By all means bring her over. Let's hear."

Labiche left and soon returned with Sergeant Gass, Charbonneau and Sacajawea. Clark looked at the Indian woman and asked, "What is it? Do you have something to tell us?"

The translation went from Labiche to Charbonneau to Sacajawea. After hearing the question she pointed as she spoke in broken English, "Cap-tan this rock is called the Beaver's Head." Then she smiled broadly from having just spoken in English. Then she turned to Charbonneau and continued in her native tongue. The translation came from Labiche. "She wants to say that she recognizes this cliff. The rock is called 'Beaver's Head' by her people. They say it resembles a beaver swimming up a stream. She says that her people sometimes meet here. There is another meeting place not far from here that they use every summer."

Clark slapped his leg and looked at Lewis, "Did you hear that, Merry? We are close to where her people meet. We sure could use a change of luck. Ain't seen an Indian in these parts at all. All the men are weary. They'll welcome seeing some friendlies and getting horses. I could use a horse, too. I can't seem to get this ankle to operate without pain."

Lewis smiled and said, "That is good news. Good news we all can use. Let's go on a short way and find a place to camp. Tomorrow I want to take some men and find this meeting place. From there I'll find the Continental Divide." Lewis lost his smile and rose up to walk away. "Tell Janey thanks for the report. I'm sure the men will be encouraged by knowing we are now close to her people and horses."

Clark, seeing Lewis' change in mood, rose up and walked after him to the edge of the camp. Hobbling toward Lewis on his one good leg, Clark asked, "Merry, what's wrong? Now is not the time to get depressed."

Lewis looked at Clark a moment in silence then said, "Bill, it's August and we're not even to the headwaters of this damned river yet. We're not at the Continental Divide yet. We haven't found the Columbia yet. Many of our men are ill. All of them are weary. Shall I go on? They all want to proceed overland. I can't blame them; I'm travel weary, too. We need horses. We can**not** proceed without horses. Pack horses, riding horses, horses, damn it, horses!"

Clark listened to his friend and then began calmly, "Merry, we're now close to contacting Indians. Janey's been seeing familiar territory and now this cliff, Beaver Head Rock. In case you don't know it, that's good news! Uplifting. The men are already encouraged with this recognizable landmark, and you should be, too. Janey said she recognized the territory before, but this is the first tangible landmark the men have seen. Yes, we can look at the dark side of things, but that's not the man I came with. You, yourself, have said you prefer to assume that the best will happen until something bad presents itself."

Lewis looked long at Clark and then said, "True."

Clark continued, "Well then, we'll do what we have always done. We will proceed on. Your idea of taking men ahead and looking for this meeting place and the Snake Indians; that's good. Do it." Then he pointed out over the land and said,

"The river has no falls. The land is what Janey said it would be. Why doubt our fate now. I believe we're close to finding friendly Indians."

Lewis replied, "You're right. Never have I seen a river remain navigable for such a long distance. I don't believe that the world can furnish another example of a river running to the extent the Missouri and Jefferson do. A river passing through such mountainous country and, at the same time, be as navigable. If the Columbia is the same, then Jefferson's dream of a Northwest Passage and a water route from west to east will be a reality." Smiling at Clark he said, "I will proceed on. I'll find the Shoshone and horses if it takes me a month."

"Now that's the man I came with," Clark said with a smile as he patted Lewis on the back. They turned to walk back to the campsite.

After reaching the others, the men engaged in light conversation. They remarked as to how much the rock resembled a beaver's head, especially when viewed from farther upriver. Conversation stayed on Whitehouse's accident. Later in the evening, a shot was heard. Shannon had spotted the campfires and was shouting as he came in through the night. He was glad he had found his companions and was no longer lost.

Joseph Field asked, "You got a big word for being lost? Maybe disoriented from your compass or something?"

"Glad to have you back." Drewyer said.

"Get yourself somethin' to eat and some rest," Sergeant Ordway said. "We'll let you catch up on your workload tomorrow."

Lewis turned to Clark and said, "Good to have our crew back together again. By the way, I have been thinking. Janey said we were near her people. That we would see them soon."

"Yeah," Clark replied in anticipation.

Lewis continued, "Well, I think we should ask her how to greet them. How to identify ourselves to them. In their own tongue."

Clark nodded as he motioned to Sergeant Gass, "Good idea. Sergeant, get Labiche and the Charbonneau's together. We have a question for them."

In a few moments the guide and his wife were standing in front of the captains with anxious expressions. Lewis spoke, "Ask her how to greet her people. How do we say we are white men?"

The translation took place, and Sacajawea nodded quickly, indicating she understood. She looked at Lewis and said very slowly, "Tab-ba-bone." Then she smiled and looked back at the translator.

Lewis looked at Sacajawea, then Clark and Labiche. "Tab-ba-bone. That means white man? Tab-ba-bone. Good. Well, I think I can remember that one. We can use our translators for the rest. When I go, I'll not return until I've found them. Should I perish in the attempt, I think I'll leave some instructions tonight. Tonight I'll write some letters."

August 11, 1805
Near Lemhi Pass, Montana

Desperate to locate Indians and horses to enable them to continue the trip westward, Lewis departs from the main party. He leaves early and takes three men with him, George Drewyer, Hugh McNeal and John Shields. They soon discover horse tracks, probably left by an Indian. Lewis is eager to follow them in search of an encounter. As they are walking across the land, following the ever-narrowing river, now nothing more than a small creek, Lewis waves an arm, signaling the men to gather around him. They immediately comply.

Lewis gave an order, "Drewyer, you keep near the stream and follow it looking for tracks. Shields, you go off to my left and look for any sign of a trail. McNeal, stay with me. Stay within sight of each other, and if anyone sees fresh tracks from Indians, signal me. Don't fire your weapon. That may scare them off. Instead put your hat over your gun muzzle and wave it in the air. Keep a sharp eye."

They proceeded to explore in this fashion for about five miles when Lewis, using his telescope, noticed something ahead. He handed his telescope to McNeal as he said, "Look. There ahead. Must be two miles off. See him? It looks like a single Indian on horseback. See him? Just there by those rocks."

McNeal studied the horizon a moment and then replied, "Yeah, I got him. Movin' real slow. Don't see any others. Think he is the only one?"

McNeal handed the telescope back to Lewis as Lewis replied, "Don't know. I'll keep looking. I don't think he's spotted us yet. He seems to be dressed different from any Indians we've seen yet. He's got a bow and a quiver of arrows, all different. Must be a Snake Indian."

McNeal said, "He's ridin' bareback. What's he using for a bridle?"

Lewis replied, "Just a light string of some sort. Amazing. Let's move toward him and make contact. Come on, we're finally going to meet some natives." He put his hat over his rifle muzzle and raised it up moving it slowly back and forth. Drewyer looked and nodded in acknowledgment. Shields pointed and nodded. Lewis was excited. He began moving toward the Indian rider with long strides.

They moved on until the distance between them was about a mile. Suddenly, the Indian spotted them approaching and halted his mount as he looked at them. Recognizing that he had caught the attention of the Indian, Lewis unfolded a blanket. He then held it by two corners and began flinging it high in the air and lowering it back to the ground.

"This is a sign of friendship," Lewis said. "The Indians of the Missouri use it to indicate that they want to sit and talk." Again he flung the blanket high overhead and lowered it to the ground. He repeated this action one more time.

McNeal said, "He ain't movin', sir. Just looking at us like a hawk."

Lewis looked around quickly and saw Drewyer and Shields moving through the grass at some distance. Looking back at the Indian, Lewis knew that the Indian could see the others coming toward him. Lewis tried to get the other men's attention but they were not looking at him. "Damn it." he said. "He may take this spread out approach of ours as an attack. We should be closer together."

"Should I fire a shot to get their attention?" McNeal inquired.

Lewis quickly replied, "No, no. I think gunfire will scare him off. He probably sees their guns as it is. Here, I'm going to leave my rifle with you and go on ahead. You stay here so we won't be so threatening. I'll take this looking glass and some beads and proceed slowly toward him. If you catch Drewyer or Shield's eye, have them hold tight. I want to go on alone."

Lewis moved on toward the lone Indian. The man remained still on his horse until Lewis was about 200 feet away. Then he turned his horse slowly and began to move away. Seeing this, Lewis began hollering, "Tab-ba-bone, tab-ba-bone," as loud as he could.

The Indian looked over his shoulder for a moment at Drewyer and Shields, who were still advancing. Then he continued to move slowly away. Recognizing the probable concern the Indian may have about their approach, Lewis turned and signaled for the two men to halt. Drewyer saw Lewis and halted. Shields did not notice and continued to draw nearer. Frustrated, Lewis continued to walk toward the

Indian and approached him to within 150 feet. "Tab-ba-bone, tab-ba-bone," Lewis shouted as he held up the gifts he had brought with him. The two looked at each other seriously for a moment, then Lewis proceeded slowly to close the gap between them.

When he was within 100 paces, the Indian suddenly turned his horse, swatted him on the rump, jumped the creek and disappeared into the willows.

Lewis' face was marked with disappointment as the Indian rode away. He turned around, slumped his shoulders and dropped his head. He stood there in silence a moment and then looked up and walked back toward the other three men. The men converged quickly on Lewis, and when they were near, Lewis simply said, "He's gone."

Drewyer said, "I think he was afraid of us. He was alone and couldn't be sure we wouldn't harm him."

Lewis looked at the men and snapped, "Shields, damn it. Didn't you see McNeal and Drewyer holding their ground. Why the hell did you keep on coming? That was a delicate moment and now we've lost it. He's gone."

Shields said, "I'm sorry sir, I didn't…"

Lewis interrupted, "You didn't think, that's all. He was alone and the four of us may have scared him. He saw you coming in on the flank with a rifle and he knew he was outnumbered. If you had held your ground like the others, maybe, just maybe, he would have let me approach and talk to him one on one. He saw your gun and probably knows its range. He left before he was within your rifle range. Simple as that."

Lewis grabbed his rifle sharply from McNeal and began walking along the track the Indian had just left. "Maybe he went to find his friends or his camp. Maybe we'll meet him again. We have no choice now. We'll try to find him."

They followed the trail, hoping to encounter a larger group of Indians. After a time they came to open ground on the north side of the creek. From there they could observe a trail leading toward higher ground about three miles distant. Lewis said, "Look up there, by the tops of those hills. If they're watching, they'll be able to see us from there. If we advance too rapidly, they may just flee again. If they're watching, let's show them we're not in pursuit."

McNeal asked, "What should we do, sir?"

Lewis replied, "Let's make a fire. We'll have some breakfast and sort out a few gifts. Act real casual. If they see us and are curious, they may approach our campfire to investigate. We'll leave a few items behind as gifts. If they find them, they'll know we're not Indians but white men."

After they had eaten, a small storm came over quickly with rain and hail. It was brief but left them soaked. More importantly, it removed any fresh signs of the trail they hoped to follow.

Drewyer said, "We should go now and hurry. The tracks won't be visible for long."

Lewis sighed and replied, "Right. We'll follow the trail as far as we can. Hugh, take the flag and attach it to a long stick. Hold it high all the while we're going forward. If they see us and the flag, they'll know we're not enemies."

The rain stopped as suddenly as it came. They proceeded on through the wet grass, trying to follow the trail. They came across an area where the Indians had been digging for roots. There were so many tracks in the small clearing that it was impossible to discern which direction they were from.

Lewis looked around and said, "Let's move over past the creek to the foot of those hills and camp for the night. We'll continue this adventure in the morning."

August 12, 1805 Continental Divide, Montana/Idaho

At first light an anxious Lewis ordered Drewyer to go out in search of any tracks or trail he might find leading into the mountains. Drewyer returned about an hour and a half later and reported that he had found nothing.

Lewis stood and looked around for a moment and then said, "We'll move off toward the mountains. Drewyer, go to my right. Shields, take the left. McNeal, stay with me. Look for fresh horse tracks or any type of road or trail. Whichever we find first we'll follow. This must be the area where they cross the mountains to hunt. This is the area Janey was telling us they meet. They're here. We just have to find 'em."

They proceeded on and soon discovered an area with bowers or conical lodges made of willows the Indians had constructed. Again they noticed that the ground all around had been dug up. Evidence of a quest for roots. Drewyer said, "Look, they dig, but for what? I can't see any plants that they're taking. If Janey were here, she might know what they're eating."

Lewis responded, "No way to know. We're wasting time here. Let's move on. We'll go back to the trail by the main stream in the lower bottom land. We'll follow it until we see fresh signs. For now, let's have the rest of the venison for breakfast, and then we'll resume our march."

They ate a relaxed breakfast and moved out. After about ten miles of travel along the stream, it turned abruptly west through a narrow bottom between the mountains. Standing by the stream, Lewis said, "This is good. If we continue ahead I believe we'll cross the divide by this evening. Soon we'll be tasting from the headwaters of the Columbia. The slope is gentle here."

Drewyer added, "Just look, this river we have been following is now coming to an end. We'll soon come to a spring, and I plan to drink right where it comes from the ground."

Lewis smiled and said, "So we all will, George."

They moved on, closer and closer to the mountain ridge above. They kept following the small stream up the mountainside for another four to five miles until they came to a spring. It gurgled clear water as it issued out of the mountainside.

Drewyer said, "This is it. The farthest point of this endless river." He knelt to drink and then stopped short and said, "Capt'n, you go first. You must be the first one to drink from the spring water of the Missouri."

Lewis stood for a moment and looked down the valley they had just come up. "You do me honor, George, thank you. This valley is beautiful. I am letting my senses become aware that I have just reached a goal, a goal I have sought unalterably for many years now. The headwater of the mighty Missouri River, right here at my feet. A river which we could easily have believed was endless after spending so many toilsome days and restless nights. Judge then, if you will, the pleasure I feel in allaying my thirst from this pure and ice cold spring water."

Lewis knelt and lowered his face to the ground until his lips touched the fountain of water. He drank long and then paused, took a breath and drank again. As he looked up Drewyer was smiling broadly. Lewis said, "It's good men, Good as I ever imagined. Go ahead, each of you. Drink as much as you wish. God knows you've earned it."

The four men each drank water from the spring and rested. Then Drewyer pointed up toward the ridge and said, "The ridge of the mountain, right there, it's only a short way up."

Shields said, "Let's do it."

Lewis said, "What you see there is the Continental Divide, a huge milestone of our journey. On the other side is the watershed of the Columbia. If we're lucky, we'll soon find another spring. It will be the Columbia. All right, men, let's move on."

With that order, they picked up their bags and rifles to move up the ridge. McNeal said, "I have been waiting for that order for a long time, sir."

Drewyer nodded and said, "So have we all."

They proceeded the short way to the ridge and stood there a moment, looking back from whence they had just come. Lewis said, "This ridge, I'm sure, is the Continental Divide. All water east of here flows into the Missouri. This ridge marks the edge of the Louisiana Purchase." He turned and looked out over the ridges of snowcapped mountains to the west. "All the water west of hear flows to the Columbia and the Pacific. As I said, this is a landmark of our journey. We may find the Northwest Passage soon." After standing on the ridge of the divide a moment, they proceeded down the westward slope of the mountain about a mile until they came to another spring.

Lewis said, "This is it, the spring that is the headwater of the Columbia. I think we should all drink again."

They all knelt and drank from the spring.

August 13, 1805

The next morning they set out early and went about six miles down a small creek and into a handsome valley. Ahead was a timber-lined valley with a gently undulating clearing. Lewis, as he was using his telescope, raised a hand to halt the others. He spoke. "There's Indians ahead, two women, a man and some dogs. See there, about a mile off, straight ahead."

Drewyer said, "Do they see us yet? We gotta be cautious. Don't want to scare these off."

Lewis nodded in agreement and said, "Right, we'll approach slowly. These people seem to be afraid of strangers."

Then smiling he excitedly said, "Maybe our luck is changing. I think they've seen us. Look, they just sat down. I think they could be waiting for us. This time, don't fan out. Stay together. McNeal, hold that flag high for them to see."

The men walked on until they were within a half mile of the Indians. Lewis turned and ordered, "Stay here. I'll advance alone. Here, keep my rifle and pack." The men stopped as Lewis handed his rifle and pack to McNeal. As he advanced toward the Indians, he shouted, "Tab-ba-bone" over and over. Much to his disappointment, the two women moved away and disappeared behind a hill. The lone man looked back momentarily, then also disappeared. As soon as they were out of his sight, Lewis quickened his pace to advance to the top of a hill for a better look from a higher vantage point. Once at the top he stared in disbelief. There was nothing. No Indians to be seen. They had disappeared into the timberline. Some of their dogs remained behind and seemed curious and came near. He knelt down and called to them, but they wouldn't come close enough for him to touch. Disgusted, Lewis stood and waved to the men to join him.

They hurried to meet him, and as they approached Lewis said, "Damn it, they're gone again. Seem to be very flighty people. They had to know we're not enemies."

Shields inquired, "What should we do? Follow 'em?"

Lewis replied, "Yes. We follow them. We need to find these people."

Drewyer asked Lewis as they walked on, "What about those dogs? Were you trying to catch one of them?"

"Yeah," Lewis said, "I thought I could tie a ribbon around one of them and maybe attach a trinket or something. When it got back to them, they'd know we are friendly."

They proceeded on about another mile. The terrain now consisted of several small ravines undulating in succession. As they rose to the top of a small knoll, they suddenly came upon three Indian women not more than thirty yards away. Seeing the men suddenly approach, the youngest one rose up, shrieked and ran away. The older woman and a child remained, evidently resigned to whatever fate would bestow upon them. Lewis laid his rifle down and hand signaled the men to halt as he moved slowly toward the woman. The old woman sat with her head down looking at the ground as Lewis approached.

Lewis kneeled down by the elderly woman, took her hand and raised her up. He said, "Tab-ba-bone" and then pushed up his sleeve to show his white skin. Next, he gave the woman some paint and beads. She smiled and accepted. The woman now appeared calm, and Lewis directed Shields to give her a moccasin awl and a looking glass. The looking glass amazed her, and she was quite taken with it. She looked repeatedly at her image in the mirror and showed the mirror to the younger girl. Then Lewis spoke to Drewyer, "Try to get her to recall the one that ran away."

When Drewyer had finished his sign language, the old woman called out loudly. Soon, the younger woman who had fled earlier, came running back, quite out of breath. Lewis painted their cheeks with vermilion paint and asked Drewyer, "Do you think you could get them to take us to their camp to meet the others? Tell her we want to meet their chiefs and warriors."

Drewyer said, "I think she understands." He then proceeded to sign with the woman. She turned and began walking away.

Lewis looked at the men a moment and said, "Well, what are you waiting for? Let's follow her."

They had moved down the river about two miles when suddenly they heard the approaching thunder of a great many horses' hooves. They stopped and looked as they saw sixty mounted warriors riding toward them at full speed. As they drew near, they slowed and then stopped about fifty paces away. Lewis looked at his men, laid his rifle down at Drewyer's feet and said, "Stay here. I'll go out."

As Lewis moved toward the group of mounted Indians, the apparent chief and two others moved forward. The chief shouted to the women who immediately stepped forward smiling and talking, raising their hands to show off the gifts just received. The chief listened a moment, slowly surveyed the four men, then gave a hand signal. Responding to the chief, all the warriors dismounted. The chief then moved toward Lewis and embraced him by putting his left arm over Lewis' right shoulder. He put his cheek next to Lewis' and said, "Ah-hi-e, ah-hi-e."

As soon as this greeting was completed, the others moved forward and began greeting the four explorers. This continued until McNeal whispered to Shields and Lewis, "I think I've had enough of this national greeting."

"Yeah," Shields replied. "Sixty some Indians is a lot of hugging, I think I hugged a couple of them twice already."

Drewyer spoke up, "The hug is tiresome, I agree, but look at those horses. Seems like I ain't seen a horse since forever. Ever see such beautiful animals?"

Lewis said, "Exactly right, George. We've found the elusive Indians and it looks like they have plenty of horses. Let's get them to sit and talk awhile. We need to let them know about the rest of our party. See if they're willing to trade for horses. Tell them about Jancy. Say we have one of their women with our second party and we'll soon be able to talk."

Drewyer looked at Lewis and said, "Yes, sir. Slow down a little. I'll do my best to let them know who we are. We've got some time here now, they're not going anywhere. First I'll ask them to sit and talk with us."

As Drewyer communicated, the Indians moved into a circle around them. Lewis had McNeal hand him some tobacco and a pipe. When he lit the pipe to pass it around, all the Indians began to take their moccasins off and set them in front of themselves. Lewis and the men copied the act as Drewyer explained, "They remove the moccasins as an act of friendship. They want to show they're serious, sincere. It seems that it's a pledge to show that if they are not truthful they wish always to go without moccasins."

Shields said, "Now that would be rough around here."

Lewis said, "I like it. It's a good signal that they are sincere and want to be friendly with us. They're willing to pledge heavily to do so. Yes, I like it."

They continued to talk when the Indian woman handed the chief the mirror. He looked at himself and said to the others in his language, "These men are strange. Like none we have ever seen. They have water that is frozen but not cold. We can see ourselves in it. They have guns but do not seem to behave like the Blackfoot or Minnetare. They give us gifts and want to smoke and talk more. I do not think it wise to kill them for their weapons. I want to know more about them."

Lewis didn't know what was being said, but he instinctively knew that they were taking his measure and that they believed his friendly gestures. He told Shields, "Give them the other gifts we brought, the vermilion, blue beads, a couple of knives and the needles." As Shields was handing out the gifts, Lewis said to Drewyer, "Tell them we're friendly, that we have come from the east and are going west. We would like to have some water. Ask them the chief's name."

Lewis smiled as he saw the gifts being individually examined as Shields handed them out. Drewyer proceeded with the translation and the chief stepped forward and spoke directly to Lewis. "Ca-me-ah-wait," he said proudly.

Drewyer said, "That's his name, Ca-me-ah-wait. He's the chief. We're the first white men they've ever seen."

They moved on to a main Indian campsite where they talked late into the evening. Lewis inquired about the direction of the westward river and if there was a larger river to be found. Drewyer made an estimate of the herd size and told Lewis that there were at least four hundred head, most of them in very good condition. They informed the Shoshone that the others of the Corps were behind and that they wanted to join them. They repeated that there was a Shoshone woman with them to improve communication. They also told them there was a strange black man. Using Drewyer as translator, Lewis asked Cameahwait to join them on the trip back to meet Clark. He asked for thirty spare horses to be used as pack animals for materials. He explained that the material they would pick up would be used for trading for their horses.

August 15, 1805

Lewis with Cameahwait and a few Shoshone began the return trip back toward a meeting with Clark. At first the Indians thought there would be an ambush of some type and did not want to go. Cameahwait indicated that he did not have fear. He finally persuaded a small group to join him on the journey to meet the other friendly white men. Soon the cautious Shoshone began to join the party a few at a time. They seemed to come from here and there until there was a large group following Lewis and the chief. Because there were no saddles for the horses, Lewis and the others each had to ride double with an Indian. They very soon became tired of this rather rough ride and told their hosts that they preferred to walk. Drewyer and Shields were dispatched to hunt and proceeded on ahead. Drewyer killed three deer and Shields an antelope. To the half-starved Shoshone, this was a time to feast. Because the men had just provided food, they now seemed worthy of trust.

Lewis informed Cameahwait that he had plans to meet Clark and the others at the fork in the river below. The chief halted the men and gave Lewis and the men necklaces to wear, perhaps as gifts in exchange for the food just provided. Lewis countered by presenting Cameahwait with his cocked hat and feather.

When they were about two miles from the river fork, it became obvious that there was no one there to meet them. The skeptical Shoshone began looking at one another and buzzing back and forth, immediately suspecting a trap. They thought that their enemies may lie in wait near the river. Lewis knew he needed to restore their confidence and quickly.

He ordered Drewyer, "Tell him that only the other white men will be here. Friendly white men. There are no Indians in ambush. Tell him I will give him my rifle as proof. It will show that if I do not speak the truth that he may shoot me with it. You others do the same."

As Drewyer translated and the other men complied by handing their rifles to the Indians. Then Lewis had another thought and spoke to Drewyer. "Remember the note I left for Clark? Well, you take them to where we left it. When you find it, tell them that the marking on the paper is from Clark, my brother chief. Tell them that he left it to let us know he would be arriving shortly and we are to wait. Tell them the note says they are having difficulty coming against the water."

Shields said, "Good idea, Capt'n. They ain't going to know any different. By the time they get to where the note is, Capt'n Clark may be there anyway. You win either way."

August 17, 1805

Clark and the others had not yet arrived. Lewis was up early, worried about keeping the Indians calm until the others could join them. He called the men together, "Shields, go out and bring us back some meat. Elk, deer, anything you get will be much appreciated. McNeal, you cook up the rest of the meat for breakfast. Drewyer, I want you to go with one of the Indians downstream until you find the others. That way he can report back to the chief that we're telling the truth. I think we're losing credibility here by waiting. They're a suspicious lot anyway. When you find our men, bring Charbonneau, Janey, York and a couple of men back with you in advance of the others. That will let them know we didn't lie. When they get here, we can use Janey to interpret. Then we'll send horses back to help bring the others up."

Drewyer and the Indian were only gone about two hours when they returned. They reported the Corps of Discovery was only a short way off. The news quickly swept through the waiting Indians and visibly uplifted their spirits. They all talked rapidly and became excited as they looked downriver and pointed. Cameahwait, hearing the news, came to Lewis and repeated the hugging gesture. Soon the Corps of Discovery came into view. Lewis waved his arms and Shields waved the flag on a long staff. Seeing their companions, Clark and the others whistled, shouted and waved.

Charbonneau and Sacajawea, anxious to meet the Shoshone, led the way with Clark and the others about a hundred paces behind. Sacajawea slowed and then stopped as she studied the faces of the Indians waiting with Lewis. She turned and placed two fingers in her mouth and sucked on them, a sign that these were her people. When she turned to look back, the Indians were approaching.. Suddenly she began jumping and running ahead. She had just recognized a girl-friend that she had not seen since her capture. As she ran, the men looked at one another curiously; they had never seen this much emotion from their stoic Indian companion.

Sacajawea shouted for joy as she ran and embraced an approaching Indian woman. They exchanged the Shoshone hug and moved in circles, first hugging, then breaking apart and looking at one another, then hugging again. As they embraced, Sacajawea said in her native tongue, "Jumping Fish, is it you? It is you! Do you recognize me, I am Bird Woman, Sacajawea. I was brought here with these white men because I could translate for them. They are good men, they work hard."

Jumping Fish was smiling and crying as she replied, "It is you! I thought you were killed. You're alive! My best friend is alive! We must talk, there is much to say. You have a baby? I have a husband now, but we do not have children yet. Is your baby a boy or girl?"

Sacajawea, with tears in her eyes, looked around as the other men began to arrive and study her with curiosity. She said, "My baby is a boy. His father is there, the one with gray in his hair. My baby is named Jean Baptiste. His father gave him a white name."

Meanwhile the captains reunited and smiled broadly at one another. Clark said, "You found the Indians. Your determination, well, it's simply admirable. I knew you'd find them when you set out. You were just going to make it happen, there wasn't going to be any other way about it. This is a good day."

Sergeant Gass said, "Look at those horses. Just look at those horses. We ain't got to pull no more. Those horses are beautiful, simply beautiful."

Joseph Field said, "Well, Sarge, since they're so beautiful, go give one of them a big kiss. Just make sure you kiss the right end."

Lewis said to Clark, "There's a good story here to tell tonight. Yes, we found the Indians and horses just across the Continental Divide. We've got a lot to share with you but just take a moment and look at some of these horses. Fine quality, wouldn't you say? Well, there are about four hundred head we can trade for." He motioned to the sergeants and said, "Get Labiche, Charbonneau and Janey together. Bring them over to the chief. That's where we're meeting. We've been waiting for good translation. Sign language has its limits." Gass nodded and moved to get the translators assembled for the captains.

Grabbing Clark's arm and pulling gently, Lewis began walking toward the Shoshone chief and the other Indians. "We met them, or found them, just over the divide. There's a small stream there, and if we can get some information and good translation, I think we'll find it flows to the Columbia."

Clark smiled and said, "Merry, this feels good, ain't no other way to say it. We've sure waited long enough to see these Indians. We were running out of river. The men were all wanting to go overland. I don't know, maybe we would have had to start portaging again."

Lewis said, "You should have seen these people. Except for their horses, they are very poor. They were half-starved and ravenous when we met them. I had Drewyer and Shields hunting, and they devoured everything that was brought in."

Clark looked about briefly and nodded in agreement, "They do have a rather lean look about them."

The Shoshone chief, Cameahwait, had assembled his important warriors around a fire. They had already removed their moccasins in anticipation of the talks. The three sergeants, along with Labiche, Cruzatte, Drewyer and Charbonneau moved over to sit with the Shoshone. Charbonneau, noticing Sacajawea still talking with Jumping Fish, shouted to her to join them. She immediately gave a small hug to her friend and moved to join the men near the campfire.

Labiche looked at Lewis and reported, "Our translation team is ready when you are, sir."

Lewis said, "Good, a bit lengthy, but we knew that. We should begin with introductions. Tell them my name and that I am a chief. Tell them Captain Clark is my brother chief. Explain that the three sergeants are lesser chiefs. Tell them that."

Labiche interrupted, "That's enough for starters, sir. It does have to go round the horn, ya know. Let's let them add their introductions, too."

Lewis nodded his approval and said, "Quite right, Private. I tend to get a little anxious sometimes. Let's just start with introductions and maybe smoke a pipe to let things warm up. These people seem to be fond of the pipe. They really like our tobacco."

Labiche began the introductions when Sacajawea suddenly widened her eyes and began to rise up. As she rose she began letting out a low but intensifying squeal. She grabbed the blanket she had been sitting on, focused her eyes on Cameahwait and began walking toward him slowly. Cameahwait, seeing her rise, took notice of her, and a broad smile came across his face. He spoke directly to her in an inquisitive manner. Upon hearing his voice, Sacajawea rushed toward him. When she reached the chief, she threw the blanket over his head and made loud weeping and laughing sounds. This continued for a few moments. The joy seemed to spread through the Indians but left the whites in anticipation of an explanation. The explanation came as Charbonneau became animated and spoke. He waved his hands wildly in the air as he pointed and spoke.

Labiche and Cruzatte listened to Charbonneau and then turned to the captains and spoke simultaneously, "She's his sister!" Then Labiche continued alone, "Janey and Cameahwait, the chief, they're brother and sister."

Drewyer said, "Well I'll be. Captain, you sure know how to pick translators." Then shaking his head he added, "What a stroke of luck. If I didn't see it, I wouldn't believe it. This is unreal, imagine, brother and sister."

Charbonneau was beaming as if the good fortune was his doing. He added more translation and Labiche spoke to the eager captains. "They're brother and sister sure enough. He's older, and he made a rescue attempt for her and her mother after they were captured. It failed, but that's how he became chief. He killed some of the enemy." Then he listened to Charbonneau again and said, "They were afraid you were leading them to the Blackfeet or Minnetare. Now they see you speak the truth. They want to see more of your strange gifts, your magic. They want to know how many horses you need."

Clark slapped his leg and looked at Lewis, "Now this is the kind of meeting I had not even dreamt of, not in my wildest imagination. Pinch me. Am I awake? This chief with all these wonderful, beautiful, magnificent horses, is Janey's brother? Damn, Merry, we're lucky today."

Lewis was smiling as he looked around to take in the scene. "You're awake all right, and sober, too. With all the work these men have been putting into our effort, I guess Providence just decided to give us a little break." Then Lewis said to Sergeant Pryor, "Have Shannon and the Field brothers get some of the Indian gifts we have. I think now would be a good time to stop carrying them and give them to the natives." Turning toward Clark, he said, "Do you see how they remove their moccasins? That's a very curious peace gesture that these people embrace. The idea is to symbolize that they're willing to go without foot covering if they are not now dealing in good faith. I like it. How about you?"

Clark looked at the ring of moccasins, removed his own and motioned for the others to follow suit. Cameahwait brought over a white robe that he offered Lewis to sit upon. Clark said, "Look Merry. His hair. Those ornaments are seashells. Those have got to be from the ocean. That means we're close. These are the first signs of objects traded from tribe to tribe all the way from the seashore to here."

Sergeant Pryor said, "It's gotta be true. They're seashells if ever I saw seashells."

The men brought in tobacco, and the smoking pipes were lit. The Shoshone enjoyed the pipe a great deal. Through the conversations, Sacajawea would sometimes become emotional and tears would run down her cheeks. But the translations, difficult as they were to complete, were captivating to both sides.

Later the hunters returned with fresh meat and there was a feast that evening. Lewis spoke to Clark as they ate, "Further up this little rivulet, there is a spring. You'll see. Cold and clear as you could ever imagine. As far as I can determine it is the fountainhead. It's the beginning of the Missouri watershed and boundary of the Louisiana Purchase. I can't tell you how good it feels to drink from that little spring."

Clark replied, "I can't wait. That'll be a celebration for every man in the Corps of Discovery. A real milestone."

Lewis continued, "Just up from the spring is the Continental Divide. From that point all I could see was more mountains. We did find a small spring on the western slope, but we really need to have these Indians show us where it goes. It's either the Columbia or a tributary to it. I want to find the fastest route to the sea we can make. Those mountains are both beautiful and horrific. We've got to learn where that stream goes."

Clark answered, "After we trade for horses, we'll load up some pack horses and head west. This really feels good. Who would have thought that the very Indians we needed most would have as their chief, the brother of our interpreter. Unbelievable, simply unbelievable. I'll mark this place on our charts and record its distance. What do you want to name it?"

Lewis said, "Camp Fortunate. I have never felt so fortunate. First, to have met the Indians after such a long search, second, to find that they are friendly, third, that they have an ample supply of very fine horses for trade, and finally, that our Indian interpreter is the sister of the chief. Trading, I assure you, will be enhanced by that relationship."

Clark asked, "Are there trees on the western slopes? We can make canoes right away and be back on the water soon as it's deep enough."

Lewis replied, "Some, but we'll need the horses for awhile anyway. Even with the current at our backs, we should use pack horses to cover as much ground as possible until we can float freely. Besides, I think we may encounter swift water, probably falls. If we're faced with another portage, I want horses. According to my calculation, the distance to the ocean is much less than that we have traveled up to now. It only follows that there will be steeper slopes over the shorter distance. The water will be swift from these mountains to sea level."

The meeting was friendly and continued on late into the evening. During that time the captains explained as long as the Shoshone were friendly to the whites, they would not have to fear their enemy tribes. There would be future trading posts with plenty of merchandise. The Shoshone were in a good location to benefit from fur trade down the Missouri. Cameahwait promised more horses for trade and understood that they could not trade their only guns at this time. They would have to wait for a different trip for that purpose. The Indians ate corn that had been brought as cargo from the Mandan. The Shoshone had never tasted corn before and it was a welcome new food for them as well as a good item for trade. The Shoshone had never seen manufactured products. They were very interested in the boats, their materials, the guns and even Lewis' dog, Seaman. York, as usual, was extremely popular. They wanted to touch him and feel his hair. They wanted to know if there were more black men coming as they thought this was a good sign and powerful medicine.

Sacajawea talked with Jumping Fish and learned how she had escaped from the Minnetare. The men were using sign language to communicate to supplement the very busy translation of Labiche, Charbonneau and Sacajawea.

In separate discussion, the captains agreed to split. Clark would take eleven men along with Charbonneau and Sacajawea to the Shoshone main camp. He would then reconnoiter down the small stream until he could determine if it was navigable or not. He would also look for suitable trees to make canoes. Lewis would follow with the main body of Indians and meet Clark on the other side of the divide at the main Shoshone camp. From there they would conclude their trading for horses and make plans for how to proceed on.

August 18, 1805

Morning found the men busily preparing to proceed westward. Lewis, aided by the translation team, traded for three good-quality horses. Both parties to the trade were well-pleased, Lewis, for the much needed horses, and the Shoshone for the materials received.

Lewis exclaimed to Colter and Sergeant Ordway, "Just look at these animals. I traded maybe twenty dollars in merchandise for them. A good deal anywhere."

Colter said, "I just traded a knife, some leggins and a shirt for this animal. They're either mighty generous or just not good at horse trading."

Lewis explained, "I think our manufactured goods have more value out here where they have never before been seen or demonstrated."

Clark took two horses as pack animals and was ready to depart by late morning. Some Indians decided to go back with Clark as far as the divide and then on to their main camp.

Two Indian men and women remained with Lewis and the rest of the Corps of Discovery. They volunteered to assist with the materials. As planned, they would meet later at the main Shoshone camp.

Clark busied himself with preparations and as he was securing a final tie on the pack horses, he noticed Lewis by himself, looking off into the distance. Clark walked over to Lewis and said, "Why so glum, Merry? Did you think I was going to leave without wishing you a happy birthday? It is today, right?"

Lewis nodded.

Clark said, "Well what better birthday present than to have established Camp Fortunate here. The definite high point of our trip since we left Fort Mandan. We've got horses, friendly Indians and a new westward rivulet to explore. What more could a man want? Happy birthday."

Lewis continued to look into the distance and spoke, "This day I complete my thirty-first year. In all probability I have now existed about half the period which I am to remain on earth. I have been thinking that I have yet done but little, very little indeed, to further the happiness of the human race or to advance information for succeeding generations. I now view with regret the many hours I have spent in indolence. I now sorely feel the want of that information which those hours would have given me had they been more judiciously expended." Then he looked at Clark and continued, "But since they cannot be recalled, I will dash this gloomy thought. I shall resolve in the future to redouble my exertions and live for mankind as I have heretofore lived for myself." He looked straight at Clark with an unblinking stare and then looked again off into the distance.

Clark stood there in silence a moment and then waved a hand in front of Lewis' eyes and snapped his fingers.

"Meriwether Lewis, you are totally and completely off the mark. Yes, you may truly have spent half your life, or you could die tomorrow, but few accomplishments, are you daft? You, more than any man I know, or even know of, have accomplished much in your thirty-one years. You have raised yourself and supported your mother and family after your father died. You have served your country honorably, even meritoriously, as much as any man I can name. President Jefferson himself, a man known for his wisdom, chose you from any number of men he could have selected. He selected you not once, but twice! Once, as his personal secretary where he consulted you on many matters of state. He selected you again to be the master of his most prized and cherished project. This expedition, our Corps of Discovery. You were chosen, Meriwether Lewis, by a wise man and not without cause or justification. Jefferson knew you had it in you. You are the spirit of this expedition. You engineered it with hours of preparation. I thank Providence that you chose me as your friend and co-captain. I am honored to serve at your side." Then he clinched his fist and lightly tapped Lewis on the shoulder as he continued, "To say you have done little to advance the happiness of the human race or its knowledge and information, you couldn't possibly be more wrong. This expedition, the Corps of Discovery, even if we stopped right here where we stand, would be a success by any measure. All that rich and fertile land we have crossed. One day that land will be farmland. There will be trading posts and forts. Cities will be built where you have led. And you say you have not advanced human happiness, nonsense. And this business of advancing information, what the hell is that? How many new plants and animals have we found? A hundred of each I'll wager, and you ain't done yet. None of these specimens are known to science. It is you, your eye to find them, your diligence to collect and record them, that will make an advance in science that will fill volumes. You have kept the spirit of these men alive with adventure. We have both witnessed a military unit like none other. Most commanders could not form a unit that would perform like these men." Turning Lewis' shoulders to look him straight in the eye, he finished, "You are a great man with a fault. These horrible fits of depression, but, nonetheless, a great man. As your friend, I would not let any man anywhere degrade you or your efforts like this, and I will NOT let even YOU continue. Now snap out of this and we'll proceed on. We have the Northwest Passage to find and a continent to conquer." Clark stood and looked at Lewis a moment and then nodded his head and turned and walked away. "Happy birthday, Merry," he shouted over his shoulder as he left.

August 29, 1805
Continental Divide, Idaho

Clark leaves Lewis and the Shoshone companions to proceed on ahead. He takes a few men with him to reconnoiter the westward flowing river. He will determine whether or not it is navigable. Lewis assumes the duties of bringing up their materials with the main body. After a few days, Clark dispatches Colter to go back to Lewis with a letter explaining that the Salmon River is impassible.

This day they are re-united again and sit to discuss the past few days and their options for proceeding. Camp is set about two hours before sundown, the Indians mixed with the expedition. Sacajawea, Charbonneau and any of the French speaking men are in the most demand for translation. Sign language is still being employed all over the campsite by both parties to supplement the demand for verbal translation.

The Shoshone camp, like the other natives, is very much taken with York. His muscular frame, dark skin and curly hair are unusual to them. They enjoy watching him dance around the fire and take turns joining in with him. Cruzatte plays the fiddle and tambourine which they find very entertaining. They add their native drums and bead shaking instruments to the music and keep the camp dancing until late. Many of the younger Indians want to pet Seaman. Due to his size, they question if he is a dog or not. They have never seen such a large dog and all are anxious to touch him. Food is becoming scarce. When the hunters bring in deer and game birds, the Indians are grateful to be able to share with the explorers. Tonight they have meat enough to go around and the mood is light.

Lewis and Clark sat together watching the men. Clark said, "I've never seen a river so impassable. Narrow, with an almost non-existent shoreline. There are many sections of steep, rapid flow. More often than not the water cuts through steep, sharp, rugged rock, whirling and cascading in every direction with white foam. Where it was smoother, I didn't see any salmon, probably because there are impassable falls farther on down."

Lewis' face was angered as he said, "We had a close call back there." Clark looked inquisitively as Lewis continued, "That stupid Charbonneau, dumb ass that he is. It seems that Cameahwait planned to take his people and leave us right away. Go east. Just leave us. He had told Janey in the morning and she had told Charbonneau. Do you know that it wasn't until later in the afternoon that he mentioned it, even then only in a casual passing, like the weather for God's sake."

Clark looked startled, "What! When did that happen?"

Lewis continued, "Just after you headed out and we got underway. I had to get Cameahwait to sit down and I used all the political wiles I could muster to shame him into staying with us. His plans were to leave us and continue on to the buffalo hunt." Then reflectively he said, "Can't say as I blame him. If I were a rail-thin chief of a lean and hungry band of Indians, I would probably want to move to the buffalo country as soon as I could myself. But Charbonneau, that idiot, no excuse there. He had to know that information like that was critical and important to know as soon as possible. Anyone would know that I'd need to know just as soon as possible. If Cameahwait had gotten away, we would have been without sufficient horses to continue on through these mountains."

Clark kicked the dirt and said, "I just can't figure him. He reaches new levels of stupidity all the time. I'm glad you got to the chief and convinced him. Glad you held them back."

Lewis said, "I have explained to Cameahwait that because he traded horses with us, the Shoshone will get guns when the other whites follow to settle the land. He says repeatedly that his people are as brave as any of their enemies, 'Pahees', he calls them. He wants guns to get buffalo to feed and clothe his people and to hold the Pahees on equal ground. The other night we shared boiled corn and beans with them. They were very appreciative and said they would like to live in a land that could provide such food. I gave Cameahwait some of the squash that we brought from the Mandan. He said it was by far the best thing he had ever tasted. To a half-starved man, I suppose anything would taste good. Bill, I have to say these people are really polite. They have no possessions to speak of. Our men have loaned them kettles and knives to use in preparing food. They are always very careful to return them after each use and thank the men."

Clark replied, "They want guns, huh? It's only natural. If I were their leader, I would want to have guns so I could hunt buffalo along with any other tribe. The reason they are so wretched and poor is they lack guns and equal footing with the other tribes." Leaning back, he added with a smile, "They are polite and I think the men have been generous with their women. They seem anxious to establish their credibility with us as good people. Fact is, with their attitude, they'll be much better off when white trading reaches them. They have the horses to be a key link in future trade routes."

Lewis looked across the camp and then said, "Your note about the river not being passable, well, it was not a complete loss, at least we know not to waste effort there. I've questioned Cameahwait about trails or passes through the mountains. He has drawn mountains and rivers on the ground for me. It's not a pretty story." Lewis looked at Clark a long moment then said, "There is no Northwest Passage. He explains that the rivers to the north are not passable. They're full of rock and rapids. His people have never traveled on the rivers to the north, but his guide, Toby, can take us to the Nez Perce to the west. He said the Nez Perce know the river that goes west to a great lake of ill taste where white men live."

Clark leaned forward and said, "The ocean. That's good. The guide they offer, can he show us the way they go?" Clark looked straight at Lewis and said in a low tone, "Too bad about there not being a passage. I was getting that idea myself exploring the stream."

Lewis said, "I can't help but believe that if the natives can cross these mountains each season with women and children, we'll be able to cross it, too, even with the burden of our cargo. I asked Cameahwait how the Nez Perce traveled over the mountains. He said they used a passage farther to the north. Said it was not a good trail. Seems like it's covered with thick timber and only berries to eat for several days." He looked at Clark and continued, "There may not be a Northwest Passage, but if the natives can pass, we can pass. Not knowing of any other way across, I would rather take the devil trail that is known than try to find a new one on my own."

Clark replied, "I agree. We're no strangers to adversity or hard work. We have packhorses now and an unshakable will to cross this land. I hate that we're heading back north again, especially after following the Missouri south for so long. I'm sure they're right, it will be tough going. Just one good look at these mountains will confirm that. If we have to, we can eat horseflesh to make it over the mountains. I'm sure you're right, it's better to go with a difficult trail than to try and find a new one. North it is, my friend."

Lewis looked up across the camp and said, "They are getting tougher to deal with. Their generosity and fair trading for horses seem to have abandoned them. Now they want to hold back some of the better stock and offer us only the culls. They did say they would provide the guide at no charge. I think we should take them up on that right away. If we don't, they may just leave us here without a guide.

Clark added, "I know what you mean about the trading getting difficult. Today, I had to trade a knife, a pistol and more ammunition than I care to mention to get a horse. I agree, we should proceed on with the horses we have and save as much of the cargo as we can for future needs, future tribes. At least we'll have some guidance. Old Toby is better than nothing. We should conclude our trade here and get going."

Lewis broke a stick and continued, "I don't know how they have stayed with us so long. Look at the chief, those fierce eyes and lank jaw line. All of them have a meager, hungry look. His people have obviously not been fed well in a while. They need to be on their way." Pausing a moment, he continued, "I had the men bury another cache of goods. I need to mark it on your charts. Not a lot of stuff, but with these steep mountains to cross there's no need to have extra weight."

Clark looked at the camp and said, "Look at them. Everyone's smiling and joking. They deserve to have a little good time, they've earned it. No telling how long it'll take to get over these mountains.

September 4, 1805

They proceed west over steep mountains, often losing their footing in the loose shale on the slopes. Several times the horses slip and fall backward. The men pull and encourage them back on their hooves. Frequently the packs on the horses are strewn all over and require repacking. During one such accident a horse rolls over and over for forty yards until it is lodged against a tree. Clark's portable laptop desk and their last thermometer are lost.

Old Toby continues to lead them through rain, sleet, hail and snow across the mountain ridges, all the while, heading north. They are cold, damp and hungry. Finally, they come to a steep descent going toward a northward flowing river. Here they meet with a small group of Salish Indians which they refer to as Flatheads. They are glad to meet another group of natives and the Salish are obviously friendly. They smoke the pipe and are welcomed as the first white men ever encountered. The Salish have an unusual means of talking that resembles clucking and guttural speech. It is so different that it has made communication nearly impossible but for a stroke of luck. A Shoshone boy lived with the Salish and they can now form a translation team.

As they sat to smoke with the Flatheads, Sergeant Gass spoke, "Capt'n, the mountains we've been in these last days are the most terrible I or any of the men have ever seen. Do you think we'll be able to take this river out? Are you sure it flows west? We'd sure would like to get heading west."

Clark replied, "Eventually it will go west, it has to. Whether it is navigable or not, now that is another question."

As they sat with the translation team in the center, they smoked the peace pipe. Sergeant Pryor said, "Capt'n, just listen to 'em talk. I ain't never heard anything like it. Clucking and gurgling, do you suppose these are the mythical lost Welsh Indians?"

Lewis said, "Well, there is a strong belief that there are Welsh Indians, from a Prince Madoc that came to the new world and settled west somewhere. Even the President was partial to the notion and spoke of it. Whether these are Welsh or not, I don't know. They certainly could be. Maybe they lost the language after generations of living in this country. Their language is distinct, that's for sure. They're not white and they have the physical characteristics of the other natives. Still, their language is so strange that we should look for any signs of ancient white ancestors. Artifacts and such, anything that we might find."

Drewyer said, "Welsh Indians or not, they have good horses, lots of them."

Just then the Salish chiefs spoke and were translated. "Where do you come from? Why are you here to visit us?"

Clark replied, "We are white men from a great and powerful nation of white men. We've just left your friends, the Snake Indians, and are headed west. We want to meet the Nez Perce and follow the river west to the great water. Do you know how to find the river that flows to the sunset?"

The translation took place and the host Indians nodded, then asked. "We know the Snake people and plan to join them soon to hunt buffalo. This we do each season. They are good horsemen and hunters. The Nez Perce people are west of here. They eat fish." Taking a stick he drew a line showing the rivers. "These rivers flow to the Nez Perce country."

Lewis said, "North, still north, if the length of that line indicates distance, we'll be going back north quite a way before we head west." Looking around quickly, he spotted Sergeant Ordway and said, "Ordway, get some tobacco and some other small gifts. Gass, help Ordway get them and give them to these friendly natives."

Ordway quickly complied and the Indians were obviously pleased that they were receiving gifts. While they were looking at the gifts, Lewis directed the translators, "Ask them if they'll trade for horses. They've got some fine looking horses."

There was much talk among the Salish, clucking in their strange language and gesturing, all without meaning to the explorers. Finally, they spoke to the translation team. "They would trade thirteen horses for the goods received from the whites. They would also take seven of the poor and sick horses that had been injured and exchange them for healthy horses."

"What a deal, healthy horses for these!" Sergeant Pryor exclaimed. "Now that's generous in any man's language. These people may talk funny, but they sure are more than friendly. Who could ask for more? I wish we had more to give them. This is the most honest extension of friendship I've seen."

Clark said, "This stock brings us to thirty-nine horses, three colts and a mule. I think our luck's holding strong."

Sergeant Gass said, "Still, horses or not, we've got some awful mountains to cross."

Lewis said, "None of that, Sergeant. Don't look at the dark side. We were just handed a stroke of luck. Tomorrow we will redistribute the load on the pack animals and lighten their burdens."

Clark looked at Lewis with a knowing smile.

The Corps of Discovery proceeded on. The Salish would move to join the Shoshone in a buffalo hunt. Northward they continued, the weather, always harsh, added to their toil. Finally, they stopped near a creek and rested where there was a small meadow for the horses. Here they allowed the horses to graze and the men to rest. Lewis asked Clark to label it 'Travelers Rest' on the charts. While there, Old Toby, the guide, informed Lewis that from this point to the place known to them as the Gates of the Rockies, was a trip over the mountains of four sleeps.

Clark said, "Four days! Labiche, have that repeated. Surely they didn't translate right. Have we come back north that far?"

The translation took place and Labiche simply looked at Clark and nodded. Lewis looked at Clark and said nothing. They had spent fifty-three days getting from the Gates to Traveler's Rest. Lewis stood, grabbed his rifle in disgust, reached for Seaman and walked slowly to the edge of camp.

Clark said to the men, "Get ready to move out."

After they left Traveler's Rest, their effort continued, perilous and difficult. The steep slopes were covered with snow and fallen timber interspersed with undergrowth that made the act of simply following one another strenuous. Both men and horses became exhausted from toil and not eating. Clark, with old Toby, led the way. They would pause frequently to confirm a trail. During one of these breaks the men had not spoken to one another for a long time. They paused momentarily to catch their breath and rest. Sacajawea, who was near the rear, was also leading a packhorse with little Jean Baptiste on her back. She began slowly to walk past each of the resting men. As she did they looked at her and fell in behind, following her lead.

Finally, Joseph Field said, "Hey, up ahead, move over and let Janey by. Do you want to know how the Indians made it over these mountains? Well, there it is. Just look. Janey ain't stopping just 'cause we did. She moved past us all one other time and led the way. Are you men going to just stand here?"

Sergeant Gass said, "Men we have been through tougher stuff than this. Remember the falls?"

Colter said, "At least we had food then."

Sergeant Pryor said, "At least we don't have to worry about grizzly bears. Besides, Drewyer's out hunting. Maybe he'll bring back something."

Shannon said, "Birds, all we been lucky enough to see are birds."

Sergeant Ordway said, "Birds add flavor to the portable soup. Let's hear no more about food for now. If Janey can make it, we all can make it. Just look at her, she doesn't look back, she just keeps plodding along."

Spurred on by the sight of Sacajawea's perseverance, the men resumed their trudging. Now they began talking about the mountains and how much longer they would be in them. They began wagering tobacco on which man could guess what hour of the day they would see the Nez Perce.

Finally, for lack of food, Clark halted the men. "Sergeant Ordway, take one of the colts for our supper tonight. We cannot sustain ourselves on meager birds."

"Yes, sir," Ordway replied as he turned to go.

Clark looked at Sergeant Pryor and Lewis then said, "In case you haven't noticed, Captain Lewis is sick. He needs food to help him to get well. I'm as wet and cold in every part as I ever have been in my life. I've been worried that our feet would freeze in these thin moccasins. Strange, it was very warm in the valley yesterday, cold and damp here on these ridges. I hate to take the colt, but there's no other food and the men are weak."

Shannon spoke up, "Capt'n, no need to explain yourself. Not a man here would take a colt unless we had to. There's just no choice, everyone's weak and hungry."

Clark stood and looked around, "See that creek. I'll name it 'Colt Killed Creek' in honor of the animal that feeds us this evening."

September 19, 1805
Bitterroot Mountains, Idaho

In order to expedite a route through the mountains, Clark moves ahead with six hunters. Should they find game, they will leave the meat

*hanging in a tree for the others as they come up. Many of the group are
ill with stomach pain, but all maintain good spirits and proceed wearily
on.*

As they advanced further, Joseph Field saw a stray horse.
He pointed and said, "Look, Capt'n, there's a horse. Do ya
think it's a wild horse?"

Clark said, "No, my bet is it's an Indian runaway. Either
way I don't want to try to catch it as a pack animal. We need
food, take it. What we don't eat, we'll leave for Captain Lewis
and the others. It'll be a welcome sight for them."

Reubin Field said, "I think this is a good sign, Capt'n. This
horse is not only food for the needy, it must be a stray from a
nearby Indian herd. That means we can't be too far from the
Indians."

Clark said, "Good deduction, Field, my thoughts exactly."

Meanwhile, Lewis, with the main body, was traveling along
narrow mountain ridges. In one case a horse lost footing and
fell nearly a hundred yards. Miraculously, the animal was not
hurt.

Lewis looked at the men, they were all weak, hungry and
cold. Many were suffering from skin eruptions caused by mal-
nutrition. Lewis said, "Our luck is changing; that horse being
spared from the fall is a good omen. Good fortune is returning, that's all there is to it."

September 20, 1805

*Captain Clark and his small contingent come down the mountainside
to a prairie where there is a band of Indians in sight. They are the Nez
Perce. Clark and Drewyer make gestures and are able to establish communication with the natives. The chief is Twisted Hair. He is friendly
and says the hungry men will be fed. Some of the Indians wear articles of*

clothing that have to have come from sailors trading on the Pacific shore. They offer salmon and camas root bread. This food, to the hungry travelers, is the first full meal they have eaten in some time. With only sign language to communicate, Clark explains that there is a larger group behind him. The other group will need help and food to reach this valley. He adds that there is an Indian woman with them and they come in peace.

Twisted Hair, a man in his sixties, looks strangely at the men. They are the first white men he has ever seen. Learning that there are more whites following in the mountains and that they might have gifts for him, he is curious. He agrees to go back with Clark to find Lewis and bring them to the encampment. Possibly he wants to learn of their strength and numbers.

September 22, 1805 Western Edge of the Bitterroot Mountains

Clark, along with Twisted Hair, met with Lewis and the main body, still laboring through the mountains.

Clark whistled then shouted, "Corps of Discovery, this is a lucky day. These are the Nez Perce. We've brought some fish, and there's plenty more where these came from."

Sergeant Ordway and Pryor moved up as Ordway said, "Captain, sure is good to see ya. Capt'n Lewis isn't well, sometimes barely able to stay on his horse."

Lewis, hearing Clark, moved up closer and said, "Nothing wrong with me that seeing Captain Clark with friendly Indians can't cure. How much farther is it, Bill?"

Clark looked at his friend and held up a hand to help him dismount. "We'll be there tonight. There's a nice prairie and friendly Indians. This man is Twisted Hair, a chief. He seems cheerful and honest to me." Then, with concern in his voice, he continued, "You don't look too good, Merry. Your bowels?"

Lewis nodded and said, "Yeah, mostly, but I ache all over. Just no strength. That horse meat you left was sure a welcome sight. Did you bring food? Everybody's hungry."

Clark pointed to the pack horses. Yeah, there's fish here and plenty of camas root and camas root bread. A word of caution though. This food seems to be strange to us and really causes abdominal pain and gas. Eat slow, some of the men got pretty ill within a few hours."

Lewis signaled to Sergeant Ordway, "Don't let 'em eat too much too fast. Captain C says his men got ill."

Ordway nodded as he handed out the food from the pack horses. Even though they had been warned, they were hungry, and hungry men do not heed warnings of eating too much.

Clark reached to his horse and pulled out an elk skin with a map drawn on it. He opened it and spoke, "Look, Chief Twisted Hair drew me a map. They've got two villages, one here and the other here. The bigger river down here, that's got to be the Columbia. He says it is five sleeps away and then another five sleeps to where there are falls." Then, with Lewis looking on intently, he continued, "See all these lesser streams. He says there are Indians all along the river now. After the falls there, he says it's a couple more weeks to the ocean."

Lewis perked up and looked around at his beleaguered men, "Did you hear that, men? Well, that is good news by God. Let's fall in behind the good captain here. Tonight we'll sleep around a campfire with a full belly." Turning to Clark he asked, "Are there trees in the valley below big enough to make decent canoes?"

September 30, 1805

All the men were sick from eating less-than-fresh fish and camas roots. The Indians evidently had established immunity, but the Corps of Discovery came down with dysentery and diarrhea. Lewis was very ill and could not do much. All the men were ill; they were at the mercy of the Nez Perce.

Twisted Hair and a group of his leaders gathered in council to discuss the white men. One lesser chief said, "We should kill them and take their guns. They have gunpowder enough for us to challenge the Blackfeet. We could hunt buffalo east of the mountains without fear. With guns we would kill many buffalo."

Another warrior said, "They have knives and kettles of yellow metal to cook. These things can be ours for the taking."

As they were talking, a woman, Watkuweis ("returned from a far country"), was bringing the warriors tobacco the whites had given. She entered the council area.

Twisted Hair said, "I have never seen white men before. These men have the power of the guns but seem friendly. They do not make us feel the power of their weapons by ordering us. They offer gifts."

The lesser chief said, "Their gifts are not worth much. Only the knives have value, and they do not offer the guns. I do not need green paint for my horse or my face."

Twisted Hair said, "The important thing is they offer gifts, they do not take. They speak of more whites to follow."

At this moment, the woman, Watkuweis, looked at Twisted Hair and the other men in council. She laid down the articles she had and spoke, "When I was with the Blackfeet as a slave, there were white men who came to trade. They treated me and all the slaves better than the Blackfeet treated us. The Blackfeet did not kill the white traders. They feared reprisal to their people. These whites offer us peace even though they have weapons. Do them no hurt, they will help us."

Twisted Hair looked at the others and then spoke, "Yes, we could kill these white men. They're sick and would not put up much fight. But they have no reason to lie to us. They say they are friendly. Their gifts are not much, but they have come over the mountains and could not carry much. Of what they do have, they give us much. That is a big thing to do. We should not kill them. Watkuweis is right, it is not good for the Nez Perce to kill men who have done nothing wrong and come in friendship."

October 3, 1805
Bitterroot Mountains, Idaho

Clark, with his map in his hand, looked over the men and spoke, "York, Drewyer, Shields, Whitehouse, Cruzatte, McNeal, Potts and Hall, you men seem to be in a little better health than the rest. Get yourselves together, get the axes, some spare axe handles, tents, bedding and the camp things. We're going to go to the junction of these rivers on the map."

The men rose and went into action. They began loading pack horses and were soon ready to leave. Clark said to Drewyer, "Twisted Hair and a few of his men will go with us. He knows we want to make canoes. He wants to show us how they do it with fire and hot coals."

Drewyer replied, "Burning them out does make sense, better than hacking away with axes all day. The fire may hollow them out as long as we watch it close and don't let it burn clean through the bottom."

Clark said, "First, we've got to find some good trees. The chief says they are there. Get Cruzatte to watch over the construction operation. He's good with canoes. I don't want to spend a lot of time on hollowing out a canoe just to have it burn through the bottom."

Cruzatte said, "Capt'n, I'll watch it close. Only got one eye and I'll keep it on the burnout. Pierre Cruzatte won't let a canoe burn through."

Colter asked, "Do you think there will be any game at the fork of those rivers? Sure am tired of fish."

Drewyer answered, "We could hunt some, especially while the canoes are burning out. There won't be much else to do. But from what the Indians have said, there ain't much game around here."

York looked at Drewyer and said, "If there be any deer in these parts, York knows you and Shields will find 'em. More'n once you've fed all us men. When those fires get goin' for the canoes, York will keep another fire goin' for some venison or antelope. That ol' chief musta got that hide with the map on it somewhere."

Clark said, "Here comes Twisted Hair and his men. Go ahead and move out with them. I'll be up with ya in a little while." Turning around, he walked over to the other men and said, "Sergeant Pryor, you, Shannon and Labiche aren't too healthy, but you are in better shape than most of the rest. I'm leaving you here to take care of them, especially Captain Lewis. The captain won't admit how sick he is, but you keep an eye on him. Feed him soup from small game if you can. Let Janey fix up something for him and the others. She seems to know what adds flavor to soup." Then turning to Pryor he said in a solemn tone, "Sergeant, the captain is ill. If he gets worse, fever or anything, you come get me on the fastest horse here. You got that?"

Clark walked over to where Lewis was lying in his tent and said, "Hey, Merry, you gonna be better in a few days?"

With a faint smile Lewis' replied, "I couldn't get much worse and still be above ground. Did you meet with Twisted Hair about keeping the horses for us?"

Clark said, "Yes, he has agreed to keep them until we return. I don't know if we can trust him or not, but then, what choice have we got?"

Lewis said, "He seems honorable enough, if I read him right. They could have killed us all, you know. Everybody was sick, they could have killed us with little effort. With that in mind, I'm not worried about the horses. If they say they'll keep them for us until we return, most likely they'll still be here. These people are tied to this river. They've got plenty of horses and our stock won't be any special burden. Still, I would brand all the horses so we could sort 'em out when we get back."

"Already branded some," Clark said, "Used your iron brand to do it. I'll have Pryor brand the rest. You get yourself better now. I need you to join me at the river fork in two days. We're headed out now to select trees for canoes."

Lewis smiled, "Bad as my stomach feels, I am excited. Just to be back on the move again. That will be good medicine for me. I can promise you we'll be there, ready to go. Think of it, Bill, when we put the canoes in the water, we'll have current with us. First time in two years."

Clark smiled and said, "Well you just use that thought to get yourself and all the others up and ready to meet us. Get things all packed up and ready to transfer from horseback to canoe."

Lewis, holding his stomach, replied, "Done, my friend."

Clark left Lewis and met Sergeant Pryor. "Remember what I said. You come get me if he turns for the worse."

Sergeant Pryor looked Clark in the eye and said, "Yes, sir, I'll take care of him. You don't look too good yourself, sir."

Clark said, "Never mind me. When we get the canoes built, we'll want to head out. Meantime, put a brand on the rest of the horses. That should keep you busy. Put the other men to work as they begin to feel better. Get everyone up and ready to move out to the river fork. Two days, hear? We should be ready by then."

Pryor nodded in acknowledgment. Clark nodded back and turned to mount his horse and catch up to the others riding north toward the river forks.

October 5, 1805 Kooskia, Idaho

The Indians called the river Kooskooske, "clear rapid water that headed west." The canoes were cumbersome and hard to maneuver, especially when fully loaded. Frequently they would catch on rocks and require time and poles to set them free. The river rapids were threatening, but there really was no other choice. They had to float the canoes in them and navigate as best they could. Old Toby, the guide, became so frightened watching them navigate the rapids that he abandoned the explorers and fled without collecting his pay. When the canoes struck sharp rocks, leaks were created which soaked the cargo and rendered them useless until the leaks could be repaired. While repairing the canoes, they unloaded the cargo to air out and dry. The men used the time to make pine tar pitch and braces for repairs.

When they came to sections of the river that were especially treacherous, the men that could not swim would portage the distance around the rapids. The others rode the canoes through the rough water. They would shoot the rapids one canoe at a time to avoid two craft in peril simultaneously. The Indians would come to watch the crazy white men try to navigate the turbulent water. When the men were near the shoreline or portaging around rocky rapids, some of the Indians would pilfer small items. Sacajawea explained that they were not intent on stealing as much as trying to collect souvenirs from strangers to prove that they had seen the white men. Lewis, threatened with losing his dwindling cargo and trading goods, became irritated. He began the practice of posting two guards to watch the materials each time they stopped lest the Indians steal their goods.

Chief Twisted Hair accompanied the travelers through the rough waters and reported that the presence of Sacajawea proved to the river residents that they had come in peace. He asked that she be put in a place of prominence to be easily recognized as a peace symbol.

Lewis recorded the languages of the Indians as they came to observe the travelers and spend time with them at the evening campsites. There were Yakimas, Walla Walla, Wanapams. The languages and customs were all similar. He deduced that they had come from the same original stock.

October 15, 1805

The Corps of Discovery was now very low on trade goods, yet they needed to trade the Indians for firewood and fresh meat. Even though the Indians continued to pilfer from them, they held to their rule of not taking anything in reprisal. They always paid for things provided by the Indians.

Coming to rest on an island in the river, the men stepped out of the canoes and began preparing a campsite. Sergeant Pryor came to Clark and said, "Capt'n, we're in luck. I found some firewood. Looks like plenty of it. Split logs left by the Indians. Should we use it?"

Clark looked at Lewis and then replied, "We have agreed not to take from the natives, but look around, do you see anyone to pay? If you signal to those on shore and ask whose wood this is so you can pay, you would find upward of fifty owners. No way to tell the rightful owner."

Lewis said, "Sergeant, they have taken so called 'souvenirs' from us at every opportunity. They're damn good at it, too. Taking this firewood is not going to do any harm. If they needed it, they would have taken it with them. Besides, Captain Clark is right, you'd never find a rightful owner."

Pryor smiled broadly, "You don't need to convince me to use wood without paying these thievin' Indians. I figure I've already paid five times over with moccasins, knives, ropes, an' well, more material than this wood is worth, that's for sure."

Pryor moved out and said, "Men, build a good fire and get some hot coals spread out. We can dry out some things. Any wood we don't use tonight, load in the canoes along the sides. We'll need it later on for sure."

Sergeant Gass said, "Cruzatte, when we get all the material out and drying, I think we should listen to your fiddle. We'll celebrate these waters pushing us along. It sure feels good."

Cruzatte said, "My fiddle is always dry, everyone is careful to watch over her for me. Tonight we'll see if York can dance after a day of river work."

York smiled and said, "Don' you worry about York bein' able to dance. Without Indians to keep an eye on, York will dance longer than any man here. Did ya notice York watching out for the fiddle out there?"

Cruzatte said, "Yeah, you had one hand on the side wall of the canoe and the other on my fiddle all the way through the rough waters. Thank you."

Whitehouse added, "York is the only one the natives won't steal from. Big medicine, ya know. Good idea to have him watching the fiddle. Ain't no Indian going to steal from a man his color and size."

York looked at Whitehouse a moment, smiled and walked over to help build the fire.

Sergeant Ordway said, "Looks like some Indians will be with us tonight. The fire is advertising our camp."

Drewyer said, "They know every move we make. Fire or not, they'll be over as soon as we camp."

Clark said, "Keep a guard on the guns and munitions. If any of them tries to steal anything, catch them and bring them to me. We are losing our trade goods. We may need to set an example."

Ordway said, "Did you notice how many are wearing cloth and sailor's coats? There's seashells everywhere; we've got to be getting close."

Lewis, walking over to the canoes to ensure they had been anchored safely, pushed one canoe up more firmly and then walked over to Clark and Drewyer. He pointed and said, "I saw some mountains over that way. They have to be the mountains on Vancouver's map. After all these months of travel over uncharted land, I think we are back on the map."

Drewyer, normally stoic, said enthusiastically, "Nothin' can stop us now. We got a river to ride. We'll be at the ocean soon."

October 16, 1805 Junction with the Columbia

The expedition set out with Sacajawea in the lead canoe. Four other canoes followed. At one point the rear canoe caught on rocks and required assistance from the ever-present Indians to set it free. The captains shared some tobacco with them to show thanks and proceeded on. They were forced to continue the practice of frequent portaging around the more rapid water sections to avoid drenching their cargo. Around midday Cruzatte, in the lead boat, shouted back to the others, "River fork ahead, a big one, looks like the fork of the Columbia."

Sergeant Pryor whistled a loud whistle and motioned that they should make camp at the fork of the rivers. All boats pulled in next to one another. There, they made camp and celebrated the first siting of the Columbia River.

Cruzatte said, "This is it, this has to be it. The Columbia River."

Lewis said, "Yes, I'm sure you're right, this is the Columbia."

Shannon said, "Columbia indeed. Look how clear and deep it is. All that snow melt. Just look at the salmon, look at them, thousands, they're everywhere."

Sergeant Ordway said, "Don't try to eat the dead ones. They've already spawned and will just make us all sick as hell again. Get the ones going upstream, they're healthy."

Shannon said, "No need to repeat that. Not a man here wants to get that visceral discontent again."

The men rested all day at the fork of the Columbia. They dried out their goods, repaired leaks on the canoes and caught fish. The captains made celestial observations to fix and record their position at this important point on the map. They smoked with the Indians and asked about the condition of the river and what landscape to expect.

Twisted Hair spoke and was translated, "You are about to enter the land of the Chinook. They are enemy to the Nez Perce and will surely kill me. They speak a strange language and no one can translate with them. They may try to kill all of you."

Clark replied, "Thank you, Chief, for your information. You say there are falls just below. Will you stay with us until we get past the falls? We don't fear the Chinook Indians. Our men are able to defend themselves against any enemy. The Chinook will lose heavily if they try to attack well-armed men."

Lewis leaned forward and added, "Chief Twisted Hair, while we're able to protect ourselves from the Chinook, our mission is peace. The Great White Father sent us here to make peace between Indian nations. We'd like you to stay with us and meet the Chinook chiefs. We'll explain to them the value of making peace with the Nez Perce."

Twisted Hair listened intently and then talked briefly with his companion. Finally he said, "The Chinook do not speak our language. They do not listen to anyone. Most important, they do not listen to Nez Perce. If I am with you, there will be trouble. They may not harm you if I am gone. They will attack if Nez Perce are with you." Then Twisted Hair looked at them and the canoes and continued, "Your boats will not ride on the water in the river rapids. No one tries this, everyone walks around. If you do not walk around, you will drown and not be found. The water makes a terrible sound as an evil spirit makes it stir. Many have gathered here to see if you will try to use the canoes. They will pick up your materials from the water on down after you are dead."

Sergeant Pryor and Sergeant Ordway looked at each other and then at the captains. Pryor spoke, "That seems pretty clear. Captains, he sounds like he knows this river well enough to know. I think we better unload everything we can and portage this section. No sense coming this far to perish."

Ordway added, "Don't want those Indians to profit from our loss. I'd rather work some than try it in risky water."

Clark looked around and spoke, "We'll select those items to be carried. Without horses we can't take everything. The canoes may ride better with some weight in them anyway. But you are absolutely right, Sergeant, we shouldn't risk when we have the option to portage."

"The canoes themselves are too heavy to portage over this rocky terrain." Lewis added, "Sort out the journals, all the rifles and gunpowder. We'll have those that can't swim and as many others as it takes handle the bulk of the material." Then, speaking seriously, he continued, "The rest will go with the canoes. Get men that are the best swimmers and boatmen. We don't have much choice here, we must proceed on."

Sergeant Ordway questioned, "All the guns and powder go with the overland crew and the river group go without arms?"

Clark replied, "Yes, the overland group needs to have all rifles primed for action. One man on shore can shoot more than one rifle if he has to. I don't like separating the men from the guns, but it is better than risking the guns over turbulent water."

Lewis nodded in agreement, "Once past these falls we'll regroup quickly. I want Janey and York to be in front of the overland group. If we're headed into potential hostile territory, seeing a woman and child has been a good peace symbol so far, it should work again with the Chinook. I want York there so they will wonder about him. So far all the Indians have thought he has special power. It may be a good defense without the use of weapons."

Sergeant Pryor said, "I like it. They'll see Janey, York and Seaman, too. They should notice the men carrying two, three rifles. We should be good."

Clark said, "With all these Indian 'observers', keep the men in close order, real close. That way they'll not tempt any thievery. We won't show any weakness that might encourage an attack. I think Twisted Hair is right, we will let him go back. No need to give any cause to question our peaceful mission."

In the morning they would continue.

October 25, 1805
Oregon / Washington

Clark busy with his charts said, "I saw a volcanic type cone mountain. I think it's Mt. St. Helens. The other one off to the south is one of the biggest mountains I ever did see. It's got to be Mt. Hood. I want to fix them on both charts, mine and Vancouver's. I'll wait until we get a little further on before I actually draw them in, just to be sure. If we're truly on Vancouver's map, we'll be to the ocean soon."

They were traveling through an area where the Indians practiced the custom of flattening the heads of children between boards so that the adults would have sloping, flat foreheads.

Drewyer said, "What do you think of these people, pressing the heads of their infants with boards? As if they were not repulsive enough."

Sergeant Pryor said, "I don't know why they do that. Reckon they think having a flat forehead is a sign of importance or beauty. Do you suppose it smashes their brain?"

Drewyer chuckled and said, "Just think, back there we called the Salish people Flatheads. I guess we should have reserved that name for the Chinook. I never saw such an ugly or strange custom."

Pryor replied, "With fresh water here, I wonder why they don't smell better? Do ya suppose it's 'cause they eat fish, fish, fish all the time?"

Lewis smiled and said, "Our job is not to try to figure out why this culture developed as it has, we just record what we see."

Drewyer said, "Talking about what we see, did you see all those dried salmon? Stacks and stacks of salmon all along the sides of their cabins."

Clark replied, "I've made note of it. I estimate ten, maybe twelve thousand pound, just in that one stack. I think there are more in each of their huts. No wonder we all got sick on bad fish."

Lewis said, "Bad fish is an understatement. None of the men want to eat fish, even fresh. They trade the Indians for meat when we can get it." Then pausing he said, "I do note they seem to have a special craft in building canoes. Those larger canoes must have come from some type of oceangoing design. We should see more of those as we continue downriver. I wouldn't mind getting one."

Ordway asked, "Did you notice those sculptured figures fore and aft? What do you suppose? Are they religious?"

Lewis answered, "Could be, or just symbols to ward off danger. More for good luck than anything."

Clark looked at Lewis and the sergeants then said, "These Indians keep stealing things. Anything left laying a moment is gone. I heard the Field brothers, Colter and Shields got so pissed they wanted to shoot them or cut off their fingers. They want to retaliate. We don't need spontaneous hostilities."

Lewis looked up sharply and said, "None of us like those sticky fingered thieves collecting the last of our trade goods as souvenirs. We must remember our mission is peaceful, we can't start a battle over trade goods. Jefferson was clear that we need to make all efforts to maintain a peaceful image. The answer to the problem is to be more vigilant. If we catch them, we can make an example of them by forcing the thief away from us, but no harsh violence. Sergeant, make sure every man understands that."

October 30, 1805
Columbia River, Oregon

The Corps of Discovery has trouble with rough water on the westward flowing river, but in comparison to the upstream travels on the Missouri, it is nothing. The men make excellent mileage each day, even with frequent required portages around falls or rapid water. Indians are very common all along the river. They live in houses built of split boards instead of the tepee homes of the plains Indians.

The Indians are very curious and flock to the river's edge to see the travelers, especially York, Sacajawea and Seaman. Frequently the Indians display cloth, hats and other items gained from earlier trade with white sailors. Many of the Indians want the captains to spend an evening with them or just sit and smoke awhile. They refuse the overtures, wanting to avoid situations where the Indians can steal from them and possibly incite the men. Another reason, equally important, is to continue on. They are concerned about the short days and late season. The men have been traveling a long time and sense the end was near. They do not want to stop. By now, the Corps of Discovery is a rag-tag group with buckskin clothing nearly falling off their backs. Seeing the Indians wearing trade articles encourages the men onward. They eagerly guide their craft through

rough waters, row strongly when there is calm water and steer deftly where there are rapids.

The expedition comes upon to a section that they call the chute, the long waterfalls of the Cascades, and has to portage around. The water continues to be very turbulent and threatening. Lewis makes notes in his journals, pointing out that many of the locals seem to have gone blind in one or both eyes. He notes that this is probably due to the sun on the water or possibly some common contaminant. The Chinook typically have teeth that are worn nearly to the gum line, most likely from eating roots with sand on them. They wear their hair loosely hanging in every direction and universally practiced the flattening of foreheads. They purposely bind their legs and ankles to create thickening of the legs, knees and thighs. The men comment that especially when compared to the handsome Nez Perce, these are the ugliest people they have seen. Their appearance, along with their propensity to steal, makes them highly unpopular with the explorers.

The corps completes a somewhat arduous portage and then camps at the bottom of the Cascades. There they make fire from ash trees, a new type of wood, and the only firewood they can find. Here they first detect the rise and fall of water level due to tidal effect on the river. Observing the tidal effect causes spirits to run high. They know they are now very close to the ocean.

November 2, 1805

George Shannon killed a deer, the first wild meat they had had in some time, welcome food for the travelers. Having traded small items for a vegetable the Indians called *wappato*, Lewis, eager to categorize all new species, questioned Clark, "Bill, do you think this is arrowhead, the Chinese arrowhead plant?"

Clark replied, "All I know is they call it *wappato*. Who knows where they got it? You're the one that studied all that stuff, you tell me. I'd be impressed if you could remember all that detail."

Lewis held a root and turned it slowly, "We're close to the ocean and with all the other trade goods we've witnessed, why not Chinese roots growing here, too? Do you think they'll sell us more?"

Clark laughed, "They'll sell you anything, anything at all. It's the price that's in question. What will you pay for a change in diet? Don't show any anxiety or the price will go up."

Lewis said, "Let Drewyer negotiate, he has a straight face and seems to make a good deal, even with tough negotiators."

Sergeant Gass came to the captains and said, "Colter and Labiche said there are some Indians coming in, looks like some chiefs. Colter said they have pistols."

Clark said, "Bring them over. We'll offer them a pipe to smoke. Maybe we can find out how much farther it is to the ocean, even trade with them if they'll deal fairly."

Sergeant Gass waved to Colter and Drewyer to come over. A small group of Indians came with them as they approached the captains. Colter had a broad smile on his face as he drew near. "Captain Clark, Lewis, you've got to hear this. These men say they are Skilloot Indians, and as you can see, they've been trading with white sailors." He chuckled with a restrained laugh as he continued, "They're real proud cause they can speak a little English. Real proud." Then he turned to Drewyer and said, "Bring 'em over and let 'em introduce themselves to the captains."

Drewyer, normally nonchalant, had a smile on his face as he turned to the Indians and said, "Go ahead, tell the captains your names."

The Indian chief, dressed in a blue flannel shirt, pistol in a sash and a hat on his head, stepped forward. He looked straight at the captains and said, "I can speak English, and I have English name." Then looking around at his companions he proudly announced, "My name is Son-of-a-bitch." Then he beamed with pride as he looked at the men to make sure he had pronounced it correctly. The second Indian stepped forward and his companion announced, "He also has English name. He is called Dirty Thieving Bastard." Then he stood triumphantly and smiled as Colter, Drewyer and Sergeant Gass laughed silently.

Clark smiled, glanced at Lewis, and said to the two chiefs, "Well, we're glad to meet you. With English names like yours we will know how to treat you with the respect you deserve."

Lewis said to Sergeant Gass, "Let the others know we have guests. Gather around, we will smoke with them. Do I need to tell you to watch all your personal effects?"

They smoked the special tomahawk pipe and Lewis asked, "How much farther to the great water?"

The chiefs indicated that it would be only a couple days downstream to the ocean. They noticed the *wappato* and asked if they could trade more *wappato* for gunpowder and knives.

Clark replied, "Our great chief has said that we must not trade guns or gunpowder. Our mission is to promote peace. We are weary travelers and want to know how much farther it is to where the river meets the great water. Are there other rivers meeting with this one? Is there flat land to make camp?"

The two chiefs talked and indicated to the captains that there was another river meeting into a bay below. Again they asked if they could trade for guns or knives. They offered fish, geese and duck in return.

Lewis used Drewyer to help translate because the English of the Indians was not fluent. "We do not want fish. We are able to get waterfowl on our own. Repeat to them that we cannot trade guns. Will they trade us one of the large boats?"

They looked at each other and quickly exchanged whispered comments. Then, they turned to the captains to announce that they would trade a boat, this one with a handsome bear figure on the front, for six rifles.

Clark, somewhat perturbed, said, "We will not trade **anything** for our rifles or our cooking kettles. We can offer only needles, fishhooks and some knives. Will you trade?"

Son-of-a-bitch talked to Dirty Thieving Bastard and then said, "We must have more. This is not a good trade. We will smoke with you and show you where the small river meets this river."

Lewis nodded, they lit the tomahawk pipe and passed it around. The guests seemed to enjoy the tobacco very much. After a short time they stood and pointed to their boats. "Come see our boats."

The captains moved to examine the larger, well-built, framed boats. The sergeants pointed out the large capacity, noting that they could load a lot more into one of these craft. The boat was hand-crafted and exhibited the figure of a large bear in front and a human image in the rear. The figures were extensions of a well-made keel. They spent a short time looking at the boat and then the Indians departed.

When they moved back to the campsite, Sergeant Gass said, "Where's the pipe? Do you have the pipe?"

Sergeants Pryor and Ordway looked around quickly as did Lewis and Clark. Then, as the five men looked around, Sergeant Gass said, "They warned us. Dirty thieving bastards said what they were. We didn't listen."

Lewis looked around and asked, "How the hell did they do it? We were watching them. It was right under our noses. They must be slick. I would rather face an Indian attack with arrows than this peaceful approach with sticky thieving fingers."

Drewyer with palms outstretched and upward said, "How can you blame them? Who is really to blame here? They identified themselves right off. Didn't they tell us what other whites had been calling them?"

Clark looked at the men, then they all laughed simultaneously. Lewis said, "Taking things silently as souvenirs or outright robbery in the dark of night, the result is the same. He is just a..." Clark and Pryor joined in unison, "Dirty Thieving Bastard."

They all laughed, and then Clark looked at Ordway and said, "Sergeant, I think they're gone for now. Set up a perimeter and post sentries. We must recognize now that they're good at lifting things. We really can't afford to fall prey to more theft."

November 7, 1805 Near the Pacific Ocean

Heavy fog covered the surface of the water all morning. It had been raining steadily the day before. The men were anxious to move out and by midmorning the fog had lifted sufficiently for them to leave. Now anxious to reach their journey's end, the men plied their oars and made thirty four miles. Suddenly Cruzatte in the lead boat let out a shout followed by a shrill whistle as he waved his arms in the air. Then the second boat fired a shot and they all pointed as Cruzatte began shouting, "Capt'n look! Just look! Tell me what you see. Let ol' Pierre know that his eye is still good."

The sky was clear as Clark stood and looked westward. Then, with a broad smile on his face, he turned to shout to Lewis and the other trailing boats. Pointing as he shouted, **"Ocean in view! Oh, the joy!"**

The men began whistling, shouting, hollering and firing their guns in a mad chorus of celebration. That evening, there was great excitement and celebration in the camp. They could hear the sound of the ocean waves crashing on the rocky shore. They were ecstatic and though they were wet and exhausted, they danced in circles and played the violin. The travel weary Corps of Discovery was truly elated. They believed they had reached trail's end.

November 25, 1805

Their earlier elation is premature. They have only reached a bay and not yet the ocean shore. It rains every day they are in the estuary. The rain is incessant, the wind strong and cold. They are pinned against rocks with no comfortable place to make camp or get a good night's sleep. Further, they are unable to advance or retreat due to overhanging rock ledges. Large trees, as big as two hundred feet long and seven feet in diameter, are carried by high tidal wave action and crash onto the shoreline near their campsite.

There they are, barely clothed, wet and cold. They have to get free to establish winter quarters. Small expeditions are sent out each day in all directions to seek a campsite and learn what they can about the surrounding area, its game and Indians.

Clark makes a journal entry as he calculates the distance they have traveled to date as 4,142 miles, most of them with tremendous effort.

Shannon, Willard and Colter spend the night with a group of Chinook Indians. The Indians steal their rifles during the night. They use sign language in an attempt to let the Indians know that there are more white men and that, when caught, the thieves will be shot. While they are conversing, Lewis and a small party join the beleaguered men. Seeing the other whites, the Chinook quickly surrender the stolen rifles.

Lewis, in an earlier scouting effort, has advanced to a cape along the ocean shoreline. He hopes to find a campground or a lookout point to *signal a passing ship. The cape offers no suitable place to camp or place from which to signal to ships. While there, he carves his name in a tree** *and names the place Cape Disappointment. Later, Clark will carve his name in the same tree and add a line which read, "By land from the United States in 1804 & 1805."*

The captains and the men have explored both sides of the river and several miles around the estuary. They have already spent too much time looking for a campsite; it is time for a decision. They meet to discuss their findings and options as to where to build a winter fort. It is an important decision.

Clark spoke loudly into the wind and said, "Sergeants, gather all the men around. We're going to consider our options. We can't stay here, pinned against these rocks. We have to move to where we can establish a decent shelter."

The sergeants motioned and soon they all gathered close to the captains. Lewis spoke, "Men, we have come a long way, a very long way. By Captain Clark's calculations four thousand one hundred forty-two miles."**

Colter said, "Every damn inch of it."

Lewis raised a hand to silence the men as he continued, "We have found the Chinook Indians on the north side, the Clatsop Indians on the south. There are lots of trees on both sides so a fort could be built with good lumber. We probably should not build close to the ocean because of the tidal action and high winds. As you know, there's a small river on the south side. We could go there and explore for a possible site. Another option would be to go back up the Columbia and winter there. If we do, we lose any possibility of signaling to a ship. A ship would mean provisions and possibly a ride home." Looking around at all the faces focused on him, he continued,

---

* Only an estimate of where that tree stood can be made.

** Incredibly accurate, to within forty miles.

"Each of you has labored hard to get here and now we have a choice. Captain Clark and I could make this choice alone. I know without a doubt that each of you would unquestionably follow our decision. But you are President Jefferson's volunteers, and Jefferson is the father of democracy. In a democracy, men vote to decide things. Captain Clark and I have decided to make this a democratic decision. We are going to vote. It will be a decision of the majority. Each of you will have a vote on where we go. The same as Captain Clark and me. One man, one vote. The choices are these: One, do we go back up to the falls? Away from this foul weather but away from the sea and a chance to signal a ship? Two, do we go to the north side near the Chinook and build a fort? Last; do we explore the south river near the Clatsop to look for a campsite? Game should be the same on either side."

Lewis stepped back and said something to Clark. Clark stepped up and said loudly, "Sergeants, take the vote. Count each vote and let me know the total."

Sergeant Pryor asked Clark quietly, "Janey, too?"

Clark said, "Yes, she came with us every step of the way. This is a democratic vote, that means every one of us."

The sergeants stood as each man came forward and voted his preference. One by one the men stepped up and voted, speaking their choice as the captains sat and watched. York stood back and watched as each of the men advanced. Seeing York observing the voting, Whitehouse smiled, grabbed his arm and pulled him forward, "Go ahead, York, you vote before me."

Sergeant Ordway looked at York and said, "What's your choice?"

York stood silent a moment and then spoke in a deep slow tone, "South side to explore for a campsite." Then smiling broadly he turned and sat with those who had already voted.

Soon everyone was sitting as the three sergeants stepped together and conferred briefly. Then Pryor turned and said to the captains. "Looks like it's explore the river on the south for a campsite."

Lewis and Clark nodded in agreement as Pryor stepped closer and said, "Do ya know, captains, this is the first time a woman ever voted on anything that I can recall."

Clark smiled and added, "And a black man."

Sergeant Pryor nodded as he turned and looked back at York and the other men, "Yes, and a black man."

Lewis was proud as he said, "This decision would please the president; the first election of any kind west of the mountains. The first election held in this new land. You men should know that he wanted democratic principle to reach to the ocean. We have established a route to the West, and more importantly, we have exercised democracy on these shores. This is a glorious moment."

Sergeant Gass said, "Well, let's get to it. The south side is waiting for us. Unless there are some of you that like it here, let's get our gear and move our butts. We've got our decision, now let's do it."

As the men began to move to pack the canoes and get ready to move, York stood silent with a broad smile. All the men were busy when Shannon noticed York's smile. "What are you grinning about, York?"

York stood straight, a strong wind blowing and light rain in his face. Ignoring the rain and discomfort of the moment, he spoke with a smile, this time in the first person, "Cause I voted."

Shannon said, "Yeah, yeah, we all voted. So what? Now we've we got to get on with it. What do you find so amusing?"

Pride in his eyes, York replied, "I voted. Ain't no property ever voted afore. Property don't vote about nothin'. Ain't nobody ever cared what property thought 'bout anythin'.

Votin' means I'm a man. A **man**. Ever' man at least once in his life should know how freedom feels." With that he stepped over and picked up a large bundle of cargo and lifted it into a canoe. He looked at Shannon a moment and then said, "Yes, sir. I feel good today. I come a long way to this campsite."

December 25, 1805
Fort Clatsop, Oregon

It is Christmas morning and the construction of Fort Clatsop is nearly complete. The men arise from their snug winter shelter and wake the captains with a volley of gunfire, whistling, whooping and shouting. Hearing the ruckus, the captains move outside to greet the men.

"Merry Christmas to everyone!" Clark shouted.

Lewis added, "A good way to start the day, men. Let's all meet and exchange those few gifts we have. Our best gift is to one another in the knowledge that by Christmas of next year we will all be home, back in the United States, with our families."

Reubin Field shouted, "That's for sure, Capt'n. Home sure sounds great. But right now I'd just settle for anyplace that wasn't rainin'."

John Shields added, "I remember how eager we all were to get started back at Fort Wood and then again at Fort Mandan. Well, that won't even compare as to how good it'll feel to head back home. All the effort it took to get here, well, it'll be a labor of love on the trip back."

All the men whooped.

Clark said, "Sergeant Ordway, get a good fire going to get some of the dampness out of the air. Looks like it is going to rain again today."

Ordway replied, "Sure would help if it would quit raining. I never knew of a place that got so much rain. Maybe it's just a bad year, but it has rained most of the time we've been here. We get slow rain, hard rain, regular rain, wind and rain, calm and rain, drizzle, fog and rain, rain and hail, showers that turn into steady rain, always some kind of rain. Easy to predict the weather around here."

Clark smiled as he said, "It is difficult, always wet like this. Damp weather can dampen a man's spirit. I know you probably would've had the fort completed long before now if it had been dry."

Sergeant Gass said, "That's for sure, no doubt about it. Our little cabins are the only dry spots around. Mud and wet lumber don't help much when you're trying to build fort walls and cabins."

Clark said to Gass, "Sergeant, today is Christmas day. As much as I would like to see us continue with work and finish the fort, I think we have sufficient shelter to take time for a holiday. We've been here a little over two weeks now. You're the best carpenter we have. How much longer will it take?"

Gass rubbed his forehead as he looked about and replied, "We got the fort walls up and secure, that's good. A fifty-foot square fence, that alone took plenty of lumber. The main gate will be ready to hang soon. Shouldn't have to worry about security after that. It's a good thing we have plenty of lumber and don't have to haul it far. We have three larger cabins framed and roofed. All done but the doors. The four opposing cabins across the courtyard have roofs started and should be done with a couple more days' work. All the inner walls and doors are moving right along. It's all coming together now. I expect we'll have it done inside a week and be able to call this construction site 'Fort Clatsop', our home for the winter."

Clark said, "Great, Sergeant, that's good. Do you need more men? I could bring in some of the hunters or men from the salt detail to help if you need them."

Sergeant Gass replied, "Thanks, sir, but I got the men I need. They're the best carpenters. Any more would just be in the way. Besides, we need the hunters to bring in food for Ordway's galley. I think he was planning a larger meal today, to celebrate Christmas. Too bad all we got is a little elk and a few fish that are on the verge of spoiling." Then looking toward the west he inquired, "How are Sergeant Pryor and the salt detail doing?"

Clark replied, "They've built a large U-shaped stone furnace just up from the tide line. There's a mouth of a small river for fresh water when they need it. The furnace is built solid to keep the kettles over the fire and designed to let them add wood and take out the ashes. Fortunately, there's not much ash from this wood. At first they had a time keeping the fires hot with so much wet wood and rain. Now they've got a rhythm to it. Boil the seawater down, keep adding more until it gets thick, then scrape the dried salt from the edges and put it in casks. They make several pounds every day. It's a steady job, hauling the timber to keep the fire going, boiling seawater and scraping salt. We should be able to use that salt for trading on the return trip."

Sergeant Gass said, "For sure, we don't have much in the way of trade goods. I hope the Indians will take salt as valuable. I know Pryor's men have been using all of our cuttings for firewood, least way when Ordway doesn't need it for the cooking fires."

At this time Sergeant Ordway approached the two men, "Capt'n, how soon can we all get together? I want to have everything cooked up and done at the same time."

Clark replied, "Now is as good a time as any. Let's get everyone together in our cabin and out of the rain. Go ahead and cook up what you have, we'll eat when it's ready."

Ordway replied, "Alright."

The men presented some gifts to the captains. Clark received a pair of moccasins from Whitehouse, Goodrich gave him a woven basket and Janey presented him with two dozen weasel tails sewn into a long scarf. Lewis gave Clark a vest, some pants and a pair of socks.

Clark gave Lewis a shirt and a pair of beaver hide moccasins. He gave the sergeants a pipe and then said to the men, "We have decided to give you men the present of six carrots of tobacco. That's half the inventory. We'd give you more but it's a good trade item for the return trip and we'll need trade materials on the trip home. We'll be replenished when we reach the caches we buried."

Shannon said, "Just talking about going home and making that our next destination, it seems real now, and it's simply music to our ears. That's the best Christmas present I could get right now."

They celebrated Christmas with a modest meal and were all in good spirits. Throughout the day they kept repeating that next year they would be home to celebrate Christmas.

January 1, 1806

Fort Clatsop has been completed just two days earlier. The final trimmings of doors and the main gate are hung. Lewis has given the order that for military security and due to their propensity to steal, no Indians are to be allowed inside the fort after sundown. The men are ordered to treat the Indians fairly and in a friendly manner. They are never to abuse or strike them and should any Indian refuse to leave when asked, the sergeant of the guard will be called to remove the offender. If an Indian requires any discipline from stealing or other criminal act, the men are to inform the captains immediately, and the captains will decide what to do. This is a military establishment and the men are to be on alert for any sign of treachery.

It is New Year's Day. The flag is raised early with a volley of shots fired to celebrate the coming of the new year. Cruzatte shouts that this year will see him in St. Louis with a pretty white woman on his arm and a drink in his hand. He announces that he will dance while someone else fiddles. All the men cheer.

January 6, 1806

The Killamuck Indians tell the men at the salt works that there is a beached whale not far away. Privates Willard and Wiser purchase some whale blubber from them and bring it back to Fort Clatsop to share with the captains and inform them of the news.

Lewis and Clark discusses the matter and decide that Clark will take a small detachment along with a few gifts and purchase some of the whale blubber as a change in diet. Sacajawea sits and listens to the men talking. She understands only a little English, and when Clark asks Charbonneau to go with the men, she stands up straight and approaches Clark. At first she is hesitant. Then she walks closer to him, wipes her hands on her hips, and begins to speak. As she speaks her confidence rises, and she moves her hands and stares at Clark.

Charbonneau translated to Drewyer who spoke to Clark. "She says she wants to go, too, Captain. She says she has been patient, waiting at the fort but thinks it is now time to go and see the great water. She says she has sat quietly and listened to the sound of the great water long enough. She must see it. Did she not travel with everyone else? Did not the mosquitoes bite her? The cactus hurt her feet? Did she not travel around the Great Falls? Did she not cross the mountains and come down the rapids? Why then, after all these days of travel is she not allowed to see the journey's end, the great water of salt? Now that there is also a great fish to be seen, she says she wants to go."

Sacajawea finished her speech and stood staunchly looking at Clark, staring him in the eye and not blinking. Clark listened as Drewyer finished the translation, then he looked at Sacajawea. There was a moment of silence as she looked at Clark, holding her gaze firm. She spoke in English, "Janey goes too, with Cap Tan."

Drewyer said, "Janey's usually quiet, but I think she has a point, Capt'n."

Clark stared a moment, then a broad smile crossed his face. He waved a hand as he spoke, "Anybody here got an objection to Janey going along? She wants to go and by God she's right. She has earned the right to see the ocean. The whale too for that matter."

Drewyer said, "I don't think there's a man among us that would stand in her way. She's proven that she will not slow us down."

They set out traveling to where the whale was beached. When they reached an observation point where the ocean stretched out in front of them as far as they could see, Clark raised a hand and stopped the party. "Charbonneau, bring Janey up here and let her see the ocean." The small group looked out over the ocean for a moment and then proceeded on toward the beach.

Clark had previously hired an Indian guide to take him to where the whale was beached. On the route south, there was a steep hill obstacle and no way around it. They climbed the hill, and as they were about to go down the opposite side, they met fourteen approaching Indians carrying whale blubber and oil. Clark agreed to purchase about three hundred pounds of blubber and six gallons of oil from them, using salt and beads as payment. Clark sent two men with the Indians back to Fort Clatsop. The rest of the party continued on to see the whale.

By the time they reached the site of the beached whale, the Indians and sea gulls had picked the carcass clean. There on the beach was a bleached white skeleton stretching one hundred and five feet long.

Reubin Field said to his brother Joseph, "Just look. Imagine what this thing must have looked like when it was alive. I wonder if it was full grown."

Joseph said, "I've heard of these animals, how big they were and all. But seeing this skeleton, well it's just impressive. What do you suppose killed it?"

Labiche said, "These animals beach themselves. No one knows why. Maybe they're are sick or just old. For some reason they decide to die on the beach, out of the water. I imagine they don't want to be eaten by sharks or other fish. Some people say they do it so the other whales won't see them die. I don't know."

Clark said, "I think you're right. They choose to die on the beach. To do so to get away from predators makes sense. It must have had a lot of flesh. I wonder how long it took to reduce it to bones. Well, anyway, we have enough blubber and oil to add to everyone's diet. I thank Providence that this whale was sent for us to eat instead of the other way around, like poor Jonah."

Sacajawea stood in awe for a few moments looking at the whale's skeleton. She slowly approached it, reached out and touched the jawbone and rubbed her hand along its edge. Then she rose and, holding her child, walked the full distance of the skeleton, taking its measure in her mind. When she reached the tail, she turned and looked back up the frame and said nothing. Having seen the whale, she walked back to the others who were in conversation regarding the amount of meat and blubber that would have been here a few days ago. Evidently her curiosity was satisfied with this examination of the whale's remains.

The Corps of Discovery is settled in for the winter. They feed mostly on elk, a few vegetables from the Indians when available and what fish they can catch. The Indians have seen the high walls of the fort and witnessed the skill and marksmanship of the hunters. Observing the marksmanship may have impressed them enough to discourage any thought of hostilities. The Indians come to visit but, as ordered, leave by nightfall. All items that can be stolen are kept in the captains' quarters for security.

The Clatsop Indians impress the men with their knowledge of English and their recollection of all trading vessels. They know the names of several ships' captains and rate them on how fairly they traded goods. They know when to expect them to return. Evidently the ships' captains have promised to return and established a schedule. The Indians can recite the names of several trade items offered to them and frequently wear sailors clothing. However, during their stay on the West Coast, not one trading vessel comes in contact with the expedition.

Lewis spends the long boring hours working on the categorization of records for all the plants and animals collected since leaving Fort Mandan. He draws detailed pictures of the animals and plants in his journal. Clark works on making accurate charts of the over four thousand miles they have traveled.

As Clark worked on the maps he spoke to Lewis, "Merry, we took many careful observations, and my charts should be accurate."

Lewis replied, "Sure they're accurate, better than anything we used on the way out here."

Clark said, "I think old Toby was right. We wasted time and miles on the trip out. From what we have charted, the headwaters of the Kooskooskie, Clark's river and Lewis' river all are north of the headwaters of the Missouri or Jefferson River. Remember the Indians indicated there was a different trail across the mountains to the buffalo prairies. In short, a lot of our toughest time could be avoided on the return trip."

Interested, Lewis rose to look over Clark's shoulder at the maps. "That's good news. Yeah, I think we wasted some time coming out. Getting lost with Old Toby didn't help. It seemed like we kept heading north a very long time. We spent way too much time in the mountains to suit me. Are you recommending a different route back?"

"Yes," Clark said, "I am. Look here, I think this is a more practical route." Clark pointed at the map as Lewis studied it. "Merry, we could avoid the falls and everything after it. We could go over the mountains and meet the Missouri at or near the Gates of the Rockies. We can use the hunting trails the Shoshone and Nez Perce use."

"Just like the Nez Perce said," Lewis replied. "You mean from the creek at Traveler's Rest we could head through a pass to the Gates?"

Clark replied, "Yes, if the Nez Perce can show us the route they take, we should be able to find a navigable pass. I'd want a guide, of course, but we should be able to cut about six hundred miles off the return trip."

Lewis answered, "We are never so ignorant as when we don't know what we don't know. We had no idea on the way out. Not knowing what lay beyond the next curve in the river, not knowing what was beyond the next mountain range really cost us time. Still, we did the best we could. It's just a damn shame we didn't locate better guidance earlier. We didn't meet with the Shoshone until we were well up the Jefferson and they're the only ones that travel the mountains regularly."

Clark said, "No matter which way we go, those mountains are high and will be covered in snow. Even a short route will tax us. We'll have to go with ample food and move quickly. I don't want to repeat our first crossing."

"You're right, of course," Lewis replied. "The men want to get out of here as soon as possible. I do too. If we get to the mountains too early, we will just spend more time with the Nez Perce. I would rather do that, wouldn't you?"

Clark smiled and leaned back as he said, "Let me see, spend time here in the rain with ugly, thieving Chinooks all around and with little to eat but elk or go visit the Nez Perce and position ourselves to move out as soon as the snow melts. I've got to think about that one awhile."

Lewis smiled and lightly brushed his friend on the shoulder as he seated himself across the table from him. "Bill, we'll head out as soon as we can. I'd like to get better canoes. If we get to the Nez Perce early, we can cross as soon as the weather breaks. I'd rather be two weeks early than one day late. With a gain in time, I want to take a small contingent and explore the Maria's River north. It's part of the purchase and therefore part of the United States. I'll take readings of its latitude at the headwaters. We can meet later downstream and you can complete the charts."

Clark replied, "I think we could split up and I'll take the Yellowstone. The Indians say it is navigable and the land around it should be a valuable addition to our charts. Future trading may find the Yellowstone to be the best route."

Lewis nodded in agreement and said, "I like it. We know the way back and this additional time will permit us to maximize our information about the area east of the Rockies. We'll leave here as soon as we can, by early April if this weather will stop raining, maybe even March. There's not a man here that wants to head for home more than me. Never have I seen such incessant rain. I've never even heard of a place with such rain. Why, in England it doesn't even rain this much."

Clark said, "I know, this is more boring than the winter at Mandan. The same diet, the same miserable weather. Knowing that our exploration is over. Knowing that only the return trip keeps us from civilization. Those thoughts make this place nearly unbearable."

March 23, 1806 Departure for home

The winter months are long. It rains every day but twelve and the sun only shines for six. While they check frequently with the Indians and the crew making salt at the ocean, the captains never learn of any vessel making port in the area. The decision has been made. They will leave Fort Clatsop today. They will give the fort structures to Clatsop chief Coboway because he has not stolen from them and appears to be an honorable man. The only canoes they have are those of hollowed tree trunks. They observe the Indians and admire their more seaworthy craft.

Sergeant Pryor approached the captains, "Colter and the Field brothers found an Indian canoe last night. It seems to be unattended, can we take it? Lord knows they've taken enough from us."

Lewis looked at Clark and then spoke, "Sergeant, our orders are to be peaceful with the natives, not to steal from them or give cause for any hostility. But, I am sure that even the president would agree that we are in an extraordinary situation. We have little to trade for an item as valuable as a boat."

Clark added, "I agree, Sergeant. We have, in effect, paid for a canoe several times over, without benefit of barter. We did trade for one boat, but we certainly can use another. They steal anything from us they can at any time they can. I would say that to take the boat would help balance the ledger."

Lewis stood silent a moment, torn between his orders and the immediate need at hand. He nodded and flicked his wrist as he said, "Do it, Sergeant. How far away is it?"

Pryor said, "Not far, sir. I got to say, taking this boat will make the men feel better about getting even."

Lewis said, "Take enough men to ensure you can handle the boat and discourage them from protesting if they discover you."

Clark looked at Lewis and said, "All this bothers you, I know, but I think it's the only choice we have. We need the boat or we'll have to add five or six more canoes. I don't recall them asking us when they stole from us."

Lewis said, "The one boat Drewyer negotiated for by trading my artillery coat will not be enough. The Indians would not trade for food or pelts. They had to have my jacket, my personal jacket. He even threw in some tobacco. God, we're not going to have much to trade when we return. Taking this boat is our only choice. It's just that I would have preferred to have been able to exchange something for it."

Pryor said, "We've heard that there is little food upriver. The salmon won't run for another month or better. Word is Indians upriver claim they're starving."

Clark commented, "Just what we need, to head into an area without much food. We have a long way to go. I think we should put more hunters out and begin drying all the elk and venison we can get."

Lewis nodded in agreement. "We'll take all the game we can. Make jerky and stow it in the canoes."

Sergeant Pryor said, "Shouldn't be hard to get men to volunteer to hunt. Get meat while we can, especially if there is none upstream. We'll increase our sentries at night to guard the supplies."

Clark added, "Let the men know we have to make it to Nez Perce country before May. They have our horses, and if we don't show, they may not wait for us. They'll just leave for buffalo country."

Lewis said, "If we can't get enough food before we enter the mountains, we'll have to use the horses to see us across. I don't want to go hungry in those mountains again."

At one o'clock the men put five canoes into the Columbia. They are an indigent group with little to trade but some tobacco and salt for the materials they will need. All other materials are needed for their own well-being. Private Bratton has been ill with a bad back and intestinal troubles. Willard is also not well. They are excused from duty and permitted to ride in the canoes. Lewis comments that once they are underway the travel alone will be the best medicine for them.

During the winter Sacajawea's child, Jean Baptiste has grown and is walking. The little boy proves to be good entertainment for the men as he learns to walk and is beginning to talk. His presence causes the men to be reminded of home. Clark enjoys the lad and gives him the nick-name of Pomp. The long boring hours of winter at the Fort are broken with Pomp dancing with the men to Cruzatte's fiddle.

April 1, 1806   Homeward Bound

The Corps of Discovery is heading home. They keep to the less rapid south side of the river and employ tow ropes to advance against the current. Where there are frequent rapids or falls, they portage around them. They meet Indians coming downstream who confirm that there is little food available in the land upstream. The salmon have not yet returned for the season. There is a brief discussion as to whether or not it is better to wait for the salmon to return to assure a food supply or to proceed on. As usual, and anxious with the spirit to get underway, they decide to proceed on. They are becoming increasingly irritated with Indian thievery and feel the urge to get back to the more friendly Nez Perce territory. They have little to offer as trade goods with the Indians except meat jerky and salt. The captains confer with the sergeants and decide they will dispatch a group of men as soon as possible to head toward the Nez Perce and regain their horses. Those men are to bring back the horses and join the main contingent so they can advance overland. The plan is simple but has difficulties. They are worried that the Indians will try to steal the horses from the men. Yet they do not want to send too many men just for security. The captains and the sergeants have to continually advise the men to be ever vigilant and not to shoot any Indian caught stealing.

April 11, 1806 Eastern Oregon

Exhausted, but continuing onward, the men are laboring against the river current in rain driven by strong, even occasionally violent, wind. The Indians are ever present and the guards have to be alert. One evening a wretch of an old man crawls into the camp just to steal a spoon. The sentry catches him and hits him with a switch as he flees. Physical violence against the Indians is prohibited, but their patience is strained to the breaking point. The men begin to lose their tempers with the Indians more and more frequently. It is not unusual to hear them ask for permission to shoot a few thieves.

It was late afternoon when York came rushing to Captain Lewis, pointing as he exclaimed, "They took Seaman, Capt'n, they took yer dog and went that way with him!"

"What!" Lewis rose up, rifle in hand. Looking in the direction York was pointing, he shouted. "When did you see him last?"

York said, "The Clatsop Indian, he told us the others had the big dog. They took him and run off."

Lewis frowned as he stomped around in a circle. "Damn them, goddamn them. I'll not put up with this any more. I've had a belly full of it." He looked around and shouted, "Sergeant Gass, come here!"

Gass came running over as some of the other men, recognizing the tone in Lewis' voice, also gathered around.

Lewis said, "Those thieving bastards just took Seaman. They just don't know when to stop; a piece of jerky, a moccasin, a tomahawk, a pipe, beads, even a damn spoon, and now Seaman. Well, now they've done it, they've gone too far. They took my dog and they're going to pay." Still raging, Lewis gripped his rifle with white knuckles, shook it and said, "I want three men to go after him. If they put up any resistance, run or try to hide, use your rifles. Let them hear gunfire."

Instantly, all the men nodded in agreement as many of them said in unison, "I'll go." Joseph Field asked, "How many can go after 'em, sir? No trouble getting volunteers for that duty."

Lewis said, "You heard me, Sergeant. Take three men and bring him back. Do anything, anything you have to, but get him back."

The men turned in anticipation toward Sergeant Gass who pointed to Colter, Thompson and Joseph Field. "You three get ready, we're heading out right now."

"Let's go!" the men said loudly. The normally tired men were charged with excitement as they quickly set out in pursuit of the Indians who had taken Seaman. When they were within sight, the fleeing Indians noticed their approach. The guilty Indians knew they would be caught. They abandoned the large dog and hurriedly moved on. Colter fired a shot and the Indians froze where they stood. As the men approached, Thompson noticed one Indian carrying an axe. He stomped over to the wide-eyed Indian, grabbed his arm and wrenched it backward in a painful grip until he dropped the axe.

Back at camp, Lewis ordered the translators to inform the Indians that if they made any future attempts to steal, insult the men by pushing them or throwing objects at them, that they would be instantly put to death.

Clark observed his friend and then said, "Feels good to vent all that anger, doesn't it? I agree with you completely, my friend. To permit it is to promote it. If we don't stop this, they will just keep getting more and more bold with their stealing and insults to the men. Taking Seaman is an example of that. That took nerve. Maybe they perceive us as being weak. We can't have that, not out here. Besides, I think the men needed to hear you take a stand. It's good for morale."

Lewis smirked and replied, "Yeah, I didn't have any trouble getting three volunteers to go with Gass to get Seaman. A show of muscle is in order here. They won't persist if we show them a little retribution and a willingness to dish out more. I don't think they're ready to die just to steal a dog, even a big dog like Seaman. You know, Bill, if it were not for our numbers, our rifles and our military order, these Indians would get aggressive and probably kill us."

Clark paused and replied, "I think you're right. They haven't exhibited much civility up to now. If they thought they had an edge, they'd use it."

Nodding in agreement as Clark spoke, Lewis paced and then shouted to Drewyer, "Go and get that chief. I want to have a brother to brother talk with him." As Drewyer left to get the chief, Lewis said, "I want to let him know in no uncertain terms that the Corps of Discovery and the United States Army will not tolerate this disrespect. If they persist, we'll have no choice but to open fire. Even a first strike. As we have said among ourselves, we need to shoot some of the thieves. Well, we are about to let them know how bad this situation has gotten."

Clark scooped up dirt and let it trickle between his fingers as he replied, "I see your point. Ain't a man here wouldn't jump to follow that order and not think twice about it. But, Merry, that's not our purpose. You are correct in sending for the chief and laying it out for him. But a pre-emptive first strike against them is out of the question. It's against Jefferson's order. Think about it, they do outnumber us. If angered with vengeance or martyrdom, they could retaliate and kill us all."

"Those cowards. Retaliate?" Lewis replied, looking Clark in the eye.

Clark continued, "Yes. They are cowardly, and as such a little show of force, some saber rattling, should get their attention. We need to get all this behind us, the quicker the better. Merry, the men will pick up on your mood, and God knows they already want to kill a few. We, as leaders, have to show restraint. We're close to being out of here. We'll get some horses and make good time. Once we reach the Nez Perce and are among friendlies, we can concentrate all of our efforts on the trip back."

Lewis nodded and replied, "You're right, of course, but it does feel good to blow off some. I still want to impress on this chief just how close they are to losing some men. I've never seen the like of these Chinook. They're without morals."

Shannon came running over and announced, "Capt'n, Drewyer is here with the Indian chief you asked him to get. Are you going to set 'em straight?"

Lewis patted Shannon on the shoulder as he smiled at Clark, "We're going to have a serious talk and let them know what is what. Then we'll see what happens."

Drewyer came over to the captains' tent with the chief. They sat in a semi-circle and used sign language to converse. Lewis explained that the stealing of his dog was the last hostile act they would tolerate. If theft persisted, some Indians would be shot. The chief listened quietly and then replied that the hostile acts were not the actions of all of his people, only a few. Lewis listened and added that he sincerely hoped that the chief could use his influence over his people and stop the stealing before there was any bloodshed. He pointed out that he and the other chiefs could control the tribesmen from stealing. Lewis went on to state that he could easily punish them for their acts. They could steal Indian horses in reprisal. He added that he would rather lose property altogether than to steal a horse of an innocent man. After Drewyer finished the translation, the chief sat silent a moment and stared at Lewis. Lewis returned an unblinking stare, and the men sat there in silence for what seemed like a long time. Then the chief rose and walked out.

Lewis said to Drewyer, "Do you think he understood everything? Was the translation adequate?"

Drewyer replied, "He understood. He understood plenty. He just didn't like it much. It was good, Capt'n, good that we let them know."

Clark said, "I'm glad we got Seaman back. I think tomorrow I'll take some men and a few trade goods and go upstream to trade for horses. Horses will expedite our way out of this neighborhood."

Lewis replied, "Excellent, Bill. I don't know how much longer we can restrain tempers. When you go to trade, keep in mind we have to have those horses. They're the key to moving faster. You know we just lost one canoe in the rapid current. That was a big loss. We now have precious little to offer in trade, but trade you must. Do whatever you have to to get them. I am not only worried about the anger of the men. I fear that I may join the anger if the chief fails to restrain his people. I don't trust myself. Besides, I want to start making miles toward home, serious miles. Proceeding on at a good pace will be the best medicine these men could get. We seem to be languishing here. In three days we have progressed a mere seven miles. That's troublesome to everyone."

Clark said with serious tone, "Losing the pirogue was a terrible loss. Some of your journal pages were among the more grievous items lost. We don't have much, some jerky and a few hides. They do seem interested in our medical treatments and abilities. Maybe that'll work as barter. I'll do what I can."

Lewis said, "Don't worry about those journal pages and samples. We're depending on you now, my friend. Anything you do to hasten our way out of these parts, this neighborhood, will be appreciated. I've got ultimate faith in your ability. Our men will be very, very happy to see horses and be able to put distance into our homeward trek." Then in a serious tone he said, "When we get the horses and can move overland, I'm going to burn the canoes. I don't want the Chinook to profit from them."

April 27, 1806

The Corps of Discovery is moving overland, over rough terrain and mostly uphill, but they are again making progress and glad to be underway. They are exhausted at day's end. Their feet and legs are in pain from their toil. They often find relief by soaking them in the cold river water after evening camp is made.

About midday, Joseph Field came running toward the captains and exclaimed, "Riders coming, over that way. Look like Nez Perce. Looks like seven men." As he pointed, all eyes looked to see the dust of horseback riders approaching.

Clark looked at Lewis, and both smiled broadly. He said, "Sergeant Pryor, Ordway, get a camp site set up. Start with our tents. Let's welcome the Nez Perce. What a relief it is to see trustworthy Indians again. It's simply beautiful!"

Pryor sprung into action as he replied, "Yes, sir, we'll have it ready in no time at all. Let's build a fire and share some jerky with 'em." He immediately began to give the men directions to set up a campsite as the Indians rode in.

The Indians were led by Chief Yellept, a Nez Perce Indian. They were from the Wallawalla tribe. He was a distinguished looking man and smiled broadly as he dismounted. He moved directly toward the captains to welcome them. The six others with him followed his lead, and soon all the men were ex-

changing greetings, nodding and listening intently as the interpreters translated.

After a brief exchange of ideas Drewyer turned to the
captains and said, "Capt'ns, this is good, real good. As you
can tell these men are part of the Nez Perce. They're
Wallawalla. This here is Chief Yellept. He's proud to say he is
chief of, I think, fifteen lodges. There are lots of people there
and horses. They have lots and lots of horses, all healthy and
good quality. He says they're glad to see us and want us to
spend some time with them. They have gifts for us and will
trade. Honestly, I don't know what we can offer them in trade,
but I didn't tell him that." Drewyer seemed excited as he continued on, "Now listen to this, they got a Shoshone woman
that lives with them. That means we can use Janey to translate
and we won't have to depend on sign language. It'll be the first
direct translations that we've had in a long time. Real translation! Seems they have a camp only twelve miles or so away. I
took the liberty to tell them that we'd go there and meet with
them. I also took the liberty to ask them to get their Shoshone
woman to come to our council meeting. I didn't think you
would mind."

Clark said, "Mind? George, you did exactly right. Did you
hear what he said? They have gifts for us. What a change."

Lewis added as he patted Drewyer on the back, "Let's
follow your suggestions as quickly as possible. We can sit and
discuss our travels for the first time in a long time. Maybe we
can learn something about the shorter mountain crossing from
them. Everyone will be happy to meet some friendly, and I
add, honest Indians." Turning to the sergeants, Lewis said,
"Sergeants, sorry to have a change of orders so soon, but we
need to break camp now and follow these men back to their
village. We'll set camp there and meet these people."

Sergeant Gass replied, "That's not a problem, sir, we
should make good time getting to the next camp. The men

will want to stay up and party a little tonight, I'm sure. What a refreshing break to have honest Indians to deal with again. Everyone will want to meet with them. Can we set minimal sentry duty?"

Lewis responded, "Minimal sentry duty is fine. Take care of it, Sergeant. Now let's see how long it takes us to get to their campsite and cook up a celebration dinner. Send eight men out to hunt ahead of the rest. With luck we'll be able to add fresh venison to the evening fare with our friends." Then he turned to Drewyer and said, "Make sure they know that we want the Shoshone woman to join us. Tell them she'll be important to our talks. Hey, tell Labiche, Charbonneau and Janey that we'll be setting up our translation circle again. I want all other translators available and ready. There'll be enough conversations going on that we can use simultaneous translations. The sign language can be a back up. Let's get going."

Clark looked at Lewis with a broad smile and added, "It's good to see you like this again, Merry. Weren't you complaining about your feet just a few hours ago?"

The men moved quickly to set up camp with the Wallawalla. When they reached the village, they were welcomed and sat around the campfires. They talked about their experiences of how they had traveled over the mountains and spent the winter on the coast. They explained the difficulties they had had with the Chinooks on the return trip. Both groups enjoyed one another's company and the conversations lasted long into the night.

The next day Chief Yellept came early to the captains' tent. Clark came out to greet him. Seeing Clark, Yellept stood straight and motioned to his men. Responding to their chief, an excellent white horse was brought up and given to the chief. Yellept took the horse's rope and handed it to Clark. Drewyer said, "It's now your horse, Captain. He wants to give the white chief a white horse."

Clark took the rope in his left hand and patted the horse on the face and neck with his right. "As fine a steed as I have ever seen. Tell the chief that I am pleased to be his friend and pleased to accept the gift. This is a good horse and I'll remember that Chief Yellept gave him to me."

Drewyer said, "There's more, he wants to know what you'll give him in return."

Clark looked at Sergeant Gass, who was standing nearby, and said, "Go get Janey, Charbonneau and Labiche." As Sergeant Gass was sending for the translation team, Clark stood and stroked the white horse while Chief Yellept stood and looked on with pride. Soon the translation team was organized and Chief Yellept spoke. After the translation, Labiche said, "Captain, the chief asks if this is not a good gift to you. He expects you to give him something in return. He's specific, sir, he wants some cooking kettles."

Clark sat silent a moment, then looked at Lewis and back at the chief. Then he laughed as he said to Labiche. "The irony of this situation strikes me as humorous. Why, it was not that long ago that the last Indian chief we met with had to be threatened because of theft. Now, here we are, in a different kind of problem because they are generous, too generous; what a twist of fate." He shook his head, looked at Labiche and said, "Tell the chief that I appreciate the gift of the horse. It's a fine animal and as good as any horse I have ever seen. But we cannot give him any of our kettles. We use these to prepare our food every day and we have many days of travel before we are home. We cannot give him any of our kettles because they belong to all the men, not just to me."

The translation went through the team and Yellept, now understanding the reasoning, sat up more rigidly, nodded slowly and then began to make gestures as he talked slowly in low tones. Finally, the translation reached Labiche. "Captain, he still wants a kettle, only one will do. He cannot give such a fine gift as the horse and get nothing in return. He would be ashamed, one kettle will be all right."

Clark looked at Lewis. Lewis remained silent, leaving the decision to his friend. Clark, with all eyes on him, paused a moment and then spoke, "I understand that he has been very generous, but tell him that I cannot give him a kettle, our men use it to prepare food. Without the kettle our travel will be slowed and every day the men will suffer. The kettles belong to everyone, without the kettles to cook our meals everyone would be paying, every day, for my horse. I cannot have everyone pay for my horse." Then looking at the chief he continued, "I understand that this is a great gift from a good and powerful chief. My gift to him must also be a personal gift, not something that belongs to all. I will give him my long knife, my sword, along with some gunpowder and shot. Ask if that will be enough. By the way, tell him if he does not take this, I will not accept the horse."

Lewis looked at Clark and then nodded in agreement. The translation team worked and soon the chief was listening to the Shoshone woman translate. She moved her hands as she spoke softly to the chief. He focused intently and then nodded slowly as he looked at Clark. Soon the translation came back. It was a deal.

Clark rose and extended his hand to Chief Yellept, "Done," he said. The chief mimicked Clark as he clasped his hand, "Done."

The men sat back down and Yellept motioned that there was more to talk about. As they proceeded over the course of the next few hours, the chief explained to the explorers that there was a different route over the mountains. Yellept then outlined a shortcut over the mountains.

Lewis turned to Clark and said, "Do you realize what we have just done? The progress we've made without traveling a mile. We have confirmed our calculations that a shorter route over the mountains does, in fact, exist. Not just gossip from Old Toby to impress us. We will cut miles, days, out of our return trip. Days, Bill, days. The men will be delighted. Those horrible mountains are suddenly not so threatening."

Clark replied in agreement, "That information alone is worth the sword, and he threw in a horse to boot. Our luck has definitely turned. Tonight, my friend, as we celebrate with the Wallawalla, I will tell Cruzatte to tune his fiddle. The sounds of an evening festival will be good for my soul."

The Corps of Discovery stayed with the Wallawalla Indians two more days and then departed. They had traded for twenty-three horses, some not in good condition. There was no complaint among the men because the horses could be put to good use and they had but little trade goods to offer in return. It was a very good deal considering the meager goods in exchange. As they departed, Lewis and Clark were presented with two fine horses from the lesser chiefs of the tribe. Lewis gave his case, or dueling pistol, and several rounds of ammunition in return. Pleased, they were now headed toward the main villages of the Nez Perce. They would soon be at the foot of the Bitterroot Mountains and able to cut eighty very difficult miles from their route. They had been gone from the Wallawallas only a few hours when two young braves came riding up hard.

Colter shouted, "Two riders coming up from the village."

Sergeant Pryor raised a hand and all the men stopped to wait for the approaching riders. Pryor said, "There's no interpreter with them. Get Drewyer and Labiche. Let's find out what the problem is."

The men all formed a circle around the captains and the two Indians as the interpreters translated. Drewyer scratched his head and said, "You ain't goin' to believe this. They came all this way after us because we left a steel trap and a couple of knives in the camp when we left."

Clark looked at Lewis, both men were astonished. Clark said, "Excellent, Drewyer, tell them they bring honor to their people by returning these things." Then, a still bewildered Clark turned to Sergeant Pryor and Lewis as he said, "Can you believe it? What a change from the Chinooks. And to think these tribes live close to one another."

Lewis reached a hand out and shook hands with the young Indians that had returned the materials. "Tell them that we are proud to know such honest people. Tell him that the Nez Perce are the friends of the white man. Tell him we have never met more hospitable, honest and sincere people on our entire voyage. We are proud to be their friends."

May 8, 1806   Idaho

The men proceed several days through rough weather and finally meet a young Indian chief named Tetoharsky, a Nez Perce tribesman. He says he will take them to the village of Twisted Hair, the Nez Perce chief. Tetoharsky tells them the chief has been expecting their return because they left their horses with him for safekeeping on the trip out. When they finally arrive to meet Twisted Hair, there is also another older, higher chief, named Cut Nose, at the meeting. At the sight of the explorers, Cut Nose and Twisted Hair immediately begin shouting and gesturing to one another. Obviously there is controversy, but the captains are at a loss to know why.

At this meeting there happens to be a young Shoshone boy who could have acted as translator through Sacajawea. However, they can not establish the usual translation chain. The heated argument between the chiefs has so intimidated the young boy that he refuses to translate to Sacajawea regarding the nature of the dispute. He will only say it is a big matter between chiefs and he can not discuss it.

Frustrated, the captains knew they must resolve whatever issues are at hand. They do not want an internal dispute to continue that can jeopardize the efforts of the expedition. Unable to translate with the Shoshone boy, they resort to sign language. Using this method, they learn that the issue between the chiefs is with regard to the stewardship of the horses left in their care. The horses have been ignored and allowed to drift. Some of the younger Indians have ridden them hard and neither chief will accept the blame. After explaining both sides of the story and seeing that Lewis and Clark are accepting the idea that the horses will be rounded up, the chiefs settle down and become more hospitable. After more discussion, they learn that there is yet another chief that they want in a group council. The captains, seeing an opportunity to negotiate with all the influential Nez Perce leaders, quickly agree to the council meeting. The council agreed upon, the group next journeys to meet with the other chief, Broken Arm. A council area has been set up in a large, 150 foot lodge, built of sticks and grass.

Greetings are exchanged and food is brought in as the leaders from both sides sit in council. Peace pipes are lit and passed around the circle of Indians and explorers. The interpreting chain consists of an elderly Shoshone woman, Sacajawea, Charbonneau and Labiche. They learn that the Indians are trying to round up all their horses. The problem is they have found only twenty-one at the time and have lost some of the saddles. Lewis tells Twisted Hair that the original agreement of paying him two rifles for keeping the horses is now changed. He will only pay him one rifle, (an old British musket they had gotten from the Chinooks), and the second rifle will be delivered when the rest of the horses are brought to them. The chiefs talk among themselves and hands move during the conversation. Finally, they agree that one rifle is fair. The chiefs promise to deliver the horses as they are found.

The next subject the captains want to discuss concerns the passage across the Bitterroot Mountains. The captains listen intently as the Indians tell them what they do not want to hear. The winter has been heavy with snow. There is still so much snow left in the mountains that they will not be able to cross to the eastern slopes for three or four weeks.

Hearing this, as it is translated, the sergeants and the captains all have grim looks on their faces. These are men that do not want to be held back by any obstacle.

Looking at Lewis, Sergeant Ordway said, "Well Capt'n, if Providence wants us to be postponed a while, this is a good place. The Indians are friendly and generous. There is food and the country is beautiful, simply beautiful. We can repair our rifles, get the horses in better condition, and prepare packs for when it is time to go."

Clark said, "And can keep checking to see when the time is right."

Lewis, normally gloomy at these times, suddenly smiled and said, "You're right, absolutely right. Let's enjoy the time we have here and not become melancholy. We'll hunt meat for jerky, hides and moccasins. We'll trade Captain Clark's medical services for food until our hunters become productive." Then looking around at the group, he continued, "We'll enjoy this place while we wait. There's no use in worrying about what can't be changed. But keep in mind, we'll move out the first day we are able to cross over. I want regular scouting reports on the conditions. Agreed?"

Clark and the sergeants nodded and said, "Agreed."

Lewis, having addressed the most pressing issue with the Indians, leaned back and said to Clark, "We have a captive audience here and translation after a fashion. I think we should let these good people know more about us."

Clark smiled and said, "I agree. We have time and the important chiefs here. I think we still have some things to show them that'll impress them with our culture. Sergeant Gass, go get a couple of men to bring back the captain's air rifle, the magnets and a compass. Get any other thing that you think would put on a good show. Have Cruzatte come with his fiddle so we can have a little music when Captain Lewis is done explaining our mission."

"Alright, sir. I'll be right back," Ordway said as he rose to leave.

Lewis summons his translation team closer to him and proceeds to explain the size, strength and power of the United States to the Indians. At each point he waits patiently for the translation loop to finish and then proceeds. He becomes animated as he explains the need for peace among all tribes on both sides of the mountains. No blood should be shed in the future. The reward for peaceful negotiations, he explains, will be trading posts and common communities. The Indians will be important because of their horses and strategic position near the mountains. He goes on to invite the chiefs to travel to Washington to meet the president. The president will know of the Nez Perce and they, in turn, will see the large and powerful United States.

The chiefs listen and seemed impressed. They say they will have to consult more before making a reply to the proposal to travel. For now they can only agree to make permanent villages on the eastern side of the mountains. These villages will only be built after the Army establishes trading posts. The captains agree. Then they put on what is considered a magic show by the Indians. Lewis fires the air rifle, demonstrates compasses, a magnet and a telescope. Those items are passed around the council. Each Indian talks to the man next to him about the marvels of the items.

The next day Lewis stood outside his tent looking at the snow-laden mountains. Sergeant Gass approached him and asked, "What do you think, Capt'n, can we make it? With the shortcut we wouldn't be up there as long."

Lewis looked down and then back at the mountains, "I don't know, Sergeant. I wish I knew how deep the snow was up there. The Indians keep saying it'll take another month. I feared this all along. Any shortcut will be welcome. I watch the river every day, it seems to be rising more and more. That's a good sign of snow melt."

Sergeant Gass said, "Well, Capt'n, I am sure if we have to wait awhile before going on, I would rather be here than just about any other place. Sure as hell wouldn't want to be back on the coast in that miserable rain."

Lewis nodded and said, "It's just the wait, pure and simple. I want to get on with it. The men want to move on. Those mountains are between us and home, a barrier to progress. I hate seeing the men lying around with nothing to do, it's not good for them. They'll get lazy and undisciplined."

Gass smiled and said, "Well, Capt'n, we been talkin' some. The men got nothin' against healing up some of our invalids while we wait. We can get our horses back in shape on this grass. And as for what to do, well, the rest of us can enter into sport with the Indians. They can ride good, they've shown us better horsemanship than I've ever seen demonstrated. We can have all kinds of other contests from tug-of-war to foot races."

Lewis looked pensive for a moment and then said, "Good, Sergeant, good. The horses should be in good shape before we attempt to cross. When we start, they may have to go a few days without grass. As for the men, I think a little sport will help morale and keep them occupied. I've seen these Indians ride, and they are good at it, real good. It's astonishing to see them ride down hills at full gallop, shooting arrows at a rolling target. Perhaps we can hone our own riding skills with competition and let them instruct our men. A good tug-of-war and a foot race will always get men going. We can set up teams and make up different games to compete. What's that game you like to play, Base, isn't it?"

Gass replied, "Yeah, Base. We couldn't play it much at Fort Clatsop because of the weather, but here, well, it's just beautiful in this valley. Everybody likes a horse race. We can combine that with foot races and throwing contests."

Lewis said, "Go ahead with it, Sergeant. Just remember we still have to keep regular duties of making rope, moccasins and keeping our rifles in good working order. Don't let the men wager heavily on the outcome of any of the contests. When we are finally ready to cross, I don't want any type of delay whatsoever."

Gass nodded and responded, "Don't worry, sir. We all know, every man, what we've got to do to move on. As soon as you give the word, we'll be moving out within a few hours." Noticing Lewis looking at the landscape, he added, "Sure is pretty up here, ain't it, sir?"

Lewis nodded and replied, "Yes, Sergeant, it's pristine, green grass, blue skies and snowcapped mountains. But from a more practical point of view, I would prefer a rolling plain dotted with buffalo and a river at my back."

Gass said, "I know. So would I."

Later that day Lewis observed the men building a large pit. "What's this for?" he queried.

Shields replied, "We are building a steam pit, sir. Put seats here and there and then put hot rocks in the center here. Pour hot water in over the rocks and make steam. It's a treatment, sir. After a while of sitting in here, the rheumatism seems to be greatly relieved and sometimes goes away for good. Capt'n Clark has already got several Indians waiting for treatment."

As they were talking, Clark approached. "We've got a regular hospital here. I've been treating ten to fifteen people an hour with eye wash. I don't know how many will come for rheumatism treatment in the steam bath. One thing for sure, Bratton will be the first to receive the steam treatments. His back has continued to bother him since we left the coast. I don't think he can withstand the rigors of crossing the mountains in his present condition. I have no idea why he has suffered so long without healing, I only hope it's not permanent. I want to try steam heat along with an onion poultice on him. Shields said he's seen steam heat work wonders. I really have nothing else to offer him as a remedy."

Bratton was treated with the steam bath. He sat in the hot sauna pouring hot water over heated rocks. Steam rolled continually from the cracks around the door. Three times he would get himself heated to a full sweat, then plunge into the cold water of the river, only to reheat himself and repeat. When he was finished, Clark put an onion poultice on his back and had him lie down.

Bratton declared that he felt better already. Due to his success, many of the Indians that had claimed back and hip ailments repeated the performance. They also declared it to relieve their pain. One elderly chief, partially paralyzed, who had not responded to any other treatment, was finally convinced to try the sweat treatment. After taking a little laudanum he submitted to the sweat treatment. To his amazement, he regained the use of his limbs and hands. The observing Indians buzzed with excitement, witnessing the success in healing the old chief. Food was brought in as payment for further treatments.

Salmon were now coming upriver adding to the food supply. They noted that the fish contained enough oil that they could be fried without adding any cooking grease or oil.

June 8, 1806

The Corps of Discovery is very anxious to move out. Every man knows the expected hunger and difficulty in crossing the mountains, but they also know it has to be done. The chiefs tell them repeatedly it is too early to attempt to cross. They say they will have to wait until July. Driven by the desire to return home, they decide to attempt a crossing anyway.

Sergeant Ordway and a detachment of men were returning from a trip to a distant river to gather salmon. They had been gone some time and the captains were starting to get concerned. Seeing them arrive, Lewis smiled broadly as he said to Clark and Sergeants Pryor and Gass, "I'm glad Ordway and his men are back. Their stock of salmon will add to our provisions." Then pausing as the sergeant approached, he said, "Good to see you, Sergeant. Get many fish?"

Ordway responded, "Yeah, seems like the more you catch, the more the river fills up with 'em again. Salmon are running real good now. Only problem is we came so damn far with 'em without salt, some of 'em are not quite edible now. I want to cook up these that are still good right away."

"Good idea," Pryor said as he motioned to two men standing nearby. "You men get some help and go get the fish the sergeant has brought in. Get 'em cooked up right away. We can eat some for supper tonight and the rest can be fried for jerky."

Lewis said to Clark and the sergeants, "I know some of the men have been trading brass buttons and other little things for roots and staple foods. What's good for the men is also good for us. Cut your buttons off and we'll send a party to trade for portable foodstuff. I'll cut the buttons from my jacket. Bill, will you do the same? The Indians seem fond of these and if they're good barter, then we should make the trade."

Clark replied, "Good idea. Those buttons ain't doing us much good anyway. Polish 'em up and I'll send York and McNeal to the village to trade."

With that, Clark summoned McNeal and York and gave them the brass buttons along with instructions to make the best deal possible for roots.

Hearing the instructions and knowing he was empowered to make such an important trade, York beamed as he said, "Don't worry none. I'll make sure ever last button gets us plenty of roots." He smiled broadly as he picked up the knapsack with the buttons, McNeal nodded in agreement as the two left for the village to negotiate for roots.

The next day Lewis and Sergeant Pryor greeted the men as they returned from their trip. Excited, a wide-eyed McNeal said, "You should've seen us. Why if we weren't somethin' to behold. York here would make the deal. He would hold up a single button like it was a sapphire or diamond, then turn it slowly in his hand an' then stick out his other hand to get the roots, playing those Indians like Cruzatte plays the fiddle. If the offer was too small or the roots of poor quality, he'd just close his fist quicker than a minute and hold it behind his back. Every time he would get more roots than they seemed willing to offer at first. They'd keep givin' me the roots until York here gave a nod. Then I put 'em in the basket. Then he began a ritual of lookin' in the knapsack like there weren't any more buttons till the Indians were all on edge. Then, when the moment was right, he'd pluck another one out and hold it up and begin all over again. I ain't never seen any snake oil travelin' salesman do a better job. All I got to say is, if you got tradin' with Indians to do - York here is your man."

York stood straight and proud as McNeal boasted of the trade.

"How many roots did you get?" Lewis queried.

York beamed as he replied, "Dropped off three heaping bushels with Sergeant Ordway, sir, all good quality, fat roots."

Lewis looked at the grinning McNeal and then at the prideful York. Nodding his head said, "Successful voyage men. Not much less pleasing to us than the return of a good quality cargo to an East India merchant."

June 16, 1806

The Corps of Discovery now has sixty-five head of horses. After weeks of grazing on lush grass, they have regained health, and most are in good shape. Lewis orders them all hobbled for the evening so they cannot wander. They are preparing to leave the Nez Perce the next day and head into the mountains.

Early in the morning, Lewis assembled the men and spoke to them, "Men, we've been detained here for nearly five weeks now due to the snow in the mountains. That's a serious loss of time in what normally should be a delightful season for traveling."

Joseph Field spoke up, "Ever one of us is ready to go, sir. We're all as anxious as a bride to move out."

Lewis replied, "I know. There is not one of you more anxious than I to see home and family, not to mention the comforts of our culture. Today we'll begin to cross these horrible mountains. With luck and perseverance we'll make it to Traveler's Rest in a few days. I'm advised that the friendly Flatheads are very likely to be there. We may be able to trade with them. We'll be in a somewhat more familiar region again. We will still have a good way to go from there just to get to the eastern slopes and on down to the Missouri. But we have good horses and a better idea of how to cross. Now don't get me wrong, this is not a cake walk. Those mountains are just as steep as ever. There will be plenty of slippery shale and fallen timber in our way."

He looked at all the men and paused for a moment before he continued. "From Traveler's Rest we will split up into three detachments. Captain Clark will take a contingent over to the headwaters of the Jefferson and then on to the Yellowstone River. He will chart that river for future navigation purposes and meet us later on downstream at the Missouri. By all accounts the Yellowstone may provide a second practical waterway to the West and we need accurate maps of it. Sergeant Ordway will take a detail to recover the buried cache of supplies and canoes left last season. It goes without saying that those provisions will be welcomed. He and his group will proceed on down to meet me later at the Maria. I will be taking a small group to journey up the Maria's River to take readings of latitude and longitude. I want to get as close to the headwater as possible. The headwaters of that river, I believe, mark the northern boundary of the Louisiana Purchase. By accurately charting those points we will stake our claim on the maps to the northern limit of this new land. When finished, we will come back down the Maria's and join Sergeant Ordway's detail. Together again we will proceed, with the river at our back, to re-unite with Captain Clark."

Cruzatte said, "That sounds better to these ears than any music I ever played. I really like the downstream part."

The men all agreed.

Clark said, "Men, these mountains are still our most immediate and biggest obstacle. You know what's there. Even though it's now mid-June, and we are just preparing to enter these mountains, we know it will be difficult. Scouting reports have witnessed in the space of twenty miles or one day's travel, all the seasons nature has to offer. That includes all the rigors of winter in its harshest form. We must be prepared, as we have in the past, to persevere and no matter what, we proceed on."

They mounted their horses, each holding a packhorse in tow, and moved east into the mountains. As they climbed in elevation, the snow was everywhere, eight to ten feet deep. The trail was completely covered, but fortunately the snow was firm enough to hold the weight of the horses. In fact, there was an advantage as the snow pack covered the obstacles of fallen timber. Climbing up and down steep ravines, over and over, the day's progress was limited to fifteen miles. They came to a point where Clark had hung meat in a tree for Lewis and party the previous year. It was a welcome landmark. They made camp and at that altitude they were in severe winter conditions.

Clark said, "Merry, travel is rough as hell here. It's colder than I thought it would be. As for finding a trail that we have never seen? I don't know. I just don't know about going on."

Lewis blew warm air over his hands and looked at the men huddling around small fires. "Damn, damn, damn," he said disgustedly. "I never hated a piece of landscape anywhere on the earth as much as I hate these mountains. I never thought I could hate mountains. It isn't enough that they preclude any chance of a coast to coast waterway. No, no, that's not enough. They are so formidable that only a seasonal crossing will be possible. Bill, I hate to lose time like this, precious time. I hate to be defeated by cold, snow, steep hills and no food. Give me an enemy I can fight, even a bear, anything but these cold, hard mountains."

Clark looked seriously at Lewis and said, "There is one thing you hate more, my friend." Lewis looked up quickly at Clark as he finished his sentence, "You hate to admit defeat. To turn back to you is to retreat. But it is obvious this is a battle we cannot win. I fear that if we persist, the mountains and this weather will devour us."

Lewis said, "Jefferson warned me on more than one occasion, he said the men and your records and specimens are too important to put at risk. When judgment declares you exercise caution, then exercise caution." Lewis looked at Clark a moment and then continued, "These men would follow us anywhere, even to death. We need to turn back. To pursue this now is folly. Tomorrow we should head back."

Clark, grim faced, said, "Merry, you are the bravest man I know and now I think the wisest. If we fall back and wait, maybe we can get some Nez Perce guides to help us. If the Indians can make it through these mountains, then by God so can we."

Lewis said, "I think I can get guides, but they'll want rifles as payment. I hate to give up even one rifle, but considering the situation, I think it would be a prudent offer."

Clark nodded saying, "I agree. Let's send a couple of men back, ahead of the rest, to negotiate with the Nez Perce for guides."

Lewis confirmed, "Done. I'll get Drewyer and Shannon to go and make the offer. It's madness at this stage of the expedition to proceed on without a guide. We can go back a ways and wait. We should go back to the last meadow lower down where the horses can feed. There are deer in the area, too. We'll wait there for the men to return with a guide."

June 23, 1806

Cheering broke out in the camp as Joseph and Reubin Field came running toward the captains. Joseph shouted, "They're back. Looks like they got three guides with 'em. We just had a stroke of luck, sir, a genuine stroke of luck."

Clark rose and walked to meet the men with Lewis close behind. "It looks as if you men were persuasive. Well done. Come join us and let us know what happened."

Shannon leapt from his horse while Drewyer and the three Indians dismounted slowly. Excitedly Shannon said, "It took some powerful negotiation, but we got ourselves good guides this time. Nothing like that Old Toby we had before." Turning and pointing at the Indians, he continued, "Those two were anxious to come. Maybe because they're the ones that gave you captains the horses. They wanted to see for themselves how we were doing and if the pass was open yet. Who knows, maybe they wanted to check on those two horses. I think they gain status for being first through the mountains. I don't care why they agreed to come, I was just glad to get them to come. The other fella is Cut Nose's brother. He wanted to gain some importance with his brother by letting the Nez Perce know if it was time to cross."

Lewis beamed, "Good job, men. We were starting to worry, you were gone so long."

Drewyer replied, "Took some negotiating. Two rifles to be exact. They promised, gave their word, that for two rifles they would stay with us. Knowing the Nez Perce, I don't doubt their word. They have told us over and over that we have to move quickly. They want to move out at first light in the morning."

As a celebration and part ritual, the Indians set two trees on fire 'to assure a safe trip and fair weather to the journey.' The men watched and warmed themselves as the trees burned.

Moving on through rough terrain there were cold nights and long days. The beleaguered men continued through the mountains without complaint of terrain or weather conditions. The horses had little to eat and were getting thin. Onward they traveled in a forced march. The Indian guides seemed to sense where the trail was under the snow. The men gained confidence, when, on those few occasions where the snow was melted, an exposed trail proved they were on the right course.

One evening before making camp, as Lewis stood with Clark, Pryor and Gass, he said, "Look at these stupendous mountains, I am filled with both awe and dread. Our Indian guides hold our very lives in their hands and they proceed with utmost confidence. To anyone unacquainted with this terrain, it would seem impossible to escape from here alive. The mountains blend together so much and to my weary eyes begin to look alike. Even though we have been to Traveler's Rest before, I doubt we could relocate ourselves without these guides."

Sergeant Pryor said, "The Nez Perce are good people. Better than any Indians I ever knew. Perhaps like birds that migrate each season they just know which way to go. I agree, sir, I'm glad you made the decision to turn back and send for them."

June 30, 1806

They had traveled 156 miles in six days. Lewis was happy and deliberate as he rode his horse through the rough terrain to where they would be able to make camp and rest. The guides told them they would be coming to Traveler's Rest soon. As they came down a steep hillside, Lewis' horse slipped. With rear hooves slipping out from under, the animal fell down the hillside. Lewis fell backward as he and the horse went down the slope, topsy turvy together. The horse let out a loud noise as the men watched in horror, seeing first the horse, then Lewis, then the horse again as they tumbled forty feet before coming to a rest. York, Colter, Whitehouse, Bratton and Cruzatte rushed down the slope to assist the captain. York's big hands grabbed Lewis by the arm and shoulder and lifted him up, "You gonna be all right, Capt'n Lewis?"

The horse was getting up as Colter and Whitehouse assisted the animal. The horse gave a loud whinny and shook itself.

Lewis looked at the horse and said, "I know how you feel. I thought I was never going to quit tumbling."

Cruzatte mused, "Well sir, I don't think you hurt him none. And since you seem to be standing straight with no bones sticking out where they shouldn't, I reckon he didn't hurt you either."

Lewis said, "That's a fair assessment, but none of you should follow my lead on that one."

York said, "No, sir, ain't none of us like that example. We're all scared for you, sir, don't want no broken bones out here."

Colter said, "I think we're real close to Traveler's Rest. Sir, you may want to walk awhile to limber up. We'll be there soon.

They arrive at Traveler's Rest and decide to camp three days to make final plans before splitting up. Lewis, as announced earlier, will take nine men and seventeen horses to follow the Nez Perce trail to the Great Falls of the Missouri. There, three men will dig up the cache and prepare for the portage around the falls until Sergeant Ordway can join them. Lewis and the other six will go on to ascertain the northern portions of the Maria's River. He hopes they can meet the Blackfeet Indians. He wants to be able to deliver his speech about the coming United States trade and the need for peace between tribes.

Knowing the whites are able to find their own way from this point, the guides ask to be released. Lewis wants them to stay and meet the Blackfeet so they can talk of peace. The Indians refuse and warn their friends to be wary of the Blackfeet. They part, wishing everyone good luck.

As planned, Sergeant Ordway leads the men coming down the Missouri, portaging around the falls and on to meet again with Lewis at the Maria's. Clark will go as far as the three forks and then proceed over the mountains to the Yellowstone River. When they separate to leave, each group wishes the other well.

July 22, 1806
Maria's River, Montana

The Corps of Discovery has divided. Clark and his group have crossed the mountains and continue on to explore the Yellowstone River valley. Lewis has proceeded to the mouth of the Maria's River. Ordway is bringing up the rear, digging up the caches of materials and portaging around the Great Falls.

Lewis and six men with seventeen horses proceed up the Maria's River to take latitude measurements of the river and thus of the Louisiana Purchase itself. They have already experienced disappointment from the discovery of damp and lost specimens stored in the cache buried last year. The men are further disappointed when Indians, at night, steal seven of their horses. Lewis decides to proceed on with only three men. He believes that the four of them can complete the mission quickly without as much chance of being observed.

Turning to Sergeant Gass, Lewis spoke low and seriously, "Sergeant, I think now that we have lost some of our horses, I'll change the plan. The Indians know the horses are here and that makes us a target. Being a target for theft is not a good thing. They may return in force and attempt to steal the rest. I want you to take Frazer and Werner and head back. You'll soon join with Ordway and the others coming downstream. Drewyer and the Field brothers will go on with me. We'll take six horses and move out fast. By splitting up, they may not follow us."

Gass replied, "Alright, sir. Do you want any of our rifles? Wouldn't hurt to have an extra shot in case of trouble. We'll be joining the others long before you get back. We won't need our guns because we'll be under their protection then. I'd sure feel better knowing you were better armed."

Lewis smiled as he grabbed Gass' arm and said, "No, Sergeant, thank you for the thought. If the Indians decide to become hostile, you'll need all your rifles. I would not feel right taking a man's rifle in this neighborhood. You're likely to be their target anyway. You'll need your arms. When you meet with the others, keep the river at your back. When you camp, be ready to put the canoes in the water quickly to defend yourselves.

They shook hands and departed.

Lewis and the three men proceeded to travel northward up the Maria's River until they reached a fork of two streams. Without question he took the northernmost tributary, Cut Bank Creek. At its most northern point, they stopped to make celestial observations. That evening clouds obscured his ability to take measurements.

Lewis said, "I want to fix the latitude here. I was hoping we would reach fifty degrees north, but it's pretty clear these waters are not going that far. I think other rivers on this prairie might go farther north. Both the White Earth and Milk Rivers carry a lot of water and just might extend as far north as fifty degrees."

Joseph Field said, "Sir, there is just no let up with this cloud cover. Do you want to go over to the Milk and set our latitude there?"

Lewis was quiet for a moment then replied, "I must admit I'm tempted." Then leaning on his rifle he said, "No, we are losing too much time, far too much time. I want to be able to return home this season. Time is becoming an enemy. There is too much land to cover and we don't have the time. We'll camp here again tonight, I'll check for clear skies later. I'm going to call this place Camp Disappointment. We'll leave here early tomorrow, readings or not."

July 26, 1806 Maria's River, Northern Montana

In the morning they began heading back south. Drewyer separated from the others and moved along the river valley hunting deer while Lewis and the Field brothers ascended a ridge to reconnoiter. Reubin Field pointed as he said, "Capt'n, look over there. There's Indians and lots of horses."

Lewis took his telescope and observed. As he did so he spoke, "There must be a herd of thirty horses or better. There's several mounted Indians, apparently looking into the valley. I think they've spotted Drewyer but ain't seen us yet."

Joseph Field asked, "Think they're Blackfeet? How many do ya see?"

Lewis answered, "If they have a man for every horse, we are hopelessly outnumbered. From what the Nez Perce told us they are mostly unfriendly. We could have difficulty with them." Pausing a moment, he continued, "We're outnumbered either way, whether we run or approach. I choose to approach. Anyway, we can't leave Drewyer down there alone. Joseph, get the flag out and show it off. Wave it high and proud. We'll advertise ourselves and get some attention. I think we're going to meet some Indians."

Obediently the flag was soon out as they proceeded toward the Indians in a slow, steady march. Noticing the men approach, the Indians suddenly became very agitated and began milling about. Then, one of the Indians broke from the group and came riding toward the men at full gallop. Seeing this, Lewis dismounted and held up his hand, waiting for the rider to draw near. The approaching Indian was dismayed by the courageous act and halted a hundred yards away. He stared at Lewis for a moment and then reigned his horse around, whipped it and left at full gallop to rejoin his companions.

Reubin Field said, "What the hell do you make of that, sir?"

Lewis said to the men, "Stay calm. Advance deliberately. If they were out to kill us, they would have all come at once. I only see eight. There may be others, but they haven't shown themselves. If there are more of them, they could be herding the other horses." As they moved onward, Lewis said in a low tone, "We're alright, but stay alert, thumb on the hammer, finger on the trigger. If they are hostile, we'll not sacrifice our journals, specimens or rifles without it costing them dearly." Without speaking, the men looked at one another and nodded. This was raw courage.

The explorers and the Blackfeet advanced slowly to within a hundred yards of one another. Then, one of the Indians moved out ahead of the group. Lewis said, "Hold here. I'll meet him one on one."

Lewis dismounted. The Indian dismounted. They walked toward one another and then met cautiously. They stood for a moment, taking one another's measure, and then Lewis extended his hand. The Indian responded by shaking his hand. Using sign language, the Indian asked for a pipe and to smoke with them. Lewis nodded and motioned for the others to advance. By this time, Drewyer had noticed the activity and moved to join his companions. It was quickly established that there were only eight Indians in the immediate area. "Only two-to-one," Reubin Field said. "We gotta feel good about that."

It was late afternoon, and through sign language they agreed to share a meal of venison, smoke the pipe and talk together. Through Drewyer, Lewis asked who was their chief. Three men stepped forward.

Drewyer winked and said, "Three chiefs out of eight men. Good thing there ain't more than eight of them or we'd have a whole passel of chiefs."

Joseph Field said, "Must be easy to be a chief around here."

Reubin Field said, "Probably get to be chief from stealing horses."

Lewis smiled and said, "I think we should humor them. I'll give them a flag, a medal and a handkerchief. That's three gifts for three chiefs. Ask them if they'll camp with us tonight. I'd rather know where they are than have them lurking around somewhere."

Drewyer translated and then said, "They are happy with the gifts and will spend the night with us. They say they are part of a large buffalo hunting party about a day's ride from here, near the mountains. The larger party has lots of pelts that they take back to trade. They have a couple of English muskets and want to get more by trading hides and furs with the Canadians."

Lewis seized the opportunity and had Drewyer translate that the Americans would give them the best deals for their trade merchandise. He went on to say how he had met many Indians of other nations and wanted to make peace among the Indian nations so trade could prosper. Trading with the white man would bring them clothing, cooking utensils, and most importantly, guns."

Lewis said to his men, "They seem willing to try to talk as long as we keep the pipe full of tobacco. Sooner or later we'll have to bed down. We'll take turns at sentry duty. Sleep next to your rifles. Tell them we have more men nearby. Say that we plan to meet with them soon. I want them to believe we have some strength."

The Indians talked among one another, knowing their conversation could not be translated. They agreed that they dare not kill these whites because there could be more nearby. If these do not return, the others, with weapons, would come to look for them. They were concerned that these whites offered trade to all tribes. That meant their enemies, or those they now intimidated, would gain parity if the proposed white gun trade were successful. They needed time to get back to their main party and tell their chiefs about these whites.

Unable to translate the spoken word, Drewyer proceeded with sign language translation. After some deliberation both parties retired for the evening. Lewis took first watch and at 11:30 PM woke Reubin Field. He whispered, "Take over Reubin, I'll sleep for now. Watch them. Keep count of them. If one leaves, wake us all up."

During the night the men rotated watch until the eastern sky was beginning to lighten from the first light of dawn. The Blackfeet continued secret conversation and signals unnoticed by the sentry. They settled on a plan to steal all the horses and rifles. They would slow the explorers and then come back later in force. At a given signal they all sprang into action.

Drewyer's shout broke the silence, "Damn you. Let go my gun!"

Lewis and the others were up in an instant. The Blackfeet's surprise attack was partially foiled by the quick reaction of the men. The campsite was instantly turned into a flurry of activity. There was chaos with dust and noise, horses whinnying, men running and cursing. Lewis called out an order, "Shoot 'em if they try to steal our horses!"

Drewyer ran after two Indians that had taken his gun and horse. One Indian fled immediately at his approach. The other, with the stolen rifle in hand, tried to hold his ground. Drewyer grabbed the rifle barrel with one hand, the mid-stock with the other. Before the Indian could point it at him he thrust the barrel forward, cracking the invading Indian in the forehead with the barrel and splitting the skin. Dazed from the blow, the Indian momentarily relaxed his grip. Drewyer stepped forward, pivoted the rifle in his hand and swung the butt of the rifle sharply upward, striking the thief squarely in the jaw. His jaw broke with a loud crack as the Indian fell to the ground, blood coming from his head and mouth. Gun now in hand, Drewyer quickly looked around to see the Field brothers engaged in combat with three men. He ran to assist them. Swinging his rifle like a club he struck one of the Indians in the midriff, sending him to the ground. The other Indian mounted a horse, grabbed another horse and fled upstream.

Meanwhile Joseph Field was still struggling to gain control of his rifle. The Indian opponent was slightly larger than he and was pulling him and swinging him around. Both men held fast to the rifle. Fearful to lose the weapon, Field took an opportune moment, quickly drew his knife and plunged it into the Indian's chest. The blade found the opponent's heart and he fell instantly as the knife was withdrawn. Just then Joseph came over and said, "My God. You've killed him! Those bastards, they were all over us. All at once! Drewyer hit one with his rifle butt; you could hear the bones crack a mile. Then he hit the other and they started runnin'." Then pivoting as he quickly looked around, he exclaimed, "Where's Capt'n Lewis?"

Drewyer, already in motion, pointed as Joseph Field wiped his knife blade on his leg. "There he goes, there! He's chasin' the Indians on foot. They're trying to drive some horses off the other way. Reubin, go and round up as many horses as ya can. Joe, let's help the Capt'n. Go. Go, now!" The men took off running. Joseph Field, being the fastest, was in the lead.

Seeing two Indians take the horses, Lewis took his rifle and immediately gave chase. The Indians had a head start, but Lewis knew he could not let thieves take his horse and be stranded in hostile country. Lewis was in such close pursuit that the Indian did not have time to mount the horse. Instead he ran along, pulling on a tether line.

Enraged with the theft of the horses, Lewis continued the chase for nearly three hundred yards. The fleeing Indians finally came to a nearly vertical bluff. One of the Indians attempted to drive the horses on while the other suddenly turned back, rifle in hand, and faced the pursuing Lewis. Lewis had been shouting all the while at them to halt. He knew they understood his meaning if not the words. For a brief moment Lewis and the Indian looked at one another. Then, the Indian raised his rifle to shoot. Seeing the challenge, Lewis quickly raised his rifle and fired first. 'Pitt cratoowh' the rifle spoke in a cloud of smoke as the Indian crumpled and fell forward. The wounded Indian then raised himself to one knee, aimed at Lewis, and returned the shot, 'pitt cratoowh.' Lewis wheeled and grabbed his left ear as the Indian pitched forward and fell.

Just then Joseph Field came up "You all right, sir?" he inquired with wide-eyed excitement.

Lewis' eyes flashed as he quickly looked around to ascertain the situation. "I felt the wind of it as it whistled over my ear. Didn't get me, did he?"

Field looked at his leader and said, "No, sir. You're alright, but I think you hit him square. He ain't movin'."

Drewyer approached and walked past Lewis toward the fallen Indian. He knelt down, rolled the Indian over and examined him. He looked over at Lewis and said, "He's dead."

Joseph Field said, "I had to kill one, too, sir. Stabbed him through the heart 'cause I couldn't get my gun back. They attacked all at once. Thought they could take us by surprise and be clear. Drewyer and I grabbed the first two, then everything just happened so fast I don't know."

Lewis said, "Where's Reubin?"

Joseph said, "He's rounding up horses. I think the Indians all ran away."

Lewis walked over to the slain Indian and looked at him a moment. Then he took a peace medallion and laid it on the dead man's chest. "They will be back after him. I want them to know who did it. They can't think that we're weak and easy prey, not any longer."

Drewyer said, "They went to get their comrades. They'll be back."

At that time Reubin Field came riding up with the horses. He shouted, "Everybody all right? I heard gunshots."

Joseph said, "Capt'n had to kill one. Almost got a bullet hisself."

Lewis stood looking around at the scene, trying to ascertain if there were any more Indians nearby. Then he said to Joseph Field, "You said you killed one?"

Field nodded, "Yes, sir. Stabbed through the heart."

Lewis looked at Drewyer and continued, "Did you kill any?"

Drewyer said, "No, didn't kill him. Broke his jaw I think. He went down and didn't move. I went on to help the Field brothers. Indians were running everywhere."

Reubin said, "Last I saw they helped the one Drewyer laid out get up on a horse, then they lit out. They're gone. I don't think they got all the horses."

Drewyer commented, "As I said, they'll be back. When they have more numbers."

Lewis said, "Men, there was blood spilled here and they'll want vengeance. Even cowards want vengeance. Let's not waste any time. Get our horses together. Take the better ones they left behind and we'll ride. We can't give them an opportunity to take advantage of us with numbers. We need to get to the river as quick as we can and meet the others. Then we'll be better able to protect ourselves."

Taking only a short time to round up their horses and selecting a few the Indians left behind, they packed their gear and headed out. Lewis said, "Pace the horses, I want to keep a steady trot as long as we can. If we come to a stream or creek, let 'em have water and then keep going. We have a hard ride ahead of us and we need to take advantage of the time it takes them to get word back to their friends. If we keep moving, we'll be out of reach."

They held the pace until midafternoon when they stopped for water and let the horses graze. They had covered sixty-three miles. An hour and a half later they resumed the pace and made another seventeen miles until sunset. They made a small campfire, killed a buffalo and ate a quick meal. When finished, they mounted up again and rode off slowly. They rode all night.

In the morning they came to the Missouri and proceeded down it only a few miles when they heard the sound of rifles. It was Ordway and the men. They would now be reunited to sixteen strong. They released the horses and took to the river where they could make steady progress. They used the white pirogue and five smaller boats.

August 7, 1806 Missouri River in Montana

Lewis' group was moving quickly downriver. Current at their back, they averaged a steady seven miles per hour. As they had done on the trip west, Lewis ordered them to cook up large amounts of meat at each evening stop in order to eliminate the need to stop for a midday meal. Lewis estimated this added fifteen miles per day to the pace and he wanted to re-join Clark as quickly as possible. As they came to the mouth of the Yellowstone he looked in all directions, but there was no sign of Clark and the others.

Sergeant Ordway shouted, "Over there, sir. They've been here. I see a campsite."

Lewis motioned with his hand and the boats pulled in near the abandoned campsite.

Joseph Field said, "Look there, on that pole yonder, there's a note on that pole." Running across the abandoned campsite, Field retrieved the note and brought it to Lewis.

"Thanks," Lewis said as he took the weather beaten note and read it, "Can't read it clear, it got wet. Captain Clark says, 'Game scarce, mosquitoes plentiful, moving on, will re-unite downstream.' Well, men, you heard it. If there's no game here, there's no need to stick around unless you want to be mosquito bait. Let's move out and put some miles behind us. We are already late and there is no profit in waiting here."

August 11, 1806 North Dakota

Lewis had been pushing the men hard to be able to rejoin the others. With the idea of hostile Blackfeet behind him, he wanted the full complement of the corps just in case. They set out early in the morning and were not long underway when Sergeant Ordway said, "Capt'n, I saw six or seven elk move along the river's edge up there. Should we pull in and get some fresh meat?"

Lewis nodded as he pointed to the shore and said, "Cruzatte, pull the pirogue in here. The rest of you pull in and anchor behind us. Sergeant, build a fire so we can cook up the meat as soon as we can. I want to be back on the river as soon as possible."

Cruzatte, the skilled river man, guided the white pirogue to a smooth landing so that the point of the boat pushed into the soft mud on the river's edge. The other canoes followed in kind and all the men jumped out and pulled the boats further onto the bank. Lewis grabbed his rifle and said, "Cruzatte, good landing. Grab your rifle and join me. We should have fresh elk before they can build a fire big enough to roast it all."

"Yes, sir," Cruzatte responded as he took his rifle and fell in behind Lewis. The two headed directly toward where the elk were last seen. Reaching the willow reeds, Lewis motioned with his hand for Cruzatte to take one side as he moved into the thick reeds near the river's edge. Soon Lewis spotted an elk, took aim and killed it. Cruzatte came over, "That's a good one sir, I saw three more movin' slow through the willows not far, just over yonder."

Lewis replied, "Good, we'll get this one on the way back. May as well take another if we can. You go that way around the edge. I'll head up through some of the shorter willows just ahead."

Cruzatte nodded and moved out, leaving Lewis to proceed through the shoreline willows. Cruzatte moved along the edge of the willow reeds, scanning the reeds with his one eye for any motion of an elk. Meanwhile, Lewis came into some taller willows and had to bend down to work his way through them. As he emerged from the willows he was still crouching when he saw another pair of elk within gun range. He paused briefly to brush mosquitoes from his face. Then, raising his rifle slowly to take aim, he sighted in on an elk. Just as he was about to pull the trigger, he felt a sudden stab of searing pain in his left buttock. His body twisted around as he fell to the ground. As he fell he heard the report of the rifle that had just wounded him. He instinctively grabbed the wound and blood oozed out between his fingers. Pain was across his face as he lay there a moment trying to move.

Gripped in pain he started to rise and look for Cruzatte, "Damn you. You shot me!" he shouted.

There was no answer.

A moment of realization that it could have been Indians flashed in his eyes. Then he shouted, "Cruzatte, I've been hit. Are you all right? Cruzatte, you there?"

No answer.

Not hearing from his companion, Lewis concluded he was dead, a victim of Indian attack. He knew his only chance for survival was to reach the others. Racked in pain and bleeding profusely, he hobbled as quickly as he could back toward the others. The pain was intense, but he knew he could not fall or be overtaken. He had to reach the safety of his men.

Sergeant Gass and Joseph Field saw the approaching Lewis first. They glanced at one another and then both started to run toward their leader. Gass shouted back over his shoulder, "Something's wrong! Capt'n's hurt! Get over here!"

The two men closed in on the struggling Lewis. As they reached him, he collapsed in their arms. Gasping, Lewis said, "Indians. I been shot. Don't know about Cruzatte. He didn't answer my call. Everybody get their rifles. We'll go after the bastards."

The men obeyed quickly and soon they were ready to go after the Indians and their missing comrade. Looking at the injured Lewis, Sergeant Gass asked, "Did ya see how many?"

His face drawn with pain, Lewis gave a strained reply, "No. I just felt it slam into my behind, next thing I knew I was spinning down. Heard the shot as I fell. Didn't see anything. I called out for Cruzatte, but he didn't answer."

Sergeant Gass said, "We'll go after 'em and get Cruzatte. You stay here, Capt'n."

Lewis said, "No. I'm going."

They all joined Lewis and started after the enemy. After a few yards Lewis collapsed from pain and could not go on. "Take me back to the pirogue. I 've got my rifle and pistol. I'll wait there. If you meet superior numbers, give them fire and retreat back to these canoes. We can defend ourselves a lot better a ways out from the shoreline. Bring Cruzatte back, dead or alive." The Field brothers helped their wounded captain back to the pirogue and then rushed off to join the others.

After a few minutes of searching, Drewyer shouted, "Cruzatte's here. Just sittin' here. Looks alright." Then turning to Cruzatte, "What the hell's the matter, man? Did you see any Indians? Did **you** shoot the captain?"

The others were closing in quickly and forming a circle around Cruzatte who was still sitting wide-eyed with a ghostly look on his face. Cruzatte rose slowly, a stunned look on his face as he looked at the circle of comrades. Then he spoke softly and slowly, "I don't know. I thought I shot an elk. Then I heard the Capt'n cussin' at me and sayin' how I'd shot him. I didn't see him. I would never shoot Capt'n Lewis, never. I'd rather die myself than shoot the capt'n. I thought I was takin' an elk."

All the men were silently watching Cruzatte, obviously in shock, trying to explain his actions. Sergeant Ordway spoke up, "Shut up, Pierre! You're making a damn fool of yourself. All of ya. Get back to the river and let's take care of the captain."

Cruzatte inquired, "How bad is he hurt?"

Ordway replied, "He made it back to the boats on his own. He was going to lead a counterattack against what he thought were Indians 'til the pain of his wound got to him. He was ordering us to come protect you, ya damn fool."

Joseph Field said, "He's shot in the butt, maybe it went clean through. There was lots of blood. I don't know how he was able to walk."

All the men began running back toward the river and to Lewis. Sergeant Gass said, "Get some elk hide. Get whatever you can find to work as bandages. We've got to make a bed for him. Got to see how bad he's wounded."

The men came over to the anxious Lewis and explained they had found a distraught Cruzatte sitting silently in shock. Lewis said nothing for a moment. He was taking short rapid breaths as he said, "Sergeant Gass, cut these clothes off me. Roll me over and see if the bullet went clean through or not. Boil up some water for clean bandages and get some bark."

Gass helped Lewis out of his bloody clothes. Ordway set to boiling water. As military men, they knew how to field dress a wound. After cutting the breeches off of Lewis, Gass said, "Well, sir, it went clean through. It doesn't appear to have hit bone or artery. Stopped in the elk hide of your breeches on the other side. All in all, sir, I'd say you were lucky with this wound. Here it is, a 54-caliber bullet. Ain't no Indians around here have that caliber."

Lewis winced and then said, "At least you don't have to dig it out of me. Have the men get some Peruvian bark poultice ready; it should fight off infection early. I'll try to pack the opening with some rolls of lint*. That should keep it free to bleed some and let it heal inside out. Don't want infection to set in."

Sergeant Gass said, "Sir, I know you're right about everything you said, we'll do it all for you as best we can. But sir, right now you're wounded pretty bad. Let us take charge now. Let us take over. You just get yourself as comfortable as possible. Try to rest and deal with the pain. I think we have a little laudanum. I want you to take that. You just forget about treatin' yourself, we're gonna take care of you."

Drewyer came over and looked at the injured Lewis, "I'm having the men clear a place in the center of the pirogue. A bed for you. We'll make it as comfortable as possible. In the center there'll be less motion to disturb you. They're all

---

* common gauze

repacking things into the smaller canoes now. They'll have it done in no time. Soon as they're ready, we'll carry you there. I don't think you should move any more than you have to. We want to keep the bleeding down. You can stay in the pirogue until you're well enough to walk."

Sergeant Gass was nodding in agreement as Drewyer spoke, then he said, "He's right, Capt'n. I'm in charge of you now and you are going to go rest in the pirogue. Do what we say until you're better."

Lewis raised his head to say something as Sergeant Ordway put a damp cloth over his forehead and gently forced him back down. "Captain, you're wounded, and we'll take charge. We'll get ya back on the river as soon as we have a comfortable bed ready. The more you cooperate, the sooner you'll be in that bed and back on the river toward Capt'n Clark and home. Take this laudanum, it'll help with the pain."

Lewis let out a deep breath as he submitted to the care of his men.

The men moved without need of orders. Some went after the first elk and began cooking the meat so they could stay on the river. Others re-packed the pirogue so Lewis could lie down. Lewis was gently lifted and carried to what would be his healing bed for several days. After the meat was cooked, the boats went back on the water. No scorn or blame was levied against Cruzatte. They understood what had happened. Lewis had forgiven him immediately upon learning he was at fault and that was that.

Cruzatte took his place as head boatsman in the pirogue, the flagship of the small river fleet. By four o'clock they came across another of Clark's abandoned campsites. There was another note on a pole. This one brought discouraging news. Sergeant Pryor had fallen victim of Crow horse thieves. He would be unable to move ahead overland to deliver a letter

Lewis had written to Heney of the North West Company. That letter urged Heney to help negotiate with the hostile Sioux to ease tension on the trip through their land. It further requested that Heney try to get Sioux chiefs to travel to Washington as a show of peace. Not being able to contact Heney meant they would have to travel through Sioux territory without benefit of peaceful negotiations.

August 12, 1806

Back on the water shortly after sunrise, the men ply the oars and work favorable currents to make rapid time. They all want to rejoin Captain Clark and the others. At 8:00 A.M. the boatman in the lead canoe shouts back that there is a campsite on the northeast shore and that it is probably white men. Lewis painfully looks to see but has to lie back down again.

With a troubled voice he said, "Sergeant, order all the boats to come around, we'll meet with those men."

As they pulled in, they met two frontiersmen, Joseph Dickson and Forest Hancock of Illinois. They exchanged brief introductions and walked toward the boats.

"You must be the other half of the Corps of Discovery," Hancock said.

Sergeant Ordway replied, "That's a fact. And we are glad to see ya. You are the first white men we have seen in over a year. Just the two of ya?"

Hancock replied, "Yeah, me and Joe. Going after beaver and whatever fur we can bring back for trade. Haven't had much luck lately. We did see Captain Clark and the other half of your men."

Lewis raised himself up partially and asked, "How far downriver are they? When did you see them?"

Hancock replied, "It was around noon yesterday. They were real friendly, too; said there was lots of beaver further west. That's good news 'cause we ain't had much luck up to now. They told us to be on the lookout for ya. How did ya get hurt?"

Lewis motioned with his hands to Sergeant Ordway. "Get my maps and sketches. These men will be the first to benefit from our experience. I'm sure they'll want us to show them what's ahead and where the beaver are." As Ordway retrieved the maps, Lewis continued. "I had a hunting accident upriver; got shot through my backside. Very sore and stiff today, but the worst of the pain seems to have passed. I'm lucky there's no infection."

Hancock replied, "Well, this is no place to be injured. Good thing you've got plenty of help to get ya better and tend to ya. Speaking of hunting, you got any powder or shot you can spare? We didn't have much and some of ours got wet."

Lewis nodded and said to Ordway, "Sergeant, get these men one of our lead canisters of powder. We can't have citizens in this country without means to protect themselves."

Ordway fetched the powder and handed it to Hancock saying, "This has a couple pounds of powder inside. See how the lid is sealed with grease and fits tight. That's Capt'n Lewis' design on how to keep gunpowder dry. It's saved us many a time."

Hancock accepted the lead canister and said, "Hey, I really want to thank you. If I had any money, I'd pay you."

They continued the conversation for about an hour and then moved out again. At one o'clock they came around a bend and Colter shouted, "I think I see 'em, waving and jumpin' up there ahead."

Clark had slowed his pace in order to wait for Lewis. He was getting concerned that his friend had not yet overtaken him. He had decided that if he did not see Lewis today that he would stay put and send a group back upriver to investigate. Meanwhile, he posted sentries to keep watch upriver for the first signs of Lewis' approach.

Shannon was on sentry duty looking upriver. When he saw the small boats coming around a bend, he began waving his arms. He saw Colter waving back at him and raised his rifle and fired into the air. From upstream, Colter returned the signal rifle shot.

Clark, standing near a tripod with a kettle over the fire, heard the shot and immediately looked up toward the west. Shannon shouted, "It's them, Capt'n. Here they come!"

Clark, anxious to re-unite with Lewis, knocked the kettle and tripod into the fire as he rushed straightway toward Shannon and the vantage point to look at the approaching boats. Excited, Clark said to Shannon, "Get all the men together. The Corps of Discovery is a unit again. Tonight we'll celebrate."

Shannon replied, "No need to go get anybody, sir. Here they all come. They heard the shots; they know what that means."

They stood on the riverbank, watching as the distant boats drew near. Sergeant Pryor said, "Sir, I don't see Capt'n Lewis. Do you see Capt'n Lewis?"

Clark's eyes were fixed on the boats, his lips tight as he scanned for his friend. He responded, "No, I don't see him." Then he moved closer to the river's edge, cupped his hands over his mouth and shouted, "Captain Lewis, is Lewis with you?"

Colter shouted back, "He's here. In the white. He got shot, and he's layin' down."

By this time the boats were near. Clark, hearing his friend had been wounded, waded into the water to meet the white pirogue as it pulled in to the shoreline. As it approached,

Lewis, lying on his belly, raised his head to assure Clark he was all right.

Clark, now waist-deep in the water, moved to the edge of the pirogue and looked down at Lewis. "You got shot? Where? What the hell happened? How long ago?" The concerned and agitated Clark waved his arms as he issued orders, "Pull this boat up and get the captain out and over to my tent. Meriwether, how bad is it?"

Lewis, still lying on his belly, turned slightly and said, "Hunting accident a few days ago. Just up from the mouth of the Yellowstone. Got hit in the backside."

Clark said, "In yer backside?"

Lewis said, "Yeah, in my ass! Bullet went clean through my ass and into my breeches. Hurt like hell, too. These good men have been taking real good care of me. Like a bunch of mother hens with one chick. I'm lucky there's no infection. Pain has let up considerably; only hurts when I shift positions. I think I'll be better in three – four weeks."

Clark, realizing his friend was not mortally wounded and would heal, let out a breath of air and said, "Merry, let's get you up to the tent. I'll get some warm supper into ya and then you can tell me just what the hell happened. Who shot ya? How did it happen?"

Lewis replied, "Hunting accident. Tried to make a quick kill on a few elk for roasting meat. I went with Cruzatte. I was bent down coming out of some reeds, ready to shoot at an elk when suddenly, wham, a stab of pain and I was down."

Clark looked at Lewis intently a moment and then laughed. With a wry smile he said, "Let me get this straight, my friend. You went hunting alone with Cruzatte, our near-sighted, one-eyed, fiddle playing boatman. The worst shot in the lot. Of all the men at your disposal, you go and choose him to go hunting with. Now you are coming out of the reeds, sneaking up on an elk. You're stooped over most likely. You're dressed in elk skin breeches and you're surprised that Cruzatte mistakes you for an elk and shoots you in the ass? Merry, do you know how bad that sounds? Do you know anybody that **ever** goes hunting with Cruzatte? He is a boatsman for God's sake, not a hunter. You go and damn near lose the best friend I ever had, not to mention a leader vital to this mission, over a choice to go hunting with Cruzatte? Merry, if your backside wasn't already sore, I think I'd give you a swift kick."

Lewis replied, "Pretty dumb, huh? At the time I just wanted to get the hunt over and get back on the river. I was hurrying things along and now I'm paying the price. Anyway, we have a lot to go over. We had some serious problems with the Blackfeet. They may be out for revenge."

The Corps of Discovery was a unit again. The men reunited and were telling one another of their adventures. The mood in the camp was light as the men feasted and told stories. Everyone agreed that together they were more powerful and less likely to be a target for any Indian hostilities. They ate elk, venison and vegetables that Clark had planned for the reunion. Cruzatte played the fiddle and York danced as the men celebrated their reunion.

Lewis explained to Clark his attempts to measure the northern latitude of the Louisiana drainage basin and the details of the hostile encounter with the Blackfeet. Clark told Lewis about the Yellowstone River and his loss of horses to the silent Crow Indians.

August 14, 1806 Ft. Mandan, North Dakota

River current lending speed to their journey, the Corps of Discovery was pleased to see the Mandan villages coming into view. The Indians recognized their approaching friends and by the time they docked, there was a welcoming party to greet them. That evening there was a council meeting and food for all. Lewis, still extremely sore, lacked mobility and was carried to the meeting. He could only lie on buffalo hides spread on the ground near the central fires. They met with the chiefs they had wintered with, Black Cat, Big White and One-Eye. Rene Jessaume, a Canadian trader, served as their translator.

After the initial exchange of greetings and expressions of concern over Lewis' condition, they proceeded to talk about recent history since the captains had left. As they relayed the story of events over the past months, Lewis and Clark listened in disbelief. They were told that Hidatsa war parties had gone west in numbers to raid the Shoshones, breaking their earlier promise to remain peaceful. Both the Sioux and Arikaras had attacked the Mandan villages. Reprisal efforts from Mandan warriors were continuing the hostilities. Even the Mandan tribes themselves seemed to be concerned with growing internal political upheaval.

It was as if the peaceful message Lewis and Clark had delivered earlier had been entirely forgotten. Lewis was dismayed and disappointed as he stared at the chiefs during the translation. Adding to their woes, none of the Indian chiefs wanted to honor their earlier promises to go to Washington. Clark tried to encourage them with promises of gifts, military weapons and future trading posts. The answer was still no. Now that the hour to fulfill their promise to visit Washington was upon them, they were reluctant to commit. The chiefs expressed fear of traveling through Sioux territory.

August 17, 1806 Leaving Ft. Mandan

It was time to depart. The reunion at Mandan was pleasant, but everyone felt the urge to move on. The two men from Illinois they had met earlier had doubled back to reunite with them again at Mandan. John Colter talked with them about joining their enterprise on their return trek west to beaver country. They urged him to see if he could join them as a partner and guide. Colter agreed to ask the captains if he could get an early discharge.

Colter approached the captains, "Capt'n Lewis, Clark, I have a request."

Clark responded, "Yes, John, what is it?"

Colter said, "Well, sir, I been talking to Dickson and Hancock. They still want to head west into beaver country. They only doubled back to see if they could get more men to join 'em. They got to thinking it wasn't a good idea going into Blackfeet country without more strength. They asked me to see if I could join 'em. I told them I would join them and act as a guide, but only if you would release me free and clear. Now that you're back in more familiar territory, what you think, sir? Can you release me?"

Lewis looked at Clark and nodded, Clark looked back at Colter, "It's a fair request and I am inclined to grant it. One condition though."

The anxious Colter said, "Yes, sir. What's that?"

Clark answered, "Go tell Sergeant Ordway about your plan. Tell him to let the other men know about it. We'll let you go only if none of the others want to go too. If any of the others want an early discharge, then you can't go. I can't afford to have diminished forces going through Sioux country and I can't show partiality by letting you go. I'll release you provided no one else asks for a similar change in his enlistment conditions."

Colter nodded and said, "Yes, sir. That's more than fair. I'll check with the sergeant right away." He turned and walked away.

Lewis said, "Good man, that John Colter."

Clark replied, "He really took to the trail. He seems like he likes the mountains and frontier more than being around any village. Men like him will help find trails and make settlements possible for those that follow*."

Lewis said, "He wants to be first in the beaver trade. Maybe even help establish trading posts. As long as we're saying our good-byes, ask Sergeant Gass to bring the Charbonneau family over. They won't be going on. We may as well pay him off."

Soon, Charbonneau, Sacajawea and little Pomp were meeting with the captains.

Clark said, "Well now Toussaint, it looks as if we are about to part company. Time to settle up. You are due some money for your horse, tepee and services. I have rounded up the exact calculation in your favor to make it five hundred dollars. That's fair I think. I must say that we found your wife, Janey, to be a significant help in gathering and preparing food all along the way. She was extremely valuable in crossing the Shoshone territory, making those difficult translations possible and making the horrible mountain crossing a little more sure. More than once she supported the resolve of the men when she trudged right along with them, little Pomp on her back. Whenever she pointed to familiar landmarks, it boosted the morale of all the men. I have to believe that any Indians observing us and seeing her and Pomp knew at once that we weren't a war party. She was a living symbol of peace. Her presence was greatly appreciated by all the men." Clark paused a moment and then picked up little Pomp as he continued, "As for your son. Well, it's no secret. I like this little fella. As long as I live I'll have favorable memories of a 'Little Dancing Pomp'. He was so loveable and entertaining moving around our evening fires, prancing with York and holding his hand. He too had to suffer the rigors of life on the trail. Those long days at Fort Clatsop would have been unbearable without his singing and playing."

Charbonneau extended his hand to take the money. He put it away and then reached out to shake first Lewis' and then

* John Colter returned west to discover what was temporarily dubbed "Colter's Hell". It is now called Yellowstone National Park.

Clark's hand. "We shared some very tough times, very tough. We too, will have our memories of the first white expedition to the West. I am not sorry we joined you; this expedition was very rewarding."

Clark looked at the little boy and then said to Charbonneau, "Toussaint, I want to repeat my offer I made back there on the river. If you ever want him to get a formal education and be raised in a city, I will be happy to raise him as my own. He'll get the best of care, a good education and have all the advantages that a city environment can offer him*."

Charbonneau nodded and replied, "Thank you, Captain Clark. I know you're sincere. This is something I will think over. Now is not the time. There are problems with the Sioux. I think we will stay here. We may come to St. Louis later."

With that they agreed to part. York took little Pomp, gave him a hug and set him back down. The boy turned and gave Clark a hug and then a grown-up handshake. Then he turned and ran to his mother. Sacajawea picked him up and said, "Good-by Cap-Tan. We will miss you."

There was a noise of weeping as a group of Indians approached. Big White had changed his mind. He and his family were going to travel to Washington. Lewis ordered the men to add another canoe and make room for the guests. Lewis, still in pain, was helped onto his belly in his bed on the white pirogue. They pushed the boats into the water and rowed out toward the favorable currents.

September 1, 1806   Teton Territory

The boats pass the Niobrara River that marks the entrance to Teton Sioux territory. Two miles on downstream there are nine Indians waving

---

* Charbonneau did bring little Pomp to St. Louis and leave him for Clark to raise. Clark took him in as one of his own and later sent him to college.

to them to come ashore. Clark ignores them and orders the men to stay away from the shoreline as they moved past the Indians. Checking quickly, he discovers one of the boats is out of sight.

Straining to look back upstream Clark asked, "Sergeant Ordway. Where's Drewyer's boat?"

"Don't know for sure," Ordway responded. "I think they may have pulled over to take some small game back there."

Clark slapped his thigh and exclaimed, "Damn it! Everyone pull in here. We'll wait for 'em to catch up."

From upstream they heard the sound of gunfire. Lewis raised up and Clark motioned for him to settle back down. "Ordway, get me fifteen men. Let's get back there and see what the hell's going on. Sergeant Pryor, Gass, stay here with the captain and set up a line of defense just off shore. Let's go! Ain't nobody going to open fire on us without reprisal!"

They moved quietly along the shoreline. As they looked up past the river bend they saw the lagging canoe, still nearly a mile upriver. Then they saw the Indians on a bluff above them.

Shannon pointed and said, "Capt'n, up there. I think they're shooting targets, just practicing."

Joseph Field said, "From here, they look like Yankton Sioux. They ain't dressed like the Teton we saw last year. What do you think?"

Clark paused and observed and then said, "I think you're right. They're just shooting targets." He studied them for a moment and continued, "I think you may be right, too, they're probably Yankton. They've noticed us and are coming this way. It doesn't look like an attack force."

They met briefly with the Indians and confirmed they were Yankton Sioux. They were younger men who wanted the explorers to smoke with them. Clark refused, explaining that they had to keep moving. By now, the trailing canoe had joined the others and was waiting. Clark and the men went back to their boats.

As the boats moved back into the river, Clark shouted out an order, "Gass, Pryor, Ordway, get your boats together. Close ranks and follow Cruzatte in the white. Stay away from the shore line. Keep close to the center of the river. Don't anyone lag behind. Everyone keep a close interval of not more than fifty yards. This is Teton territory. I don't want to stop on the shore at all. Run silent, don't shoot at anything unless I order it. When we do stop, it will be on a sandbar island, safe, and something we can defend."

Rounding a bend they see the chief, Black Buffalo, with a small group of warriors. He shouts that he wants the men to stop. Clark refuses, shouting back that they will not forget Teton treachery. Black Buffalo strikes the ground three times with a lance. A symbol of making an oath among the Indians.

September 3, 1806 Near the Great Bend of the Missouri

Lewis has recovered enough to walk gingerly about. Clark and the others insist that he only indulge in small exercise as earlier, more strenuous attempts, have weakened him. In late afternoon they encounter a large trading party coming upstream. The leader is James Aird, and he warmly greets them. They provide the men with fresh tobacco and the first taste of whiskey they have had since July of 1805. They camp and exchange information. Aird says there are many that think they are dead, but Jefferson still holds hope on their safe return. He is grateful to have accurate information about the river. Lewis and Clark listen intently to the news he brings about the country.

Clark said, "I can hardly believe it. On July 11, 1804, Aaron Burr killed Alexander Hamilton in a duel! In a duel! Jefferson is re-elected, that's good."

Lewis said, "Burr and Hamilton never lost much love for one another. Still, a duel does surprise me. Zebulon Pike exploring into the Southwest, now that's news. I wish we knew more."

Clark said, "Let's get an early start in the morning. I want to read a newspaper."

In the morning Aird and his men headed upstream, and the Corps of Discovery moved downstream. As they proceeded south, each day they would see travelers moving upstream. After reaching lower Missouri, the men all let out a cheer at the sight of a cow grazing, the first domestic livestock any of them had seen in a long time.

As they approached La Charette, the men asked permission to fire a salute. It was granted and the salute was answered in kind from the citizens gathering on the shoreline. Everyone was overwhelmed at seeing the men, the general word being that they had perished.

September 23, 1806
St Louis, Missouri

They were in civilized country again. Houses and places of business were along the shoreline. At noon, they pulled in to St. Louis.

Shannon shouted, "Capt'n, can we..."

Clark raised his hand, anticipating the question and replied, "Of course. All hands fire your weapons on my signal. Let's let them know we're home!"

The volley of gunfire brought people into the streets and running toward the river. Lewis was greeted by Peter Chouteau, a friend from the winter of 1804. He immediately accepted an invitation to spend the night in his home. His first obligation was to set to writing a letter to Jefferson that his 'darling project' was now complete.

The letter would be mailed in the morning. The expedition of the Corps of Discovery was over.

October, 1806 St. Louis, Missouri

Lewis, Clark and their crew are constantly approached to discuss their trip and describe the country of the West. They are heroes and people travel to St. Louis to see them. This is a preview of the national acclaim they will receive. It is a good time for all the men.

One day, Clark and York go to a general store to purchase materials and supplies. Clark parks his buckboard outside the store and walks through the store selecting items. As he selects items, York carries them to the buckboard and the storekeeper writes them down. The last item selected is a sack of beans. Clark walks over to pay for the goods while York carries them outside to add to the stack of materials that has been already selected.

As York is stacking the bags, a boy with a dog comes running toward the store, anxious to see the famous Captain Clark. The dog barks as the boy approached the store, causing Clark's team of horses to make a sudden jerk. The motion, in turn, causes the stack of materials in the buckboard to shift. York reaches out and grabs the shifting sacks. He is holding them precariously as Clark comes out of the store.

York shouted, "Hurry, Capt'n. Calm the horses. The load's shiftin! I don know if I kin hold it."

Clark moved and grabbed the horse to settle it. As he did so, the other men that had gathered around the store looked at one another with a surprised stare. One man said, "Did you hear that? That nigger shoutin' and givin' orders to a white man like that? And the white man is his master. Just who the hell does he think he is?"

Another man said, "Ain't never heared a nigger talk like that. He's Captain Clark's black, ain't he? He's a big one but still, no nigger got a right to talk to any white like that."

Hearing the racist comments, Clark looked quickly at York, then at the onlookers. At the moment, helping York seemed as natural as anything, but here they were in St. Louis, in slave country. York's actions were strictly forbidden. Clark knew this was trouble.

The men moved up as two of them grabbed the now frightened York and pulled him back. The sacks of beans and tobacco fell to the ground.

One of them said, "We can tie this nigger to that post or to the wagon wheel there. Where do you want to beat him?"

Clark, still somewhat astonished at the swiftness of the re-action to York's comments, looked at the men and then said, "No, I don't want to beat him here in public. I'll take him to the storeroom in the back of the general store. He'll get it good back there. He don't often act up like this. I don't know what's got into him. I'll give him some lashes back there, that should get his head straight." Clark took York's arm and said, "Come with me, boy."

The spectators seemed satisfied that Clark was going to punish York and stepped aside, mumbling comments to one another as Clark and York went inside the store.

Clark said to the storekeeper, "Can you let me use your back room there. I got a temperamental nigger here and I need to set him straight."

The storekeeper nodded and said, "Sure, Captain Clark. Take all the time you need." He walked over and opened the door to the backroom. As York and Clark entered, he handed the captain a buggy whip. "Here you go."

Once inside the storeroom and away from the others, Clark turned and looked at the wide-eyed, panic stricken York. The two stood there a moment looking at one another, then York's eyes shifted to the whip in Clark's hand.

Clark said, "Never mind, York. I'm not going to beat you. But we've got a problem here. We're back in civilization now. You know you can't talk to me or any white man like that."

York stepped back, took a deep breath, and said, "Capt'n, for over two year, we been out there on that trail together. I never heard the word 'nigger' once in all that time. The men, they began to accept ol' York as soon as we got away from this, what you call civilization. We pulled ropes together until we were sore from where they cut into our shoulders. We swatted mosquitoes and flies. We ate, drank and slept together. York was always there, side by side, no more, no less, than any one of the men. I was given a rifle. I was showed how to shoot it. I hunted with the men. I faced the Indians and grizzlies with the men. They took me as an equal, not a nigger slave. I was an equal out there."

Clark gazed, mildly astonished at the usually quiet York and listened.

York, seeing that Clark was allowing him to speak, continued, "The Indians thought this black skin was special. They never thought I was inferior. They thought I had spiritual powers and wanted to touch me. A lot of them came a long way jus' to touch me. But capt'n, all this didn't make me a man, didn't make me free until we got to the big ocean."

Then, his voice cracking with emotion, he continued, "It was there we voted on where to make camp. Out there, you and Capt'n Lewis let me vote. There was no question of it. No one said, 'You ain't gonna let the nigger vote.' No, I voted and votin' made me feel free." Tears now in his eyes he took a deep breath, exhaled and said, "Just like I told young Shannon out there on the ocean when he asked me why I smile so big. I told him. Property don't vote, sir. No, property don't vote about nothin'. Only free men vote. Feelin' free is a feelin' you don't forget once you felt it. Not ever. Feelin' free is somethin' you don't want to give up after you have felt it." Then stepping closer and looking Clark in the eye, he said in a low tone, "Let me go, Capt'n. Let me go back with anyone. The next boat headed up the Missouri. I'll go with anybody goin' into that wild country. This nigger would rather work hard and even die out there, feelin' free, breathin' free, than live in this city with all the comforts of civilization."

Clark stood there in silence, looking at a man that he had known nearly all of his life, a man that for the first time was speaking like a man. The words seemed strange coming from the normally submissive York, but in his heart he knew they were true.

Finally, he said, "Damn it, York. I don't know what to do with you. I can't beat you and I can't set you free. I'm going to whip this post so they can hear the sound of the lash out there in the store. When we leave here, have the front of your shirt open. Look down like you've just been beat." Pacing the floor a moment Clark turned and said, "York, if I let you go now, you have no money. A black with no money will have trouble and wind up getting hanged. If I let you go with fur traders, they may kill you 'cause they just don't know better." Then, waving a finger in the air, he said, "Here's what I propose. You stay with me. To everyone it'll look like you're still just my slave. We'll agree on pay of...of $25 a month plus room and board. I'll set aside that amount each month for you. In a few years you'll have money to buy some land or a business. Then you can be free. In the meantime, the politics of the country may change. There are those in office that oppose slavery and there could be new laws any time now. It's your choice. Stay on for pay in secret or go upriver with white fur traders you don't know."

The two men stood and looked at one another for a moment, then they both broke into a smile. York extended his hand and said, "I'll stay with you sir, you're all I know."

Clark took his hand and said, "Done."*

Then Clark proceeded to lash the post in the storeroom to feign giving York a beating. When he was done he said, "Just remember, you must act like a slave. Next time they may catch

---

* Six years later Clark emancipated York. He started a freight business hauling cargo up and down the rivers.

us away from a private storeroom and I'll have to beat you
with witnesses."

York said, "Yes, sir."

They left the storeroom and proceeded to the buckboard.
York loaded the bags, still on the ground, onto the wagon and
the two left.

December 30, 1806 Washington, D.C.

*They are heroes, the first national, non-war heroes anyone has ever
seen. The whole country is wild about them, from schoolchildren to elderly.
Everyone talks of Lewis and Clark. Newspaper reporters are hungry for
any scrap of information they can get. Since arriving at St. Louis in the
fall, the captains and the men have enjoyed the limelight of immense
popularity. There are frequent parties, posing for portraits and auto-
graphs of those that can write. On the commercial side, just being present
at a store enhances business. Lewis always insists that Clark be recognized as a co-captain. Soon the names Lewis and Clark are forever
linked as if they are one. Interest in the West, the land and the Indians,
peaks to an all-time high. Newspapers that carry any information about
the western lands sell quickly. The captains and the men of the Corps of
Discovery are constantly being featured and quoted. Everyone is talking
about them, their courageous trip and the marvels of the new land. People
everywhere are planning excursions into the new western land to harvest
the fur trade or settle on the beautiful and bountiful prairies described in
the newspapers.*

*There is no question any longer, the Louisiana Purchase is a good
thing for the United States. It unites the country as no other force can.
Now even the man-in-the-street begins thinking of the United States as
one country, extending from coast to coast. It becomes everyone's 'Manifest
Destiny' to inhabit the continent. It is the fulfillment of Jefferson's dream,
to build an empire based on democratic principle.*

*Lewis spends time in Albemarle County, Virginia, with his family
and friends. Clark spends time with his brother and then with Julia
Hancock, his intended bride-to-be.*

*The President holds a gala welcome dinner for them. They sit in a
large room as the featured guests at one of several long tables.
Conversation in the room becomes still as Lewis, Jefferson or Clark
speaks. Jefferson is beaming with pride. His political, scientific and
personal ambitions for the new country are being accomplished in the
personification of Lewis and Clark.*

In response to comments regarding remuneration for the
men, Lewis was clear as he said, "Gentlemen, my application
to Congress for remuneration for our men will be that each
man on my list be given a large parcel of land, three to four
hundred acres, in addition to twice the pay of his enlistment.
These men have willingly suffered everything that cold, hunger
and fatigue, in full measure, could possibly impart. A commander could not have had a more dedicated group of men.
They have more than earned any amount Congress agrees to
award them."

Pausing a moment, Lewis stood and directed his speech
toward the congressmen in the room. "With respect to the exertions and services rendered by our esteemed man, Captain
William Clark, in the course of our late voyage, I cannot say
too much. If any credit be due for the success of the arduous
enterprise in which we have been mutually engaged, he is
equally with myself entitled to your consideration and that of
our common country. Regarding recognition of Captain Clark,
my views are well-known; the expedition would not have been
possible without him and his capable command. Therefore, I
insist that whatever measure of payment Congress awards me,

that Captain Clark receive an exact equal payment." Looking at a table of generals, he continued, "Be it known that this request is endorsed by our President. Regardless of whatever rank the War Department chooses to carry for William Clark on its rolls, William Clark was, in every respect, a co-commander the entire length of the expedition." Smiling broadly, Lewis slowly seated himself.

Jefferson nodded as he applauded Lewis' comments. Then he looked around the room and said, "I anticipate that Congress will not delay in settling on a fair and just remuneration as per Captain Lewis' request." Turning to Lewis, the president asked, "Share with us a little of the potential for trade you briefed me on earlier."

Lewis paused while the room silenced again. "As you all know by now, there is no all-water passageway to the Pacific. There are very difficult mountains between the headwaters of the Missouri and Columbia. But there is good news too. At this most difficult spot on the map, there are friendly natives. Two large bands of Indians inhabit those mountains, the Shoshone and the Nez Perce. Both of these tribes were very friendly toward us. These Indians have large and handsome herds of horses and they are willing to trade them at very fair prices. Their horses will aid in establishing roadways and regular portage over those mountains. With little effort these tribes could provide the location for large trading establishments and thus bridge the difficult mountains as economically as possible. The established route would be faster than an all-water trade route around the Cape of Good Hope. Now then, I should point out that due to the harsh weather in this region, the trade would be restricted to crossing between mid-June and September. I can easily imagine the promotion of great annual trade fairs at the Nez Perce establishment. Without question the lands of the great prairies are rich and will be good for fur trade and home-steading. The establishment of trading posts and cities will provide political stability between the Indians and add strength to the sovereignty of our great country. There is no reason to doubt that our great nation can now spread influence beyond the Louisiana Purchase to the Pacific Ocean."

The room was filled with applause followed by the buzzing of multiple conversations, men nodding, pointing and engaged in side conversations over what Lewis had just said. One reporter for a Philadelphia newspaper asked, "Mr. Lewis, what can you tell us of the potential for fur trade in the Louisiana Territory?"

Lewis snickered at the obvious question, "Well sir, if you would listen carefully or read the reports we have been giving, you would know. I can tell you now that the Missouri River and all of its branches, from the Cheyenne upwards, abound more in beaver and common otter than any other streams on earth. Particularly that portion of them lying within and near the Rocky Mountains." Lewis looked around. Knowing he had every ear in the place on him, he continued. "Gentlemen, I can tell you with assurance that if the government will only aid, even in a very limited manner, the enterprise of its citizens, I am fully convinced that we shall shortly derive the benefits of a most lucrative trade. The land is unbelievably rich. In the course of ten to twelve years a tour across our continent by the route mentioned will be undertaken by individuals with as little concern as a voyage across the Atlantic is at present. Those discoveries that we have made in this new land will not long remain unimproved. People were streaming into the land even as we were returning."

President Jefferson, like the others, listened intently as Lewis spoke. When Lewis finished, Jefferson looked around the room and then said, "I could not be more pleased with the outcome of this noble expedition. They have documented the

land, its minerals, its flora and fauna. Thanks to these explorers, we now know the number and disposition of the
native tribes that inhabit the new territory. We know the
friendly from the hostile, the languages they speak. That alone
is information valuable enough to merit the cost of the expedition." Then looking at Lewis, Jefferson continued, "I would
like to announce that I have urged the American Philosophical
Society to elect Meriwether Lewis as a valuable member of
that prestigious fraternity."

The room filled with applause and Lewis looked at
Jefferson and said, "I am deeply moved and honored, Mr.
President. Thank you."

Jefferson raised a hand and said, "There is more. I am
commissioning Charles Peale of the Philadelphia museum to
paint portraits of you and Clark. Those portraits will hang in a
place of honor for all of our citizens to come and see for years
to come."

Again the room filled with applause. When the applause
stopped, Jefferson said, "I am building a museum of native
Indian artifacts. The first items placed in that museum will be
those specimens and articles you have brought back from the
expedition."

Clark said, "Big White will be pleased to see that. He and
his people are very impressed with the cities and culture they
have seen so far. I am sure he will be honored that the natives
have a special building to display their culture. Taking that information back to his home will prove that our message to
them was true. It will help establish the idea of promoting
trade with the United States. This is very good. I hope to see
it as soon as possible."

As the conversation continued through the evening, one of
the senators came over and stood by the president. Seeing the
senator approach, they stopped talking and looked up at him.

The senator looked at the two explorers and with a smile said, "We are sure glad to have you back. When you left we thought you would be back in eighteen months. When you didn't come back, many of us, and I must confess I was one, thought you had met with dire consequences. You were gone so long that some said you may as well have gone to the moon." The senator smiled as he looked at the explorers.

After a moment of hesitation Clark said, "Well now, senator. You give us the same crew of men and a ship that will fly the skies, and **we will go** to the moon."

The senator laughed as he repeated Clarks last words, "A ship that will fly the skies,...go to the moon..., why I never...." He stopped his chuckling sentence short as he looked at the serious stare in the faces of Lewis, Clark and Jefferson. He started to continue, "The moon. Can you imagine such a silly notion of ...."

Jefferson looked sternly at the bungling senator as he interrupted his awkward speech, "These men are explorers, senator. Fom the heels up they are true adventurers. They do not take lightly any remark in jest regarding expeditions of **any** kind. While you, whose entire life is politics in soft chairs, may not understand such rugged men as these, let me assure you of this. If there ever could be a ship that could fly the skies and go to the moon, it **will be** men such as these that will be on board."

The somewhat embarrassed senator stood there in silence a moment and then walked away. When the dinner was over, Jefferson said, "I want you two to come to my office. I have Clark's maps spread out on the floor awaiting the opportunity to go over them inch by inch. I don't care if we are up all night. I want to see and hear more about key points on your journey."

Following Jefferson's request, the men spent many hours going over the maps spread out on the floor in the oval office.

October 11, 1809 Grinders Inn, Tennessee

In the years following the expedition, Lewis, no longer challenged by the rigors of the expedition, did not adapt well to being governor of the Louisiana Territory. Lewis was suffering from depression, exacerbated by creditors presenting him with unpaid invoices from the expedition. He was experiencing a troublesome governorship over the Louisiana Territory with its own set of financial and political problems. He decided to go to Washington and see President Madison. He would plead his case for more funds to pay for the debts of his office and remedy the situation.

On the way to Washington, he continued to have episodes of depression. His usual remedy for depression was hard work or the uplifting personality of his friend, William Clark. At this time, he had neither.

When he approached Grinders Inn, a sort of bed and breakfast stop, his depression had climaxed. He was disoriented and moody. Near sundown he told Mrs. Grinder, "It is a lovely evening. I think I will sit here and watch the sundown and evening progress. I await the arrival of my friend, Bill Clark."

Mrs. Grinder looked at her guest strangely. Lewis was alone and Clark was far away in Missouri. Saying nothing she left the despondent Lewis alone. Later that evening, Lewis took two pistols, held one to his head and the other pointed toward his chest. He fired them simultaneously.

- THE END -

Epilogue

Meriwether Lewis – A very prolific scientist/explorer, Lewis was ever alert, always looking to discover new plant and animal species. Even when the expedition was going through perilous times, the vigilant Lewis would take time to document new findings. In all, he catalogued one hundred twenty-two animal species and one hundred seventy-eight plant species previously unknown to science and the civilized world. His descriptions often included drawings and were always painstakingly made to be thorough and accurate. When possible he included samples.

Lewis' descriptions of the native Indians, their clothing, speech, and customs were the first and most accurate available to help understand the Indians west of the Mississippi.

Lewis planned well for the trip. When returning to St. Louis he still had ample supplies of paper and ink, (his journals were extremely important to him), and enough gun-powder and lead to make the trip again.

Lewis' suicide was almost expected by Clark. While there was question of possible murder in the press, those that knew him best, Jefferson and Clark, never doubted that it was suicide. He was an exemplary leader on the trail, facing the rigors of weather, Indians, topography and insects. Later, when becoming a government administrator, he was the antithesis of his trail persona, he managed poorly as a government ex-ecutive and failed. He simply could not adapt well to administration. He made three attempts to seek a wife but was unsuccessful. Jefferson, even with repeated urging, could not get him to write about the expedition. His depression, held at bay during the expedition, came back on him with such force that it proved to be more than he could handle.

William Clark - Clark was a success after the expedition. He received equal pay to Lewis and an equal land grant, $1,228 and 1600 acres. He became brigadier general of the Missouri militia and was appointed as Superintendent of Indian Affairs for the Territory of Upper Louisiana. He was also governor of the Missouri Territory until 1820.

Clark married Julia Hancock and named his first-born son, Meriwether Lewis Clark. He also adopted the two children of Sacajawea and Toussaint Charbonneau, Jean Baptiste (Pomp) and a daughter, Lisette. They both lived in his home and were educated in Missouri.

His expertise as a cartographer made the early maps of the West the only dependable source of information. The accuracy of his maps is uncanny. From St. Louis to Portland, they were accurate to within forty miles, a feat most of us could not duplicate today.

Clark died of natural causes in St. Louis on September 1, 1838 at the home of his son, Meriwether Lewis Clark.

As a recent presidential act, President William Clinton posthumously promoted Clark to the rank of captain.

Sergeant Nathaniel Pryor - After the expedition Pryor went to live among the Osage Indians in Oklahoma. Clark named him as a sub-agent for Indian affairs. Pryor married an Osage woman and had a family of unknown size. He died June 10, 1831.

Sergeant John Ordway - Ordway made some journal entries of his own, encouraged to do so by Lewis. He was further encouraged by the newspapers of the time. He was paid $300 for his journals and many of his entries are referenced today. He married a New Hampshire woman and moved to Missouri where he claimed his 320 acres of land and settled down.

Sergeant Patrick Gass - Gass was elected by the men to be sergeant after Sergeant Floyd died. Gass took credit for coining the name "Corps of Discovery" and used that name on his version of the journals. Gass was alive when the Civil War broke out and, at 94 years of age, he made an attempt to volunteer for service. Gass was the longest lived member of the expedition and died April 2, 1870 at age 99 in Wellsburg, West Virginia.

George Drewyer - His real name was spelled Drouillard, but the captains spelled it Drewyer throughout the journals. Lewis referred to him as the most skilled hunter and woodsman of the men. He had cool judgment and was courageous. Lewis frequently chose him on short expeditions. He was trusted without question throughout the expedition. He delivered Lewis' first letters to Jefferson to the postmaster.

Drouillard later returned to the three forks area for beaver pelts. He frequently avoided the Indians, saying that because he was half Indian, he could not be captured. He met his fate in a final battle scene. He evidently killed several Blackfeet in the skirmish, but they eventually subdued him. His mutilated body was send downriver in a canoe.

Sacajawea - Sometimes spelled Sacagawea. The name meant 'Bird Woman'. The men affectionately called her Janey. She was captured at a very early age by the Minnetare and held as a slave. At age 14, Toussaint Charbonneau won her from an Indian as payment for a gambling debt. He married her and she became his second wife. Because the captains only allowed one woman, Sacajawea was chosen. She died in South Dakota on December 22, 1812, at age 25. The cause of death was supposedly 'putrid fever.' Eight months later, Clark would adopt her two children.

Toussaint Charbonneau - The eldest member of the expedition, he was a translator and cook. He had poor river ability and was self-centered. He lived among the Mandan Indians until he died at age 80.

Jean Baptiste Charbonneau – Youngest member and Sacajawea's infant child, he made the entire trip. The men, especially Clark, loved to watch the boy play during their winter stay at Fort Clatsop. Having a child around helped break the boredom and reminded the men of home and family. He was nick-named 'Pomp' by Clark. Clark named a large rock outcrop in Montana "Pompeys Pillar", where he carved "Wm Clark, July 25, 1806" in the rock face. It is still there, protected by park rangers and is the only visible sign of his passing.

Clark adopted the boy after his mother's death and raised him as his own. He was educated in St. Louis. He later went to Germany for six years as a guest of the aristocracy. In 1829 he returned to the United States and became a mountain man. He briefly was employed as a scout for the Mormons and also worked as a hotel clerk in Auburn, California. In 1866, at the age of 61 he died of pneumonia while seeking gold in Montana. He is buried in Danner, Oregon. His gravesite is listed in the National Register of Historic Places.

York - Clark's slave was the first black man to cross the continent and the first black man to vote in America. Little is known except that in 1809 Clark permitted him to go to Kentucky. Clark officially emancipated York in 1816. He then started a freighting business in Kentucky and Tennessee. He died of cholera about 1831.

John Colter - After leaving the expedition at Mandan, he returned to western Montana. He was the original "mountain man" of the early West. He later supplied Clark with supplements to his maps of the Yellowstone area. In describing the geysers and phenomena of the area, it became known as 'Colter's Hell', today's Yellowstone National Park.

He and John Potts were captured by the Blackfeet, stripped naked and given a head start on an execution race. Potts was killed but Colter survived, and the story became an American legend.

Credits for Paraphrasing and Quotations

Pp. 1 and 2 from Ambrose p. 59. Thomas Jefferson's description of Lewis' job as personal secretary.

P. 2 from Ambrose p. 59, "retain his rank and right to promotion."

P. 11 from letter of Thomas Jefferson relating to Meriwether Lewis, Monticello, August 18, 1813. Heritage Press, Volume One, page xix. Portions of the same letter are repeated in Ambrose p. 484.

P. 19 from Ambrose pp. 98, 99 paraphrase quotation of Lewis' letter to Clark.

P. 26 from Ambrose p. 104 paraphrase quote Clark's acceptance letter to Lewis.

P. 29 list of supplies from Ambrose p. 88 paraphrase Lewis notes of list of materials taken.

P. 35 Ambrose p. 118 paraphrase, "the men from Kentucky were sworn into the Army in a solemn ceremony."

Pp. 46, 47 paraphrase near mutiny at Ft. Wood from Ambrose pp. 130, 131.

P. 47 paraphrase refurbishment of keelboat Ambrose p. 128.

P. 48 paraphase Lewis' letter of credit, merchants being first to profit Ambrose p. 123

P. 52, "the peculiar situation…which is enclosed." is a quotation from Dearborn's letter March 26, 1804. Ambrose p. 154.

P. 87 lead in narration paraphrase Ambrose p. 139.

P. 87 positioning of the men on the boats, paraphrase Ambrose pp. 145, 146.

P. 88 paraphrase Ambrose p. 146, "Pirogues ahead ....
Voyagers grease."

P. 100 paraphrase Ambrose p. 149, "deer tracks, they're as thick as cattle...around a farm." From Clark June 30.

P. 160 paraphrase intro from Ambrose p. 152 Clark's entry.

P. 110 paraphrase tobacco carrot Ambrose p. 155.

P. 116 paraphrase Lewis entry, "if they displease the Great Father...consume as fire consumed the grass..." from Ambrose p. 157.

P. 126 from Ambrose p. 159, "... as lenient as your oaths will allow." Then, paraphrase running the gauntlet.

P.129, 130 paraphrase Big Horse's nudity, Ambrose p. 160.

P. 133, "sergeant in Corps of Volunteers for Northwestern Discovery" Lewis' journal from Ambrose p. 161.

Pp. 136, 137 from Ambrose p. 162 paraphrase Pryor regarding Yankton and Yankton meeting.

P. 139 paraphrase from Ambrose pp.163, 164 Arcawechar.

P. 140 paraphrase description of land from Ambrose p. 165.

P. 147 paraphrase add coyote and mule deer from Ambrose p. 168.

P. 148 paraphrase eighty lodges camp at next river from Ambrose p. 168.

P. 162 Clark quote from journal, "...bad humored island..." from Ambrose p. 171.

P. 188 paraphrase description of Arikara boats and crossing from Ambrose p. 179.

Pp. 191, 192 paraphrase ranking of chiefs and York as a spirit being from Ambrose p. 180.

P. 194 paraphrase grabbing your boat, Not one would dare. Ambrose p. 180.

Pp. 195, 196 paraphrase Chief Hay from Ambrose p. 181.

P. 207 paraphrase, "Many of our people ... dissapointed with small gifts..." from DeVoto p. 61, Ambrose p. 185.

P. 258 paraphrase, "Lewis journal entry observing his crew and small craft...two thousand miles in breadth..." from Ambrose p. 212.

P. 261 paraphrase, "white pirogue flagship..." from Ambrose p. 213.

P. 266 paraphrase Lewis' entry of April 14, 1805 from DeVoto p. 95.

P. 273 river measurements, Lewis' journal entries from DeVoto p. 101.

P. 283 paraphrase bear measurements, Lewis journal from DeVoto p. 105.

P. 284 paraphrase Lewis' entry regarding curiosity about bears from Ambrose p. 219.

P. 287 paraphrase Lewis' entry regarding Milk River from DeVoto p. 107.

P. 289 paraphrase river accident scene from Ambrose p. 225.

P. 293 paraphrase bear hunting incident from Ambrose p. 224.

P. 302 paraphrase tree scene burning, Clark's journal entry from DeVoto p. 112.

P. 313, "...of the heretofore boundless Missouri." Lewis' entry fromDeVoto p. 118.

P. 323, "Lewis' journal entry of visionary enchantment." From DeVoto p. 123, Ambrose p. 228.

P. 325 paraphrase bear killing incident, Lewis' entry from DeVoto p. 124.

Pp. 328, 329 paraphrase discussion regarding river choice. Lewis' journal entries from DeVoto p. 126 , Ambrose p. 230.

P. 331 paraphrase Lewis' journal from entries DeVoto 125

Pg332 paraphrase river measurements from Lewis' journal from Ambrose p. 230.

P. 335, 336 paraphrase Lewis re: returning back down Maria's river, Ambrose p. 232, DeVoto pp. 130, 131.

P. 343 Naming Maria's River, Lewis journal entry, DeVoto p. 132.

P. 350, "...this is the most beautiful sight I ever beheld." Paraphrased from Lewis' journal entry. DeVoto p. 137.

P. 353 paraphrase Lewis journal entry. Confrontation, bear, badger, buffalo from DeVoto, p. 139, Ambrose p. 238.

P. 402, "...I don't believe the world...river, running to the extent...as navigable as they are." Lewis journal entry, DeVoto p. 184.

P. 409 paraphrase, "Judge then...pure and ice cold water." from Lewis journal entry DeVoto p. 188.

P. 425 paraphrase Lewis' lengthy 31st birthday journal entry. from DeVoto p. 206, Ambrose p. 280.

P. 430 paraphrase, "Lewis ...great lake of ill taste where white men live." from DeVoto p. 211.

P. 436 paraphrase Clark journal entry, "wet and cold in every part as I ever have been" from DeVoto p. 240, Ambrose p. 293.

P. 458 Clark's entry, "Ocian in view! O! the joy." from Ambrose p. 310.

P. 506 paraphrase…who was their chief. Three men stepped forward. from Ambrose p. 388.

P. 507 "damn you. Let go my gun!" Lewis' journal entry From Ambrose p. 390.

P. 509 paraphrase wind of the bullet Lewis' journal entry From Ambrose p. 391.

P. 513, "damn you. You shot me." Lewis' journal entry from Ambrose p. 396, Devoto p. 445.

Pp. 535, 536 Lewis' comment in letter to Jefferson. Paraphrase recognition to Clark from Ambrose page 411.

P. 537 paraphrase rivers and trapping beaver and otter from Ambrose page 408.